AGRICULTURAL POLICY REFORM

Global Environmental Governance Series

Series Editors: Konrad von Moltke and John J. Kirton

Global Environmental Governance addresses the new generation of twenty-first century environmental problems and the challenges they pose for management and governance at the local, national, and global levels. Centred on the relationships among environmental change, economic forces, and political governance, the series explores the role of international institutions and instruments, national and sub-federal governments, private sector firms, scientists, and civil society, and provides a comprehensive body of progressive analyses on one of the world's most contentious international issues.

Also in the series

**Governing Global Biodiversity:
The Evolution and Implementation
of the Convention on Biological Diversity**
Edited by Philippe G. Le Prestre
ISBN 0 7546 1744 0

**Linking Trade, Environment, and Social Cohesion:
NAFTA Experiences, Global Challenges**
Edited by John J. Kirton and Virginia W. Maclaren
ISBN 0 7546 1934 6

**International Equity and Global Environmental Politics:
Power and Principles in U.S. Foreign Policy**
Paul G. Harris
ISBN 0 7546 1735 1

Agricultural Policy Reform

Politics and process in the EU and US in the 1990s

WAYNE MOYER
*Rosenfield Professor and Professor of Political Science,
Grinnell College, Iowa*

TIM JOSLING
*Professor and Senior Fellow, Institute for International Studies
Stanford University, California*

LONDON AND NEW YORK

First published 2002 by Ashgate Publishing

Reissued 2018 by Routledge
2 Park Square, Milton Park, Abingdon, Oxon OX14 4RN
711 Third Avenue, New York, NY 10017, USA

Routledge is an imprint of the Taylor & Francis Group, an informa business

Copyright © Wayne Moyer and Tim Josling 2002

The authors have asserted their moral right under the Copyright, Designs and Patents Act, 1988, to be identified as the authors of this work.

All rights reserved. No part of this book may be reprinted or reproduced or utilised in any form or by any electronic, mechanical, or other means, now known or hereafter invented, including photocopying and recording, or in any information storage or retrieval system, without permission in writing from the publishers.

Notice:
Product or corporate names may be trademarks or registered trademarks, and are used only for identification and explanation without intent to infringe.

Publisher's Note
The publisher has gone to great lengths to ensure the quality of this reprint but points out that some imperfections in the original copies may be apparent.

Disclaimer
The publisher has made every effort to trace copyright holders and welcomes correspondence from those they have been unable to contact.

A Library of Congress record exists under LC control number: 2002074456

ISBN 13: 978-1-138-71999-6 (hbk)
ISBN 13: 978-1-138-71996-5 (pbk)
ISBN 13: 978-1-315-19524-7 (ebk)

Contents

List of Figures   *viii*
List of Tables   *x*
List of Boxes   *xi*
Preface   *xii*
Acknowledgements   *xiv*

Chapter 1:	**Introduction**	1
1.1	Agricultural Policy Reform in the US, EC/EU and GATT/WTO	1
1.2	The Progression of Agricultural Policy Reforms in the US, EC/EU and the GATT/WTO	3
1.3	The Analytical Framework	7
1.4	Central Themes in Policy Reform	8
Chapter 2:	**The Analytical Framework for Farm Policy Reform**	10
2.1	Introduction	10
2.2	Explaining National Policy Decision Making	10
2.3	Models of EC/EU Multilevel Decision Making	18
2.4	The Dynamics of the Decision-making Process	24
2.5	Application of Decision Making Approaches to Farm Policy Reform in the US, the EU and the GATT/WTO	28
Chapter 3:	**The Search for an Agricultural Policy Paradigm Shift**	29
3.1	Introduction	29
3.2	Paradigm Shifts in Agriculture	30
3.3	The Conditions for a Paradigm Shift	36
3.4	Reform in OECD Countries	43
3.5	Farm Policy Reform and International Pressures	47
Chapter 4:	**Reform Frustrated: The Uruguay Round, 1986-1990**	49
4.1	Introduction	49
4.2	Negotiating Agricultural Trade in the GATT	49
4.3	The Place of Agriculture in the Uruguay Round	55
4.4	The Uruguay Round Agricultural Negotiations	59
4.5	Relationship between Trade and Domestic Policy	64
Chapter 5:	**The 1990 US Farm Bill - Reducing the Budget, but Minimizing the Pain**	77
5.1	The Development of the 1990 US Farm Bill	77

	5.2	Analysis	85
	5.3	Assessment	89

Chapter 6:		The 1992 MacSharry Reform of the CAP	96
	6.1	The Development of the MacSharry Reforms	96
	6.2	Analysis of the Reforms	103
	6.3	Assessment of the Reforms	107
	6.4	Conclusion	116

Chapter 7:		Reform Revived: The Dunkel Draft, the Blair House Accord and the WTO Agreement on Agriculture	118
	7.1	Introduction	118
	7.2	MacSharry Reform Unlocks the Door	118
	7.3	Bilateralism in Action: The Blair House Accord	120
	7.4	The Accord Revisited: Blair House II	122
	7.5	Explaining Negotiating Success	122
	7.6	The URAA and Domestic Policy Reform	134
	7.7	Market Access	135
	7.8	Export Competition	136
	7.9	Domestic Support	136
	7.10	The "Peace Clause"	138
	7.11	Experience with the Implementation of the Agreement	139
	7.12	Effect of the URAA on Domestic Policy in the United States	139
	7.13	Implementation in the European Union	140
	7.14	Explanations for the Success of the Round	142

Chapter 8:		The FAIR Act of 1996 - Decoupling Payments from Production	144
	8.1	The Development of the FAIR ACT	144
	8.2	Analysis	158
	8.3	Assessment	164
	8.4	Conclusion	172

Chapter 9:		Agenda 2000 - New Reforms for the CAP	174
	9.1	Development of the Commission Reform Proposals	174
	9.2	The Agenda 2000 Debate	183
	9.3	Analysis of the Agenda 2000 Proposal	193
	9.4	Assessment	204
	9.5	Conclusion	211

Chapter 10:		The 2000 Agricultural Negotiations	212
	10.1	Introduction	212
	10.2	Building on the Uruguay Round Agricultural Agreement	214

	10.3	The US and the 2000 Round	221
	10.4	The EU and the 2000 Round	222
	10.5	Timing of the Negotiations	224

Chapter 11:		**Reform Compared: Similarities and Differences between the US and EU**	**229**
	11.1	Introduction	229
	11.2	US and EU Policy Changes Compared	229
	11.3	The MacSharry and FAIR Act Reforms Compared	231
	11.4	The US and EU Policy Processes Compared	232
	11.5	Comparison of the Impact of Trade Negotiations on EU and US Domestic Policy Reform	236
	11.6	Lessons for the Causes and Consequences of Reform	238
	11.7	Evidence of Paradigm Shifts in US and EU Policy Changes	240

Chapter 12:		**The Future of Agricultural Policy Reform in the EU and the US**	**242**
	12.1	Introduction	242
	12.2	The Climate for Further Reform of Agricultural Policies	243
	12.3	The Path of US Reform	250
	12.4	The Path of EU Reform	252
	12.5	Instruments for the Reformed Policies	253
	12.6	Prospects for Further Reform of Agricultural Trade	253

Bibliography — *258*
Index — *267*

List of Figures

Figure 1.1:	Comparison of US and EU Farm Policy Expenditures (1970-2000)	2
Figure 1.2:	Comprehensive View of Agricultural Policy Reform in the US, EU and WTO (1984-2000)	6
Figure 2.1:	Linked Policy Games in the US, EU and GATT/WTO	23
Figure 2.2:	The Dynamic Agricultural Policy-making Process	25
Figure 3.1:	Producer Subsidy Equivalents (PSE) for OECD Countries (1997-2000)	37
Figure 3.2:	World Wheat Stocks and Prices (1980-1986)	42
Figure 4.1:	Decision-making Process for EC/EU Agricultural Trade Policy Formation	52
Figure 4.2:	Total Value of US and EU Agricultural Exports (1980-1986)	57
Figure 4.3:	World Prices of Selected Commodities (1980-1990)	57
Figure 4.4:	US and EU Exports and Producer Subsidy Equivalents (1980-1986)	58
Figure 4.5:	World Wheat and Corn Prices (1985-1991)	70
Figure 4.6:	US and EC Outlays for Agricultural Policy (1985-1991)	71
Figure 4.7:	US and EU Wheat Stocks (1985-1991)	72
Figure 5.1:	Bargaining Process for US Agricultural Policy at the Time of the 1990 Farm Bill	78
Figure 5.2:	US Exports, Federal Support and Farm Income (1980-1990)	86
Figure 5.3:	US Farm Spending, Producer Prices, Stocks and Exports (1985-1990)	87
Figure 5.4:	US Federal Budget Deficit (1980-1992)	87
Figure 6.1:	Decision-making Process for EC/EU Agricultural Policy Formation at the time of the MacSharry Reform	97
Figure 6.2:	EAGGF Spending Compared to Guideline	103
Figure 6.3:	EU Cereal, Dairy and Beef Stocks, Intervention Prices and Export Subsidies	104
Figure 6.4:	EU Agricultural Income (1985-1992)	105
Figure 6.5:	German Budget Surplus / Deficit (1987-1992)	114
Figure 8.1:	US Budget Deficit (1990-1997)	159
Figure 8.2:	US Agricultural Exports, Total Trade Balance and Agricultural Trade Balance (1990-1997)	160
Figure 8.3:	World Prices for Wheat and Corn (1990-1996)	161
Figure 9.1:	EU Agricultural Income Levels and Intervention Stocks (1992-1997)	194
Figure 9.2:	EU EAGGF Farm Policy Spending (1992-1997)	195
Figure 9.3:	Agenda 2000: Projected Agricultural Expenditures (1994-2006)	196

List of Figures

Figure 9.4:	Commission Projections of Ending Cereals Stocks (1995-2006)	197
Figure 9.5:	Commission Projections of Ending Beef and Veal Stocks (1995-2005)	198
Figure 9.6:	Commission Projections on EU Wheat Exports and the URAA Limit	199

List of Tables

Table 3.1:	Three Competing Paradigms of Agricultural Policy	32
Table 3.2:	Producer Subsidy Equivalents (PSE), Nominal Protection Coefficients (NPC) and Nominal Assistance Coefficients (NAC), OECD Countries, 1986-1998	37
Table 9.1:	Agenda 2000: Agricultural Expenditure Projections, Billion Euro, in Current Prices (assumes two per cent inflation per year)	179
Table 9.2:	EU Budget Payments and Receipts (1996)	191
Table 9.3:	Comparison of MacSharry and Agenda 2000 Reforms	192

List of Boxes

Box 9.1:	The Cork Declaration	178
Box 9.2:	Agenda 2000: Rural Development	182
Box 9.3:	Agricultural Policy Objectives	202

Preface

This project was launched in 1996 when the authors, discussing the significant changes to agricultural policy embodied in the 1992 MacSharry reforms in the EU, the 1995 Uruguay Round Agreement on Agriculture, and the 1996 US Federal Agriculture Improvement and Reform (FAIR) Act, decided that these reforms were significant enough to justify a sequel to their 1990 book, *Agricultural Policy Reform: Politics and Process in the EC and USA*. They met in Minneapolis in the summer of 1997 to develop a research design for the new book.

Work began during the 1997-98 academic year, when Wayne Moyer had a sabbatical. He spent October to January in Washington, DC, where he did research at the National Center for Food and Agricultural Policy and conducted the Washington interviews. During the remainder of the sabbatical, from January to August 1998, he was a Visiting Scholar at Wye College of the University of London (now Imperial College at Wye), carrying out the EU research, and making trips to Belgium, France, Germany and Ireland to conduct interviews. Tim Josling conducted his part of the research at Stanford and also in Oxford, where he taught at Stanford's program from January-March 1998. Moyer and Josling met several times over the course of the year in Washington and the UK to discuss their work, and subsequently in California and in Iowa.

Valuable inputs into our work were an April 1999 symposium on agricultural policy developments in the EU and a June 2000 workshop on policy changes in the EU and the US in relation to the WTO, both sponsored at Stanford by the European Forum, Institute for International Studies. The mix of economic analysis and political science needed to explain the reforms of the 1990s came out clearly in both meetings. With their respective disciplinary perspectives (Moyer as a political scientist and Josling as an economist), the authors found such discussions as stimulating in explaining the significant reforms of the 1990s as they had in their earlier work evaluating the more incremental changes of the 1980s.

Josling and Moyer are grateful to the many people who helped in one way or another with this project. They especially wish to thank Stefan Tangermann and David Orden and the anonymous reviewers who read the entire manuscript, providing detailed and very helpful comments. They also are grateful to Allan Buckwell, Berkeley Hill, Dale Hathaway, David Harvey, Ray Hopkins, Wade Jacoby, Philip Lowe, Rob Paarlberg, Clive Potter and Michael Tracy, who each provided helpful advice at one point or another during the course of the project. Special thanks are due to Hathaway, Buckwell and Tracy in other respects as well. Hathaway, the Director of the National Center for Food and Agricultural Center, provided Moyer with office space and helpful suggestions about people to interview in the Washington phase of the research. Buckwell was a superb host for Moyer at Wye College, welcoming him to academic life there, providing extremely valuable insights about the EU process, and contributing guidance on the Brussels interviews. Tracy shared his vast knowledge of the Common Agricultural Policy and provided a fine list of people to interview, many from a perspective different than that of the anglo-saxon policy analyst.

The authors owe a huge debt of gratitude to Rachel Anderson, Josling's research assistant at Stanford University, for helping with the research, preparing the tables and charts, keeping track of revisions and getting the final manuscript ready for publication. Her careful and tireless work made a major contribution to the quality of the final product.

Moyer greatly appreciates the assistance provided by Grinnell College, and in particular the Rosenfield Program endowment for providing him with generous research support to undertake this project. He also wants to thank Grinnell College students Gordon Rice and Kenneth Yeung for research assistance.

Finally, the authors want to thank their wives, Helen and Anthea, for their unflagging support and encouragement as this project progressed, even if it spread over a somewhat longer period of time than we had originally anticipated.

Acknowledgements

A series of 37 in-depth interviews was conducted on a non-attribution basis by Wayne Moyer with participants, former participants and close observers of the United States and European Union agricultural policy processes. These interviews took place in Washington DC, during the period from November 1997 to January 1998; and in Brussels, Bonn, Paris and London, during the period from March to June 1988. The domestic policy interviews focused generally on how agricultural policy is made in the USA and EU, with specific discussion of the 1990 and 1996 US farm bills, the 1992 MacSharry reforms and the 1999 Agenda 2000 reforms of the EU Common Agricultural Policy. The international policy interviews focused on the GATT Uruguay Round trade negotiations. The authors wish to thank the various people who were interviewed for giving willingly of their time, for speaking candidly, and for sharing their insights. These individuals were extremely helpful in piecing together the puzzles in US and EU agricultural policy formation and in the Uruguay Round Negotiations.

The authors owe a debt of gratitude to Dr. Dale Hathaway of the National Institute for Food and Agricultural Policy, Washington, DC, Professor Allan Buckwell at Wye College of the University of London, and Michael Tracy, former director in the Secretariat of the European Council for assistance in scheduling the interviews, and for sharing their considerable expertise in private conversations.

List of Interviews in Europe Completed During Spring 1998

1. **Frans Andriessen** - Former EU Agricultural Commissioner and External Affairs Commissioner
2. **Dirk Ahner** - Director, Directorate A, DGVI, European Commission
3. **Isabelle Albouy-Delponte** - Brussels Representative - Cerealiers de France
4. **Isabel Boussard** - Ingenieur de Recherche, Fondation Nationale des Sciences Politiques
5. **Noel Devisch** - President Belgische Boerenbond, Brussels, Belgium
6. **Helene Delorme** - Directeur de recherche a la FNSP, Centre d'Etudes et de Rescherches Internationales, Paris France
7. **Rainer Eberle** - German Ministry of Foreign Affairs
8. **Deterd Goeman** - German Ministry of Agriculture
9. **Eckart Guth - Director,** Directorate A, DGXIX, European Commission, formerly DGI
10. **Ulrich Maas** - German Ministry of Agriculture
11. **Ray MacSharry** - Former EC Agriculture Commissioner

Acknowledgements xv

12. **Mary Minch** - Former Cabinet Member of Ray MacSharry, now DGVI
13. **Rolf Moehler** - Former Deputy Director General, DGVI, European Commission
14. **David Roberts** - Deputy Director General, DGVI, European Commission
15. **Erhard Schwinne** - German Ministry of Agriculture
16. **Theodor Seegers** - German Ministry of Agriculture
17. **Peter Witt** - German Ministry of Agriculture
18. **Risto Volanen** - Secretary General of COPA
19. **Natacha Yellachich** - World Wildlife Fund European Policy Office, Brussels

List of Interviews in Washington, DC

1. **John Campbell** (telephone) - Deputy Undersecretary of Agriculture 1990 and currently Vice President Agricultural Processing, Omaha, Nebraska
2. **Keith Collins** - Chief Economist USDA and **Joseph Glauber** - Deputy Chief Economist, USDA
3. **Kenneth A. Cook** - President Environmental Working Group, Washington DC
4. **Charles F. Connor** - President, Corn Refiners Association, former aide to Senator Lugar and former Chief of Staff, Senate Agricultural Committee
5. **Susie Earley** - Office of the US Trade Representative
6. **Bruce L. Gardner** - Professor, Department of Agricultural and Research Economics, University of Maryland and former Assistant secretary of Agriculture for Economics
7. **Ralph Grossi** - President American Farmland Trust
8. **Vernie Hubert** and **Howard Conley** - Minority Staff, House Agriculture Committee
9. **Julius Katz** - Deputy US Trade Representative 1989-1993
10. **Kendall Keith** - President, National Grain and Feed Association
11. **Senator Richard Lugar** - Chairman Senate Agriculture Committee
12. **Eugene Moos** - Undersecretary of Agriculture for International Affairs and Commodity Programs
13. **Joe O'Mara** - Chief Agricultural Policy Negotiator - Uruguay Round of the GATT
14. **Bill O'Connor** - Policy Director, House Agriculture Committee and formerly Chief of Staff to Secretary of Agriculture Madigan
15. **Robert Peterson** - President, National Grain Trade Council
16. **Charles Riemenschneider** - Chief of Staff, Senate Agriculture Committee 1990-1994
17. **Craig Thorn** - Director Europe, Africa and Middle East Division USDA Foreign Agricultural Service
18. **Ann Tutwiler** - Central Soya Cerestar and President, IPC

Chapter 1

Introduction

1.1 Agricultural Policy Reform in the US, EC/EU and GATT/WTO

Industrial country agricultural policy in the post-World War II era has been highly protectionist, commodity based, market distorting and dominated by domestic politics. The agricultural sector has therefore lagged behind in the general trend of deregulation and market liberalization that has permeated most sectors of the economy. The problems this has created have spilled over into the international arena. Subsidies have been paid to farmers largely on the basis of production and financed by consumers, leading to the build-up of embarrassing surpluses, the disposal of which has proved increasingly disruptive to the international market for agricultural goods. The United States and the European Community (EC) can share much of the blame for the export of the surplus capacity, though major importing countries such as Japan have kept many of their markets closed and smaller countries have also maintained high support levels for many crops.[1] By the mid 1980s, the costs of agricultural policy in many countries had grown to unacceptable levels, and the disruption of agricultural markets had created international conflict.

As a result of increasing costs and market disruption, both the EC and US began to undertake reform of their agricultural policies. The policy changes in the 1980s were analyzed in a previous book (Moyer and Josling, 1990).[2] During the 1990s, more significant reforms were undertaken in both Europe and America, accompanied by the inclusion of agriculture into the liberal international trade regime of the World Trade Organization (WTO). We have diagramed these changes and the interplay between domestic and international reform in Figure 1.2.

---

[1] We will use the term European Community (EC) in our discussion of policy-making in Europe prior to the 1993 Maastricht Treaty, which created the European Union (EU).
[2] It is not easy to define agricultural policy reform. The notion of reform is essentially subjective. A policy change seen by one group as reform could be viewed by another as a modest revolution in policy, or as an improvement in program administration. The definition employed in this book will be the same one used in our 1990 work. Reform is *a significant shift in policy direction, usually involving changes in policy instruments, arising from general dissatisfaction with the current operation of the policy*. The connection between policy reform and the appearance of a new paradigm for agriculture is discussed in Chapter 3.

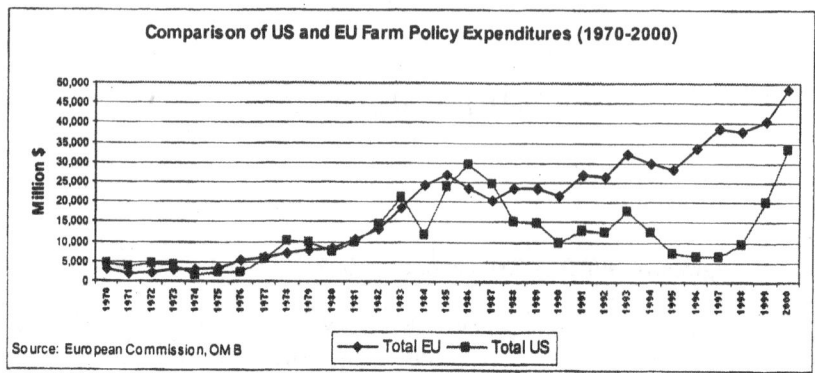

Figure 1.1: Comparison of US and EU Farm Policy Expenditures (1970-2000)

These reforms, overall, have significantly liberalized agricultural policy, but have not succeeded in stemming the growth of government farm spending.[3] Indeed, the continuing high cost of government support for agriculture has provided a strong impetus for successive reform efforts.

In our earlier work, we analyzed the reforms of the 1980s. This book will explain in detail the progression of domestic farm policy reforms in both the US and EU for the 1990s, the international agricultural trade reforms in the GATT and WTO, and the interplay between domestic and international reforms. What provided the impetus for each reform? How does one explain the timing and content? How did the reforms of the 1990s follow from those of the 1980s? Why have the reforms generally been liberalizing with greater market orientation and the de-coupling of government farm payments from production? But, why has liberalization not gone even further? Why, with the farm population declining in both the US and EU, have policy-makers been unable to control farm spending?

A number of previous works have attempted to explain agricultural policy reform. Writing for the 1980s, Moyer and Josling (1990) saw reform in the US and EU driven by budget pressures, but slowed by compartmentalized policy processes dominated by the farm policy community. For the 1990s, a number of scholars have shown that the MacSharry reforms were driven both by international pressures generated by the Uruguay Round trade negotiations and by the domestic unsustainability of the CAP (Tangermann (1998), Swinbank and Tanner (1997) Coleman and Tangermann (1997), Patterson (1997). These authors also see the completion of the MacSharry reforms as instrumental for the successful completion of

---

[3] Reforms are considered liberalizing if they make policy more market-oriented. EU agricultural price supports rose from $6 billion in 1977 to $39 billion in 1997, though over this period the EU increased its membership from 9 to 15 countries. Support expenditures in the US show more up and down fluctuation, but still increased over time. Outlays rose from $4 billion in 1977 to $25 billion in the peak year of 1986, then declined to $6.4 billion in 1997, before rising to $28 billion in 2000 (Moyer and Josling, 1990, p.xvi; USDA, 1997).

Introduction

the Uruguay Round Agreement on Agriculture. Patterson explains the linkage between domestic and international reform in terms of multi-level bargaining games, while Coleman and Tangermann see the influence of intersecting CAP and GATT games. Webber (1997,1998) argues that both CAP reform and the GATT negotiations were strongly influenced by intergovernmental politics between France and Germany. Vahl (1997) makes the case that the supra-national EC Commission played a critical leadership role in negotiating a GATT agreement acceptable to the EU and in then selling that agreement to member states. Coleman, Skogstad and Atkinson (1997) find that a shift in thinking about agriculture policy from a *state-assisted* paradigm to a *market liberal paradigm* is associated with agriculture policy reform in the US, EU, Canada and Australia. They note that corporatist policy networks lend themselves to a cumulative, negotiated, problem-solving trajectory to paradigm change whereas state directed or pressure pluralist networks are more likely to be associated with crisis-driven change. Coleman, Atkinson and Montpetit (1997) conclude in their study of agriculture policy during the 1990s in the US, EU and France that systemic retrenchment and obfuscation helped governments overcome the resistance of entrenched farm lobbies in producing significant policy change. They also find that when agriculture was introduced successfully into international trade negotiations, the domestic rules of the game and players at the table were reconstituted in ways that promoted reform. Finally, they note the importance of two systemic variables - rules and practices that structure the roles of groups in policy-making, and the ideological position of the ruling party in the legislature - in explaining farm program change. Orden, Paarlberg and Roe (1999) downplay the importance of the Uruguay Round in promoting US agricultural policy reform in the 1996 FAIR Act, arguing that the election of a Republican congress in 1994 and rising commodity prices were far more important.

All of these works provide valuable insights. However, each represents only a partial analysis focusing on specific policy decisions rather than examining the full progression of policy reforms in the US, EU and the GATT between 1980 and 2000. Ingersent and Rayner (1999) provide an excellent overview of reform during the entire time period, and for an even longer time span, identifying the economic trends that promoted change. But they do not consider the process and politics shaping the reforms that finally emerged. This book will contribute a more complete explanation of how politics and process, influenced by past policies, national and international economic trends and political developments, shaped farm policy reform.

1.2 The Progression of Agricultural Policy Reforms in the US, EC/EU and the GATT/WTO

Before discussing in detail our argument, it may be helpful to layout in sequence the various steps toward policy reform in the US, EU and the GATT between 1980 and

2000.[4] The first important development in this time period came when the EC, facing a farm spending crisis, took a significant step toward policy reform with the decision in 1984 to impose dairy quotas (see Moyer and Josling, 1990, Petit, 1987). This did little to liberalize trade in dairy products, though it did reduce EC milk surpluses and stabilized expenditures for dairy support. The US farm crisis of the mid-1980s contributed both to the reforms in the 1985 US Farm Bill and to the efforts to liberalize agricultural trade in the GATT Uruguay Round negotiations. The US had lost export market share partly as a result of the strong dollar, partly because loan rates had been set too high in the 1981 Farm Bill, and partly because of EC competition fueled by export subsidies (see Moyer and Josling, 1990, Chapter 9).

With GATT negotiating differences with the EC so pronounced, the US was not under much pressure to liberalize agriculture policy in the 1990 farm bill, which was completed just before the Heysel Conference. In fact, the bill provided for increased subsidies through the Export Enhancement Program as a "bargaining chip" to pressure the EC to agree to reduce export subsidies in the GATT negotiations (Orden, Paarlberg and Roe, p.98). However, a liberalizing impetus was created by the large US budget deficit, which led to the establishment of the "triple-base" program, dividing farmer's base acreage into three categories: land with crops eligible for deficiency payments; required land set-aside under the Acreage Reduction Program (ARP); and 15 percent of base acreage on which farmers could grow whatever they wanted, but not receive deficiency payments.

The MacSharry reforms, along with the reports of two GATT panels that ruled against EC oilseed subsidies, made it possible for the US and EC to bridge their differences, and reach the Blair House I agreement in November 1992.[5] Domestic support was to be reduced 20 percent, tariff barriers cut by 36 percent and export subsidies reduced by 36 percent in expenditure and 21 percent in volume. Both parties agreed to create a new "blue box" for US deficiency payments and EC compensatory payments, not subject to challenge in the GATT for a period of time (the Peace Clause).[6] This agreement was unacceptable to the government of France, facing angry farmers in a tough parliamentary election campaign. Following the victory of the conservatives in the election, the French were able to force further negotiations. These negotiations produced the Blair House II agreement in December 1993, which dealt with French objections by extending the Peace Clause from six to nine years and by delaying export subsidy cuts to allow the EU to dispose of its stocks without a collapse in prices. This agreement was accepted by the other parties of the GATT, thus

---

[4] See Figure 1.2 for a graphic representation of this sequence of events.

[5] This agreement was more or less along the lines suggested by WTO Director General Arthur Dunkel in his December 1991 draft. Blair House is the US government's official residence for state visitors in Washington, DC.

[6] The "blue box" created a third category of subsidies in addition to the "green box" and "amber box." Green box subsidies were allowable in that were perceived not to distort markets. Amber box subsidies, perceived as market-distorting, were to be reduced.

allowing the Uruguay Round to be completed with the March 1994 Marrakesh agreement, and the creation of the World Trade Organization.

With the 1990 US Farm Bill about to expire, debate on new farm legislation began in early 1995. The Uruguay Round Agreement on Agriculture (URAA) provided only minimal constraints to the debate in that the domestic support reductions of the 1990 Farm Bill met URAA requirements, while export subsidies had declined due to increasing world prices. However, the Uruguay Round enhanced the attractiveness of liberalized domestic policy in that it portended greater openness in international markets. The Federal Agriculture Improvement and Reform (FAIR) Act, approved in April 1996, marked a significant liberalizing departure from previous farm legislation. It de-coupled farm payments from production by abolishing deficiency payments and ARP set-asides. Farmers could grow whatever they wanted on their land, and receive whatever they could get in the market. To cushion the adjustment, they would receive acreage based compensatory payments, adjusted for average yields over the previous five years, under Production Flexibility Contracts. These payments would gradually decline over the six years of the farm bill's duration.

The FAIR Act has not played out as intended. Conceived at a time when farm prices were high, it was anticipated that the costs of farm support would decline over time, even though they would rise in the short run. However, the sharp decline in world prices led to the US congress to pass emergency farm bailout measures in 1998, 1999 and 2000, which have produced the largest levels of farm support ever, reaching $28 billion in 2000.

The FAIR Act, by de-coupling farm payments from production, served notice to the EU that the US would be willing to abolish the "blue box" in the next round of WTO agricultural trade negotiations due to begin by the end of 1999. Moreover, the EU had other reasons to undertake further reforms. Agricultural spending had actually increased after the MacSharry reforms, and would continue to increase, without further policy change. None of the EU members was willing to pay the increased cost, particularly Germany, the largest contributor, which was burdened by the huge expense of integrating former East Germany. Another impetus was the prospective entry into the EU of the former communist countries of Central and Eastern Europe. Extending the MacSharry compensatory payments to these countries would break the CAP budget. Projections showed that EU export subsidies would soon exceed Uruguay Round limits and would have to be reduced.

The EU Commission, recognizing the realities, proposed an Agenda 2000 reform package in June 1997. This proposal continued and intensified the MacSharry reforms, calling for further significant price cuts for cereals, oilseeds and beef, with reduced support for dairy and increased compensatory payments. There was also a new emphasis on spending for rural development and agri-environmental measures. The Agenda 2000 package was finally approved by the April 1999 Berlin summit, after the price cuts were weakened and the dairy reforms delayed.

6	*Agricultural Policy Reform*

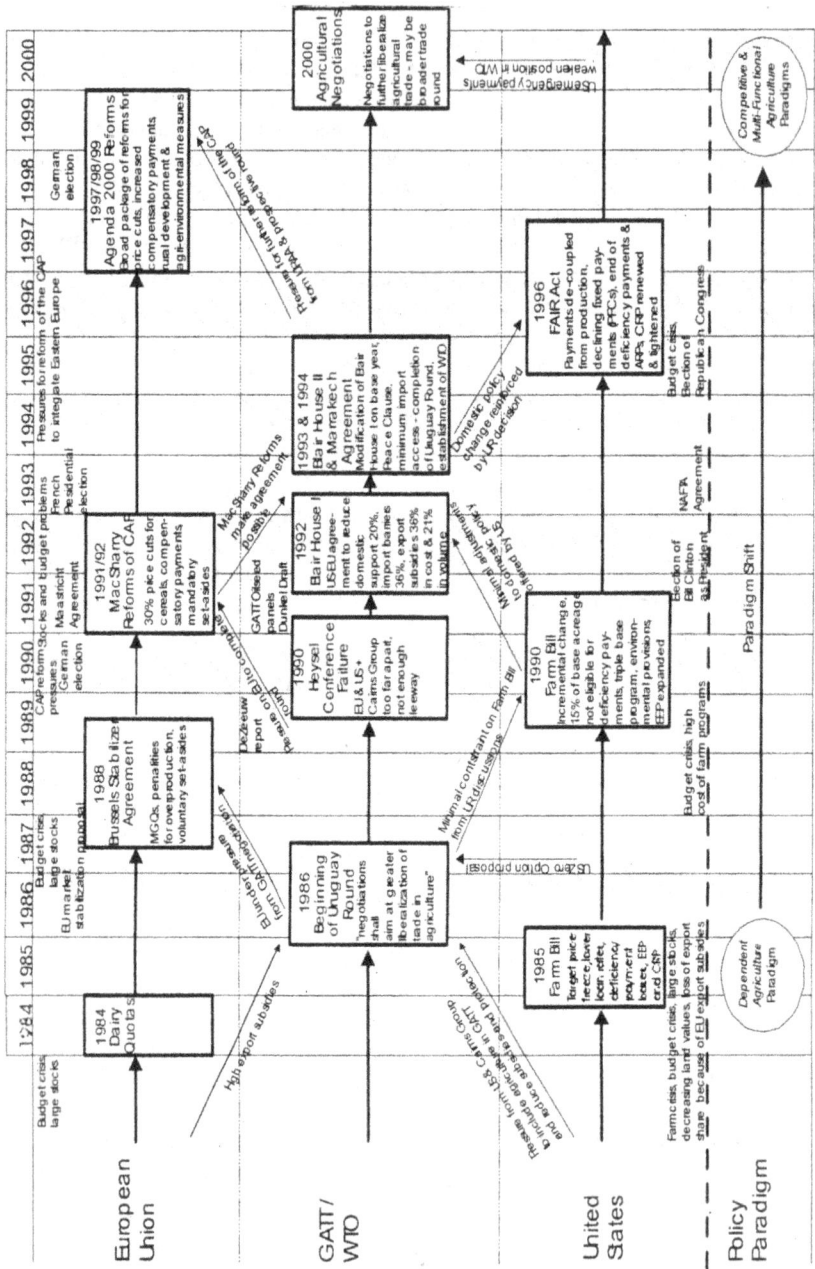

Figure 1.2: Comprehensive View of Agricultural Policy Reform in the US, EU and WTO (1984-2000)

Introduction

The WTO agricultural trade negotiations began seriously in the summer of 2000 after being side-tracked by the break-down of the Seattle Conference in November 1999. As in the Uruguay Round, there are serious negotiating differences between the US (and the Cairns Group) on the one hand and the EU on the other.[7] The US proposes further liberalization through the reduction of tariffs and the elimination of export subsidies and would limit agricultural spending to a proportion of total production. The EU, though willing to contemplate further reductions in domestic supports, import barriers and export subsidies, insists on retaining the "blue box" for compensatory payments. It also wants recognition of the multi-functionality of agriculture. This would exclude from WTO disciplines payments to preserve the country-side, small towns and villages, or to compensate farmers for the loss of market share to those whose costs are lower as a result of not having to provide these public goods.[8]

There are a number of puzzles in this reform sequence that this book will attempt to explain. Why, for example did US and EU policies tend to converge? Is there any reason to believe that these policies will converge further in the future, or are they likely to diverge? Why did agricultural policy expenditures in the EU increase after the approval of the MacSharry reforms and in the US after the FAIR Act? To what extent did the Uruguay Round Agreement on Agriculture constrain subsequent domestic agricultural policy reform in the US and EU? Is the WTO process likely to constrain future reform?

1.3 The Analytical Framework

In our previous book, we examined the steps toward US and EC agricultural policy reform in the 1980s using an analytical framework that explained the decision-making process operating in response to a wide range of factors. These included economic trends and shocks, political developments, group and national interests, outside political inputs (lobbies, academic writings, pressures from allies and other trading partners), inside political inputs (the positions of various political actors and how they are formed), and the interplay between different actors (see Moyer and Josling 1990, Chapter 1). We analyzed decision-making using a series of conceptual models including rational national actor, public choice, organizational process, bureaucratic politics and partisan mutual adjustment. In this book we will build on this conceptual framework, adding to our conceptual focus the nature of paradigm shifts, the importance of path dependency analysis, and the importance of multi-level and linked bargaining games.

---

[7] The Cairns Group proposal calls for export subsidies to be cut by at least 50 percent from 2004, before being entirely phased out (*Agra Europe*, June 23, 2000, p.EP/4).

[8] Agriculture is viewed as a provider of public goods not only in the EU but increasingly in the US, where the multifunctionality perspective is becoming well-established. Of course, the term multifunctionality is not favored in US official documents that discuss the role of agriculture in providing environmental and other rural amenities.

1.4 Central Themes in Policy Reform

This book will argue that agricultural policy in the US and EU is highly path dependent; that it takes a crisis to produce non-incremental change. The farm policy community has been dominant in shaping the content of the reforms that have been implemented, though it does not control whether there will be reform, or indeed the timing of reform. The policy inertia is so great, and the vested interest of the farm community in the policy *status-quo* usually so significant, that the impetus for reform must come from the outside. This may be in the form of economic pressures, political pressures, or some combination of both. When change appears inevitable, the farm policy community has taken action to avoid losing control of policy. It has been able to shape the reforms because of its expertise and positioning in the policy process. Thus the implemented reforms have only gone as far as necessary to remove the external pressures for change, and have tended to minimize the harm to the farm community. While perceived budget pressures were a catalyst for reform in every instance of significant policy change, the farm policy community has been strong enough to protect farm spending, even to ensure its increase in the MacSharry and FAIR Act reforms.

The paths of US and EU farm policy have changed significantly in the 1990s accompanied by changes in the dominant way of thinking (the policy paradigm). In both the US and EU, the prevailing view of agriculture over most of the post-war period has been based on the notion that farming was unable to compete either internally with the non-farm sector for resources, or with farming overseas. The major role of government was to find and secure markets for farm products. Government would provide border protection, buy surpluses, impose production quotas, support prices and provide export subsidies.

The escalating costs of subsidies, combined with domestic economic policy reform and growing pressures to bring agriculture within the GATT/WTO international trade regime undermined this paradigm. The increasingly dominant view of agriculture in the US is that the farm sector can stand on its own two feet. Government policy performs the twin tasks of giving competitive farmers a "level playing field" on which to compete, while at the same time putting a low safety net under those who cannot play on that field. Supply control is seen as unnecessary and undesirable. Policy instruments include de-coupled payments to cushion the transition from previous policies.

Shifting views of agricultural policy in both the US and EU have probably contributed to the liberalizing reforms that have been instituted, and to convergence in US and EU agricultural policy. But, such shifts do not necessarily assure that the EU and US will be able to agree on further liberalizing reforms or that US and EU farm policies will converge further. A different new paradigm may be taking hold in Europe. In many countries of the EU, agriculture is viewed as a provider of public goods in addition to, and in many ways as important as its role as a producer of raw

Introduction

material for the food industry. The market for commodities inadequately rewards the farmer for such public goods as a pleasant-looking and environmentally friendly countryside. Appropriate instruments for policy include environmental payments, either as a reward for providing public goods or as compensation for the loss of market share to those whose costs are lower as a result of not having to provide the public good. The clash of these seemingly inconsistent ideas of the nature of agriculture and its place in society promises to keep the debate about farm policy reform lively for years to come.

The plan for the book is as follows. Chapter 2 will lay out the analytical framework for the study of policy reform. Chapter 3 will include a discussion of the notion of a paradigm shift and discuss its impact on agricultural policies in several OECD countries. Chapter 4 will analyze the collapse of the Uruguay Round, up to the failed December 1990 meeting. Chapter 5 will discuss the 1990 US Farm Bill and why it produced only incremental change to US farm policy. Chapter 6 will examine the development of the MacSharry reforms of the CAP that signaled a major shift in policy in the EU. Chapter 7 will cover the bi-lateral negotiations between the US and EC at Blair House, which served as a catalyst for the final Uruguay Round Agreement on Agriculture. Chapter 8 will analyze the 1996 US Farm Bill, assessing the impact of the Uruguay Round, the US budget crisis and a shift of political control in the US Congress. Chapter 9 will discuss the EU's Agenda 2000 and how it has been influenced by the Uruguay Round, the 1996 US Farm Bill and the prospective entry into the EU of the countries of Central and Eastern Europe. Chapter 10 will discuss the future of agricultural policy reform and the prospects for the next round of talks in the WTO. Chapter 11 will make comparisons between process and policy in the US and EU. A final chapter will attempt some conclusions on the possible future of the reform process and how this may be influenced by recent developments in the political and economic environment.

Chapter 2

The Analytical Framework for Farm Policy Reform

2.1 Introduction

Policy reform is a complex process involving political and economic forces acting in a specific institutional environment. The first task for the analyst hoping to understand this process is to develop a framework into which the various elements can be placed. The analytical framework used in this book builds on that used in our 1990 book (Moyer and Josling (1990), Chapter 1) that focused on the farm policy reforms of the 1980s. In this chapter we discuss a number of alternative approaches to understanding agricultural policy reform. Each of these approaches illuminates certain aspects of the policy process, though none of them by themselves provides a full picture. After a discussion of some of the main types of models that have been used for explaining policy making, we attempt a heuristic approach for integrating insights from several of these models. But the policy making model is only the first step in the process of developing a framework. The decisions on farm policy are made at various levels, national, regional and multilateral. We discuss the particular problem of multilevel political processes, first in the context of trade negotiations and then with respect to the European Union, which itself illustrates a particular type of two-level game. Finally, we raise the issue of the dynamics of policy reform, exploring the notions of path dependency of the reform process and of paradigm shifts in the perception of agriculture's place in the economy and the objectives of farm policy.

2.2 Explaining National Policy Decision Making

The analysis of farm policy reform necessarily implies the adoption of a model of the process of decision-making at the national level. The literature provides a wide menu of analytical constructs from which to choose. They differ in the basic objective function specified or implied and in the complexity with which the actual decision process is represented. Each can be instructive as a way of looking at a particular issue. None can by themselves illuminate all the aspects of agricultural policy formulation and change. The main features of four of these models of national decision making are discussed below.

Rational Choice Models

Rational choice models come in different flavors. Two of these varieties are discussed here. One set of rational choice models focuses on the policy maker as an individual actor playing a role on the national scene. The other focuses on group or institutional behavior, and is usually called "public choice".

The rational actor The rational (national) actor is by assumption a calculating central decision-maker with the power both to make and to implement decisions.[9] The actor develops a clear set of goals, with priorities rank ordered, consistent with the national interest. A variety of options are considered for every decision, on the basis of cost-benefit analysis, and the most efficient option is chosen. Governments can pursue economic, social or political goals or a combination of these objectives. The essential nature of these models is that policy is made through analysis and not as a result of "politics". Not surprisingly, the presence of such an actor is often assumed in economic discussions of policy: the analysis is by implication based on an economic calculus of costs and benefits rather than the study of the political process. Perhaps more surprising is the popularity of such models among political scientists. But clearly the ability to use more precise models of political behavior, and to come to predictions of policy choice under the assumption of rationality is appealing.

It is important to note that the rational actor does not only take economic effects into account. In agricultural policy, the rational actor would no doubt add a number of objectives to the economic calculations of costs and benefits of commodity production. Such an actor could work to assure a fair standard of living for farmers, to save the family farm, to conserve the natural environment, to ensure adequate food for consumers, or to maintain vigorous and pleasant rural communities. The agricultural policy process rarely approximates the rational actor model because there usually is no unitary actor. However, this model has usefulness for analysts in that it provides a standard of judgment for the policy process. For instance, if saving the family farm is indeed the goal of society then one can ask what are the most efficient means of achieving this goal, and how closely does the government policy square with the most efficient means.

This model has the advantage in that it is relatively easy to apply, since it requires no knowledge of the workings of the policy process. It needs only an understanding of the goals of policy and of how costs and benefits are assessed. It is not, however, very useful in explaining the selection of goals or the rank ordering of priorities, since these are matters of value choice more than analysis. The rational actor model does not get

---

[9] The rational actor is elucidated in Allison & Zelikow (1999), Chapter 1. In the economics literature a "benign dictator" makes policy choices with the best interests of the country in mind.

very far in specifying the available options, since these have a basis both in the ideas circulating in the policy process and in institutional capabilities. It is also not very useful in explaining actions when power is divided, and when bargaining and politics are involved.

In our 1990 analysis, we showed that the "rational actor" model had some limited usefulness in analyzing the introduction of EC dairy quotas and budget stabilizers and the policy outcomes in the 1981 and 1985 US farm bills. There were clear goals in each instance (such as limiting budget costs and protecting farmer income), and a limited number of options were considered. However, it is difficult to explain the policy outcomes even in these cases as efficient results based on cost-benefit analysis.

Public choice models Public choice models also fit into the rational choice category. In this set of models, rationality is shifted to the level of the individual or group maximizing utility subject to constraints.[10] Individuals with common interests combine together to form organizations in order to protect their interests. These organizations develop interests that are not always identical to the interests of their constituencies. Government agencies have their own interests. The role of particular institutions is very important. Elected officials can be counted upon to do whatever it takes to maximize votes. Bureaucrats will work to strengthen the position of their organization and their own position within the organization. The openness of the process and the degree of accountability are also matters of significance. The resources that an individual or group is willing to commit to a given issue will depend on how much is at stake.

Public choice analysis is certainly very useful for the agricultural policy analyst. In particular it provides insights about the groups that try to influence policy. It helps explain why the farm lobby continues to dominate the policy process, even though its constituency is small and declining in number as farm size increases and machinery is substituted for labor. Farmers cannot easily move their fixed capital resources and have an attachment to their land. Hence, they have a strong incentive to mobilize. To use the terminology of Alfred Hirschman, denied easy exit, they exercise strong political voice (Senior Nello, 1984, p.269). Increasing this incentive is the fact that farmers receive massive financial benefits from government, which they feel compelled to defend. The farm lobby's mobilization is enhanced by the fact that farmers are a relatively homogenous group, with common interests. Farm organizations have the ability to hold the loyalty of farmers, even when interests diverge, in that they provide private benefits to members, such as life insurance. Bureaucrats in agricultural ministries have an incentive to given special attention to the demands of farm groups, as they need the support of these groups to ensure policy implementation. Consumers and voters are less directly affected by farm policy. Thus, they have less incentive to commit the resources necessary to influence farm policy.

---

[10] Senior Nello (1984) gives a useful summary of this approach and a full biography. She later updated this (Senior Nello, 1997), applying the "New Political Economy" approach to agricultural policy formation in the European Union.

Even though they are far more numerous than farmers, consumers and voters, who are highly heterogeneous in their interests, have far more difficulty organizing collectively to influence agricultural policy.

Public choice, however, still has some limitations for policy analysis. Decision-makers often have competing interests and conflicting loyalties, making it difficult to determine in advance how they will act. For instance, agricultural ministers have a loyalty to the national government as well as to farmers. Bureaucrats in agricultural ministries have an interest in preserving the influence of their organizations, which may sometimes put them at odds with the farm lobbies. When policy makers have multiple values to consider, their behavior is not easy to model. There is substantial evidence from the psychological literature that individuals have difficulty making trade-offs between values (Jervis, 1976; George, 1980). The decision-making context is often critical in influencing their actions. Public choice analysis does not fully explain multiple policy goals or options, the influence of the decision making structure, or the impact of bargaining dynamics.

In spite of these limitations, "public choice" proved to be very helpful in our analysis of policy reform in the 1980s. Lobbies took positions that one would have expected based on their interests and the farm lobby showed a predictable intensity of involvement. Within the EC, national agricultural ministries appeared highly responsive to the positions of entrenched farm lobbies. Farm lobbies also exercised a perceptible influence on both the EC Agriculture Directorate-General (DGVI) and the US Department of Agriculture (USDA), although these bodies showed some complexity in their activities. DGVI had to strike a balance between the often-conflicting positions of national farm lobbies, on the one hand, and, between farm interests and broader Commission goals, on the other. USDA had to balance farm interests with the broader priorities of the Administration. The EC and US decision-making processes, by placing primary legislative power in the hands of bodies closely linked to farm interests, respectively the Council of Agriculture Ministers and the House and Senate Agriculture committees, helped magnify the asymmetrically strong influence of farm lobbies in policy outcomes.

The Organizational Process Model

The organizational process model fills some of the gaps in rational actor and public choice analysis.[11] It starts from the assumption that policy is not made by a monolithic single actor, but rather by a constellation of loosely allied organizations on top of which leaders sit. Power is fragmented and problems are factored. Each organization has responsibility for a narrow set of problems, which encourages organizational parochialism. Organizations tend to be reactive, rather than pro-active, particularly when they are large and complex. They tend to pursue organizational goals, rather than the broader goals of the community or nation, or at least to put an organizational spin

---

[11] For a full discussion of the Organizational Process model, see Allison & Zelikow (1999), Chapter 3.

on the broader goals. The organizational response to a problem is usually a programmed one, based on repertoires and standard operating procedures. Organizations do not easily manage conflicts between goals, but rather give sequential attention to goals. They tend to satisfice in choosing options, which is to say that they search for an acceptable option, not the best option. Organizational decisions usually show considerable inertia, with only incremental change. Policy at time (t) is best explained by policy at time (t-1). However, when threatened, organizations can sometimes show resourcefulness in proposing new solutions, designed to preserve their influence.

The organizational process model is useful in explaining organizational positions. It also helps explain why coordination between organizations is sometimes poor. For agriculture, it helps to explain compartmentalization, where policy is made in farm ministries, with little influence from other ministries. Organizational process helps explain the goals actually pursued and why these goals often differ from broader national goals. It also goes a long way toward explaining which options are considered and adopted as policy. Knowledge of organizational structure and process is absolutely essential for understanding agricultural policy implementation. However, the organizational process model cannot stand alone as a full explanation of the workings of agricultural policy. This model's greatest limitation is that it provides little insight into the bargaining process. It does not explain the interaction between different elements of the bureaucracy, and between elements of the bureaucracy and elected or appointed officials. It postulates a process, but makes no allowance for the interaction of different agencies or the interplay with outside actors.

The organizational process model proved helpful for explaining the inertia in both EC and US agricultural policy processes during the 1980s (Moyer and Josling, 1990). The compartmentalization of policy processes, with both executive and legislative functions handled by bodies with a strong commitment to the standard operating procedures of present policy, made it very difficult to insert new ideas into the policy debate. The "new" policy options of dairy quotas and budget stabilizers for arable crops in the EC, and fixed bases and yields for the US only got serious consideration after policymakers became convinced that there was no alternative to changing existing policy. Policy change came about largely through satisficing (finding an acceptable solution). EC policy-makers settled on milk quotas only after rejecting the two other principal alternatives (increasing the co-responsibility levy and cutting prices) as unworkable. Arable crop stabilizers were adopted because of the perceived difficulty in administering quotas for cereals and the unacceptability of major price cuts. Stabilizers were a variant of guarantee thresholds, an SOP previously implemented in the CAP. For the US, the unacceptability of lowering target prices made freezing base acreages and yields acceptable as a way of stanching budget costs, while still retaining deficiency payments.

The Government Politics Model

The weakness of the organizational process model in downplaying the importance of bargaining is remedied in the government politics model, which focuses specifically on the political process. Policy is seen in this model as the resultant of bargaining, often at a number of different levels.[12] As with the public choice interpretations, the government politics model focuses on the individual, but here the emphasis is on the interaction between individuals - the bargaining game. The structure of decision making is very important, such as who gets to sit at the bargaining table at each stage of the process. Role-playing is also very significant and the model recognizes that "where you stand depends on where you sit." The government politics model is concerned with the power resources of the various actors and their ability to bring these resources to bear. Rules and procedures are extremely important. The government politics model is also concerned with bargaining strategy, tactics and coalition building.

The government politics model is often used in the narrow sense of bargaining within the bureaucracy, where the positions of bureaucrats reflect parochial organizational interests. However, the model has applicability to a much broader range of bargaining. Examples include bargaining between bureaucrats and appointed or elected officials, between actors in the executive branch of government and those in the legislative branch, and between officials representing different levels of government. The model can also help to explain the interactions between officials representing different state or national governments; between the representatives of national governments and inter-governmental organizations; and between lobbyists and officials of state governments, national governments, or inter-governmental organizations. The strength of the government politics model is that it provides insights into the various compromises reached as policy is developed, and into how policy coherence is often sacrificed for political acceptability.[13] This model furnishes the framework for showing how different policy processes bias policy outcomes in different ways.

The principal limitation of this type of model is that it is very difficult to use it to predict in advance the outcome of a bargaining process. The positions of individual actors often depend on complex influences related to background, ideology, reference group, previous experience and the bargaining context as much as on decision-making role. Predicting the dynamics of bargaining is also elusive. Bargaining is influenced by a variety of variables difficult to assess in advance, such as the personal interplay between actors and the dynamics of a particular group. Bargaining processes have a tendency toward inertia, causing the outcomes of subsequent games to differ only

---

[12] For a full discussion of the Government Politics model, see Allison & Zelikow (1999), chapter 5.
[13] David Harvey (1998) develops a model for agricultural policy change, which involves bargaining between players including WTO & world traders, economies in transition, EU less favored areas, the EU bureaucracy, EU taxpayers, EU commercial agriculture and EU environmental and conservation groups. He argues that the power of various groups will be enhanced to the extent that they develop policies with a high degree of coherence, legitimacy and sustainability.

incrementally, particularly if the actors do not change and if the final decision requires a high degree of consensus. This is because the bargaining costs of making a major shift in policy are likely to be far higher than continuing the present policy with some adjustment.

The government politics model proved useful for explaining why the reforms proposed for the EC and US in the 1980s were attenuated as they worked their way through the policy process, with provisions added that did not seem closely linked to the reform goals. At each stage of the bargaining process, those advocating reform had to make compromises and side payments to build a winning coalition. There was a little something for each of the important farm interests in the EC dairy quota and arable crop stabilizers decisions and in the 1981 and 1985 US farm bills. The prominent position of individuals representing farm constituencies in the legislative arena of US House and Senate Agriculture committees and the EC Agriculture Council ensured that reforms would be designed in such a way as to minimize damage to farm interests. The principle of decision by consensus practiced by the EU Agriculture Council, and, to a somewhat lesser degree, by US congressional committees, helped ensure long debates before farm legislation could be finalized. It also put a premium on leadership that could broker an agreement acceptable to multiple farm constituencies.[14]

Partisan Mutual Adjustment

The partisan mutual adjustment model, explicated by Charles Lindblom, overlaps government politics in that it focuses on bargaining (1959; 1965; Lindblom and Braybrooke, 1963). This model explains why policy change tends to be incremental, and provides a normative justification for outcomes resulting from bargaining and politics rather than cost-benefit analysis. It argues that synoptic decision-making analysis (considering all the variables) is deficient. There may be no consensus over goals or their rank ordering. Even if there is consensus over goals, it may not be possible to identify in advance the costs and benefits of all of the alternatives. The net effect can be to promulgate significant policy change, which one accepts unquestioningly since it comes from "analysis," but which in fact may be seriously flawed, because of incorrect assumptions.

Moreover, Lindblom argues that partisan mutual adjustment has distinct advantages. First, it is often possible to get agreement over means, even when there is no consensus over ends. Second, in a bargaining process, every important value is likely to have a representative. In the discussions that take place, the pros and cons of various alternatives may actually be better analyzed than if the burden of analysis is

---

[14] In the EC, the French and German agriculture ministers, Michel Rocard and Ignaz Kiechle, both serving as presidents of the Council of Agricultural Ministers, played significant roles in brokering the final agreements respectively, on dairy quotas and arable crop stabilizers. In the US, House Agriculture Committee Chairman Tom Foley, and Senate Majority leader Bob Dole, played strong leadership roles in developing the 1985 Farm Bill (see Moyer and Josling, 1990).

placed on any central decision-maker. Third, since decisions tend to be incremental, they are easily reversed upon receipt of negative feedback. Finally, partisan mutual adjustment adds legitimacy to decisions since those who have an interest in the outcome will have had a chance to participate in the process. Legitimacy is achieved at the expense of policy efficiency. But, in a democratic process, legitimacy may be even more important than efficiency. Agricultural policy reform achieved through partisan mutual adjustment is likely to be slower than reform imposed by a central actor trying to maximize efficiency, but farmers will probably accept the changes.

The Lindblom argument about the advantages of partisan mutual adjustment depends on the representation of all of the relevant values and interests. They also depend on accountability of decision-makers to their constituencies. If these conditions are not met, both efficiency and legitimacy may be sacrificed. The assumption of the responsiveness of individuals and organizations to negative feedback is questionable. Evidence from the literature of psychology would indicate that decision makers look for feedback that supports their decisions and find ways to discount or ignore negative feedback (Jervis, 1976).[15] Hence, decisions reached through partisan mutual adjustment may be far more resistant to change than Lindblom assumes.

Our previous analysis showed that partisan mutual adjustment pervaded agricultural policy decision-making in both the EC and US during the 1980s. In the EC Agriculture Council and US Senate and House Agriculture committees, the accommodation was largely between individuals representing narrow agricultural constituencies. The debate was rarely over the goals of policy, but mostly over debating the levels of policy instruments such as price support levels and deficiency payments, trying to reach a consensus minimally acceptable to all represented constituencies. When external pressures forced new options on the policy agenda, such as dairy quotas, arable crop stabilizers and deficiency payment limits, the discussion focused on how these options impinged on the represented interests, with the proposals evolving to maximize acceptability.

Policy network analysis combines the insights of organizational process, government politics and partisan mutual adjustment. A policy network is an organizational arrangement created to facilitate intermediation between state actors and organized interests (see Adshead, 1996 and Daugbjerg, 1999). State actors and constituency interests are mutually dependent on each other to achieve their goals, and form a policy network whenever they exchange resources regularly. There is usually an inner circle of constituency groups who position is privileged, either because of some specific administrative arrangement (the established right of a group to be consulted), or because of the resources that the group can deliver. The outer group has legitimate reason for access to policy, but a weaker claim. Those in the inner circle dominate the policy process. Groups outside the network often have great difficulty gaining access. Policy networks are normally strong defenders of the *status quo*. The existing policy usually is beneficial to both the constituency groups and to the state actors, and both uncertainty and bargaining costs are associated with change. When change is

---

[15] See also the discussion on path dependency analysis later in this chapter.

necessary, policy networks will generally work to keep it incremental, so as to minimize the uncertainty and ease the adjustment. For agriculture, policy networks consist of bureaucrats administering policies, legislative bodies and farm interest groups.[16] These communities vary over time in their cohesiveness and even in their membership. The EU farm policy network includes the Directorate General for Agriculture, The Council of Agriculture Ministers and national and EU farm organizations. In the US, the farm policy network includes of the US Department of Agriculture, the House and Senate Agriculture Committees and commodity groups and general farm organizations.

2.3 Models of EC/EU Multilevel Decision Making

Social scientific inquiry into the European integration process has produced a growing number of models for multilevel decision-making, such as is the hallmark of the EU political system, which try to identify the most powerful actors, and/or to explain patterns of policy decisions or choices. Douglas Webber has identified seven basic models from the literature (Webber, 1997). Four of these models (neo-functionalism, intergovernmentalism, multi-level governance, and European bureaucratic politics) are discussed here.[17] These models provide alternative views of decision-making in the EU, and can be integrated in the Allisonian analytical framework described above. Each provides a set of questions for the analyst to consider and a way of formulating the policy questions.[18]

Neo-functionalism

The concept of neo-functionalism draws its inspiration from the observation that applying supra-national solutions to problems in certain policy areas appears to create inexorable pressures for the extension of these solutions to others. Specifically, it holds that integration tends to "spill-over" from one policy area to another, as a result of the experience of working together. This creeping integration has implications on the lobbying efforts of private actors as well as on the distribution of competencies among levels of governance. Rooted in the study of EU integration, it predicts that as private actors shift their loyalties from national to EU political organs, the power of national governments will wane, and that legitimate and powerful EU institutions will develop which will be capable of autonomously developing policies and imposing them on the member states.

---

[16] These are sometimes referred to an "iron triangles."

[17] The other three models: transactional exchange, institutionalist, and epistemic communities are not discussed here because they seemed less helpful for our analysis.

[18] Our discussion of the various models for EU decision-making borrows heavily from Webber (1997), pp.2-7.

Neo-functionalism operates at the level of alternative layers of decision-making: within each layer the analyst must still decide how to model decisions. To the extent that Community institutions have achieved dominance, it is possible to contemplate a EU rational actor pursuing community interests. At organizational process and governmental politics levels, the focus becomes, respectively, the norms and routines of community institutions and bargaining between Community institutions.

Neo-functionalism applied to agricultural policy would therefore focus on issues such as the extent to which the locus of agricultural policy lobbying has shifted from the national to EU level. To what degree can and do EU policy-makers develop agricultural policy options based on Community interests rather than the interests of member states? To what extent can the EU institutions impose their policy options on member states? Is there a tendency for the scope of agricultural policy to increase over time, as a result of the revealed benefits of collective action? And, is the power of the EU supra-national institutions increasing over time in determining agricultural policy?

Inter-governmentalist Theory

Another theory of multilevel decision-making rejects the federal tendencies of neo-functionalism, and asserts that the dominant actors in any international system remain the governments of the member states. Treaties and other apparent constitutional manifestations of collective decision-making are in fact just convenient strategic alliances that will survive only as long as national interest requires them. In the realist tradition of international relations, intergovernmental theory argues that the EU institutions are still dominated by the governments of the largest member countries, in particular because the EU depends on these governments for resources. Major EU decisions are essentially lowest common-denominator bargains struck between the largest members, whose governments strive to protect their sovereignty.[19] Intergovernmental models focus attention on the bargaining between member states, and the ability of member states to impose their views on EU institutions. Similarly, in looking at the WTO and its rule-setting and tariff-reduction activities, intergovernmental theory would emphasize the importance of the strong actors and the fact that any deals made are dependent upon their agreement. The largest nations bring the other member states along by making side-payments, or by implicit threats of adverse consequences.

The questions for the agricultural policy analyst are therefore of the following nature:

- to what extent are EU decisions on farm policy really bargains between the large members, such as France and Germany?
- do EU institutions have their own agricultural policy power resources, which allow them to influence policy outcomes?

---

[19] Andrew Moravcsik (1991) in his analysis of the Single European Act, sees the governments of the three major states - France, Germany and the United Kingdom - as the dominant actors.

- what is the balance of influence among the EU institutions and between EU institutions and member governments?
- What is the role of the large countries in the WTO discussions of agricultural policy?

Multi-level Governance Model

Somewhere between neo-functionalism, with its inevitable drift towards federal structures, and the intergovernmental model with its insistence on the dominance of the largest member states, is a theoretical approach that accepts that member-state governments are the most important actors in the international bargaining process, but argues that decision-making competencies are shared. Multi-level governance theorists assert that supranational institutions exercise an independent influence on policy outcomes, that national governments no longer are the exclusive representatives of the interests of national groups institutions, and that the integration process has significantly eroded national sovereignty. A variant of the multi-level governance model ascribes the balance of power between different actors to institutional structures and arrangements, including such things as informal "rules of the game" as well as formal legislative, or decision-making procedures. Thus "institutions matter" over and above the nation states that set them up. These models can thus focus the government politics analysis described above on the bargaining between Community supra-national institutions and member states. Government politics analysis focuses on decision-making rules, norms and procedures within the intergovernmental governance structure.

Among the questions raised by this type of approach for the study of agricultural policy reform are:

- what are the independent agricultural policy bargaining resources of EU institutions?
- to what extent do EU institutions mediate the demands of various agricultural interest groups?
- to what extent has the development of EU rules, norms and procedures for agricultural policy eroded the influence of national governments?
- how does the structure of the EU agricultural policy process enhance the influence of certain actors and reduce the influence of others?
- which actors gain influence from the structure of the decision-making process, and which actors lose influence?

European Bureaucratic Politics

A final model of multilevel decision making for EU-Member State relations is a variant of the government politics model to which we referred earlier. EU politics is seen as de-politicized, decentralized and sectorally fragmented (Webber, 1997, p.6). Below the level of the European Council, the dominant policy actors are not elected politicians, but rather officials from national ministries and Commission directorates-general (DGs). Policy outcomes depend on bureaucratic interaction and bargaining. Government departments and DGs are seen as quasi- autonomous actors, with their own goals, producing policies that are the product of "loosely organized and flexible policy communities" (Webber, 1997, p.6). In the EU, policy communities cluster around the functionally differentiated Council of Ministers. Policies are not coordinated to the same extent as national government policies, since there is no EU government. "Policy communities" can be distinguished from other kinds of networks by the high level of their insulation, close and stable relations of mutual interdependence between their members and stable membership.[20] They tend to exert an influence toward policy stability rather than toward policy change.

The questions here are:

- to what extent are government agriculture ministries and the EU Directorate-General for Agriculture) really quasi-autonomous actors?
- how tightly knit and how influential are the agricultural policy communities in each EU member state?
- what is the bargaining balance between DGVI and national agricultural ministries?

Multi-level Bargaining Games

The concept of multi-level governance can be taken one stage further by emphasizing the relationship between the decision processes of the various levels of government. National bargaining models focus on the policy-making process when the bargaining all takes place in one policy arena, as in the making of domestic US agricultural policy, where all the crucial bargaining takes place in Washington. However, this does not give a full representation of the bargaining when decisions are shared among multiple levels of government. For this one needs a two-level game, such as has been suggested to describe EU policy-making. In this case, even though the Commission and Council of Ministers operate in Brussels, the Council of Ministers, which represents EU member governments, cannot act until the members receive instructions from their home governments. This implies bargaining in both national and EU arenas and between the EU Commission and national governments. Neither does the single level schematic take into account the interplay between bargaining inside the US and the EU at one level, and between the US and EU in the GATT/WTO at another level. Often these different but linked games occur simultaneously.

Robert Putnam in his article, "Diplomacy and Domestic Politics: The Logic of Two-level Games" makes some operational points to guide the use of this type of analysis (Putnam, 1988). The first is to identify the importance of the relative size of

---

[20] Webber derives his definition from the work of Rod Rhodes and David Marsh and Jeremy Richardson. For a discussion of the concepts of policy network and policy communities in the EU, see Richardson 1996, pp.6-11.

domestic win-sets in international negotiations. The size of the win-set is determined by the distribution of power preferences and possible coalitions (explainable in terms of bureaucratic politics); the domestic political institutions (the greater the necessary majority for ratification the smaller the win-set, and the greater the power of the Executive the larger the win-set); and the strategies of international negotiators. Putnam notes that the larger the domestic win-set, the greater the possibility that this win-set will overlap with the win-sets of other parties in international negotiations and hence the greater the probability that an international agreement. Paradoxically, a small domestic win-set relative to the win-sets of other parties actually provides bargaining advantages in international negotiations. If a nation's domestic win-set is small, the credibility of its international bargaining position is increased, because its negotiating partners know that it cannot deviate very much from its stated position without losing the ability to ratify any agreement which is reached. International negotiators have an unequivocal interest in maximizing the win-sets of their negotiating partners, but mixed motives with regard to the image they present about their own win-sets.

A second important point that Putnam makes is that not only do domestic politics influence international negotiations, but also that international negotiations may catalyze domestic outcomes, which could not be achieved exclusively through domestic bargaining (Putnam, 1988). Often the factions in the divided domestic political debate are stalemated. But, when offered the possibility of a deal that is within the win-set (the range of acceptable solutions) for a winning domestic coalition, strong pressures develop for domestic decision-makers to align themselves in support of the deal. While other outcomes, while they may be preferable to some, are uncertain at best, the deal is attractive because it is a certainty. Thus, whoever represents the country (usually the Executive) gains a lever in international negotiations to manipulate the domestic debate. There are also reverberation effects between international negotiations and bargaining at the national level, which can be either positive or negative. For example, the EC agreement on the MacSharry reforms to the Common Agricultural Policy had negative reverberations in France, which endangered the referendum on the Maastricht agreement.

Coleman and Tangermann, in their paper, "Linked Games, Supranational Mediators and Agricultural Trade" (1997) go one step further. They note that often nations are involved in sets of simultaneous negotiations, which have different agendas, different rules and a different mix of actors, yet are linked to each other in their outcomes. For agricultural policy in the 1990s, they see a CAP game and a GATT game played out simultaneously. They argue, for example, that the failure of the December 1990 Brussels Conference (originally scheduled to conclude the Uruguay Round of the GATT), exerted strong pressure on the EC to reform the CAP. The MacSharry reforms, in turn, made successful completion of the Uruguay Round possible in that the EC win-set was increased to the point where it overlapped with win-sets of the US and Cairns group.

Coleman and Tangermann further argue that linked games provide opportunities for mediation by supra-national organizations. Supra-national organizations may be either strong or weak mediators depending on their power. They use the example of the EU Commission as a strong mediator and the Director-General of the WTO/GATT as a weak mediator.[21] They argue that the Commission was successful in manipulating both CAP and GATT games because of its power to represent the EU in the GATT game, and to set the agenda in the Council of Ministers (and hence in the member state governments) in the CAP game. The WTO/GATT Director General, without the authority to set the agenda in the GATT game could only confront negotiators with issues and choices.

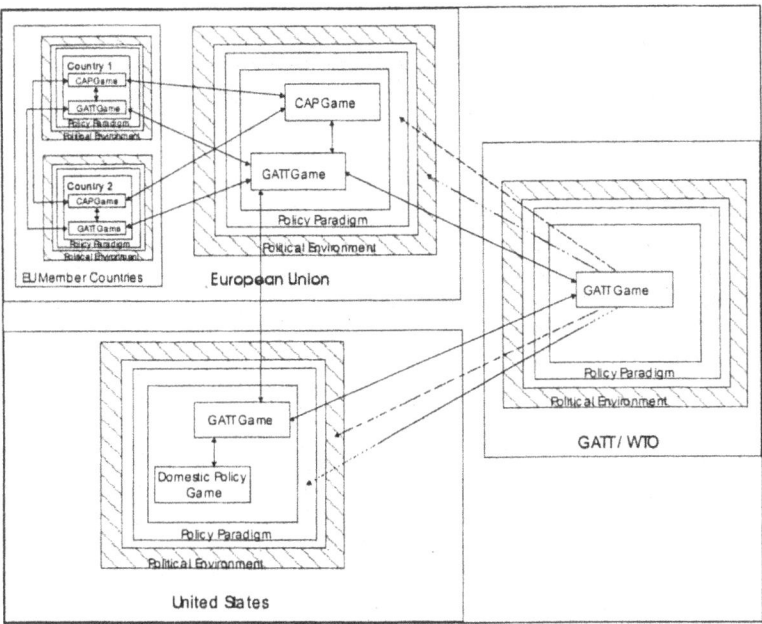

Figure 2.1: Linked Policy Games in the US, EU and GATT/WTO

Figure 2.1 illustrates two linked games important during the 1990s; the domestic agricultural policy game for the US and EU (which is one level for the US and two-levels for the EU), and the GATT/WTO game, representing the bargaining process which led to the Uruguay Round Agreement on Agriculture (URAA). The two games continue today, with the implementation of the URAA and with the renewal of WTO agricultural trade negotiations on the horizon at the turn of the century. This game adds bargaining at the level of the GATT/WTO to the domestic processes of the US and

---

[21] Coleman and Tangermann aptly use the term mediator for the GATT Director General, but the EC Commission would seem better described as a catalyst for action. The WTO should perhaps be considered as an intergovernmental organization in that it is member states that make the decisions.

EU. It is a two-level game for the US and a three-level game for the EU. Not only do the games intersect, but also the GATT games can affect both the policy paradigms and political environments at other levels. When games are multi-level and/or are linked, one can make some generalizations about how the bargaining process will differ in predictable ways from single level bargaining games.

2.4 The Dynamics of the Decision-making Process

All of the approaches to decision-making analysis discussed thus far are static in nature. To fully understand the dynamics of decision-making, one must understand the impact of previous decisions and the economic and political context in which decisions are made. Three alternative dynamic processes are discussed here with potential use in the study of reform. The first emphasizes the sequential nature of the policy process, that decisions in one time period are determined in large part by the decisions in a previous period. A variant of this brings in the path-dependence of decision making as a constraint on the simpler notion of a sequential policy process. A third concept stresses the significance of paradigms in policy formulation. Thus the dynamics comes not just as a result of the role of the status quo or past history but as a reflection of the prevailing set of ideas, explanations and presumptions that underlie policy. Policy change is therefore conditioned by the way actors perceive the problem and the impact of instruments and arrive at their determination of interest.

Sequential Decision Processes

A schematic of a dynamic policy-making process is shown in Figure 2.2. The decision-making process at time (t) operates in response to economic trends (changes in key economic indicators such as gross national product, rate of inflation, trade balance, food production, commodity prices and farm income), and economic shocks (such as a national financial crisis, drought, floods, and the BSE crisis). The decision making process also responds to political developments (examples would include the re-unification of Germany, the Maastricht Treaty, and the election in the US of a more ideologically charged Republican Congress in 1994) and political shocks (such as the 1989 collapse of the communist governments in Eastern Europe). Previous policy decisions often influence economic trends. Economic trends and shocks may contribute to political developments, though reverse causality or mutual causality is possible. The possibility also exists that economic trends/ shocks and political developments will operate independently of each other.

Economic trends and shocks and political developments influence the way states, groups and individuals define their agricultural policy interests. But the influence in moderated by the political environment, which we will define as the range of issues which policy-makers feel are important at the moment, how they define the need for action, and the sense of parameters for a politically viable response. The influence of economic trends and shocks and political developments is further moderated by the agricultural policy paradigm, which we define as the conceptual template guiding agricultural policy, which includes the way policy actors think about policy, the underlying assumptions, the discourse employed, and the analysis utilized (Hall, 1993).

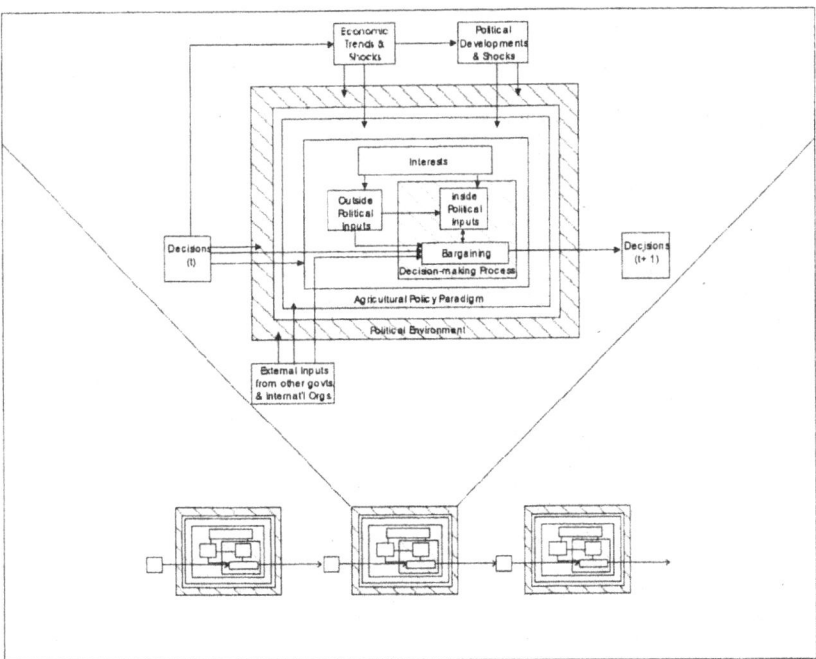

Figure 2.2: The Dynamic Agricultural Policy-making Process

Policy actors fit into two groups: outside political inputs and inside political inputs. Some examples of the former are farm, agri-business and environmental organizations, academics, the press and public opinion. They are considered outside inputs in that they influence policy-makers, but do not par1ticipate directly in decision-making. Inside political inputs are the actors who participate in the decision-making process, including representatives of the bureaucratic services, appointed officials and directly elected politicians. The positions which actors take and the intensity of their commitment are strongly influenced by their conception of political and economic interests. Decisions are the resultant of bargaining, reflecting the relative power, skill and will of the actors. They may be influenced by external inputs from other governments and international organizations. Decisions also reflect the structure, rules and norms of the decision-making process. The schematic is dynamic in that it represents how decisions at time (t-1) influence decisions at time (t), which in turn influence decisions in time (t+1).

Our previous analysis of agricultural reform during the 1980s showed both EU and US policy processes strongly resistant to reform as long as decision-making remained in the hands of the EC Directorate-General for Agriculture and the Council of Agriculture Ministers, and the US Department of Agriculture and congressional agriculture committees. The close linkages between farm lobbies and agricultural policymakers, along with strong public sympathy for farmers, worked to perpetuate the status quo. It was only when budget crisis developed, creating a zero-sum game between agriculture and other priorities that outside actors could force agriculture policy-makers to institute reforms. Yet, the detailed design of EC dairy quotas and arable crop stabilizers, and limiting deficiency payments in the US, was left to the agriculture policy establishment.

Path Dependency

The policy schematic suggested above gives some sense of the importance of policy history in understanding today's decisions and predicting those for tomorrow. Yet, all past decisions are not equally important. There are critical junctures where decisions are made which set policy off in new directions. These decisions are usually difficult to reverse, creating path dependence.[22] Margaret Levi provides a vivid description of the meaning of path dependence:

> Path dependence has to mean, if it means anything, that once a country or region has started down a track, the costs of reversal are very high. There will be other choice points, but the entrenchment of certain institutional arrangements obstruct an easy reversal of the initial choice. Perhaps the better metaphor is a tree, rather than a path. From the same trunk, there are many different branches and smaller branches. Although it is possible to turn around or to clamber from one to another - and essential if the chosen branch dies - the branch on which a climber begins is the one she tends to follow (Levi 1997, p.28).

This conception of path dependence, where preceding steps in a particular direction induce further movements in the same direction, is linked to the idea of increasing returns (Pierson, 2000, p.252). The *relative* benefit of the current activity compared to other possible options increases over time. Putting it another way, the costs of switching to some previously plausible alternative rise. Increasing returns are self-reinforcing or positive feedback processes.

There are a number of reasons why policies tend to be self-reinforcing. First, there usually are significant start-up costs for new policies. Once these have been incurred, it is easier to proceed by developing the policy rather than sink additional start-up costs for another new policy. Some of these start-up costs are in developing new standard operating procedures, which are much easier to refine than to change. The more complex the policy, the greater the start-up costs. Second, new policies establish mental images, which serve to filter incoming information and feedback. The process thus becomes most receptive to feedback legitimating the core policy decision. Third, knowledge is gained from the operation of a policy. This knowledge is more

---

[22] For a detailed discussion of path analysis, see Pierson, 2000, and North, 1990.

likely to be valuable in further development of an existing policy than in implementing a new policy. Fourth, the bargaining and coordinating costs of adjusting a current policy are usually much less than the bargaining and coordinating costs of developing a new policy, thus creating a strong incentive toward continuing the current policy course.

An impetus to depart from an existing policy path only occurs when it becomes crystal clear the current policy is untenable. Thus, the analyst focusing on path dependency pays special attention to the moments when existing policy becomes untenable and inquires about the circumstances leading to the selection of a particular new direction of policy, as opposed to choosing other plausible directions.

A number of critical moments appear during the 1980s and 1990s for US and EU agricultural policy. The first of these was the 1984 EC milk quotas decision. Why were milk quotas imposed (supply controls) rather than price cuts or co-responsibility levies (greater market orientation)? Our 1990 analysis provided an explanation based on the anticipated feasibility of administering quotas through dairies and the political unacceptability of imposing price cuts (Moyer and Josling, 1990). Another critical moment came with the institution of the MacSharry reforms of the CAP in 1992. Here, we will have to explain why greater market orientation was pursued with price cuts and compensatory payments, rather than increased supply controls. The critical change in US farm policy came with the 1996 FAIR Act, which de-coupled farm payments from production. How did the situation leading to greater market orientation here compare to the situation that produced the MacSharry reforms in Europe? The successful completion of the Uruguay trade round with the inclusion of agriculture within the liberal international trade regime of the WTO established a new agricultural trade policy path, so we will have to explain why this occurred in 1994.

Paradigm Shifts

A third type of dynamic process is captured in the notion of paradigm shifts. Peter Hall, in his article, "Policy Paradigms, Social Learning and the State" (1993) notes three distinct kinds of change in policy: Type 1 changes, where the levels (or settings) of basic instruments are adjusted; Type 2 changes, in which the hierarchy of goals remains the same, but basic techniques used to attain them are altered; and Type 3 changes, where the hierarchy of goals itself changes, which then implies changes in the types of instruments used and in the settings of those instruments. Changes of Types 1 and 2 tend to be made within an interpretative framework of ideas and standards (a paradigm) that specifies not only the goals of policy and the kinds of instruments that can be employed to attain them, but also the very nature of the problems they are intended to address. Type 3 changes depend on paradigm shifts. Changes of Types 1 and 2 tend to be incremental, whereas Type 3 changes are normally more drastic.

Type 3 changes are by their nature disjunctive. They are as likely to be sociological as scientific in origin. The choice between paradigms can rarely be made on scientific grounds alone. The movement from one paradigm to another will ultimately entail a set of judgments that are political in tone. The policy outcome will depend not only on the arguments of competing factions, but on their positional advantages within the broader institutional framework, on the ancillary resources they can command in the relevant conflicts, and on the exogenous factors affecting the power of one set of actors to impose its paradigm on others.

Issues of authority are likely to be central to the process of paradigm change. Faced with conflicting views from the experts, politicians will have to decide whom to regard as authoritative, especially in matters of technical complexity, and the policy community will engage in a contest for authority over the issues at hand. The movement from one paradigm to another is likely to be preceded by significant shifts in the locus of authority over policy. Issues of policy experimentation and policy failure are likely to play a key role in the movement from one paradigm to another. Like scientific paradigms, a policy paradigm can be threatened by the appearance of developments that are not fully comprehensible within the paradigm. As these accumulate, ad hoc attempts are generally made to stretch the terms of the paradigm to cover them, but this gradually undermines the intellectual coherence and precision of the paradigm.

Therefore, the movement from one paradigm to another that characterizes third order change is likely to involve the accumulation of anomalies, experimentation with new forms of policy and policy failures that precipitate a shift in the locus of authority over policy and initiate a wider contest between competing paradigms. The contest may well spill beyond the boundaries of the state itself into the broader political arena. It will only end when the supporters of the new paradigm secure positions of authority over policy making and are able to rearrange the organization and standard operating procedures of the policy process so as to institutionalize the paradigm.

2.5 Application of Decision Making Approaches to Farm Policy Reform in the US, the EU and the GATT/WTO

In subsequent chapters, we will try to create a comprehensive overview of the entire agricultural reform process in the US, EU and the GATT. We will explain how rational national actor, public choice, organizational process, and government politics models, applied to multi-level and linked bargaining games, influenced by economic trends, political developments and political and economic shocks, explain the pace and content of agricultural policy reform up to the present. We will ask how much policy-makers have learned from past experience. We will also examine the development of the paradigm shift, which was influenced by the reform process and later contributed to this process. Finally, we will make some speculations about what the current state of reform and the institutionalized new paradigm tell us about further changes in agricultural policy in the first decade of the new millennium.

Chapter 3

The Search for an Agricultural Policy Paradigm Shift

3.1 Introduction

The period since 1985 has been one of remarkable change in domestic agricultural policy. This change was most apparent in the developing and middle-income countries of Latin America, where agricultural policy reforms were part of a package of economic policy changes induced by a combination of external pressures and shifting notions of the role of the state (Williamson, 1994). In retrospect, it is notable that politicians in these countries did not shy away from the inclusion of agricultural markets in the overall reform of economic policy. In most cases, difficult decisions had to be made in the face of opposition from rural constituencies, and governments often showed considerable fortitude in pursuing economic policy reform in agriculture. Domestic reforms then allowed countries to bring agriculture within the scope of trade policy reforms, generally involving the removal of non-tariff barriers and the setting of low fixed tariffs against imports.[23]

In the major industrial countries, however, agricultural policy reform came only reluctantly in the period up until 1990 and with a great deal of domestic opposition. The farm policies in these countries had become so entrenched that they seemed almost to be immune from external pressures. Some high-income countries, such as Sweden, did undergo radical reforms of agricultural policy, following the lead of New Zealand in the mid-1980s. But for every reform there are many more examples of reform delayed and watered down. The Common Agricultural Policy (CAP) of the EU was perhaps the most resistant to change. In our previous book, on reform in the 1980s, we had to stretch the definition of reform somewhat to include the 1984 and 1988 changes in the CAP (Moyer and Josling, 1990). In retrospect, we spent most effort explaining why the CAP had survived pressures that might have been thought enough to lead to change. The US farm policy did change somewhat more noticeably in the direction of "reform", in the 1981 and 1985 Farm Bills, but again at a pace dictated by domestic political resistance from the agricultural sector.

Most industrialized countries fell somewhere in between the radical shifts of the developing countries and the snails-pace incrementalism of the US and the EU.

---

[23] An earlier discussion of domestic farm policy reform in the context of agricultural trade policy reform is to be found in Josling (1998).

Canada offers a good example of such a country with an ambivalent record over this period. New instruments were introduced which emphasized such elements as crop insurance and direct payments at the expenses of open-ended price supports. But supply control still dominated the import-competing sectors and the export industries still benefited from federal subsidies and state marketing. Japan began to move away from the tight control of internal markets and imports, but only in those sectors where domestic production was not adequate to meet demand.

The situation changed quite appreciably in the 1990s. The changes in the EU's Common Agricultural Policy (CAP) in 1992 and the 1996 Farm Bill in the United States represent very significant shifts in direction for farm policy and qualify more readily as "reform" - as will be detailed in the following chapters. Canada dropped its rail subsidies for western grains and converted quotas to (rather high) tariffs for sensitive import products. In Japan the Basic Law that governs the role of the government in agricultural markets was modified in the direction of privatization, though the task of bringing down domestic prices was hardly begun. The industrial giants seemed at last to follow the lead of the middle-income countries in adapting their agricultural policies to the new global realities. However, by the end of the decade there were indications of backsliding, as countries tried to protect their farmers from low world prices. And the breakdown of the WTO Ministerial in Seattle, though not caused by disputes over agriculture, delayed the start of another round of talks on liberalization of agricultural trade.

The aim of this book is to explore and explain the changes in farm policy in the US and the EU during the 1990s, with reference both to domestic pressures and to the parallel developments in the GATT/WTO. This chapter employs the framework of the previous one that laid out a way of looking at farm policy changes as the resultant of a set of forces in political and economic arenas. It attempts to address questions such as:

- Has there been a paradigm shift in farm policy in developed countries, or have we just observed incremental reform?
- How can one explain the different pace of reform in different countries, such as the apparent slow reform in the larger countries?
- What is the role of international institutions in promoting reform, and can these institutions play a role in the paradigm shift?
- What is the connection between reform in the US and the EU and that in other countries?

3.2   Paradigm Shifts in Agriculture

The idea of a new paradigm for agricultural policy was explored explicitly by Coleman, Skogstad and Atkinson (1997).[24] They argue that there has been a change from a state-assisted to a market-liberal paradigm. In the former paradigm, the state

---

[24] The discussion of paradigms in agricultural policy draws on Josling (2000).

considers that the agricultural sector contributes importantly to national policy objectives and that special support is required to ensure the welfare of farmers. In the latter paradigm, agriculture is treated much like other sectors in the economy. Competitive markets should be the main source of income for commercial farmers, though public programs can still exist in areas where the market is inadequate. To Coleman, Skogstad and Atkinson, paradigm shifts can come slowly over time, reflecting a changing balance in the political debate, rather than in a Pauline conversion of politicians to a new faith. They detect movement toward the market-liberal paradigm, well-advanced in the US, and proceeding more slowly in the EU (1997, pp.297-298).

Tweeten has also argued strongly for the emergence of a new paradigm. His "new economic paradigm" for (US) agriculture is characterized by the idea that agriculture is no longer the backward, non-competitive sector that it was once thought to be (Tweeten, 1999; Tweeten and Zulauf, 1997). Such a sector was thought to require government assistance to deal with the triple jeopardy of weather and disease, concentration in upstream and downstream activities, and a chronic tendency toward overproduction. Instead, the sector (or that part of it which produces the bulk of the output) is now recognized as competitive both with other sectors of the economy (generating roughly comparable return on resources) and on international markets (at least when not facing undue foreign subsidies). Again, government programs are limited to correcting for externalities, particularly in the environmental area, and perhaps to helping farmers manage risk.[25]

Other authors have been more cautious in interpreting policy changes as evidence of a paradigm shift. Orden (2000) points out that there has not been a true Kuhnian paradigm shift, as the underlying economic models that have been used to analyze farm policy have remained unchanged. The analogy with macroeconomic paradigm shifts, in which there were theoretical developments in parallel with policy changes, can therefore be misleading. Farm policy is still driven by demands for income protection and supported by entrenched political actors with the implicit support of the electorate. Orden however finds one important element of a paradigm shift for agriculture: analysts no longer assume that a chronic farm income problem has to exist based on the inability of the farm labor market to equilibrate. Thus the intellectual interpretation of the "farm problem" has indeed changed even if there has been little fundamental change in other assumptions, political or theoretical, underlying policy.

The general argument that US farm policy now takes for granted that the agricultural sector is basically competitive, is therefore broadly accepted. But the same cannot be said for policy discussions in Europe. The lively debate in the EU on farm policy reform is certainly not predicated on an efficient sector that can duel the US, Australia and Canada for market shares in emerging regions. This suggests that although the "old" paradigm may have broken down in Europe, it is not being replaced

---

[25] Orden (2000) finds one important element of paradigm shift for agriculture in that analysts no longer assume that a chronic farm income problem has to exist based on the inability of the farm labor market to equilibrate. However, he does not see fundamental change in other assumptions.

by the same new paradigm that appears evident in the US policy debate. In fact, two new paradigms appear to be vying for the title of successor to the old view of agriculture as a sector in need of support. These are identified in Table 3.1, together with the policy objectives and instruments implied by the new paradigms. In addition, the implications for trade rules are suggested, as well as the explicit sub-paradigm for the nature of the world market. A brief discussion of these paradigms is necessary before tracing their manifestation in the development of farm policy.[26]

Table 3.1: Three Competing Paradigms of Agricultural Policy

	Dependent	Competitive	Multifunctional
Nature of Agriculture	• Low incomes • Not competitive with other sectors • Not competitive with other countries	• Average incomes • Competitive with other sectors • Competitive in world markets	• Incomes from farming inadequate • Producer of under-rewarded public goods
Policy Objective	• Government needed to find markets • Supply control necessary	• Move towards free market • Relax supply control	• Preserve countryside • Keep family businesses viable
Policy Instruments	• Border protection • Surplus buying • State trading • Export assistance	• Decoupled payments in transition • Risk management • Low safety-nets	• Environmental subsidies • Protection against "mono-functional" agriculture
Main Supporters	• Farm organizations • First-stage processors	• Larger farmers • Agricultural processors and traders	• Small-farm groups • Farmers in remote areas
Trade Policy Aims	• Avoid restrictive trade rules	• Market access • Remove export subsidies • Constrain domestic support	• Moderate pressure on agriculture • Allow subsidies under trade rules
World Market Paradigm	• World market unstable • Prices depressed and no basis for domestic policy	• World market stable and reliable if domestic policies are reformed • World prices best guide for domestic policy	• World market reflects "mono-functional" agriculture • Prices inadequate for supply of public goods

---

[26] For a fuller discussion of these paradigms see Josling (2000).

The Dependent Agriculture Paradigm

In order to highlight the changes inherent in the adoption of each of the two new paradigms it is useful to briefly characterize the "old" view of agriculture as a dependent sector unable to compete either internally with the non-farm sector for resources or with other agricultures overseas. This view, which has been dominant in post World War II Europe, the US and most other industrial countries, held that major role of the governments was to find and secure markets for farm products. Over time this role expanded to managing the quantities produced, through domestic production quotas. Farmers themselves were in general left to focus on the production of commodities. The implicit social compact was that the government would provide border protection, buy surpluses and assist with exports if they were in excess of the commercial sales possible on world markets. Such surpluses frequently emerged, as technical change tended to outstrip demand growth. Support for this paradigm came from the mainstream farm organizations and from first-stage processors, whose profits appeared to be linked to the level of domestic production. Even countries that were major exporters of farm products subscribed broadly to the notion that agricultural market supports were necessary for a viable rural sector.

The trade policy implications of such a view of agriculture were patently obvious for years. Trade rules could not be allowed to get in the way of the management of domestic markets. In particular, Articles XI and XVI of the GATT were designed to ensure that agriculture was relieved of some of the disciplines applied to other traded goods.[27] Moreover the GATT waiver granted to the US in 1955 and the choice of the ambiguous "variable levy" and "export restitution" instruments by the EU in 1962 made it clear that countries were not prepared to submit their policies to international discipline. Behind this determination to keep trade rules weak in agriculture was a particular view of the functioning of world markets. Commodity prices were seen as low and unstable, and not a sound basis for domestic policy. This view of a market characterized by chronically weak world prices became self-fulfilling, as interventionist policies promoted surpluses that came up against insulated markets.

The Competitive Agriculture Paradigm

The main feature of the competitive agriculture paradigm is the view that the sector can stand on its own two feet. Government policy is defined in this paradigm as performing the twin tasks of giving the competitive farmers a "level playing field" on which to compete while at the same time putting a safety net under those who cannot play on that field. Eventually the non-competitive farmers will leave the sector. Supply control is not only unnecessary but also undesirable: why handcuff a competitive sector and give the market to others? Policy instruments include decoupled payments

---

[27] Article XI allowed quantitative restrictions in cases where there was domestic supply control and Article XVI implicitly condoned export subsidies for agricultural products (see Josling, Tangermann and Warley, 1996).

where a transition is needed from the previous policy. Emphasis is switched to such issues as risk management and low "safety-nets" in lieu of price support. Such policy directions generally have the support of large farmers and their organizations as well as of agricultural traders and processors.

This trade-friendly paradigm has been accompanied by (and perhaps reflects) a shift in the composition of the groups that have political influence in agricultural policy (Josling, 1999). This is in part connected with the move away from commodity-based support systems. The "decoupling" of support from output has in turn had a profound impact on the range of trade policy choices in the sector. It essentially means that a country can recast its trade policy for agricultural goods to be consistent with that for non-agricultural goods. Shifting from price supports to income insurance schemes, for instance, gives the possibility of relaxation of import regulations. One is substituting financial instruments for physical commodity market intervention, generally at lower cost. Similarly, production constraints previously needed to limit government payments on export subsidies would no longer be needed if the compensation payments to farmers were not influenced by market price. The decline of commodity programs liberates trade policy, just as the de-linking of price from income liberates social and environmental policy.

In the absence of externalities in commodity markets a major role of governments is to run a trade policy that supports the competitive parts of agriculture along with a policy to improve competition at home. This implies that governments agree to restrictions on their ability to intervene in markets in exchange for agreements by others to do the same. Market access needs to be improved by tariff reductions; export subsidies should be removed as they grossly distort world markets, and domestic support payments that escape the disciplines imposed at the border have to meet certain criteria. This is essentially the set of rules that emerged from the Uruguay Round. In other words, the competitive paradigm is enshrined in the Agreement on Agriculture. The implicit world market paradigm that supports this domestic view of a competitive agriculture is of a sector that is essentially stable if domestic policies are reformed.

The Multifunctional Agriculture Paradigm

The primary challenge to the new market-oriented paradigm has come from Europe. In recent years, farm politicians in many EU members have adumbrated a "paradigm" of their own, of a "multifunctional" agriculture sometimes referred to as the "European Farming Model" (EFM). This argument is often dismissed as merely a mixture of political posturing for position at the WTO and of the repackaging of some bland facts about the significance of farm activities in rural areas. But it is also the case that there are real differences in perception between Europe and (say) the US about the place of agriculture in the modern economy. Population density and farm size are not unrelated to the political (and economic) relationship between agriculture and other sectors. One does not have to be a closet protectionist to recognize that Holland has a serious problem of groundwater pollution, or to acknowledge that Austrian meadows give pleasure to millions of town-dwellers in winter and summer. The question is whether these differences show up as nuances of an essentially similar agricultural model or whether they lead to incompatible policy sets, which, in turn, constrain the reform of the international trade system?

The main characteristic of the "multifunctional" paradigm is that agriculture is viewed as a provider of public goods in addition to, and in many ways more important than its role as a producer of raw materials for the food industry.[28] The market for commodities inadequately rewards the farmer for such public goods as a pleasant-looking and environmentally-friendly countryside, or a stable social infrastructure built on small towns and villages. Appropriate instruments for policy in such an agriculture include environmental payments, either as a reward for providing the public goods or as compensation for the loss of market share to those whose costs are lower as a result of not having to provide those public goods. Support for this view of agriculture comes predominantly from small farmers and those in remote areas. So far there does not seem to be a consensus among environmental groups that this is a good way to formulate policy toward the environment: presumably there is the potential conflict of interest if the total sum that society wishes to devote to environmental stewardship is constrained.

One key question is what are the trade policy implications of a multifunctional view of agriculture? It is often argued that multifunctional agriculture needs protection from the lower-cost supplies from those countries whose agricultural sectors are not asked to bear the burden of countryside preservation, rural development or societal stability. This is based on a "world market" view of a European agricultural system handicapped by small-sized units and by demands and regulations imposed by a crowded continent, and therefore unable to meet the challenge laid down by the sparsely populated "new world" suppliers. Far from being competitive, border measures are still needed for the viability of such an agriculture. But one can also argue that providing additional public goods through the taxing of private goods at the border is pretty inefficient. In other words, the issue is not whether but how to give the support. And the support could well be given in a way that does not spread the burden to others.

Not all countries in the EU, or farmers in any one country, fully buy into the notion of a multifunctional agriculture. Many European farmers also see themselves as part of a competitive core, and have begun to question the restrictions that the CAP has put on them in the name of saving them from "unfair" competition from abroad. This view is particularly prevalent in the UK, Denmark and Sweden. It is also possible to argue that the European Commission is using the multifunctional argument for domestic consumption, to set up something that can be defended at the bargaining table without having to support the continuation of export subsidies and high tariffs. If multifunctionality means paying producers directly for the amenity value of their

---

[28] For a critically constructive discussion of the concept of multifunctionality and the problems surrounding the measurement of the contribution of agriculture to public goods see OECD (2001).

farming or their care of animals rather than through distorted prices for output then the concept is not so inconsistent with the competitive paradigm.

3.3 The Conditions for a Paradigm Shift

The conditions under which one would expect to see a shift in policy paradigms include dissatisfaction with existing policies and instruments, shifts in the external environment, and broader ideological and political climate change. At the heart of the pressures on farm policy are fundamental trends in the sector itself. Advances in technology and structural change in agriculture increased yields, but domestic market growth was slow. The choices were to control supply, an unpopular solution with farmers; to store the surpluses against the next period of shortage; to export with generous subsidies, thus distorting other countries markets; or to lower farm support prices. This last option can be made more palatable by paying compensation to those who were disadvantaged. Until the mid-1980s most countries tried a combination of supply control and surplus disposal, with some attempts to constrain price increases. The situation began to change in the period after 1985, as countries both modified their domestic policies and then later incorporated new trade rules into the Uruguay Round Agreement that reinforced the domestic policy changes.

Orden, Paarlberg and Roe have framed the policy reform strategy as choosing one of four options: a "cut-out" is a quick termination of price supports without compensation; a "buy-out" is a quick termination with compensation; a "squeeze-out" is a slow reduction in price supports without compensation; and a "cash-out" is a slow compensated cut in prices (Orden, Paarlberg and Roe, 1999, p.8). In our terminology, a buy-out and a cut-out are likely to be clear evidence of a paradigm shift, though there are not too many cases in the US and the EC where such options have been tried. A squeeze-out is the traditional way in which poorly-performing policies get changed, when the forces for reform overcome the bureaucratic inertia and the power of vested interest. A cash-out has been the instrument of choice in the reform of the 1990s, both in the US and in the EC. Whether a cash-out necessarily is evidence of a paradigm shift is debatable. But when policy paradigms shift instruments such as cash-outs are a convenient way of making the transition.

The effects of these policy changes can be seen in the OECD aggregate statistics that monitor the development of farm policies. The transfers effected through specific policies for a range of commodities have for a number of years been captured by the OECD in their calculation of the "Producer Subsidy Equivalent" (PSE), the payment that would have to be given to offset the income effect of a removal of those policies.[29] The total value of this part of the transfer rose slightly from $247 billion to $259

---

[29] The OECD have recently renamed the measure the "Producer Support Estimate" in deference to countries that wanted to avoid the use of the term "subsidy" in view of possible political and legal connotations of that word. Happily the acronym has been preserved. For convenience the original name is used here.

billion over the decade (see Figure 3.1 and Table 3.2) but fell again to $245 billion by the year 2000. Relative to the value of output, the PSE for the products considered for the OECD member states was estimated at 33 percent in 1996-68 and 34 percent in 1999, down from 41 percent in the period 1986-88 (OECD, 1999). Expressed with the border price as a base, the level of protection (called by the OECD the Nominal Protection Coefficient) for producers fell from around 70 percent to about 50 percent over the decade, and appeared to fall further to 30 percent in 2000. Calculated on the basis of market prices (i.e. not including direct payments) the level of protection (called by the OECD the Nominal Assistance Coefficient) fell over the period from 60 percent to 30 percent. However, this improvement was largely the result of firm world prices in 1996, and was largely reversed when these prices collapsed after 1997.[30]

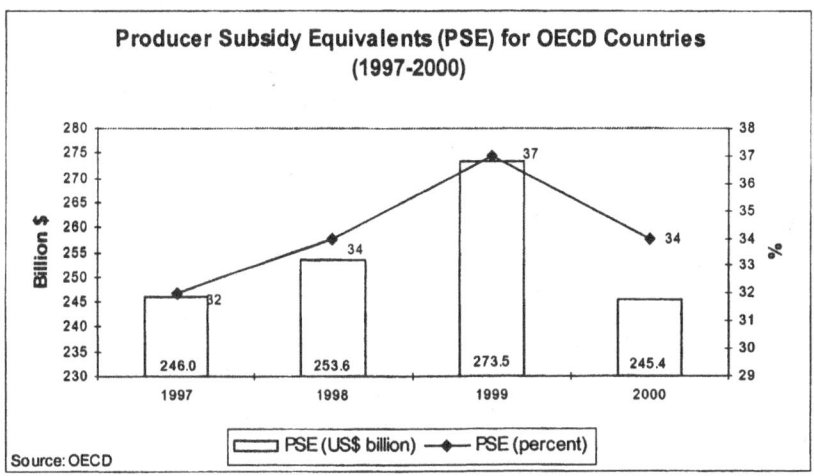

Figure 3.1: Producer Subsidy Equivalents (PSE) for OECD Countries (1997-2000)

Table 3.2: Producer Subsidy Equivalents (PSE), Nominal Protection Coefficients (NPC) and Nominal Assistance Coefficients (NAC), OECD Countries, 1986-1998

	1986-88	1991-93	1996-98	1999	2000
PSE (US$ billion)	247	292	259	274	245
PSE (percent)	41	39	33	37	34
NPC	1.7	1.7	1.5	1.5	1.4
NAC	1.6	1.5	1.3	1.6	1.5

Source: OECD (1999, 2001)

---

[30] These numbers tend to confirm the impression from the average unweighted *ad valorem* agricultural tariffs of a level of protection of about 40 percent for agriculture as a whole.

The OECD calculations split the Producer Subsidy Equivalent (PSE) into that which is given through market price support (MPS) and that which comes from direct payments and "other" support (not commodity-related). In 1986-88 market price support made up 77 percent of the total subsidy equivalent for all the OECD countries taken together. By 1996 the MPS had dropped to 60 percent of the PSE. this rose to 65 percent in 2000 as a result of weaker world prices. The change is primarily due to the MacSharry reforms in the EU. The share of MPS in PSE in the EU dropped from 85 percent to 59 percent in 2000. By contrast, Japan still relies predominantly on market price support: the ratio of MPS to PSE in 2000 is at 91 percent, marginally higher than in 1986-88.

The New Paradigm in Domestic Policy

It can be argued that the combination of reform in the developed countries and in the middle-income economies represents the emergence of a new paradigm for domestic policy towards the agricultural sector which is much more trade-friendly as well as more efficient. This paradigm shift has been away from the manipulation of the commodity price level as the main way to assist the agricultural sector towards the payment of direct payments to farm families on the basis of present or past activities. Early signs of this shift in developed countries were the adoption of commodity-based deficiency payments in place of price supports, so that consumer demand could respond to market prices. These deficiency payments over time have become decoupled from present production so as to reduce the incentive to over-produce. The decoupled payments have in some cases been targeted to various environmentally-friendly farming practices. Income insurance and crop insurance schemes have also been introduced to act as a stabilizing device for rural areas. Developing countries have avoided the budget cost of such programs and generally moved to remove impediments that hindered agricultural production.

The shift occurred because the old paradigm was clearly inappropriate in an open world economy and a less regulated domestic market. Commodity price intervention rewarded farmers according to their output of the product, regardless of the state of the market. Farm output and structures responded to the policy signals rather than consumer demand, and agriculture became dependent upon further government assistance to dispose of surpluses. Moreover, environmental groups began to point out that farming systems geared to high price policies were creating problems for the water supply, for worker safety, for public health and for the preservation of plant and animal species. Targeting payments to the farmer has the advantage of being more direct, involves less distortion in production incentives, can be tied to environmental standards, and allows the consumer to chose more freely among competing products (OECD, 1994).

The change was resisted at first by farmers who would prefer to be paid "through the market", however much that market was distorted by border protection and export subsidies. Moreover, the world market was often deemed, with good reason, to be unreliable and unstable. What convinced governments to change was in part a growing awareness that the policies were not achieving their objectives: farmers who needed help the most were not the ones who had the most product to sell. In part it was a recognition that the operation of such policies in different countries effectively offset each other, so that a coordinated removal of such policies would have less impact on farmers than a unilateral change by one country. It was also a reaction to the growing political visibility of environmental groups in many countries, and to the need for farmers to be more responsive to "green" concerns. Coupled with these specific reasons was the more general change in the role of governments in the marketplace. As the notion that governments could or should control prices began to be replaced by the idea that market forces should be the main determinant, the end of commodity price support was in sight.

Change in Political Influence of Agriculture

This change in paradigm has been accompanied by a shift in the political influence of agriculture. This has in part to do with the general unpopularity of programs that support particular groups at the expense of the consumer or taxpayer. But in the case of agriculture it may also be connected with the move away from commodity based support systems. If the government supports the price of a commodity, by restricting imports, subsidizing exports, buying up surpluses or taxing substitute products, then it usually needs to work through the processing sector or the wholesaler to implement the policy. Sugar policies are operated largely through sugar beet factories and cane refineries. Dairy policy is implemented through the dairies and creameries that take delivery of farmers' milk. Grain policies involve storage and shipping of cereals through merchants and middlemen. Oilseeds policies involve oils and meals from the crushing activities as well as just seeds and beans. When the basis of farm payments is the output of commodities, there is some coincidence of interests between the processor and the farmer. When the farmer gets paid compensation bonuses on the basis of historical hectarage and regional yield, the processor has less interest in the profitability of the domestic producer and is more willing to import the raw material and look for the cheapest source of supply.

Internal Forces for Change

As it turned out, domestic policies in the developed countries were, in the process of changing, if more for domestic than external pressures. The same issues were faced in country after country. Three domestic pressures can in particular be isolated. The first internal pressure came as a result of changing market balance in the traditional temperate zone agricultural commodities coupled with a shift in the set of acceptable agricultural policies. Traditional agricultural policies were not able to cope with the changes in cereals, oilseeds, dairy and beef. Advances in technology and structural change in agriculture increased yields, but domestic market growth was slow. The choices were to control supply, an unpopular solution with farmers; to store the surpluses against the next period of shortage; to export with generous subsidies, thus distorting other countries markets; or to lower farm support prices.

Until the mid-1980s most countries tried a combination of supply control and surplus disposal, with some attempts to constrain price increases. The situation began to change in the period after 1985, as countries came under pressure to both modify their domestic policies and incorporate new trade rules into the Uruguay Round Agreement that reinforced the domestic policy changes. Prices were reduced in an attempt to lower incentives and stimulate consumption. This price-reduction option was made more palatable by paying compensation to those who were disadvantaged.

Meanwhile a second contributing factor to the agricultural policy paradigm shift was beginning to be significant. The agricultural sector had been changing at a rapid rate, making the old style agricultural policy mechanisms less relevant to the needs of the industry. The support of raw commodity prices in the market through the withholding of supplies or the buying up of surpluses effectively breaks the link between producer and consumer. Just as the market was getting more sophisticated and differentiated, the policy was sending the message to farmers to "produce low quality goods for government stocks". Just when supply chains were being set up for the provision of goods to supermarkets, farmers were being encouraged to take land out of production and live on payments for keeping farmland idle. Clearly the vast expense of farm policy was not helping farmers to meet the challenges of providing for modern consumers. The farmers that prospered were those that took advantage of the changed conditions and began to service the differentiated market.

A third "internal" factor also began to have an impact on agricultural policies over the 1990s. The rise of environmental consciousness in OECD countries, together with increasing concern over food safety and the conditions under which livestock is reared. These concerns began to impinge on agricultural policies primarily through the presumed link between intensive, chemically-dependent farming practices and the cleanliness of water supplies, the health of the food supply and the habitat for wildlife. Thus the domestic farm policies came under pressure to change in a way that would reduce the conflict between chemical farming and a safe environment. This pressure is still increasing in most of the OECD countries to modify farm policies to incorporate more directly the needs of the environment in farming decisions.

The Role of Trade Policy in the New Paradigm

Two sets of external constraints can be identified as shaping farm policy in the developed countries in the past dozen years. One is the rise of regional trade blocs as elements of commercial policy. This has sometimes encouraged more liberal agricultural trade and sometimes worked in the other direction. In the Americas the trend has been for the emergence of regional trade blocs to support the move away from protected national commodity markets toward integrated regional markets for agricultural goods. This is clear in the case of the US and Mexico, where the prospects are for a single regional market with modest external protection for most commodities within a few years. Mexico coordinated its domestic policy reform with the signing of the NAFTA, using the latter as an additional reason to undertake the former. Even Canada, which opted out of the single North American market for sugar, dairy and poultry products, has felt obliged to modify a number of its policies to facilitate the development of NAFTA. The US has perhaps felt the impact of regional trade pacts on domestic policy the least, but that is likely to change with the discussions on access of Brazilian and Argentinian agricultural exports into the US under the terms of the FTAA.

In Europe, where regional markets are protected from third country imports, regionalism is not a major force for liberalization. The expansion of the European Union to include countries of Central and Eastern Europe has raised the specter of more countries falling within the protectionist orbit of the CAP.[31] But in one respect regionalism is having a constraining effect even on the CAP. The political attractiveness of negotiating free trade agreements with South Africa and the Mediterranean countries, along with the desire for commercial purposes to gain access to Mexico and the MERCOSUR countries, are making it increasingly awkward to have an agricultural trade policy based on the CAP and hence inflexible with regard to access.[32]

In Asia, regional integration has lagged behind other regions, and it would be misleading to give credit to regionalism for any changes in Japanese or Korean agricultural policy.[33] One should however acknowledge that bilateral pressure from the US on these two countries probably has had some liberalizing results, whilst at the same time leading to resentment and conflict. On a more positive note, the Closer Economic Relations Agreement between Australia and New Zealand has certainly changed the context in which agricultural policy is framed in those countries, and has presided over the creation of an open trans-Tasman market.

The second external factor in the change in agricultural policies has been the introduction of new rules for agricultural trade at the multilateral level. It is generally agreed that the completion in 1993 of the Uruguay Round of trade negotiations marked the first time that effective international constraints had been put on domestic agricultural policies. The Uruguay Round Agreement on Agriculture (URAA) put in place a set of rules that has already gone some way toward shaping the development of such policies. Bound tariffs have replaced non-tariff import measures, export subsidies

---

[31] It should however be pointed out that Finland and Austria "decoupled" some of their farm support policies in the process of joining the EU. Their previous price levels had been higher than those of the EU and their farmers would have taken a substantial cut in income in the absence of direct income payments by way of compensation.

[32] Access problems are particularly difficult with respect to the supply-control commodities (dairy and sugar) and the commodities in chronic surplus (cereals and beef). Other difficulties are related to regional concentration of producer interests (such as Spain and Italy for olive oil, Italy for rice, and France, Germany, Spain and Italy for wine) which make it difficult to consider liberalized access for these products.

[33] The apparent agreement within APEC to move to a free trade and investment zone would appear to qualify as a major constraint on Japanese and Korean policy. However it is too soon to point to any concrete results from this statement of intention.

have been curbed and domestic programs have been codified on the basis of their potential to distort trade.[34]

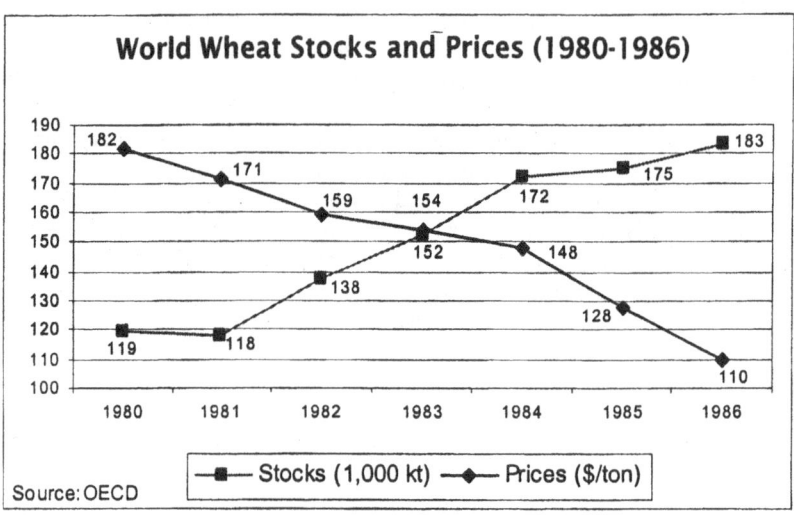

Figure 3.2: World Wheat Stocks and Prices (1980-1986)

The extent of progress made in agricultural trade reform can be judged by contrasting the current situation with that which prevailed prior to the Uruguay Round. World markets for the major temperate zone agricultural products had been in disarray for two decades before that, as the surpluses of the 1960s gave way to shortages in the 1970s, with the vagaries of weather exacerbated by destabilizing trade policies.[35] The 1980s began with a brief "shortage" of grains, caused largely by a surge in demand but again made worse by the reaction of the major countries, and then a long slump in the prices for wheat (and other traded commodities) associated with a build up of stocks (Figure 3.3).[36]

By the middle of the decade, as the Uruguay Round was about to begin, soaring budget costs from farm programs were conflicting with pressures for fiscal restraint. It became widely recognized in the US and Europe that the situation was rapidly becoming untenable. In earlier trade negotiations, the farm policies of the major industrial countries had been required to make only relatively minor changes to bring them into conformity with the agreements. Thus the key question for the Uruguay

---

[34] See IATRC (1997) for a more complete discussion of the Uruguay Round results and Josling (1998) for the need for further reform of the agricultural trade rules.

[35] The classic analysis of the problems of agricultural trade over this period is D. Gale Johnson (1975).

[36] The behavior of commodity markets over this period is discussed fully in Hathaway (1987). See also Chapter 6 of Josling, Tangermann and Warley (1996).

Round was whether there would be the will to engage in a set of multilateral talks that would effectively put constraints on domestic agricultural policies.

3.4 Reform in OECD Countries

Reform of agricultural policies has many common elements among the OECD countries. Study of reform in one country can help explain changes in others. This section highlights some of the reforms in countries other than the EU and the US, Mexico, New Zealand, Canada and Japan. Each shows aspects of the reform that spread over the 1990s to include most of the industrialized world.

Policy Reform in Mexico

Mexican policy toward the agricultural sector has changed equally dramatically over the past few years. After the high budget cost of the programs of the 1980s, as a result of policies which generally kept the prices high for farmers and low for consumers, economic reform was bound to bring some adjustment. However the speed of adjustment was notable. The parastatal agency which had regulated the market for basic foodstuffs, CONASUPO, was relieved of most of its powers, and private importation was allowed of all products except for milk powder and the most sensitive commodities, corn and beans. Domestic sectors felt the pressure immediately, with the dairy industry in particular undergoing contraction, but the cost of imported feeds declined and the fruit and vegetable sector expanded. A politically bold reform of the land tenure law followed, allowing peasants the ability to buy and sell their shares in communal holdings ("ejidos") and borrow on the basis of such holdings. Finally, high prices for the major ejido products were cut and replaced in the PROCAMPO program by payments guaranteed over a period of fifteen years. These payments are essentially decoupled from current output and represent another example of a policy shift away from commodity price support. They have recently been incorporated in a package of policy measures called the Alliance for Agriculture (Alianza por el campo) that includes investment incentives and infrastructural improvements. It is too early to say whether these policy reforms will generate a strong competitive agricultural sector, but they certainly represent a bold step in the direction of such an outcome.

The Mexican case illustrates most clearly the link between domestic policy reform and the negotiation of regional trade pacts. Without serious economic policy reform extending to the agricultural sector, it would not have been possible to contemplate a NAFTA that would include free trade in agricultural goods. The same story can be repeated in many other countries of the region.

Policy Reform in New Zealand

Among the developed countries the lead in the policy reform race was taken by New Zealand, in 1985. Facing a deepening economic crisis, the new Labor government took a bold approach to economic reform, introducing monetary stringency, deregulation of the economy, and trade liberalization. The reform included a sweeping overhaul of the agricultural programs that had become unwieldy and ineffective.[37] Several of the programs had been introduced in part to offset the negative impact on the traditional rural export sectors, such as sheep and dairy, of tariffs on manufactured inputs, high interest rates and exchange rates which made them uncompetitive. Farmers were therefore assumed to benefit from the reforms in the rest of the economy, which lowered costs through tariff reform, and through exchange rate adjustment. The programs that were cut included the price support schemes for livestock products, subsidies on capital and on the use of inputs, and tax breaks for landowners. In addition many of the marketing boards that had been set up as government-sponsored monopolies lost their market power. The wheat and poultry industries were deregulated, and there was a partial deregulation of the liquid (town) milk sector (Sandrey and Reynolds, 1990).

The results were closely watched in case they had some relevance for other reforming countries. Output and land prices fell initially, not least because interest rates were high and the exchange rate was unrealistic.[38] But within two years the agricultural economy had rebounded and become profitable again, now in the absence of governmental support. Reform of the marketing system led to a surge of entrepreneurship in foreign markets and a diversification of the export base. Farmers themselves seemed to be reconciled to life without subsidies, though much of this reflects the generally well-structured farm sector and the absence of too many uncompetitive sectors in the industry. Moreover the programs that had been removed were of rather more recent origin than the farm policies of the United States, Europe or even Japan. The lessons were perhaps more applicable to a middle-income country with favorable agricultural prospects but with a counter-productive mix of agricultural policies giving inappropriate signals to an otherwise competitive farm sector.[39] However in practical terms it gave New Zealand a new authority in international discussions of farm policies, as being willing to make dramatic policy changes of the sort being suggested to others.

---

[37] Assistance to agriculture had grown to about 10 percent of the total public expenditure. For a small economy dependent upon livestock export earnings these subsidies imposed a heavy burden. The political conditions that allowed these reforms are discussed in Williamson (1996).
[38] Total agricultural output fell from $7.6 billion in 1985 to $6.9 billion in 1986, but had rebounded to $7.6 billion by 1988 and by 1990 was up to $9.9 billion. Real farmland values declined from 70.2 (1982=100) in 1985 to 42.4 in 1988 but started to rise again in 1989. Total assistance to agriculture fell from $1060 million in 1985 (23 percent of output) to $209 million (3 percent of output) in 1990. All figures are from Sandrey and Reynolds (1990).
[39] See Valdés, *op. cit.* for a discussion of the similarities and differences between the Chile and New Zealand experiences.

Canada and Farm Policy Reform

Canadian policy toward the agricultural sector has been in a process of modification for some years. Rather than experience a discreet "reform" it has been changed by a series of modest improvements. Many of these have been in the direction of reducing government involvement in commodity price support. In fact, it was among the first of the major countries to explore the range of income policy alternatives to straightforward price support. Starting in the 1980s there were a number of attempts to reduce the degree of market intervention in favor of direct payments intended to stabilize producer incomes, including the Gross Revenue Insurance Program (GRIP) and the Net Income Stabilisation Account (NISA) that took over from the main Federal price support programs. These experiments gave Canada a special role in the discussion of decoupled payments during the Uruguay Round and some useful experience in implementing the regulations that emerged. New policies in Canada are closely matched to the WTO green-box criteria, thus enjoying the shelter against international challenge afforded by the Peace Clause.

Among major agricultural countries Canadian farm policy stands out in two respects. First is the sharing of responsibility between Federal and Provincial authorities. Although other federations face similar problems of coordinating the conflicting views of their constituent states and provinces, in no other case are these views so diverse. Different views from Province to Province merely exacerbate the problem, as does the continuing controversy over the constitutional status of Quebec. That Province has the largest dairy production and is the most ardent defender of the principle of Provincial Marketing Boards with powers to control access to their market. Agricultural marketing issues are thus entangled with those of the survival of the Canadian federation in its present form. As a result of federal-provincial sharing of responsibilities, the Federal agricultural ministry has limited responsibility over agricultural market institutions, though federal agencies administer some parts of the dairy policy and the federal government has charge of the main parastatal marketing organization for Western grain exports, the Canadian Wheat Board (CWB).

The second aspect of Canadian policy of interest is the existence of barriers on trade among provinces. There have been a number of attempts over the years to achieve a free market within Canada. Agricultural goods, particularly when marketed through the Provincial Boards, are subject to restrictions on inter-provincial trade. The consequence has been the slow emergence of national food companies in these areas that might be competitive in international markets. And once again such interprovincial tensions within the country limit the effectiveness and cohesiveness of external policy.

Implementation of the Uruguay Round Agreement in Canada reflects the importance of these two issues. The biggest change was the introduction of tariffs in the commodities, mainly dairy and poultry, where supply is managed by the Provinces through their Marketing Boards. As discussed above, the way in which this change was effected was to introduce tariffs at such a high level that no imports were likely to enter, other than the minimum market access granted under the Agreement. Thus the effect of the change was to preserve the control of the domestic market for the immediate future, but to set the industry on a course toward increased competition once the high levels of protection are eroded.

Japanese Revisions to the Basic Food Law

It was suggested that one of the most worrying prospects for world agricultural trade is that of the larger Asian countries following Japan in its own brand of farm protectionism. The nature of agricultural protection in Japan is somewhat different, at least in emphasis, from that in Europe and other industrial countries.[40] First of all support is concentrated in a small number of commodities. Rice in particular is much more heavily protected than are the basic food grains such as wheat in Europe. Other food grains are supported incidentally, as a way of encouraging diversification away from rice and discouraging substitution in consumption. Oilseeds and animal feed ingredients, by contrast, are imported with fewer restrictions. Beef protection is high in Japan to perpetuate a profitable sector that sells high quality (and high price) beef to discerning consumers. Although dairy and sugar are accorded high levels of protection in Japan, as in Europe, they are less crucial to the social and political fabric of the countryside.

As with many aspects of Japanese life, public and private agencies interact to form a web of supporting institutions for the farm sector. In Europe firms tend to deal at arms length with public agencies, and the agencies themselves operate with more transparency. This difference shows up in both the internal marketing of farm products and the importation of foreign goods. With few exceptions, marketing and importing in Europe are done by private wholesale concerns: Japan has parastatal marketing agencies which still control imports of several products and a mixture of cooperative and private interests that resist competition on the domestic market. The privatization, deregulation and liberalization of the wholesale sector is one of the more critical issues which affects trade with Japan. In the next round of negotiations on agricultural trade the issue of state trading and its relation to domestic marketing is bound to be central. But in addition the level of protection is still extremely high compared with other developed countries. Moreover, the changes in the modality of farm policy that have been evident in other industrial countries have yet to be undertaken in Japan. Farm income support rests still very heavily on price support and supply management and the move to "decoupled" payments has been slow.

The awareness of these issues of high prices and rigid marketing systems has increased in Japan in recent years. The strong yen that followed the Plaza Agreement in 1985 made the price difference between domestic and imported foods more noticeable. Imports of grain (other than rice) and oilseeds were joined by other products such as beef, citrus fruits and processed vegetables. More recently the country has imported significant quantities of fresh vegetables to complement the domestic supply. The marketing and distribution system was itself tested by this import

---

[40] A comprehensive account of the state of Japanese policies around the time of the Uruguay Round is given in ABARE, 1988.

surge. Traditional channels for the distribution of domestic products were not easily adjusted to the new source of supply. Small retail stores found themselves in increasing competition with variety stores and even supermarkets. It was clear that significant adjustments were necessary.

In April 1994, the Agricultural Policy Council (APC), a body set up to advise the Government on future policies, published a report on "The Direction of Policy Development in Japanese Agriculture in a New International Environment". This report emphasized the fact that the food system, both the price supports for farmers and the state-controlled distribution channels for the major products, was under challenge from abroad. It recommended modifications in the system to allow for more private involvement in marketing and to adjust the instruments of support to be consistent with the direction of multilateral trade rules. Some aspects of the APC report have already found their way into legislation. The Government abandoned the Food Control Law and put in its place the New Staple Food Law of 1995 that goes some way to deregulating the system for rice. However, some of the improvements merely legitimize changes that were taking place through the expansion of unauthorized rice sales. And in some respects the controls on the sector have actually increased. Much more remains to be done to before the Japanese consumer can be assured of a reliable flow of quality foodstuffs at reasonable prices from the farmers of the world.

3.5 Farm Policy Reform and International Pressures

The widespread attempts at reform of national agricultural policies and the negotiation of modified trade rules in the last half of the 1980s were mutually supportive. Though the US and the EU adhered steadfastly to the notion that their own domestic policies were not negotiable in trade talks it was becoming increasingly clear that trade and domestic policies were intimately connected, and that progress on one front required movement on the other front as well. Thus the saga of the Uruguay Round negotiations on agriculture forms an important backdrop to the process of domestic policy reform. Though changing trade rules and modifying domestic support are conceptually separate, the politics and the process are closely intertwined.

One important link between them is the state of world markets, which often drives countries to react in similar ways. If countries react to shrinking markets abroad by restricting their own imports, such reactions lead to trade tensions. If countries react by seeking to expand their exports by means of subsidies, conflicts again emerge. The obvious cooperative solution is to restrict the ability of countries either to put up trade barriers or to subsidize exports in times of weak markets. Then the burden is shared and the trade system survives unscathed. Domestic requests for assistance and income support can be given in other ways that do not distort trade patterns so egregiously. The first phases of the Uruguay Round were in essence an attempt to put this realization into practice.

The apparent need for agricultural trade reform can thus be linked in large part to the world market situation that prevailed prior to the Uruguay Round. World markets for the major temperate zone agricultural products had been in disarray for over two decades, as the surpluses of the 1960s gave way to shortages in the 1970s, with the vagaries of weather exacerbated by destabilizing trade policies.[41] The 1980s began with a brief "shortage" of grains, caused largely by a surge in demand but again made worse by the reaction of the major countries, and this was followed by a long slump in the prices for the main traded commodities.[42] By the middle of the decade, soaring budget costs from farm programs were conflicting with pressures for fiscal restraint. It became widely recognized in the US and Europe that the situation was rapidly becoming untenable (Moyer and Josling, 1990).

The reaction to this crisis was a combination of actions in a number of institutional settings. The problems had already been studied and remedies discussed in international organizations. The two policy related exercises which were most significant were the mandate given by governments to the Organization for Economic Cooperation and Development (OECD) Trade and Agriculture Committees to investigate the link between domestic policies and agricultural trade (the 1982 Trade Mandate), and a decision in the same year to establish a Committee on Trade in Agriculture (CTA) within the GATT. These deliberations led eventually to the incorporation of agricultural trade reform firmly in the stated goals for the new Uruguay Round of trade negotiations, along with a Ministerial Declaration by the OECD in May 1987 supporting the development of more "market-oriented" agricultural policies. The political stakes were raised when President Reagan chose to take up the issue at the G7 Summit held in Tokyo in July 1987. He persuaded his fellow summiteers to give the issue high priority. Perhaps for the first time, agricultural policy and trade reform were at the top of the political agenda.

---

[41] The classic analysis of the problems of agricultural trade over this period is D.Gale Johnson (1975).

[42] The behavior of commodity markets over this period is discussed fully in Hathaway (1986).

Chapter 4

Reform Frustrated: The Uruguay Round, 1986-1990

4.1 Introduction

If the depressed prices of the mid-1980s, along with escalating budget costs and sporadic trade conflicts generated activity at the international level, these stimulants were not enough to bring reform to the trade system nor to force reform on the reluctant political systems of the EC and the US. The two agricultural "superpowers" were destined to face a protracted struggle in the Uruguay Round before agreement could finally be reached on new trading arrangements. Their own domestic farm policies would prove to be formidable obstacles to trade reform. This chapter details the first four years of the Uruguay Round, which were dominated by conflict over the appropriate way to reform the GATT rules, and more fundamentally the degree of discipline that should be exercised at the international level over domestic farm policies. The experience of these four years emphasized the relative impotence of international structures to influence policy in the US and the EC, though mid-size and smaller countries were modifying their policies with some alacrity, as discussed in the previous chapter. But before discussing the negotiating positions of the US and the EC in the Uruguay Round it is useful to describe in brief the way in which each organized itself for the conduct of the negotiations.

4.2 Negotiating Agricultural Trade in the GATT

The main GATT decision-making body (until the emergence of the WTO in 1995) was the GATT Council, made up of representatives from the governments of GATT members ("contracting parties" to the GATT, which strictly speaking was a set of articles provisionally applied rather than a full-fledged international organization that could have members). The contracting parties were represented in Geneva by ambassadors.[43] These ambassadors served on GATT committees, notably the Council

---

[43] For smaller countries this diplomatic representation includes responsibility for the United Nations agencies that are located in Geneva, such as the UNCTAD, the UNESCO and the ILO. The largest countries have separate representations for the UN and the GATT/WTO. The smallest countries maintain no permanent representation though they may send officials for particular meetings.

on Goods, which had overall responsibility for decisions. Such decisions were taken by contracting parties on a consensus basis.[44] Occasionally, the ambassadors gave way to trade ministers from their capitals in a GATT Ministerial session, which was the only body that could take decisions amending articles or initiating trade rounds.

Each country has its own way of ensuring that its representation in Geneva accurately reflects both policy decisions taken in the capital and the political interests that have influenced such policies. This delicate balance is not always maintained, as was evident at several points in the Uruguay Round when negotiators appeared to exceed their mandates.[45] But negotiators in general have an interest in reaching a conclusion, and are not averse to pushing domestic policy-makers to modify their mandates. This can lead to tensions between interest groups and trade negotiators, which have to be resolved periodically. The different "levels" of the policy game can therefore come together in sometimes unpredictable ways.

One of the key aspects of the structure of negotiations in agriculture is the relationship between agricultural ministries and trade officials. In most countries the trade ministry takes prime responsibility for the overall conduct of the talks. But the agricultural ministry usually makes proposals and is frequently in a position to veto any proposal that is deemed politically impossible. In the case of the US and the EC this relationship proved of significance as the Round progressed. The US is represented in trade talks by the Office of the US Trade Representative (USTR), a part of the Executive branch of government, which is expected to liaise with other departments, the legislative branch and the public. In the case of agriculture, the lead is taken in practice by the Foreign Agricultural Service (FAS) of the US Department of Agriculture (USDA) in conjunction with the office of the Secretary of Agriculture. Draft papers in the Uruguay Round originated with the FAS and were then discussed by a committee including other parts of USDA, as well as USTR, before being cleared by the Secretary. At this stage they were considered by an inter-agency committee, including representatives from the Department of State and the Office of Management and Budget (OMB). USTR took responsibility for turning these USDA texts into proposals for the negotiating table. Thus the origin and perspective of such proposals reflected the priorities of the USDA, and more specifically the export side of USDA, i.e. the FAS, rather than those parts of the agency that deal with domestic programs.

In the case of the EC, the position is somewhat complicated by the division of labor between the Brussels bureaucracy and the member states. The Treaty of Rome that set up the EC gave to the Community institutions (the European Commission and the Council of Ministers, restrained by the European Court of Justice and advised by the European Parliament) the sole power to enter into trade treaties with other countries.[46] The Commission is given the responsibility to negotiate such treaties and

---

[44] By convention, countries were referred to as the CONTRACTING PARTIES when they took decisions.

[45] In the case of the EC, such discussions were often quite open and the rebuke of the Commission almost public.

[46] The relevant authority was in Articles 110-116 of the Rome Treaty, now renumbered as

Reform Frustrated: The Uruguay Round, 1986-1990

the Council has to approve the outcome.[47] The Commissioner for External Affairs has overall responsibility for the negotiations. The overall objective of the EC trade policy was also specified in the Rome Treaty, to promote the "harmonious development of world trade, the progressive abolition of restrictions on international trade and the lowering of customs barriers" (Article 131 [ex 110]).[48] The support for the Commissioner came from the Directorate General for External Affairs (known historically as DG-I[49]). The manifestation of the Council that maintains oversight and the right of final approval is the Foreign Affairs (General) Council. The European Parliament has no formal role in the negotiation of trade agreements, though it does retain a veto right under Article 300 [ex 228] (Hix, 1999, p.338).

In the case of agriculture, the situation is somewhat different. By agreement (not mandated by treaty) the lead negotiator is the Commissioner for Agriculture. The Commissioner gets support from the Directorate-General for Agriculture (formerly known as DG-VI but now renamed the Agriculture DG). The body that has oversight during the negotiations is the Council of Agriculture Ministers. Figure 4.1 provides a general schematic for the complex Commission - Council process, indicating that it operates in a context influenced by past policy decisions, economic trends, economic shocks, political developments and sectoral interests. The EC process specifies the mode of interaction between national governments and the GATT negotiating team, via the Council. But the EC position is also influenced by outside inputs such as press and public opinion, EC consultative and lobbying bodies and by organized interest groups from member states.

Articles 131-134 of the most recent revision of the EU Treaty (the Amsterdam Treaty).

[47] The mandate for trade negotiations comes from a body traditionally called the Article 113 Committee (now the Article 133 Committee), essentially a subcommittee of the COREPER, which also maintains a watching brief during the course of the negotiations. The name is derived from the article that set up this structure.

[48] Though not always evident in the agricultural area, the Commission has indeed taken a relatively liberal line in many of its trade policy initiatives.

[49] We use the current designations for the Directorates-General in describing the operation of the EC/EU agricultural policy process, with the historical abbreviations in parenthesis. In our discussion of the MacSharry and Agenda 2000 reforms, and the Uruguay Round, we will employ the historical abbreviations in use at the time.

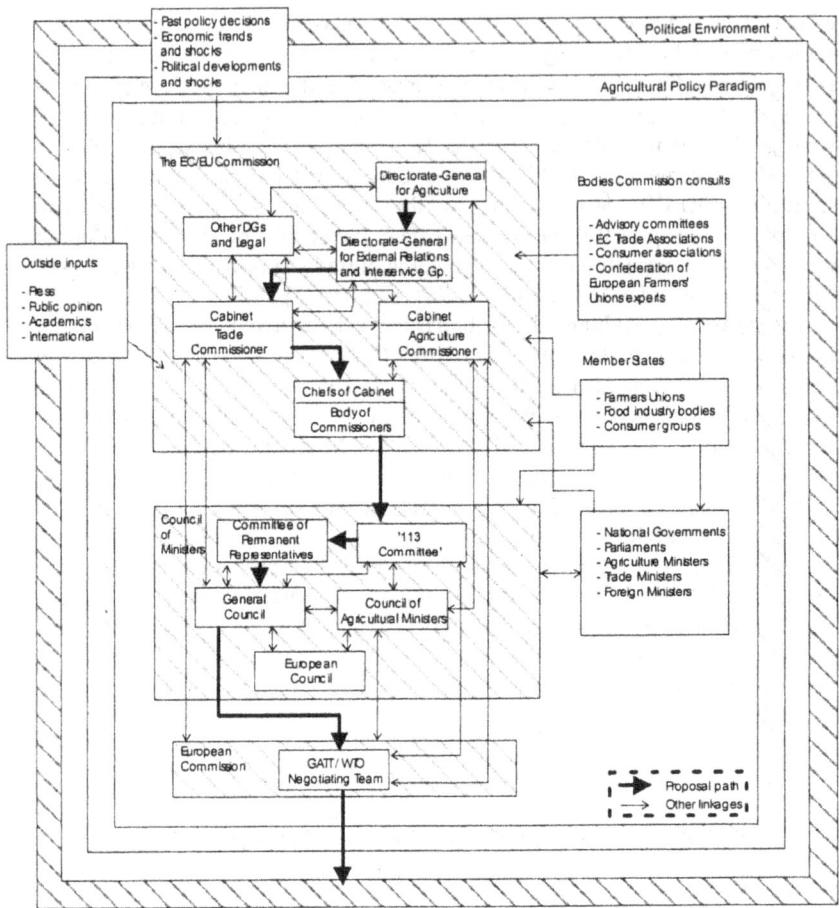

Figure 4.1: Decision-making Process for EC/EU Agricultural Trade Policy Formation

The first stage of the EC policy-making process takes place in the European Commission, which performs the executive function.[50] Agricultural trade proposals are

---

[50] Insights from Graham Allison's *Organizational Process* model would suggest that each of the included organizations is likely to see agricultural trade policy differently, influenced by its own organizational interests and priorities, and to take positions consistent with those interests and priorities. This model also would also suggest that change in organizational position is likely to be inherently incremental, even in a dynamic environment, with stable parochial perceptions, satisficing and standard operating procedures exercising a strong influence. On the other hand, *Public Choice* theory would emphasize that policy is the outcome of the way in which the preferences of egoistic institutions are combined in the political process. A *Government Politics* approach helps explain the bargaining outcomes, with its attention to the

Reform Frustrated: The Uruguay Round, 1986-1990   53

formulated in the Agriculture DG (DG-VI), then submitted to the Inter-Services working group which coordinates the various Directorates with a stake in the policy.[51] The membership varies with the issue, but the Agriculture DG (DG-VI) always presides. The Inter-Services working group members report to the various cabinets of the "most interested" commissioners, which meet together on a regular basis.[52] For agriculture trade policy, the External Affairs and Agriculture Commissioners always appear among the "most interested". Proposals are sent on to the Heads of Cabinet for the 17 Commissioners, who screen the proposal before forwarding it to the Commissioners for debate. The Commissioners must approve a proposal by simple majority vote before it is finalized.

The Agriculture DG (DG-VI) tends to dominate this phase of the policy process. This body is the largest Directorate-General in the EC, largely because the CAP is currently the most active and completely integrated EC policy. It has most of the Commission's expertise on agricultural policy questions, expertise which is critical when changes are considered which may affect the highly complex Common Agricultural Policy. The Agriculture DG (DG-VI) has a vested interest in the CAP in that its power and many of its jobs depend on the elaborate regulatory mechanisms for EC agriculture. Moreover, it administers the CAP and must implement any policy changes. EC farm lobbies have close links with the Agriculture DG (DG-VI), and this adds a sectoral interest dimension to the bureaucratic concerns.

The External Affairs DG (DG-I) comes to agricultural reform from a rather different perspective, in that its constituency is far broader than agriculture and includes groups from the industrial and services sector. The External Affairs DG (DG-I) derives bargaining strength in that it is responsible for coordinating together EC positions for the various GATT negotiating groups and actually leads the negotiations for all the groups except agriculture. The breadth of its responsibilities also constitutes a weakness, in that the External Affairs DG (DG-I) is spread too thin to devote much in the way of human resources to agricultural trade policy.

Debate among the Commissioners tends to be dominated by those with dossiers directly affected by matters under consideration. Other Commissioners not directly affected tend to conserve their bargaining resources for matters more central to their interests. Trade policy debates during the Uruguay Round were strongly influenced by the practice of submitting proposals separately for the different GATT negotiating groups. Thus, agricultural trade proposals were considered separately from trade policy proposals in other sectors, which were prepared by different Directorate-

---

structure of decision-making, rules and procedures for bargaining, and action channels controlling access to the process and power resources of the various bargaining actors. For a more complete discussion of how EC agricultural policy can be explained by these models, see Moyer and Josling (1990), chaps. 2-4.

[51] For a discussion of the function of the Inter-Services working group see Anna Murphy, (1990), vol. 2, p.119.

[52] The Inter-Services Group itself decides whether a proposal should be submitted to the full college of Commissioners for their approval or be passed on directly to the Article 133 Committee (formerly known as the Article 113 Committee).

Generals, though coordination occurred in the External Affairs DG (DG-I) and the Inter-Services working groups.

After an agricultural trade proposal leaves the Commission it goes to the Article 133 Committee (formerly known as the Article 113 Committee), which consists of the senior civil servants from the trade and other ministries of national governments.[53] Each delegation will have a representative from the Ministry of Agriculture who will tend to take the initiative, thus ensuring that national agricultural interests are considered. In the discussions, the External Affairs DG (DG-I) serves as the representative of the Commission, but the Agriculture AG (DG-VI) is also present. The Article 133 Committee never votes and discussions continue until consensus is reached.

When approval is reached, the proposal goes to the Committee of Permanent Representatives (COREPER), who screen the proposal for the agenda of the next General Affairs Council, where it will usually be considered by foreign trade ministers.[54] The General Council also tends to decide by consensus, though the formal voting rule is by Qualified Majority.[55] The Council of Agricultural Ministers makes recommendations to the General Council. It also maintains direct links with the Article 133 Committee and the Trade negotiators. When the General Affairs Council approves a proposal it creates a negotiating mandate for the Commission, which has the sole power to represent the European Community in trade negotiations.

National governments have very significant influence on EC policy decisions. As already noted, the Council of Ministers and the Article 133 Committee are composed of representatives from the various national governments. Thus, as a practical matter, the Commission must take national positions into account before preparing any agricultural trade policy proposal if it harbors any hope of Council approval. The

---

[53] In this discussion of the policy process we use the current designation for the trade negotiations committee, the Article 133 committee, with the historical designation, the Article 113 Committee, in parentheses. In the discussions of the Uruguay Round negotiations, we use the historical designation in use at the time. The Article 113 Committee operates at two levels. When major policy issues are discussed, the national governments are represented by the chief civil servants from the various ministries. When the issues are less significant, more junior officials represent their home governments.

[54] COREPER has two parts: Part I consists of the Deputies to the Ambassadors, which usually deals with agricultural trade issues, and Part II, consisting of the Ambassadors, which rarely deals with CAP matters, concentrating on more general issues. The General Affairs Council can also consist of Foreign Ministers, but is not usually so constituted for GATT matters.

[55] The EC had 12 members at the time of the Uruguay Round. France, Germany, Italy, and the U.K. each with 10 votes in the Council of Ministers; Spain with 8 votes; Belgium, Greece, the Netherlands and Portugal with 5 votes; Denmark and Ireland with 3 votes; Luxembourg with 2 votes. A Qualified Majority required 54 votes and a Blocking Minority required 23 votes. The rules for a Qualified Majority prevent the four large states from acting without support from at least some of the smaller nations.

sectoral nature of Council decision-making tends to ensure that national positions on agricultural trade will not be well-coordinated with positions on other trade issues. This is easy to understand when one considers that the dominant voice in agricultural trade is the Agriculture Council, which consists of farm ministers from national governments. It follows that national agriculture ministries, which, of course, have mastered all the complex details of the CAP, will have the initiative in preparing position papers for cabinet consideration. The agriculture minister will thus enter cabinet discussions from a very strong position. Since the agricultural trade stance is considered separately from position on other GATT issues, other cabinet members are disadvantaged in arguing against the agriculture minister. They must discuss agricultural policy details that neither they nor their departments normally have any incentive to learn. It is not easy to talk about how agricultural trade policy must be consistent with positions on other GATT/WTO issues when the focus of the discussion is limited to agricultural trade.

Even if national cabinets can balance agricultural interests with other priorities, it is still the agriculture minister who represents the cabinet position in the EC Agriculture Council. He has strong incentives to interpret his mandate in the way most favorable to his country's domestic agricultural interests. Agricultural policy is so complicated that the only government agency likely to fully understand his actions is the national agricultural ministry, which shares similar interests. Overcoming these problems will still not lead to much policy flexibility in the Agriculture Council, unless they are overcome in every member country at once. This is because the Council's practice of unanimity allows the most recalcitrant member government to block policy flexibility.

4.3 The Place of Agriculture in the Uruguay Round

Agriculture was destined to play a central role in the Uruguay Round of trade negotiations from the start. The emphasis placed on agriculture came in part from the countries who saw closed markets and restricted trade opportunities as anomalous with the more liberal trade regime in manufactured goods. In part it stemmed from a source of frustration that rules for agricultural trade were not precise enough to be useful either in preventing disputes or in resolving disputes once they had arisen. But the main emphasis came from a widespread sense that the systems of domestic farm support had become too costly and troublesome, that these programs were in large part responsible for the chaos in world agricultural trade, and that an international solution to these domestic problems was necessary to provide the basis for modified trade rules and an agreement to lower external protection.[56]

This link with domestic policies set the Uruguay Round talks on agriculture apart from previous rounds of trade negotiations. It was also the factor that made the

---

[56] The role of domestic policies and the anomalies in the treatment of agriculture in the GATT were documented in Hathaway (1987).

negotiations so prolonged and the final agreement so difficult to reach. The focus on national agricultural policies was necessary to resolve the fundamental problems that had beset the treatment of agricultural trade in the GATT from the start. Unlike many areas of trade policy, it was never easy to separate the issue of agricultural trade rules from the conduct of domestic farm policy. Given the political strength of groups that had a stake in these domestic policies, trade policy tended to take a back seat. Had the issue not been tackled in the Uruguay Round, any resulting trade agreement would have been of doubtful value to agricultural markets. Accordingly, one of the most interesting aspects of the Round was the extent to which domestic agricultural policy reforms were encouraged by the negotiations, and the extent to which these reforms are now effectively locked in by the terms of the Agreement. To explore this link it is necessary to follow the stages of the talks in the light of what was happening to agricultural policy on the home front.

The Uruguay Round was not initially conceived with agricultural trade in mind. The origins of the Round go back to 1982, a time when protectionist sentiments were rising, in particular in the US, as a result of the fear of Japanese competition.[57] The Tokyo Round had finished in 1979 with a somewhat weak agreement on curbing non-tariff import barriers and the negotiation of a number of Codes to tackle issues such as anti-dumping measures, the use of export subsidies, and the existence of different standards. However, the Codes had not proved a great success, and non-tariff barriers proliferated. Agricultural trade had benefited a little from the reduction of some quantitative trade restrictions, notably by Japan, but no substantive degree of liberalization had been possible. The two commodity agreements concluded in the Tokyo Round, for dairy products and for beef, were not designed to liberalize trade. It had not proved possible to reach an agreement on the international management of grain stocks. With high agricultural prices on world markets at the start of the Tokyo Round in 1974, market liberalization appeared less pressing than stabilization.

Agricultural markets were again firm in the period after the Tokyo Round, with major countries experiencing record agricultural export earnings in 1981. This contributed to renewed concerns about food shortages in world markets rather than surpluses from domestic policy excesses. Against this backdrop, the early plans for agriculture in the upcoming round were focused on rule changes, to assist the settlement of disputes. The GATT Committee on Agriculture that was appointed in 1982 was intended to look at such rule changes, but downplayed the issue of trade liberalization as presumably too difficult to achieve. The OECD also decided to investigate the nexus of trade and agricultural policies, and gave a mandate to the Trade and Agriculture Committees to look into the reasons for the conflict between domestic and trade objectives. The OECD Trade Mandate focused on the changing modalities of domestic policies as the improvements needed in the trade system, and

---

[57] A discussion of the achievements of the Uruguay Round as a whole is found in Schott (1994). The story of the treatment of agriculture in the GATT, from its early days through the Uruguay Round is to be found in Josling, Tangermann and Warley (1996).

was concerned as much with methodological questions of support measurement as how to negotiate reductions in that support.

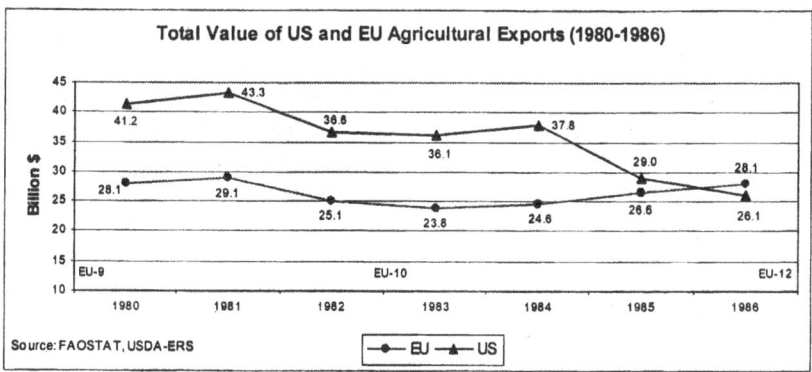

Figure 4.2: Total Value of US and EU Agricultural Exports (1980-1986)

By 1986, when the Uruguay Round was launched, the world market for agricultural products had changed dramatically. Exports contracted rapidly as demand from developing countries weakened in response to the lingering debt crisis. US agricultural exports, in particular, fell precipitately from their peak in the early 1980s, though EC agricultural exports held up with considerable expenditure on subsidies (Figure 4.2).

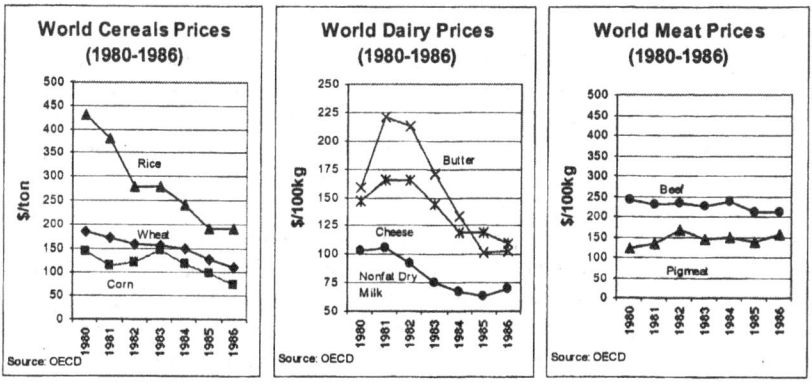

Figure 4.3: World Prices of Selected Commodities (1980-1990)

World cereal prices were on a downward slide, reaching their lowest point for many decades (see Figure 4.2), followed by prices of dairy goods after a brief surge in 1981. As a result, agricultural support costs escalated on both sides of the Atlantic. Export subsidy programs were reintroduced in 1983, and trade disputes became more common and more bitter.

In the European Community, subsidized exports became the main outlet for surplus production, at an increasingly high cost. Small and medium-sized exporters of agricultural goods began increasingly to suffer under the burden of the export market competition of the two agricultural "superpowers".

Support levels rose as world markets weakened. The OECD's index of support, the Producer Subsidy Equivalent (PSE) rose steadily over the first part of the 1980s, mirroring the reduction in exports (Figure 4.4). In the US, transfers to farmers climbed from $15 billion in 1980 to $45 billion in 1986. Support in the EC increased from $20 billion to over $60 billion in 1986. Few government programs in history could have generated such a dramatic and largely unintended increase in transfers over a period of five years.

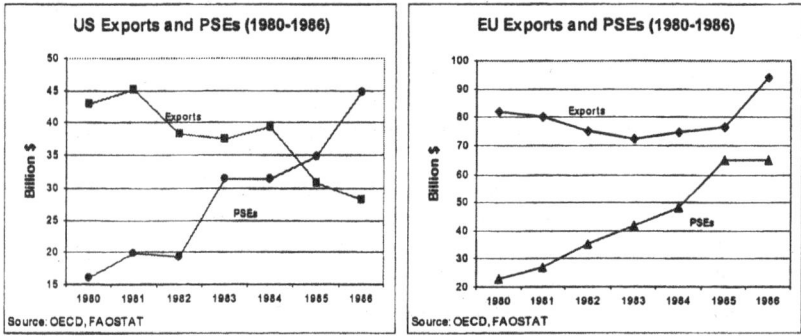

Figure 4.4: US and EU Exports and Producer Subsidy Equivalents (1980-1986)

In this situation, the prospect of the Uruguay Round as a solution to the disarray in world markets began to look more attractive. By the time that governments met in Punta del Este in September 1986 to launch the Uruguay Round of trade negotiations, a general consensus had been reached that it was necessary to reform agricultural policies in order to achieve trade liberalization in agriculture.

The ministers at Punta Del Este set themselves an ambitious target. The negotiations were to last for four years, culminating in a final ministerial meeting in December 1990. So as to consolidate gains and to keep the negotiators to schedule, a mid-term ministerial meeting was agreed for December 1988 at Montreal. In the event, the timetable slipped somewhat, leading to the first "crisis" of the Round, as the Montreal meeting ended without agreement, to be rescued in April 1989 by some shuttle diplomacy, and to the second crisis as the Brussels (Heysel) meeting also collapsed in disarray. Agriculture was mostly to blame for both crises, and was largely responsible for causing the round to last for over seven years. Agricultural policy reform at home, at least in the US and the EC, was lagging behind the pace being set by the trade negotiators. The trade "tail" was unable to wag the domestic policy "dog".

4.4 The Uruguay Round Agricultural Negotiations

The agricultural negotiations in the Uruguay Round of GATT talks can conveniently be divided into three stages.[58] In the first stage, countries exchanged ideas as to the approach to be taken to agricultural trade and the way in which negotiations should proceed. This stage began in 1986, with the launch of the Round at Punta del Este in September, and continued through the "mid-term meeting" in Montreal.[59] Though interesting ideas emerged as to how to reform agricultural trade, political accord was elusive. It appeared that agriculture was about to sink the Round. This process was rescued from disaster by the April 1989 "mid-term review" which emerged from the ashes of the failed Montreal meeting, and began a second phase which ended with the December 1990 Ministerial meeting in Heysel, Belgium, where the abortive attempt to come to a negotiated agreement on agriculture spilled over into the inability to complete the round on time. The third stage of the talks of the negotiations began a couple of months later, and was made possible in large part by the EC's reform plans for the CAP. This third stage is discussed in Chapter 7 after a discussion of that reform.

The Round was launched amid high expectations, at least on the part of those who saw the opportunity for the elusive agricultural policy reform. The content of the Punta Declaration was certainly encouraging. There was explicit mention of the need to keep agriculture an integral part of the process, though it would still be considered by a separate committee. Negotiators agreed on the "urgent need to bring more discipline and predictability to world agricultural trade", and set the objective of achieving "greater liberalization of trade in agriculture" by "bringing all measures affecting import access and export competition under strengthened and more effective GATT rules and disciplines". Thus for the first time, domestic policies were brought within the scope of trade negotiations, though it was not clear how they were to be negotiated. This was the first task: to agree on a modality which would both be effective in reforming trade rules and opening up markets and be broadly consistent with the realities of domestic policies and politics. The tension between the desire to regulate the trade distorting impact of domestic policies and the need to bring along domestic constituencies in the process permeated the Round and is still evident today.

The talks got off to a lively start. In July 1987, the US unveiled its proposal for the improvement of the trade system by eliminating all trade-distorting farm programs over a ten-year period. All that would be left would be what became known later as "decoupled" payments, i.e., those not tied to output, together with genuine food aid and domestic nutrition and poverty programs. The OECD PSE measure, which aggregated the effects of diverse policy instruments into a subsidy-equivalent, was

---

[58] For a more detailed account of the Uruguay Round agricultural talks see Josling, Tangermann and Warley (1996). Other accounts are to be found in Ritson and Harvey (1997), Rayner, Ingersent and Hine (1998), and Swinbank and Tanner (1997).

[59] This stage was described in our earlier book on agricultural policy reform in the 1980s, and will be discussed here only briefly (Moyer and Josling, 1990).

suggested as a possible mechanism to embody these commitments. Governments would table "country plans", which would then be discussed internationally. At the end of the ten-year period (i.e. 2000) a new set of rules could be introduced which would govern this liberal agricultural trade system. The boldness of the Reagan Administration proposal is still impressive, even though it may have had the effect of delaying a result in the Round. It matched the unsuccessful attempt to remove all domestic programs (see Chapter 5) in the Administration's 1985 Farm Bill proposal, declared "dead on arrival" at Congress. From the start, the "zero-2000" proposal was equally unlikely to survive as an agreed outcome to the discussions, but it proved a convenient platform from which the US team could look down on the other delegations scrambling to regain the initiative.

The EC countered with a two-part proposal in October 1987 that appeared to offer a radical departure to traditional policy positions but also to be firmly anchored in the past. The first stage of the EC plan would be for coordinated action to shore up world markets, thus saving budget cost and removing some of the tensions over the use of export subsidies. Only when that was done would a second stage kick in, to reduce price supports (paying farmers compensation) and bind support (and export subsidy) levels.[60] The US was encouraged that the EC was at least in principle willing to negotiate down domestic support levels, but was scornful of the call for short-term market strengthening, with its hint of market sharing and its reminiscence of the Baumgartner/Pisani plan from the Kennedy Round (see Josling, Warley and Tangermann, 1996).

This first phase of the talks produced more heat than light and culminated eventually in the stalemate in the negotiations at the Ministerial meeting in Montreal in December 1988. The US insisted that the EC agree to the long run objective of elimination of price supports over a defined period. The EC argued that such an objective was politically unacceptable at home, and that the most important task was to firm up world markets. Thus the period leading up to the Montreal meeting was one of rising frustration and invective, with neither side making much attempt at forging a compromise.

The Montreal meeting itself proved a disappointment. There had been reasonable progress on several negotiating fronts, and the US was pushing for an "early harvest" agreement on those less contentious topics such as the liberalization of trade in tropical products and the periodic review of countries trade policies. The EC pushed hard for the principle of "globality", keeping all the components of the talks together as a package. In the end, failure to reach an agreement on how to proceed with the

---

[60] The newly-formed Cairns Group, of 14 small and medium-sized exporters, emerged with a proposal that would have entailed an immediate freeze on price supports followed by a phased reduction, until finally a new set of rules could be introduced to regulate agricultural trade. A separate proposal by Canada (also a Cairns Group member) argued in similar vein. A late entrant by Japan in the list of proposals supported the restraint of export subsidies but maintained that importing countries should be allowed to keep the level of protection needed to maintain the social position of agriculture - an early indication of the importance of "non-trade concerns".

agricultural talks caused the package to come apart. The search for an appropriate phrase which would at the same time satisfy the US that it had an agreement to phase out supports and the EC that it had defended them proved elusive – despite the resort to a thesaurus by at least one of the delegates. The Cairns Group delegates walked out of the Ministerial when it was clear that no deal on agriculture was possible, in essence to prevent the possibility of the US and the EC deciding to cut a deal to sideline the agricultural component of the talks.

After some deft diplomacy by the GATT Director-General, Arthur Dunkel, the talks were rescued in April 1989, when countries finally agreed to a "midterm" package of measures. This package had an important agricultural component, laying down a freeze in support prices (the first time such an agreement had been possible) and indicating the timetable for the rest of the negotiations. More significantly, it included a political commitment to the improvement of import access, to the curbing of export subsidies, and to a "progressive reduction in trade-distorting subsidies". The phrase that had proved elusive in Montreal had turned up in Geneva four months later.

The Comprehensive Proposals

The second phase of the agricultural negotiations was able to begin. This consisted of an elaboration of the negotiating ideas by each (major) participant, leading to "comprehensive" proposals that could be blended eventually into a common document on which all parties could focus attention. It was in this stage that the form of the final agreement began to take shape. As important as the agreement in Geneva, new negotiating teams were in place in the US and Europe. Carla Hills took over the post of US Trade Representative in the incoming Bush Administration, replacing Clayton Yeutter, who moved to Secretary of Agriculture. The post of chief negotiator for the EC (Commissioner for External Affairs) went to Frans Andriessen, who had been Commissioner for Agriculture. A new Commissioner for Agriculture was appointed: Ray MacSharry had both farming links and experience in the financial portfolio in Dublin. The new teams thus were thoroughly familiar with the issues, and the talks were reinvigorated by the progress apparent in the April Agreement.

The papers on specific topics soon followed the April Agreement. In what turned out to be a seminal move, the US proposed a strategy, which would focus on new rules to guide both domestic policies and trade in agricultural products, in sharp contrast to their original paper of 1987, which advocated constraints on support levels. Non-tariff import barriers were to be converted into tariffs. Export subsidies were to be banned. Domestic policies were to be categorized into those that were acceptable, i.e., minimally trade-distorting, those that were objectionable and therefore had to be banned, and those which were somewhere in between and therefore had to be reduced.[61] The use of an aggregate measure of support, such as the PSE, which had been envisaged in the July 1987 paper as a way of monitoring the phase out of all trade

---

[61] This is an example of the "traffic light" approach to domestic subsidies: the terminology changed a few months later as governments began to refer to these policy categories as "boxes".

distorting policies, was now limited to the measurement of these "amber" box policies. The Cairns Group broadly supported the US approach on tariffication, the elimination of export subsidies and the categorization of domestic support.

The EC, however, argued against the use of rules to target individual policy instruments. Though the Community reluctantly agreed to a form of tariffication, it insisted on adequate safeguards against low world prices (i.e. the maintenance of something like the variable levy mechanism) and the ability to "rebalance" protection by raising some tariffs as others were reduced. The EC resisted strongly the control of export subsidies, arguing that these were necessary aspects of market management – and by implication that the EC exporters would not be competitive without them. In place of the "rules" approach, the EC argued for an across the board cut in support levels, by means of an instrument similar to that proposed by the US in 1987. The "Support Measurement Unit" had one crucial difference from the PSE: support was measured relative to a fixed "reference price" rather than the (variable) world price. The argument was that governments should not commit themselves to support levels over which they had little control.[62]

Though the "comprehensive" proposals were relatively clear statements of the positions of the protagonists, it is not clear that the US and the EC were any closer to an agreement than they were in late 1987. The US had switched from championing a sweeping approach to negotiating constraints on individual policies. The EC had gone from arguing for commodity-specific world market price-supporting measures to be followed later by modest support cuts to proposing a "global" initiative for a reduction of support across all border and domestic instruments. The two ships had passed in the night.

The link between the trade negotiations and the reform of domestic policy became apparent during the second phase of the negotiations. During the first phase, the Reagan proposal had been considered as so unrealistic that neither US nor European farmers took it as a credible threat to their programs. US farm groups could give it support without really having to come to grips with the realities of a subsidy-free world. Unlike New Zealand, the chance of sweeping de-regulation was remote. EC farm groups could berate the proposal as unrealistic without having to offer specific alternatives. In the second phase, actual policies were under discussion and the impact on farmers became clear. The US proposal for tariffication would have required changes in both US and EC domestic support legislation. Abandoning export subsidies would require other means of surplus disposal or supply control. Getting rid of price-linked domestic subsidies would likewise have had a dramatic impact on farm programs. By contrast the EC proposal disciplined no particular instruments, and sought to assist the development of domestic policy by avoiding "disharmonies" among commodities.[63]

---

[62] The tension between the benefits of flexibility of domestic prices to assist world market adjustment and the fixity of support prices to maintain farm incomes underlay much of the discussion at this time. The "flexibility" argument eventually won out.

[63] The disharmonies sometimes had themselves an origin in the GATT, such as the effect of

The Chairman's Draft

The first document that attempted to pull all of these ideas together was prepared by the Chairman of the Negotiating Group on Agriculture, Aart de Zeeuw, in June 1990. The "Chairman's Draft" benefited from intensive discussions in Geneva, both within the Agriculture Group and in informal meetings of delegates. The structure of the proposal was built around that of the US and the Cairns Group, calling for tariffication of non-tariff border measures, curbs on export subsidies, and classification of domestic support. In addition, the draft included provisions for maintaining current access through tariff quotas based on a proportion of current consumption. Countries were to present lists of concessions consistent with the proposed agreements, which could then form the basis for the remaining stage of the negotiation. The main element that was missing was the quantitative dimension: how deep was to be the cut in tariffs, export subsidies and domestic support? It was as if the exporters were being granted the rules that they desired and the importers could set the pace at which these rules were implemented.

This document represented a substantial and comprehensive draft agreement, and was welcomed by most of the delegations. But it still did not command full support as "a basis for negotiations". The EC felt that it followed too closely the US/Cairns Group line and rejected it. To accept it as the basis for negotiations would have implied abandoning the elements that were absent from the draft, such as rebalancing, and accepting constraints on export subsidies. It was still widely assumed in Brussels that the CAP could not be operated without the ability to increase export subsidies when required. Pressure increased on the EC to respond more positively, as only a few months were left before the December meeting in Brussels. A high level attempt to reach an agreement was made at the Houston Summit in the summer of 1990, when President Bush and his Canadian counterpart took it upon themselves to lobby the EC Commission along with the German, French, Italian and UK delegations, but the European politicians would only agree that the draft provided the "means to intensify negotiations" (Houston Communique: 11 July 1990: pt.23). However, less than one week later, the General Affairs Council declared that the DeZeeuw Report was only "one way to intensify" the agricultural negotiations (*Agence Europe,* 18 July 1990: 6). The EC retreat was due to the Council feeling that the Commission had gone past its mandate. Time was running out on the Brussels ministerial.

In the fall of 1990, the national delegations tabled draft "final offers" based largely on the Chairman's proposal. The US tabled a proposal in October 1990 to cut both tariffs and domestic support by 75 percent and to cut export subsidies by 90 percent, over ten years. Tariff quotas would be implemented to guarantee access over the transition period, and a tariff ceiling of 50 percent would apply at the end of that period. The Cairns Group tabled offers which broadly followed the same lines. The

---

binding oilseed tariffs at zero at a time when competitive animal fats and cereal-based feed ingredients were supported at high levels.

EC, however, was anxious to make sure that its own offer of November 1990 did not prejudge the outcome and exclude the elements that had been in their Comprehensive paper. Thus their offer comprised a 30 percent cut in "support" across the board over five years. This included guarded support for tariffication if accompanied by "rebalancing" (the introduction of tariffs on oilseeds, protein crops and corn gluten feed at a level comparable to that of cereals) and adequate safeguards. But it avoided offering any direct cut in export subsidies - though the suggestion was made that the reduction in export subsidies that followed from the support reductions could be calculated if other countries so desired.

Though with hindsight it is clear that it would have been difficult to complete a deal, the Heysel meeting in December 1990 raised some expectations that an agreement could be reached on agriculture, thus allow the Round to be completed on time. The task for reaching such a compromise fell to Mats Hellstrom, the Swedish Minister of Agriculture who was in the Chair of the Agricultural Group when they met at the Ministerial level. Hellstrom had had a major hand in reforming Swedish agricultural policy, and was keen to reach an agreement. After intensive bilateral discussions he circulated a "non-paper" with elements that he thought might form the basis for an agreement. The essence of this Hellstrom Draft was a 30 percent reduction in support, tariffs and export subsidies over five years, as suggested by the EC, but from a base more recent than that proposed by the EC. This would have taken the cuts to a level close to that envisaged by the US plan. But fortune did not smile on this attempt at a compromise. It won approval from the US and the Cairns Group and even an initial response from the EC Commission that was "cautious but broadly positive" (Josling, Warley and Tangermann, p.155). But the agriculture ministers, not coincidentally meeting in Brussels at that time, treated it less well. The French and Irish ministers considered that the Commission had exceeded their negotiating mandate (technically true) and Commissioner MacSharry retreated somewhat from his support of the Hellstrom draft. The talks in other areas were abandoned as the agricultural negotiations collapsed, as the Cairns Group once again decided to walk out rather than face the prospect of an agreement without an agricultural component.[64]

4.5   Relationship between Trade and Domestic Policy

Several important questions arise from this brief account of the events of the early stages of the Uruguay Round. First, how could the domestic policy-making process countenance the removal of control over policy to a set of international rules and processes alien to most rural politicians and remote even to most food industry

---

[64] Despite the useful position papers put forward by the Cairns Group over the negotiations, perhaps their most notable function was to keep pressing for agricultural agreement when many in the US and the EU would have gladly "postponed" the agricultural component to allow other parts of the negotiations to be concluded. Both the Kennedy Round and the Tokyo Round had been terminated with a hurriedly patched agricultural component that satisfied few countries. (Josling, Warley and Tangermann, Chapters 4 and 5.)

stakeholders? The answer in previous trade rounds could have been that domestic interests were somehow excluded from the discussions, and had little idea of what was going on in the negotiations. In the Uruguay Round the veil of secrecy was lifted. By the end of the Round, every lobbyist and politician knew the score. Even in the lead up to Heysel, the press coverage was extensive and the involvement of the private sector was profound. Some may have believed that an agreement would not be possible, and that the talks were therefore an exercise in shadow boxing with little practical content. It is not easy to see how one could support such a contention in the face of the quickening pace of globalization in the 1980s and the shift in the levers in other policy areas to the regional or multilateral level. The most constructive explanation would be that politicians had by the late 1980s come to accept that agricultural policies do not work in a vacuum, that one country's policies impinge directly on others, that global markets need agreed rules, and that open agricultural systems can be dynamic and profitable. In other words, the Dependent Agriculture paradigm was breaking down.

A second question is how was it possible for countries to go as far as to offer the deregulation of the domestic agricultural industry (or at the least the reinstrumentation of farm policies) at the bargaining table in Geneva? Why, if powerful domestic interests were likely to be disadvantaged by trade reform, were such proposals ever put forward? One answer could be that the processes of domestic policy and trade policy were so disconnected in agriculture that the trade policy process could set the agenda without having to face the issue of acceptability by the domestic policy actors. This undoubtedly happened in some countries, where trade and economic ministries regarded agricultural ministries as "part of the problem", to be circumvented in trade negotiations. In the US and the EC the situation was more complex. In both instances the agricultural departments were intimately involved in the trade talks. But there was also tension between the trade and agricultural agencies engaged in the talks, with trade ministers pushing for greater liberalization. While negotiators met in Geneva to confront their trading partners, US officials sat through interagency meetings trying to decide how agricultural goals meshed with broader commercial and strategic objectives. European officials had an even trickier problem, having to cope not just with differences between trade and agricultural goals but between diverse national trade objectives, particularly those of France, Germany and the UK. In the end the US proved to have the greater flexibility in taking initiatives and reacting to suggestions. The EC position tended to be locked in by tortuous agreement in the Council of Ministers, with those countries unhappy with the direction of events only too willing to object that the Commission was exceeding its mandate.[65]

---

[65] The concept of a negotiating mandate is itself problematic. The essence of negotiations is to have the flexibility to move to an agreement when advantageous. One element in this is to know more about the "bottom line" of the other parties than they do of yours. The EU, with its very public "internal negotiation" of a mandate to be taken to the table tends to produce an inflexible, defensive position. Added to an inflexible CAP, this put the EU negotiators in an unenviable situation.

The complex, compartmentalized EC decision-making process contributed to inflexibility as can be seen by assessing the "government politics" of the situation.[66] With a negotiating proposal having to clear DGI, DGVI, the Agriculture and External Affairs Commissioners, the Commission, the "113 Committee", COREPER, the Agriculture Council and the General Council, the bargaining costs of promoting a new initiative were very high. The net effect of considering agricultural trade proposals separately from trade proposals in other sectors was that most of the commissioners had difficulty seeing the implications for their dossiers, which reduced their incentive to assess critically agricultural trade issues. Thus, the Commission discussion tended toward a debate between the Agriculture Commissioner, defending the CAP, and the External Affairs Commissioner promoting the broader trade interests of the EC. The Agriculture Commissioner had the advantage in this debate, commanding the full resources of DGVI to back his position, along with the support of the farm lobby. He also benefited in that other commissioners tend to defer to the agricultural expertise that he represents and to accept his view as worthy of special consideration as his dossier would be most strongly affected by an agricultural trade agreement. At the Council level, the practice of seeking consensus in both the "113 Committee" and the Agriculture Council, meant that any new initiative must have near unanimous support from EC member governments, usually reflecting the lowest common denominator.

The interests of the member nations were so diverse that the lowest common denominator was often hard to find. France did not want to reduce export subsidies and Germany did not want to cut domestic prices, while the UK wanted both to lower domestic supports and liberalize trade. Paeman and Bensch note that the Agricultural Council systematically emasculated Commission proposals, seriously impeding the EC's ability make innovative moves in the Uruguay Round (Paeman and Bensch, 1995, p.109). The open Council debate further impeded negotiating effectiveness by eliminating any uncertainty about the EC's acceptable minimum position.

The US had made a radical proposal with Reagan's zero-option in 1987, but was not very flexible in making use of the "high ground" that this established. There was remarkably little deviation from this position until the April 1989 Mid-Term agreement. Orden, Paarlberg and Roe argue that the zero-option was a rational bargaining move as a means to jolt GATT negotiators out of the overly cautious style that had failed to produce significant reforms for agricultural trade reforms in the past (OPR, 1999, p.97). It also made good procedural sense for a lame-duck president to take an extreme position at the beginning of negotiations, which could be modified when his successor took office. It was a good political move for dealing with US domestic farm lobbies who were nervous about the GATT process (OPR, 1999, p.97). Farm lobbies were reassured first because the proposal was unlikely to be accepted abroad and therefore no real threat at home. Second, because all distorting subsidies would have been eliminated, the administration did not appear to be making arbitrary decisions about which countries, regions or commodities would have to bear the

---

[66] For a more detailed discussion of the implications for trade policy of the EU decision-making process see Moyer (1993).

heaviest burdens of reform. Third, de-coupled payments were not ruled out, so the zero option could be presented to reformers as a cut-out proposal, but at the same time could be presented to farm groups as a de-coupled cash-out, leaving US farm subsidies unharmed (OPR, 1999, pp.97-98).

There was little to be lost and much to be gained from staking out the "high ground," forcing the EC to react and be on the defensive.[67] As such the tactic worked remarkably well, at least in the first stage of the talks. The proposals of 1987 were much more imaginative than most observers would have thought likely.[68] But the question remains as to why the US negotiators hung on to this proposal long after it was clear that they were not going to convince the EC to agree?

What Went Wrong at Montreal?

Understanding of policy can be gained from failures as well as successes. It is therefore useful to consider the first of the two "breakdowns" of the GATT negotiations, each largely as a result of an impasse on agriculture, which threatened the future of the trade system. Was the problem at Montreal one of inadequate time for preparation, lack of motivation on the part of major countries, imperfect knowledge of partner responses, or just bad timing? It is difficult to argue that two years was too short a time for countries to prepare their positions on trade reform in agriculture. Indeed the succession of papers suggesting negotiating modalities seemed well thought out, if mutually incompatible. Nor can one really argue that the EC and the US did not understand each others positions at Montreal, though there may have been some doubt in the minds of the EC negotiators about how long the US would cling to the Zero Option proposal. It seems clear in this case that the failure of Montreal was in large part a lack of political will to make the necessary compromises.

The main issue at Montreal was whether the goal of the agricultural negotiations should be the elimination or the "substantial reduction" of agricultural subsidies, or as Paeman and Bench put it, "arms reduction" or "complete disarmament" (PB, 1995, p.134; see also Vahl, 1997, p.92). The report of the Trade Negotiating Committee identified the fundamental points of disagreement and set out the possible options in a straightforward, no nonsense style. The very structure of the text seemed to leave little room for compromise (PB, 1995, pp.134-135). The EC may have felt constrained to stand its ground because the Commission was very closely watched by the Agriculture Council, representatives of the European Parliament, and by farm groups (Vahl, 1997, p.92). American pressure may have hardened the EC position by drawing attention to

---

[67] Paeman and Bensch note that the zero-option allowed the Americans to "seize the initiative in the agricultural negotiations and to determine its parameters. Better still, they had succeeded in routing the European Community, which by now was in a state of some confusion" (PB, 1995, p.107).

[68] Experienced ex-negotiators such as Dale Hathaway were predicting a more modest scope for the talks that would essentially have involved commodity-specific bargains on a "request and offer" basis (Hathaway, 1987).

the agricultural negotiations, thus stimulating member states to closely monitor the Commission (Vahl (1997), p.111).

There does appear to have been a possibility of a deal at Montreal, at least to the extent of an agreement between the US and the EC on the conduct and objectives of the Round. Clayton Yeutter, the US negotiator, was apparently prepared to abandon the Zero Option but was opposed by the Agriculture Secretary, Richard (Dick) Lyng. Lyng was aware of the opinion of many farm groups (including the heavily protected sugar and dairy producers which had the least interest in liberalization) that only the zero-option would guarantee them a "level playing field" in international trade (Orden, Paarberg and Roe (1999), p.98). But had Yeutter made that move it is likely that Frans Andriessen, the Agricultural Commissioner, would have been able to accept the deal (interview). This would have prevented the hiatus in early 1989 and may have made it possible to adhere to the original four-year timetable for the Round.

In the end, new US flexibility came in time to contribute to the successful April 1989 Geneva Mid-Term Review (see Paeman and Bensch (1995), p.141; Orden, Paarlberg and Roe (1999), p.99). The Bush administration which had taken over in Washington and Clayton Yeutter replaced Dick Lyng as Secretary of Agriculture. The US now abandoned the Zero Option, bringing the US position close enough to that of the EC to allow agreement on the basic goals of the negotiations. The EC also felt the need to make concessions. After Montreal, fears were expressed that a US - EC trade war would ensue. At the first meeting between the Commission and the new US administration, the Commission President, Jacques Delors tried to cool things down. (Vahl (1997), p.92). He stressed that there was consensus on the source of the problem in world agriculture, namely that subsidies were too high. In addition, Frans Andriessen, who now had moved from Agriculture Commissioner to External Affairs Commissioner, argued that the EC had to reconsider its position in the agricultural negotiations if it were to avoid isolation again (Vahl (1997), p.92). He was given a little flexibility by the General Affairs Council after he assured the member states that he would take their positions into account, and that the Commission would cooperate closely with the "113 Committee" and, if necessary, COREPER (Vahl (1997), p.93). Still, the Agriculture Council took a firm stance to defend the CAP and reaffirmed its intention to play a central role in the GATT agricultural negotiations (Vahl (1997), p.93).

The US shifted away from the notion of across the board reductions in protection through the use of an aggregate measure of support toward an instrument specific approach which essentially targeted actions taken by major countries and devised rules to contain them. This approach constituted a much more direct attack on the CAP, and signaled an attempt to constrain the choice of instruments used rather than their level of use. Meanwhile the EC was warming to the idea of using an aggregate support measure as it appeared to give the most flexibility to the CAP while reinforcing the general attempt to keep support costs down. Implicit in the EC position was concern about the US tariffication approach, which was seen as a threat to the EC's variable levy (Vahl, 1997, p.111). This was made explicit by the new Commissioner for Agriculture, Ray MacSharry, when he outlined the EC position on agriculture in

October 1989 (Vahl (1997), p.111). The Commission, in its December 1989 proposal, had partially accepted the idea of tariffication, but only under a number of conditions. These included the concept of re-balancing, highly unpopular in the US, of increasing protection against products that had been allowed to enter the EC untaxed since the 1960s. These products were, notably, products which competed with cereals, such as oilseeds (Vahl (1997), p.112).[69]

The change in strategy on the part of the US was not unconnected to a shift in the influence of different agencies within USDA on the direction of policy. The Economic Research Service (ERS), that had favored the aggregate measure of support, found itself losing influence to the Foreign Agricultural Service (FAS) that was from the start more skeptical of such an approach. In the case of the EC, the change in heart may have been connected with the results of the Organization for Economic Cooperation and Development (OECD) studies which showed the US and Canada with surprisingly large Producer Subsidy Equivalents (PSEs) in the late 1980s. The Commission position also reflected a very divided Agriculture Council. Germany worried about tariffication and the possibility that EC price support would have to be reduced too much, while the United Kingdom and the Netherlands favored a more far-reaching contribution to the GATT negotiations (Vahl (1997), pp.112-113). The demand for re-balancing reflected a long-standing wish, especially of France, a large producer of cereals.

Why the Heysel Stadium Conference Failed

If the Montreal stalemate signaled a need for greater flexibility on the part of the main protagonists, the second crisis of the Uruguay Round illustrated other aspects of the relationship between domestic and trade policy. The response to the June 1990 De Zeeuw draft agreement provided an early warning that the differences between the US and EC were still too great for agreement to be reached by the upcoming Heysel Stadium conference. The reactions of most GATT members were positive, and a majority began to emerge for adopting the text without amendment (Paeman and Bensch (1995), p.171). The Cairns group in particular was especially vocal in its support. The US view was more cautious, calling the text "a viable basis for negotiation" (Paeman and Bensch (1995), p.171). There was opposition among developing countries, particularly agricultural importers who felt their interests had been ignored. But, by far the most serious objections came from the European Community. Commission agricultural policy decision-makers regarded the proposal as highly biased toward the Americans (Paeman and Bensch (1995), p.172). Other reactions in the Community were mixed. COPA's demand to reject De Zeeuw's paper altogether was echoed by France and Ireland (Vahl (1997), p.116). The other member nations, while expressing their criticism, favored acceptance with amendment. The consensus norm in the Agriculture Council meant that the EC could go no further than

---

[69] Rebalancing was the EU's answer to American criticism of the EU's oilseeds regime that in mid-December 1989 culminated in a GATT ruling against the EU (Vahl, 1997, p.112).

say that the De Zeeuw draft was "a means of intensifying negotiations." On July 17, Rolf Mohler, the European Comission's agriculture negotiator, delivered the EC's comments on the draft agreement without pulling any punches. A row ensued between the EC on one side and the US and Cairns group on the other (Paeman and Bensch (1995), p.172). The US and Cairns Group felt compelled to react publicly to counter all the EC's criticisms. The crisis blew over, but no progress had been made in bridging the gap in US and EC positions. The European Community was so divided about how to proceed in the GATT agricultural trade negotiations that it was unable to meet the October 15 deadline for submission of "final offers."

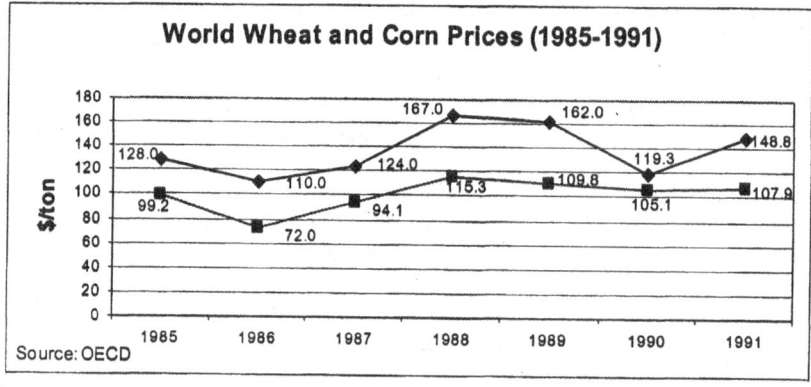

Figure 4.5: World Wheat and Corn Prices (1985-1991)

To underscore how strongly EC agricultural interests felt about preserving the CAP and how reluctant national and Commission leaders were to challenge the farm lobby, it is instructive to examine how the "final" EC GATT proposal developed. The outline for what was to become the EC final negotiating proposal was presented informally by Agriculture Commissioner MacSharry at a meeting of the "Quint" group of Agriculture Ministers (EC, Canada, Japan, Australia and US) at Dromoland Castle in Ireland at the end of July, even before it had been discussed either in the Commission or in the Council (*Agra Europe*, Aug. 3, 1990: E/1). MacSharry said the EC would be willing to concede a reduction of support of 30 percent from the base period of 1986 to 1988 based on the SMU. Since about 15 percent of that amount had already been achieved by 1990, that left only another 15 percent to be accomplished. Export subsidy reductions could be no greater than the decline in domestic support, and a decrease of import barriers would have to be accompanied by rebalancing. MacSharry's action indicated that he rather that the External Affairs Commissioner Frans Andriessen now held the initiative.[70]

---

[70] Commissioner Andriessen was pre-occupied at the time with the problem of dealing with the newly democratic countries of Central and Eastern Europe.

MacSharry's GATT proposal received EC approval only with great difficulty. When first presented to the Commissioners in mid-September, it was not approved, because a significant group of Commissioners (Andriessen, Bangeman and Brittan) thought his support reductions too small. However, the message from EC national capitals seemed supportive of MacSharry and the full Commission approved his proposal almost intact, with the exception of allowing an 8 percent increase in soybean imports to make rebalancing more palatable to the US But when the proposal was debated in the Agricultural Council at an emergency meeting on October 8, it was rejected. The main objection was that the Commission had made no attempt to gauge the impact on farmers of the proposed cuts (*Agra Europe*, Oct.12, 1990: E/4). For many of the Agriculture Ministers, notably those from Germany and France, the cuts were acceptable only if farmers could be provided with compensatory aid to cover their losses. *Agra Europe* noted that the Agriculture Council action exemplified the traditional unwillingness of this body to offend the farm lobby, passing the responsibility on to others - in this case the trade ministers meeting as the General Council (*Agra Europe*, Oct. 12, 1990: P/1). But, the trade ministers were not anxious to take the lead, and refused to act until the Agriculture Ministers had rendered a formal opinion.

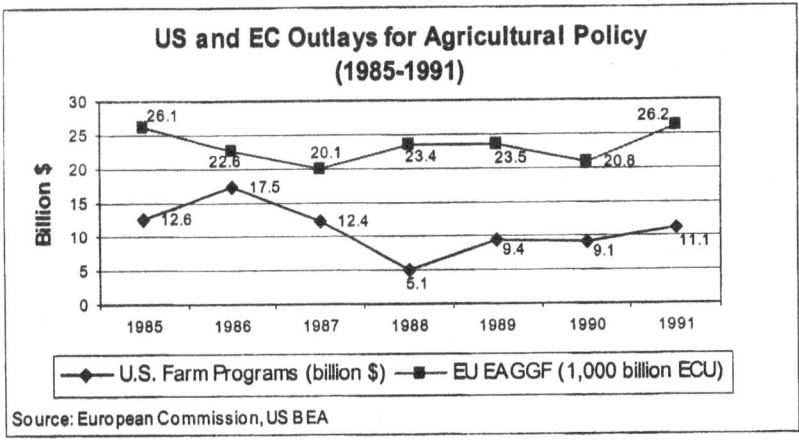

Figure 4.6: US and EC Outlays for Agricultural Policy (1985-1991)

In the event, the EC proposal did not receive approval until early November, almost three weeks after the October 15 deadline. The Agriculture Council took the proposal up again on October 19, but still couldn't act, so it went to a joint Council consisting of the agriculture and trade ministers on October 26, with both MacSharry and Andriessen as Commission representatives. But agreement still could not be reached, so the proposal was put on the agenda of the European Council, meeting that weekend. However, the Heads of Government refused to decide the issue and sent it back to the Agriculture Ministers. Finally, the proposal was approved in a somewhat emasculated form: the link between the decline in domestic support and reductions of export subsidies and import barriers was removed (*Agra Europe*, Nov. 9, 1990: P/1). The main barrier to agreement was again the French-German alliance, illustrating the constraints placed on EC agriculture policy by "intergovernmental politics". The German government liked the compensation provisions that had been added to the proposal, but refused to vote against the French, who had great difficulty accepting the dilution of Community preference and the reduction of export subsidies (*Agra Europe*, Nov. 2, 1990: P/1). The forthcoming parliamentary election on December 1 strengthened German resolve to hold the line on agriculture. Even though German industrialists were pressing for a GATT agreement, the last thing that Chancellor Kohl wanted to do was to alienate the farm lobby (Paeman and Bansch (1995), p.178). The German Farmers Union traditionally delivered 80 percent of its vote to the CDU and CSU, the parties central to the governing coalition (Patterson, 1997). *Agra Europe* commented that the EC's behavior confirmed that the Community was only prepared to reduce agricultural support as much as it was forced to do so by internal pressures. Any amount of external pressure for protection reduction would clearly be secondary to internal pressure (Nov. 9, 1990: P/2).

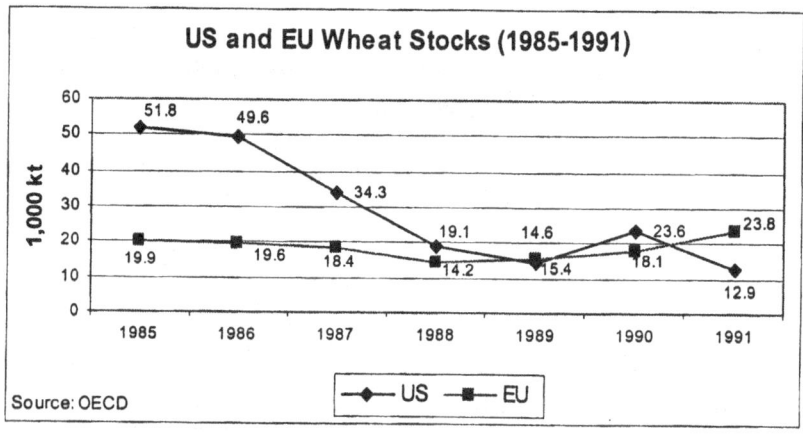

Figure 4.7: US and EU Wheat Stocks (1985-1991)

There is a sense in which the GATT Ministerial conference that was held at Heysel Stadium in December 1990 was doomed from the start. Carla Hills, and her deputy with chief responsibility for agriculture, Julius Katz, were determined that there be no agreement to end the Round without a deal on agriculture. So were the Cairns Group, of smaller exporting countries. But economic trends had improved sufficiently to weaken the interest for an agriculture agreement in both Brussels and Washington (see Orden, Paarlberg and Roe (1999), p.100). The high internal farm budget pressures within both the US and EC, which during the initial phase of the Uruguay Round had sustained a sense of reform urgency were much reduced by 1990. The summer drought in the US during 1988 drove up crop prices on world markets (Figure 4.5). In the US the rising world market price had finally constrained farm budget outlays, which fell rapidly (Figure 4.6). In the EC, the 1988 cereals stabilizers agreement had also temporarily reduced farm budget pressures. The strong world market also temporarily reduced government stocks in the US and the EC (Figure 4.7).

The EC was also somewhat distracted by other events. The momentous decision to form an Economic and Monetary Union (EMU) had recently been taken, and an Intergovernmental Conference (IGC) of the EC members was getting underway in Rome, designed to lead to a Treaty change that would extend the EC institutions' competency to include monetary union.[71] The parliamentary election in the first week of December in Germany also provided a distraction. The major event of the period was the political transformation of Europe, made possible by the fall of the Socialist regimes in Central and Eastern Europe and the tearing down of the Berlin Wall. Though this had only indirect consequences for the GATT talks, it had the effect of distracting EC politicians and began to absorb the time and energies of the Brussels bureaucracy. Though no one was quite sure what would be the outcome of the dramatic changes in Central Europe, it was clear that they would have a major impact on the EC and indeed on the configuration of the Atlantic Alliance. In addition, conflict was heating up in the Persian Gulf, the first post-cold war security threat. Against this backdrop the European politicians might be forgiven for spending less time thinking about the issues of trade in agricultural goods.

Failed Efforts to Reform Domestic Policy through Trade Negotiations

The US and EC had shared interests at the beginning of the Uruguay Round in 1986 in seeking agricultural policy reform through international trade negotiations. Agricultural policy expenditures were rising in both Europe and America along with increasing commodity stocks, while the economic situation of farmers was deteriorating. High government expenditures had only a limited effect on farm income, as much of the money went for surplus storage and disposal. Effort to dispose of surpluses on an international market depressed by the Third World debt crisis had led to export subsidy competition between the US and EC, which in turn had generated political conflict. Efforts to limit surpluses through domestic policy reform had not been very successful. In the EC, only the dairy sector had been reformed, with the 1984 imposition of quotas. In the US, the freezing of deficiency payment base acreages and yields along with the creation of the Conservation Reserve program was having some effect, but much more was needed.

The Reagan administration and the European Commission (more reluctantly) sought to control surpluses and expenditures through the Uruguay Round, and hence attain goals that they could not achieve through domestic US and EC policy processes. Put in terms of multi-level linked bargaining games, they hoped for the synergistic

---

[71] The IGC (or to be more exact, two IGCs in parallel) led to the Maastricht Treaty, which added common foreign and security policy and mandated cooperation in justice and home affairs, as well as paving the way for a single currency.

effect described by Putnam, where international negotiations can exercise a transforming influence over domestic political processes (see Putnam, 1988; Coleman and Tangermann 1997; Moyer, 1993). There was reason to hope that international trade negotiators committed to trade liberalization would be better able to withstand pressures from the farm lobby than either the EC Agriculture Council or the US congressional agriculture committees.

The failure at Heysel showed a synergistic effect between domestic agriculture policy and international trade negotiation. However, it was domestic policy that constrained international negotiations. Part of the explanation stems from the inability of either the US or EC to distance the agricultural policy community and farm lobby from the negotiations. Both the US and EC had to rely heavily on their agricultural policy bureaucracies in preparing negotiating positions, in order to get the necessary expertise for dealing with the myriad complexities of agricultural policy. DGVI and USDA actually led the agricultural trade negotiations. Farm lobbies could not be kept away because the negotiations were highly visible. Liberal trade interests had to follow all the trade sectors under negotiation, and gave the agricultural negotiation much less attention than the farm lobby - as would have been predicted from the literature on public choice.

The US had one advantage in this respect in that the congressional agricultural committees could be kept at arms length until the conclusion of the Uruguay Round, when the entire agreement would be brought to Congress. With Fast Track procedures in place, the agriculture committees could not propose amendments to an overall agreement, as Congress could only vote the entire package up or down.[72] The EC Agriculture Council, on the other hand, could not be kept at arms length, and in fact had to approve all major Commission initiatives. This reflected a national government constraint on the Commission. France, Germany and Ireland prevailed in their insistence on the inclusion of the Agriculture Council at the heart of the negotiation process.

At least one unsuccessful effort was made to limit Agriculture Council influence. The Commission wanted to move toward an agreement on agriculture and thought it had streamlined its decision-making process to allow flexibility and responsiveness. The intent at that stage was for the Commission negotiating team to exercise as much leeway as possible in the negotiations, going only to the Council of Ministers when absolutely necessary, but working closely with the "113 Committee" of national representatives in Geneva. The Commission planned to work directly through the General Council, without having to submit its proposals to the Agriculture Council. To put this in the terminology of the three-level GATT bargaining game, the Commission hoped to restructure the bargaining process to allow the EC negotiators sufficient room to reach an agreement, which could never be approved in advance by the interaction of the EC and national policy processes. Once this agreement was reached, it was hoped that the benefits for sectors other than agriculture would be sufficient to change the

---

[72] The Agriculture Committees would, however, write implementing legislation, which would be instrumental in how the US carried out its commitments. See Moyer, 1993.

bargaining balance at both levels, when the choice would be a certain (though less than perfect) deal or no deal at all (see Putnam (1988), p.446).

This procedure worked, to a degree, in considering the EC's response to the De Zeeuw Draft, but there was a flaw and the results should have indicated that problems lay ahead. The flaw was that the Commission response to De Zeeuw was prepared by the DGVI representatives, who led the agricultural group negotiating team. Their critical response was then forwarded to DGI, which took a more positive view. But DGI was disadvantaged in that it was reacting to DGVI rather than initiating the response. The response went directly to the General Council, but not before Agriculture Commissioner MacSharry had sharply criticized the De Zeeuw Draft. The General Council could then not accept the De Zeeuw Draft as a basis for negotiations and would only go so far as to say that it could be used as a means of "intensifying negotiations" (*Agra Europe*, July 27, 1990: E/1).

The problem in the General Council was more serious than dealing with a response drafted by the section of the Commission with the greatest vested interest in the CAP. A further bargaining constraint also appeared in that the EC member governments were still far from consensus that significant changes in the CAP should be made in the GATT. The most serious opposition came from Germany and France, which managed to preserve their agricultural alliance. The German government, with an agricultural sector at that time consisting largely of small farmers, who did not export very much, had little intrinsic problem with the sections of De Zeeuw which would reduce export subsidies. However, it expressed serious reservations about domestic price cuts. The French government on the other hand, relying heavily on agricultural exports for its balance of payments strongly opposed to reductions in export subsidies, though it could have accepted price cuts. Not surprisingly, the German government supported the French government on export subsidies, while the French government supported the German government on price supports. After Heysel, industry interests in a number of EC countries (particularly Germany) began to prevail over agriculture, which would later have an important influence on the perspectives of heads of state and government (see Chapter 6).

The attempt to exclude the Agriculture Council from consideration of GATT proposals backfired. When this body met on July 24 1990, the day after the EC response to the De Zeeuw Draft was submitted to the Trade Negotiating Committee of the GATT, it took action to place itself in the center of the debate. The Agriculture Council appointed a high level working group consisting of member state representatives for agriculture to shadow the agricultural trade negotiations and declared that it wanted to be updated on the current status of the talks at each subsequent meeting as long as the GATT negotiations continued. Given the public sympathy for farmers, and the strength of the EC farm lobby, this action was not challenged either by the EC Commission or any national government.

The US made an attempt, with the zero-option, to reach a trade agreement that would have transformed domestic policy (the synergistic effect predicted by Putnam). But, it managed to get this accepted by the farm lobby at least in part because the consensus was that the EC would never accept this proposal. If the EC had accepted the zero-option, then Putnam's synergistic linkage might have been achieved, but of course American perceptions of EC politics were proved correct.

Chapter 5

The 1990 US Farm Bill - Reducing the Budget, but Minimizing the Pain

5.1 The Development of the 1990 US Farm Bill

The 1990 US Farm Bill debate took place in a context not very auspicious for agricultural policy reform. To be sure there was a large federal budget deficit, but government farm spending was rapidly declining. The unusually hot and dry summer of 1988 had caused a major crop shortfall, with the result that commodity prices had increased and stocks had fallen. The farm economy was well on the way to recovery from the depressed conditions of the mid-1980s, and there was a general perception in the farm policy community that the 1985 Farm Bill had been a success. There was little pressure for change from the Uruguay Round negotiations that were stalled at the time because of EC reluctance to cut domestic price supports, import barriers and export subsidies.

The farm bill development followed a very traditional process, as illustrated in Figure 5.1. In this process, administration recommendations are formulated under the supervision of the Secretary of Agriculture, with input from the various branches of USDA, the White House, Cabinet departments and Executive Agencies.[73] The Secretary's recommendations, cleared by the White House are sent to Congress, serving as inputs for House and Senate Agriculture Committees, which each write their own farm bill. In the House, the process starts with hearings in commodity subcommittees of the House agriculture committee, followed by the formulation of proposed legislation in the full agriculture committee. This bill then is taken to the floor of the full house for debate and approval. The process is similar in the Senate, except that the Senate agriculture committee does not parcel out its work to subcommittees. After bills are passed in both houses of Congress, they are reconciled in a conference committee consisting of members of both House and Senate agriculture committees. The Conference report then goes to both houses, where it may either be accepted without amendment or rejected. If accepted by both houses, the bill goes to the President, who may either sign the bill or veto it.[74] If signed by the

---

[73] For a more detailed discussion of the traditional US agricultural policy process see Moyer and Josling (1990), p.121.

[74] If the President signs the bill it becomes law. If there is a Presidential veto, the bill only becomes law if it subsequently is approved by a 2/3 vote in each house of Congress.

President, the bill becomes law, where the primary responsibility for implementation lies with USDA. The development of the 1990 Farm Bill through this process is described below.

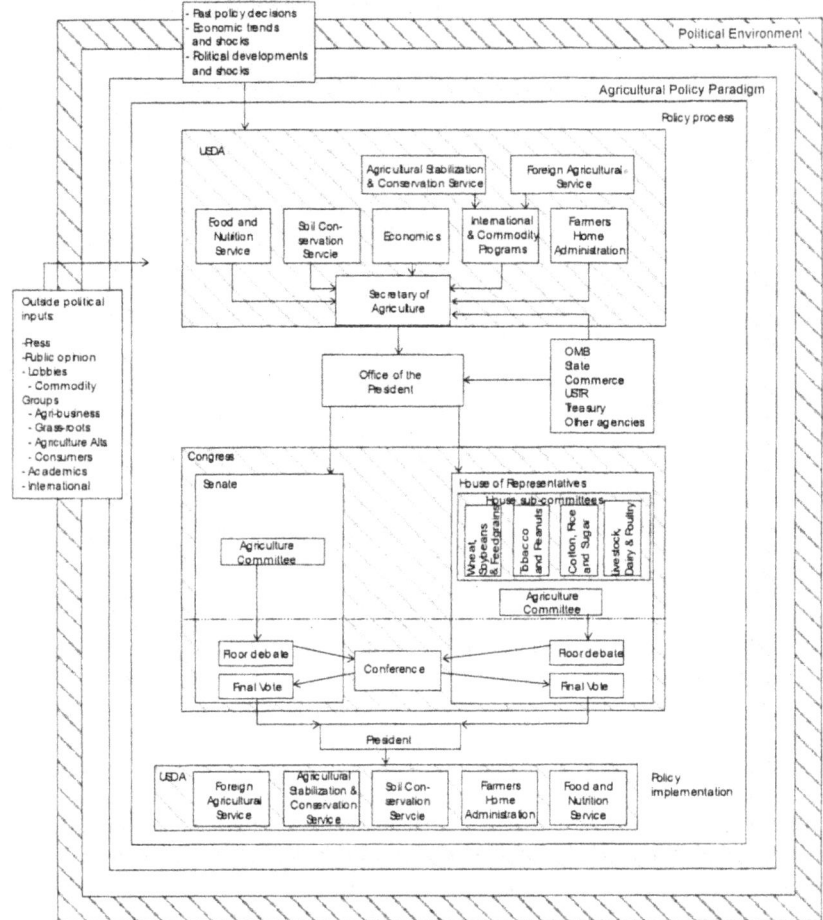

Figure 5.1: Bargaining Process for US Agricultural Policy at the Time of the 1990 Farm Bill

The US Department of Agriculture began its planning for the 1990 Farm Bill in the summer of 1989. The Office of the Undersecretary for International Affairs and Commodity Programs was given responsibility for preparing the administration proposal to Congress. Task forces were established to prepare documents relevant to the various aspects of the farm bill. They made their reports to a central planning group.[75] This group met frequently, sometimes every day. The work of some of the task forces, such as the one for forestry, did not stir up much controversy. The reports of other task forces, particularly those related to commodities, conservation and the environment, and international programs, engendered much discussion. Pros and cons of specific ideas were debated extensively prior to formulating policy recommendations. Representatives of the Office of Management and Budget and the White House Economic Office sat in on the discussions, but there was not much Presidential involvement in shaping the USDA recommendations. The central planning group tried to steer clear of lobbyists by keeping a low profile, but the commodity groups were able to exercise influence by heavy lobbying in ASCS. The environmental lobby also had input into the process by lobbying the newly appointed Assistant Secretary with responsibility for conservation and the environment.

Cautious Recommendations from the Bush Administration

The Bush Administration proposal for the farm bill was formulated in November and December 1989, and submitted to Congress in February, 1990.[76] Instead of following the usual practice of sending Congress formal legislation to retool farm programs, Secretary Yeutter offered a pragmatic package of recommendations, some detailed and some not so detailed. Though it was clear that farm spending would be a target for reduction, given the budget deficit of $161 billion, the administration made no recommendations about how farm spending should be cut. The proposal called for more flexibility for farmers to respond to market signals. More specifically, it called for overhauling the base acreage system. Previously, if a farmer planted a crop other than the one for which he had a base, he lost part of his subsidy payments, and his base shrank in the future. To change this, the administration recommended its Normal Crop Acreage (NCA) scheme, where each farmer would have an overall base including all acreage planted in any program crop, as well as acreage planted to oilseeds (soybeans, sunflowers and rapeseed) (Cochrane and Runge 1992, p.57). Farmers could produce whatever program crops they chose on NCA acreage. The administration characterized the NCA proposal as "flexible base."

Flexibility was also a key element in the Administration proposals for dealing with environmental problems resulting from agriculture. Yeutter argued that allowing farmers to respond to market signals would make them more efficient and frugal in their use of synthetic pesticides and fertilizers, and would encourage them to rotate their crops (1990 CQ Almanac, p.326). The administration wanted to provide farmers with incentives to become better environmental stewards. It proposed extending the

---

[75] This group included Undersecretary Crowder, his deputy John Campbell, Assistant Secretary for Economics Bruce Gardner, his deputy, Dan Sumner, Chief Staff Economist Keith Collins, and Keith Bjerke, the administrator of the Agriculture Stabilization and Conservation Service (ASCS).

[76] "1990 Farm Bill, Proposal of the Administration," February, 1990, USDA, frequently referred to as the "Green Book."

Conservation Reserve Program (CRP), under which farmers were paid to take environmentally fragile land out of production. New land enrolled in the CRP would have to meet tougher erosion-control standards if returned to production. Farmers would be paid to withdraw land susceptible to groundwater contamination from production. Existing cropped wetlands would be eligible for CRP payments beyond 1990, the deadline for enrolling fragile land in the program. Farmers who agreed to take land permanently out of production would be offered payments.

The administration made recommendations increasing its discretionary authority to set loan rates and to adjust ARP programs, hoping to further its aim to make farm policy more market-oriented. Under the 1985 Farm Bill, the Secretary of Agriculture could set the loan rate for wheat and feedgrains at 75-85 percent of the average price received by producers during the previous five years, excluding the high and low years.[77] The loan rate could not be reduced by more than five percent a year, or more than 20 percent for the duration of the farm bill. However, the 1985 Farm Bill raised the loan rates for cotton and rice, giving the Secretary little authority to lower them. The administration proposed that the 1990 Farm Bill calculate loan rates for all commodities using the 1985 formula for corn and soybeans. For acreage reduction programs (ARPs), the administration wanted to change the way set-asides were calculated, taking into account projected market use and exports in addition to carry-over stocks.

The 1990 farm legislation that emerged from Congress could not be considered major reform of agricultural policy. The outcome was quite different from what the administration had envisaged but it did address some of the administration goals. The newly created "triple-base" program was designed both to limit farm spending and to give farmers more flexibility in their planting decisions. The CRP program was re-authorized and expanded to include existing wetlands. There were also measures to encourage farmers to take better care of the environment. However, the Secretary of Agriculture did not get the flexibility he requested to set loan rates.

Congress Formulates a New Farm Bill

House of Representatives The hearings and debate process in the House agriculture sub-committees produced recommendations that seemed to ignore the budget deficit, adding $14 billion in farm subsidy increases. These recommendations would have increased target prices for wheat and feedgrains by 10 percent over the subsequent five years (the same amount that they had declined since 1987) and have increased loan rates between 7 cents and 30 cents for wheat and feedgrains[78] (1990 CQ Almanac,

---

[77] The loan rate is the price a farmer gets when he puts his crop into government storage upon harvest. If the market price rises above the loan rate, the farmer may sell his crop and repay his loan. If the market price falls below the loan rate, the farmer is relieved of his debt obligation by forfeiting his crop to the government, making the loan rate in effect a floor price. Acreage reduction programs (ARPs) are unpaid land set-asides required by the government as a condition for receiving the benefits of federal farm programs.

[78] Target prices are artificial prices set by government representing the prices that it is thought

p.327). However, the full committee drastically scaled down these recommendations. A task force convened by committee chairman, E. "Kika" de la Garza, D-Texas, recommended freezing target prices for major commodities at 1990 levels for the next five years and limiting dairy spending to existing levels (1990 CQ Almanac, p.327). This recommendation was challenged by a group of junior Democrats, who had hoped to go home for the Memorial Day recess promising farmers large increases in crop prices. They backed a plan by Iowa Democrat Dave Nagel that would have reversed the course of the 1985 Farm Bill, which had brought US prices more in line with world market levels. However, the senior Democrats joined a nearly united bloc of Republicans to reject this challenge and accept the task force recommendations. The committee did not change the sugar or peanut programs in significant ways. For dairy, the Committee agreed to set a five-year floor on the government price support level at $10.10 per hundredweight - the existing level, with the Secretary authorized to impose marketing controls in surplus years.

Environmentalists managed to prevent a broad loosening of existing law, by threatening action on the House floor (1990 CQ Almanac, p.130). The Conservation section of the bill included support for the swamp-buster program, which denied government subsidies to farmers who drained and planted wetlands, although penalties for first time violations were reduced. Also included were incentive payments to farmers to reduce water pollution and a new five-year program to retire 2.5 million acres of wetlands from production. However, the environmental lobby was unable to gain House Agriculture committee support for many of their more ambitious proposals to build on the mandatory controls of the 1985 law, such as requiring farmers to keep records of their pesticide use and reduce their use of agricultural chemicals in polluted areas.

The trade section of the bill did not engender much controversy in the House Agriculture committee. Recommendations of the Subcommittee on Department Operations, Research and Foreign Agriculture were accepted to extend for five years several programs which subsidized exports of US commodities and provided food aid to needy foreign nations (1990 CQ Almanac, p.330). Authority was expanded to donate government owned commodities to aid programs meeting poverty reduction criteria established by the World Bank. In addition, the Secretary of Agriculture was asked to maintain a stable level of commodities for use in the PL-480 food aid program. Appropriations for the Export Enhancement Program (EEP) were authorized at not less than $500 million for each of the following five years. The scope of the Targeted Export Assistance program (TEA) was expanded by permitting its use to stimulate exports in countries with market potential - not just where there were unfair trade practices, as existing law required.

The House Agriculture committee finally completed on the 1990 Farm Bill on June 14, 85 days after it began deliberation, acknowledging that there was no money

---

farmers should be getting for their commodities. Deficiency payments are given to farmers calculated on the difference between the target price and average market price.

for a major policy change, and little sentiment for one among farmers (1990 CQ Almanac, p.326).

The debate on the floor of the house was highlighted by an attack on the Committee bill by a coalition of urban Democrats and suburban Republicans led by Rep. Charles E. Shumer D-NY and Rep. Dick Armey R-Texas, who wanted to slash farm spending. The centerpiece of this assault came in the form of an amendment to deny crop subsidies to farmers with gross adjusted incomes of more than $100,000 a year, but this effort failed by a vote of 327-91. The House also rejected calls to close loopholes that permitted widespread evasion of a $50,000 limit on income support subsidies and a $250,000 cap on government benefits paid to individual farmers.[79]

The sugar program was also attacked, with an amendment by Rep. Thomas Downey D-NY and Bill Gradison of Ohio, which would have imposed a 2-cent cut to the 18-cent-per-pound price support. This amendment failed by a vote of 271-150.

The House did make a few changes to the Agriculture Committee Bill. In one of the closest votes in the debate, it adopted an amendment by Rep Peter Defazio, D-Ore to adopt a national standard governing what foods could be labeled organic by a vote of 234-187. It also accepted a "circle of poison" amendment greatly restricting the export of pesticides considered too dangerous for use in the US.

The House passed its version of the 1990 Farm Bill easily on August 1, by a vote of 327-91. In general, income-subsidy levels were frozen for crops such as wheat, corn, cotton and rice. Some potentially expensive changes were made in the calculation of loan rates, but the bill did not greatly increase overall payments to farmers. However the threat of a presidential veto was evident. Rep. Edward Madigan of Illinois, ranking Republican on the Agriculture Committee, said that Budget Director Richard Darmen told him that "if anything like we passed today was put before the president, he would veto it" (1990 CQ Almanac, p.331). The House Agriculture Committee estimated that the bill would cost $55 billion: this was $2 billion more than the five-year budget allocation. It was anticipated that another $8 billion to $20 billion might have to be cut from the bill pending a White House-congressional budget agreement to trim the deficit (1990 CQ Almanac p.331).

Action in the Senate In the Senate Agriculture Committee, Chairman Patrick Leahy D-Vt. and senior minority member Richard Lugar, D-Indiana built a bi-partisan coalition, which produced an omnibus farm bill, containing a package of modest changes in federal crop subsidy programs. The bill froze income subsidy levels for wheat, corn, cotton and rice as well as dairy products. The bi-partisan coalition was opposed by a group of Democrat "prairie populists," including Senators Daschle (S.D.), Kerrey (Neb.) Harkin (IA) and Conrad (N.D.). These senators wanted to raise target prices

---

[79] At the time, a farmer could collect payments from three different entities: his own farm (which was eligible for the maximum $50,000 and $250,000) and two other farming operations in which he was allowed half ownership. From these three entities, a farmer could legally double his government largesse for a total of $100,000 in income subsidies and $500,000 in total benefits. All this was retained by the House, but the $250,000 limit was reduced to $200,000.

and strip the power to lower loan rates from the Secretary of Agriculture. However, they failed in a series of test votes, even though concessions were made. Growers of wheat, feed-grains and soybeans were offered marketing loans, which previously had been available only for cotton and rice. Marketing loans (harvest time advances from the government using the crop as collateral) required a farmer only to repay as much of the loan as he received in the market, with the remainder of the loan kept as a subsidy. In another concession to the "prairie populists," the committee put new constraints on the power of the Secretary of Agriculture to lower loan rates. For every one-cent reduction, farmers would have to be given an offsetting 0.75-cent payment before planting.

In other action the committee voted to keep the dairy price support at the existing $10.10 per hundredweight for the subsequent five years, although the Secretary of Agriculture was authorized to take measures to control production if surplus dairy products exceeded seven billion pounds per year. The Committee voted to bar the Secretary from buying up and slaughtering entire dairy herds, which had been authorized in the 1985 Farm Bill, but which had aroused opposition from cattlemen. The Committee voted to renew the sugar program with few changes, rejecting amendments by Senator Lugar to cut sugar price supports and do away with the sugar program. It also voted to renew the peanut program.

The Senate Agriculture Committee included strong environmental provisions in its farm bill. It agreed to toughen some elements of the swamp-buster provisions and to relax other, but keep the essence of the 1985 law intact. In separate action, the committee offered to create conservation programs that would give farmers financial incentives to enroll wetlands in government easements and to prevent contamination of ground and surface water as a result of agricultural practices. For the first time the committee voted to require farmers to keep records of their use of certain potentially harmful pesticides. The Secretary of Agriculture was also encouraged to enroll one million acres of wetlands over five years in the Conservation Reserve Program (CRP). A tough "circle of poison" provision was approved which would have banned export of any pesticides that the EPA had not approved for use in the US.

The Farm Bill sent to the Senate included a number of measures designed to promote food exports and food aid. It sought to reform the 1954 Food for Peace Program by providing food grants to the poorest countries. It also created a new "Food for Freedom" program described by one committee aide as a "mini-Marshall Plan" to help the new democracies (1990 CQ Almanac, p.337). The bill also created a new marketing-assistance program in improve the nation's competitive posture and put more punch behind the Export Enhancement Program (EEP), where spending was authorized for $900 million in 1991 and between $500 Million and $900 million from fiscal 1992 through fiscal 1995.

The Senate approved its five-year farm bill on July 27 by a 70-21 vote. This bill largely accepted the recommendations of the Senate Agriculture Committee and reaffirmed the basic course of US agriculture policy set in 1985. Floor debate took only six days, a sharp contrast from 1985, when a sharply partisan Senate had debated the measure from October 25 to November 23 (1990 CQ Almanac, p.339). Appeals by farm state lawmakers to raise subsidies and direct more government payments to small, family-run farming operations were rejected.[80] But, with the exception of the federal honey program, which was abolished, proposals to lower payments or eliminate crop programs were also defeated (1990 CQ Almanac, p.339). Faced with the threat of a Presidential veto, the Senate accepted an amendment by Senators Lugar and Leahy to cut $3.5 billion out of the bill. However, it rejected an amendment by Senator Harry Reid (D-Nev), which would have barred farmers with gross sales of more than $500,000 from most federal subsidies.

Conference action and the creation of "triple-base" The House-Senate Conference was impeded by the contentious federal budget debate between the White House and Congress. When finally congressional budget makers instructed them to come up with $13.6 billion in cuts, they did so reluctantly. The conferees did not cut target prices and loan rates, but adopted the "triple-base" option.[81] This option gave farmers receiving subsidies a third category of land in addition to the acreage on which they received subsidies, and the land the federal government required them to idle, as a condition for receiving federal benefits. In this third category of land, farmers could grow whatever they wanted, though they would not receive any subsidies on this land. The final 1990 Farm Bill placed 15 percent of each farmer's base acreage in this third category. Other savings were achieved by changing the way deficiency payments were calculated, by levying assessments on other subsidized crops that did not receive direct payments (dairy, sugar and peanuts), and slashing other government loan programs.[82] Direct lending by the Farm and Home Administration (FmHA) and Rural Electrification Administration was replaced with government guarantees on private loans.

Environmental organizations had expressed fear that the Conferees would reject several sections from the controversial conservation title, which had been inserted in order to win support for the bill on the Senate and House floors. But their fears were exaggerated. The conferees agreed to re-authorize the Conservation Reserve Program, directing the Secretary of Agriculture to add 6 million acres of land to the 34 million acre reserve, including one million acres of wetlands. The bill also provided for a voluntary program offering farmers incentives to reduce and prevent water pollution from agriculture. However, the Conference dropped the "circle of poison" provision from the bill.

---

[80] The targeting debate had little support in the South. Cotton and rice, have much higher planting and growing costs than cereals, so need larger farms to be profitable. Only the "prairie populists" pushed this issue (interview-Reimenschneider).

[81] "Triple-base," had been formulated earlier in the farm bill debate by Representative Charles Stenholm (D-Texas), as a means of fitting farm program costs into the Balanced Budget Act equation (Madison, p.1085).

[82] Even though dairy and sugar producers would have to pay assessments, the overall sugar and dairy programs were frozen in place. Producers would receive the same level of government subsidy as before, but they would have to return part of the subsidy.

The prospects for presidential approval of the farm bill improved significantly after an October 12 meeting between Secretary of Agriculture Yeutter and senior House and Senate conferees. At the meeting Yeutter agreed to provisions in the House bill setting the loan rate for wheat and feedgrains at 85 percent of the previous five-year moving average, rather than the 75-85 percent band included in the 1985 Farm Bill. In return, Yeutter requested and received changes in the sugar and dairy sections of the bill which had strayed too far from the free-market approach favored by the administration (1990 CQ Almanac, p.350).

Farm state legislators got one more major concession in the final conference - a provision directing the Secretary of Agriculture to increase export subsidies and ease production restrictions if the ongoing Uruguay Round did not reach an agreement to reduce export subsidies. This threatened an all-out agricultural trade war if the European Community was not more forthcoming in its willingness to liberalize trade.

The Conference report won overwhelming approval in the House on October 23, by a vote of 318-102, and in the Senate, on October 25, by a vote of 60-36. The farm bill then went to the President, who signed it on November 28. In his remarks on signing the bill, President Bush expressed no reservations, viewing the legislation as a continuation of the shift toward market-oriented policies and a good base for maintaining pressure to reduce worldwide agricultural subsidies. He said, "increased flexibility in planting choices contained in the 1990 Farm Bill will allow farmers to break out of the traditional farm program straitjacket, which bound them to produce the same crop year after year, regardless of market opportunities" (CQ Almanac (1990), p.351).

5.2   Analysis

The reform process in the 1990 Farm Bill can be understood in the light of previous policies, economic conditions and political developments. This section relates these factors to the outcome of the policy process.

Perceived Success of Previous Policy Inhibits Change

The 1985 Farm Bill, by lowering loan rates, had made US agriculture policy more market oriented, and had been successful in promoting exports.[83] Farm exports had grown above $40 billion in 1989, roughly back to their 1981 peak, after having dropped below $30 billion four years before (Figure 5.2). Farm income had been stimulated by maintaining target prices at high levels, and had virtually tripled since 1983. The Conservation Reserve Program (CRP) created by the 1985 Farm Bill, with the authorized removal of 34 million acres of production by 1990, provided significant guaranteed income for farmers. More taxpayer dollars were spent on agriculture

---

[83] Serendipitously, the dollar weakened during the last half of the 1980s, which also contributed to export growth.

between 1985 and 1990 than at any time in US history. Yet, farm spending had become the fastest shrinking portion of the federal budget. Federal farm program expenditures had dropped from $25.8 billion in 1986 to $10.5 billion in 1989, back to their more "normal" levels. Farm support expenditure clearly reflects the health of the export sector, not least the cereals economy. High exports of wheat on rising world markets (Figure 5.3) corresponded to high producer prices and low stocks. Spending on farm programs declined rapidly as a result of the improved market. Even though the decline in farm spending was in part due to the 1988 drought, which scorched millions of acres of cropland across the country, the 1985 Farm Bill was perceived to have been a success, both inside and outside the agriculture community.

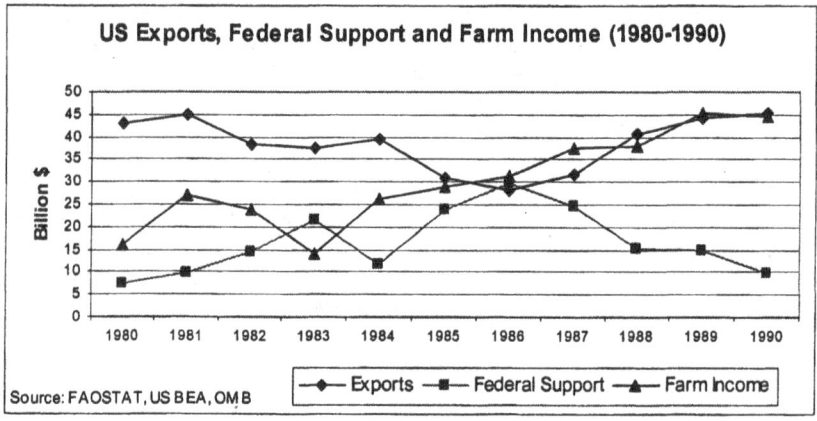

Figure 5.2: US Exports, Federal Support and Farm Income (1980-1990)

Effects of the Budget Deficit and the Improving Farm Economy

There were some economic trends in 1990 that worked to change the 1985 Farm Bill and others that worked to preserve it. Chronically large federal budget deficits augured strongly for policy change, with a deficit of $161 billion projected for 1991 (Figure 5.4). The Balanced Budget and Emergency Deficit Control Reaffirmation Act of 1987 (known popularly as Gramm-Rudman) mandated deficit targets of $64 billion for 1991 and zero by 1993. Agriculture was a prime target for any deficit reduction package. However, the impact of the budget deficit in shaping the farm bill was delayed, because the full constraint only became clear when the farm bill got to the Senate-House Conference. After the House had rejected a budget summit agreement on October 5, the conferees were finally told by congressional budget writers to come up with $13.6 billion in five-year deficit savings.

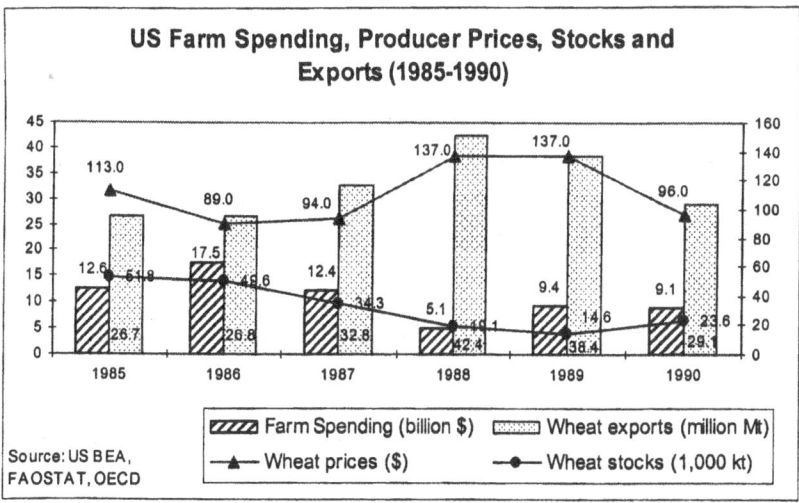

Figure 5.3: US Farm Spending, Producer Prices, Stocks and Exports (1985-1990)

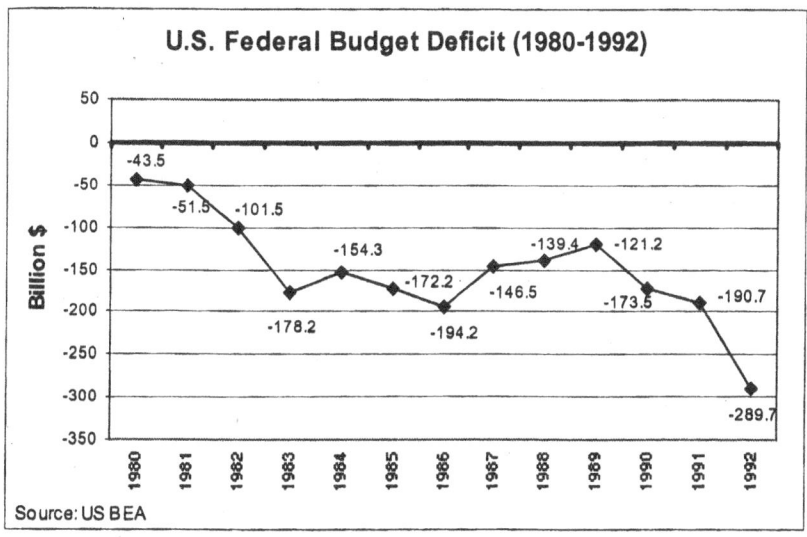

Figure 5.4: US Federal Budget Deficit (1980-1992)

The economic trends working to maintain the 1985 farm legislation related mostly to the improved health of the farm economy. As we have mentioned, farm spending had declined to manageable levels, commodity prices were up, stocks were down and exports had increased. Net farm income had increased from $28.8 billion in 1985 to $45.3 billion in 1989. The percentage of farm income coming from federal payments to farmers throughout the period of the 1985 Farm Bill had been quite high, rising from 38.1 percent in 1986 to 44.8 percent in 1987, then declining to 24.0 percent in 1989. The economic situation of farmers had greatly improved in the period from 1985 to 1990, with a great deal of this improvement provided by government payments. These trends created strong incentives for the farm community to lobby vigorously to preserve the benefits achieved in the 1985 Farm Bill. The easiest way to preserve these benefits would be to use the 1985 legislation as a template for the 1990 Farm Bill, making marginal adjustments.

Little Impetus for Change from Domestic Politics and the Uruguay Round

Two major political developments stand out as significant for the 1990 Farm Bill debate. First, 1990 was a congressional election year. All of the members of the House Agriculture Committee and 9 of the 19 members of the Senate Agriculture committee were up for re-election (CQ Weekly Report, May 12, 1990, p.1648). A major issue in these election races was which party could appear more generous to farmers given the tightly constrained budget. The 1985 Farm Bill debate, a brutally partisan affair, was perceived to have been injurious to the Republican Party. Populist Democrats had portrayed Senate Republicans, several of whom were up for re-election in 1986, as co-conspirators with the Reagan administration in a plot to get the federal government out of agriculture in the midst of the worst farm depression in years (1990 CQ Almanac, p.324). Three Republicans from farm states were defeated for re-election - Mack Mattingly of Georgia, James Abnor of South Dakota and Mark Andrews of North Dakota - and the GOP lost control of the Senate. The victorious Democrats -Wyche Fowler of Georgia, Tom Daschle of South Dakota and Kent Conrad of North Dakota - all became members of the Senate Agriculture Committee. Given the improved situation of agriculture in 1990, neither Democrats nor Republicans had much incentive to argue for drastic changes in farm policy.

The GATT Uruguay Round trade negotiations constituted a second important political development. The Uruguay Round was proceeding toward a December 1990 ministerial meeting in Brussels, where it was hoped a new multilateral trade agreement could be finalized. However, the agricultural negotiations were proceeding glacially. The US had dropped its demand for the end of all trade distorting subsidies and import barriers and supported by the Cairns group, was now calling only for very significant reductions. However, the European Community was dragging its feet. Tied up in internal political debate, the EC was unable to come up with a negotiating proposal that seemed promising for an agreement (see Chapter 4). Secretary of Agriculture Clayton Yeutter, who had been US Trade Representative in the Reagan administration, was committed to an agreement, which meant that the administration had to keep domestic agriculture policy consistent with the US GATT negotiating position. However, the pressures from the Uruguay Round for domestic commodity price cuts were not very strong, given the reluctance of the EC to reduce the high price supports of the Common Agricultural Policy. There were pressures in Congress to increase funding for the export enhancement program as a "bargaining chip" to force the European Union to agree to export subsidy reductions.

A Political Environment for Incrementalism

The political environment for the 1990 Farm Bill debate was clearly to preserve the status quo - not to make radical changes in the 1985 farm legislation. The 1985 Farm Bill had been expensive, but costs had declined rapidly. Significant pressures to change farm policy had not been generated either in the farm community or outside. Neither Democrats nor Republicans had any incentive to make farm policy a major partisan issue. There were no significant outside pressures for change generated by the Uruguay Round. The budget deficit would have to be addressed, but the incentive was to adjust existing programs not transform them.

The Developing Strength of the Competitive Agriculture Paradigm

The shift in thinking about agricultural policy from the Dependent Agriculture paradigm to the Competitive Agriculture paradigm was well-advanced. US policy-makers had become convinced that future prosperity for American farmers could only be ensured if export markets were open to receive the surplus generated by American agricultural productivity. The alternative was unacceptably high cost domestic agriculture policy propping up commodity prices, either maintaining huge expensive stocks, which could only be exported with subsidies, or requiring huge set-asides. This certainly implied that the US work to lower foreign trade barriers, and be willing to lower domestic trade barriers in return, but it also implied competitive US agricultural commodities. As one key 1990 farm policy-maker noted in an interview, "politicians admitted that price makes a difference." The 1985 Farm Bill, by lowering loan rates, made US farm products more competitive. The perceived success of this endeavor strengthened the belief in a market oriented US farm policy. The establishment of "triple-base" was an incremental step forward in de-coupling farm payments from production.

5.3   Assessment

There are a number of puzzling aspects of the 1990 Farm Bill debate that the analytical framework of the book helps us to explain. Why in a situation of budget crisis did the administration submit only general recommendations and why the emphasis on planting flexibility? Why did the House of Representatives agriculture subcommittees, knowing that farm spending would have to be slashed initially recommend farm bill provisions that would have increased spending? Why in the Senate did farm state legislators divide between "prairie populists" from the Midwest and a bi-partisan coalition from the rest of the country? Why, with the increased emphasis on competitive agriculture, was it not possible to reform the protectionist dairy, sugar and peanut programs? How can we explain the strong environmental provisions? Finally, why did "triple-base" emerge in the House-Senate Conference as the vehicle for limiting farm program costs?

Administration Cautiousness Explained

Why did Secretary of Agriculture Clayton Yeutter only submit the "Green book" of policy recommendations to Congress rather than a draft farm bill as his predecessors had done, and why did he make no specific recommendations about target prices? Government politics provides an explanation. The Reagan administration farm bills had generated partisan attacks when submitted in 1981 and 1985, and then had generally been disregarded by Congress. The Bush administration did not want to become a target in the 1990 Farm Bill debate and hoped to maintain negotiating influence as the farm bill progressed through Congress. The administration believed that general recommendations, avoiding specific reference to target prices, would promote both of these objectives (interview). Also, it seemed foolish to get too specific when there was not yet any agreement between the Executive and Congress about how much the agriculture budget should be cut.

Why did the administration place such a strong emphasis in increasing the flexibility that farmers would have, without being more specific than recommending a "flexible base" acreage, on which farmers could plant whatever program crop they wanted? The rational (national) actor model would suggest an explanation for flexibility. Since the goal of the administration was to make farm policy more market-oriented, farmers had to be able to respond to market signals. This meant that they had to be given more leeway in what crops they planted on farm program land. Planting freedom also had become something of a political issue for farmers, who resented having government tell them what they could plant. The word "flexibility" was carefully chosen because this would appeal to the farm community. Policy-makers wanted to avoid using the word "decoupling," which had earned a bad name in the 1985 Farm Bill debate. The administration was not very specific, because it thought the appeal of the concept of flexibility would be weakened if the concept was well-demarcated.

Overlooking the Budget Crisis in the House of Representatives

Why did the House Agricultural sub-committees raise target prices, loan rates and the overall cost of agricultural spending at a time when it was common knowledge that the farm budget would have to be cut? This outcome has all the earmarks of government politics. The House Agriculture sub-committees are constituency committees, with the majority of members coming from districts producing the commodity covered by the committee (see Moyer and Josling (1990), Chapter 5). Thus the environment was ripe for commodity group influence. Then, there were incentives for posturing. Even though sub-committee members knew their recommendations would be cut by the full

Agriculture committee, it was good politics to show support for the constituency back home by advocating increased farm assistance.

Why did a split develop between junior House Democrats, who wanted significant increases in target prices and loan rates, and more senior Democrats joined by Republicans, who wanted to marginally increase the status-quo? A government politics explanation based on the different perspectives of the junior and senior members helps to answer this question. The senior members of the committee remembered the adverse consequences of the 1981 Farm Bill, which raised price support levels well above market prices (1990 CQ Almanac, p.327). The lessons of the 1981 Farm Bill were not so indelibly engrained in the minds of junior congressmen, who focused on the current plight of farmers. The attitude of Rep. Dave Nagel, D-IA was typical. He argued that as many as 500,000 farmers would leave agriculture over the following five years if Congress merely froze support levels – "I don't want the blood of those farmers who leave their farms on my hands," he said (1990 CQ Almanac, p.327).

Why did the full House, with the great majority of members not representing agricultural constituencies, vote down efforts to limit the government subsidies that prosperous farmers could receive? Again, government politics provides an explanation. The advocates of subsidy limits were disadvantaged by the structure of the process. By the time the farm bill got to the floor, where they could exercise their majority, it was a highly developed package of compromises, which could not easily be disturbed without splitting the coalition whose support was necessary to ensure successful passage. But there were other problems. Representatives Armey (R-Texas) and Schumer (D-New York), the subsidy limit leaders, were perceived as "antifarmer," and their amendment was seen as designed merely to cut the agricultural budget, not help family farmers (1990 CQ Almanac, p.332). Surprisingly, the AFL-CIO worked against Armey-Schumer, noting in a letter to members that "the exclusion of big producers seems enticing on the surface," but "the amendment would make farm programs inoperable" (1990 CQ Almanac, p.332). Insiders suggested a vote-trading deal. In return for a vote against Armey-Schumer from pro-labor Democrats, farm state congressmen would support a textile protection bill coming to the floor shortly thereafter (1990 CQ Almanac, p.332). Interestingly, the opponents of Armey-Schumer received support from several environmental groups, including the National Audubon Society and the National Wildlife Foundation, who argued that kicking large farmers out of federal farm programs would hurt environmental quality, because to qualify for federal payments, farmers had to submit to numerous environmental controls, including a ban on draining wetlands and plowing highly erodible land.

Why did the 1990 Farm Bill survive efforts to cut farm spending on the House floor? Part of the explanation again lies in the fact that the farm bill, by the time it got to the floor, was so delicately balanced, that any disturbance would undercut the rural-urban-environmental coalition necessary to ensure passage. Paradoxically, the prospect of having to make deep cuts before the end of the year - either from a budget summit agreement or from automatic cuts under the Gramm-Rudman anti-deficit law, may have helped to weaken cost-cutting efforts on the floor. Deputy Under Secretary of

Agriculture John Campbell, a close observer of the House process, observed, "People figure: 'why should we vote against farmers? Why should we do the right thing and take a political hit for it, if the summit is going to take care of it?'" (1990 CQ Almanac, p.331).

"Prairie Populists" Joust with a Bi-Partisan Coalition in the Senate

Why did debate in the Senate divide between a bi-partisan coalition, led by Chairman Patrick Leahy (D-Vt.) and leading Republican Richard Lugar, who basically wanted to continue the status-quo of the 1985 Farm Bill, and a group of "prairie populist" Democrats, who wanted to increase support prices? The creation of a bi-partisan coalition was probably due to a number of factors. One important factor was obviously the general level of satisfaction with the 1985 Farm Bill within the agricultural community. Another was memory of the long brutal partisan committee fight over the 1985 Farm Bill. In the absence of strong pressures to change farm policy, why engage in another bitter partisan fight? The "prairie populists" had a different political perspective. They saw support for increases in target prices and loan rates as good politics. After all, three of them (Kerrey D-Neb., Harkin D-IA, and Daschle, D-SD) had won election to the Senate in 1986, after blasting their incumbent Republican opponents for supporting the cuts in the 1985 Farm Bill.

The Resilience of the Dairy, Sugar and Peanut Programs

Why was it not possible, in the context of a budget crisis, to cut dairy, sugar and peanut programs on the floor of either House or Senate, where agriculture was not the dominant constituency? Public choice theory provides the explanation that the recipients of the benefits of these programs had made a much stronger effort to mobilize efforts to preserve them than their opponents, who represented more general consumer interests. The proponents of the peanut and sugar programs were strengthened in that they were largely self-supporting and did not place a major drain on the agriculture budget. It was difficult to undercut the dairy program because dairy price support outlays had declined from over $2 billion in 1986 to about $500 million for 1990. Government politics provides a supplemental explanation. With the farm bill largely shaped in the agriculture committees, the proponents of the sugar, peanut and dairy programs could count on receptivity to their point of view as legislation was drafted. In addition, the support of legislators with peanut, sugar and dairy interests was critical to crafting the coalition necessary to passing the 1990 Farm Bill. By the time the bill got to the floors of the House and Senate, the farm bill had a momentum difficult to reverse, particularly since major changes might endanger passage of the bill.

The Strength of the Environmental Lobby

Why did both Senate and House write strong environmental provisions into their respective versions of the 1990 farm bill, particularly on wetlands, given the criticism in the farm community of the environmental section of the 1985 Farm Bill? Looking at the situation through the lenses of the government politics model helps with the explanation. The environmental lobby was well-organized and had gained strength between 1985 and 1990 (Cochrane and Runge (1992), p.58) There was a receptive audience among the public which could understand wetlands and water pollution issues much more easily than target price and loan rate issues. To antagonize the environmentalists was to endanger the entire farm bill. Besides, it was not a zero-sum game. The demands of the environmentalists could be satisfied without endangering the benefits of farm income support programs. In addition, strong environmental provisions would strengthen the perception that farm subsidy programs preserve the environment. The House and Senate Agriculture Committees had different motivations. The House Committee was responsive to the environmentalists, largely, because of the fear that environmentalists could jeopardize the farm bill on the House floor. In the Senate Agriculture Committee, the environmental movement had a strong advocate in chairman, Patrick Leahy (D-Vermont), who took a keen interest in environmental issues and had close contacts with environmental organizations. The environmental lobby, however, was limited in what it could accomplish when it came in direct conflict with important agricultural constituencies. The limits on the export of pesticides banned in the US (the so-called "circle of poison") was dropped in the Conference after a potent attack from pesticide companies and farm organizations, which argued that American jobs, not the safety of the food supply, was at stake (1990 CQ Almanac, p.349).

"Triple-base" as an Acceptable Outcome

Why did the Senate-House Conferees settle on the "triple-base" option? We can see this outcome as the result of government politics in the form of partisan mutual adjustment. "Triple-base" was a political bargain between the administration and farm interests. The administration offered farmers planting flexibility in return for surrender of part of the deficiency payment guarantee (see Cochrane and Runge (1992), p.57). We get another perspective by looking at "triple-base" as the outcome of rational political choice. The Conference, faced with a mandate to make deep cuts in the agriculture budget, had to find the most politically painless way to achieve this goal. Cutting target prices would unambiguously signal to farmers that their incomes would fall, and hence would generate major political problems. The impact of "triple-base" was more ambiguous - deficiency payments would be reduced to be sure, but farmers would gain in the ability to decide what to plant. There was always the chance that they could pick a crop for the unsubsidized land that would be very profitable on the market. Triple base was not a new idea. Representatives Charles Stenholm (D-Texas) and Pat Roberts (R-Kansas) had favored using this concept as a means of making the budget savings required of agriculture, but kept it under wraps until the Conference, the most politically acceptable place to make cuts (1990 CQ Almanac, p.330). Still another perspective is provided by network analysis. Faced with the necessity of change, "triple base" met the need, minimizing the uncertainty and necessary adjustment.

The acceptance of "triple-base," highlights an important point in this analysis and in our previous work on agricultural policy reform in the 1980s (see Moyer and Josling, 1990). Agricultural policy reform comes only when it is mandated from outside the agriculture policy community, usually by a budget crisis (real or perceived). But, outsiders do not dictate the substance of what changes will be made. Faced with the inevitable, insiders strategically placed in the action-channels of the agricultural policy process take the initiative, and are usually able to ensure the minimum change necessary to satisfy the external mandate, making the substance of the change such as to minimize the pain to the agricultural community.

The Impact of the Uruguay Round

Since one of the purposes of this book is to address reform as a sequential process, with domestic and international efforts influencing each other, it is important to address the impact of the Uruguay Round on the 1990 farm bill. This impact was more subtle than that of either budget or environment (see Cochrane and Runge (1992), p.58). The farm bill had to be consistent with the US GATT negotiating position to drastically reduce market-distorting subsidies and trade barriers. Loan rates had to be kept down and target prices had to be kept in check to control domestic spending for agriculture. While it might be argued that the budget deficit and paradigm shift in agricultural policy thinking would have argued for the same kind of policy, the presence of Uruguay Round negotiations strengthened the hands of the proponents. They could respond to arguments for increased target prices and loan rates from the "prairie populists" that such a course of action was inconsistent with the US GATT negotiating position. The Uruguay Round provided legitimacy to the shift to the Competitive Agriculture paradigm, which influenced the farm bill debate. Even if the Uruguay Round was proceeding glacially, analytical studies on the economic benefits of a successful liberalizing trade round, the broad participation of the world's nation-states in the negotiations, and the defensiveness of nations opposing trade liberalization, all provided reassurance of the value of a market-oriented agricultural policy.[84]

---

[84] It has been suggested that the increase in analytical studies associated with farm legislation in the US and EU with the Uruguay Round, and the formation of such associations as the International Trade Research Consortium (IATRC) and the International Policy Council on Agriculture and Trade (IPC), gave rise to *epistemic communities* - networks of "professionals with recognized expertise and competence in a particular domain and an authoritative claim to policy-relevant knowledge, sharing the same normative and principled beliefs, the same causal beliefs, the same notions of validity, and a common policy enterprise" (Webber (1997), p.7; see also Haas (1992), p.3,). Such groups can often exercise significant policy influence.

Had the European Community and Japan been responsive to the US GATT negotiating position, strong international pressures might have developed for the US to sharply pare back farm income supports in the 1990 farm bill. However, the actual pressures did not measure up to this potential when the EC and Japan were unresponsive. The failure of the Uruguay Round to produce an agreement on agriculture may have impeded policy liberalization by contributing to some illiberal measures in the 1990 Farm Bill (see Cochrane and Runge (1992), p.58). The bill included a provisional clause that if no GATT agricultural agreement was reached by June 30, 1992, the Secretary of Agriculture was permitted to spend an additional $1 billion on export subsidies. The secretary was also required to enact a marketing loan program on wheat and feed grains. These measures were instituted as "bargaining chips" to pressure the EC to make GATT concessions (see Orden, Paarlberg and Roe (1999), p.99). The synergistic effect in the linked GATT- US domestic policy bargaining games was a negative one in that it strengthened the power of commodity lobbies rather than weakened them.

Incrementalism Explained

The 1990 US Farm Bill represents only incremental change from the 1985 farm legislation, moving further in the direction of decoupling payments from production with the establishment of "triple-base" acres. Path dependency theory is helpful in explaining this incrementalism. The 1985 Farm Bill took a significant step along the decoupling path begun in the 1960s). This legislation lowered loan rates, froze base acreages and yields and created the Conservation Reserve Program (CRP). "Triple-base was a logical extension of the 1985 Farm Bill's "50-92" (later "0-85") provision, which entitled wheat and feed grain producers to collect 92 (later 85) percent of the deficiency payments on their permitted acreage even if they used half (later all) of those acres for conservation purposes rather than planting crops. The feedback from the 1985 Farm Bill by 1990 was highly positive. The costs of farm programs were declining rapidly, exports were increasing and farm income was rising. Farmers also seemed happy with the guaranteed income provided by the CRP and the "50-92" provision. There was thus every incentive to continue down the de-coupling path, making only marginal adjustments to the 1985 legislation.

Lindblom's concept of partisan mutual adjustment is also helpful in explaining the incrementalism of the 1990 farm bill. With positive feedback from the 1985 Farm Bill, the 1990 farm legislation was left largely in the hands of the House and Senate agriculture committees, which, predictably, only adjusted the accommodation (legislative log-rolling) reached in 1985 between the various farm commodity groups. Conservation provisions were strengthened and urban nutrition programs and food stamps received continued support to gain the votes necessary to pass the 1990 farm bill.

Chapter 6

The 1992 MacSharry Reform of the CAP

6.1 The Development of the MacSharry Reforms

The reform of the Common Agricultural Policy (CAP) under the guidance of Ray MacSharry, the EC Commissioner for Agriculture, is perhaps the most striking and significant change in the domestic agricultural policy of a major country or economic area in the post-war period. Understanding the process of reform and the conditions under which it took place is important to the study of the broader reform process. This chapter explores the events leading up to the May 1992 meeting of the Council of Agriculture Ministers at which, under the chairmanship of Arlindo Cunha, member states agreed to change the direction of the CAP. The change had highly significant implications for the path of reform of the international trade system in agricultural goods, as is discussed in a subsequent chapter.

The MacSharry reforms had to go through a complicated EC policy process similar to that diagramed in Figure 6.1.[85] In this process, CAP reform proposals are generated in the Commission by the Agriculture Commissioner and the Directorate-General for Agriculture (DGVI). After approval by the Commissioners, they are sent to the European Parliament (EP) for an opinion and to the Council of Ministers for approval. The Council cannot act until the European Parliament has rendered an opinion, although it is not bound by that opinion. The Agriculture Council seeks consensus, reflecting the legacy of the Luxembourg Compromise, although the voting rule, and increasingly the practice, is decision by qualified majority.[86] The MacSharry

---

[85] For a more detailed discussion of the "traditional" EC agricultural policy reform process see Moyer and Josling (1990), chapter 2.

[86] Though it never had legal status, the Luxembourg Compromise, accepted in 1965, when France returned to participation in EC institutions after a six months absence, allowed a member state, by citing "vital national interests," to block action by the Council of Ministers. When "vital national interests" were invoked, a majority of the members would support the state making such a declaration. The Luxembourg Compromise was last invoked in 1988, when Greece blocked the agriculture price package. A qualified majority is the number of votes that will prevent the four largest states (France, Germany, Italy and the UK) from acting without the support of the smaller members. In the EC 12 Agriculture Council that considered the MacSharry reforms, France, Germany, Italy and the UK had ten votes each; Spain had 8 votes; Belgium, Greece and the Netherlands had five votes each; Denmark and Ireland had three; and Luxembourg had two votes. Out of total of seventy-six votes, a qualified majority required fifty-four and a blocking minority required twenty-three votes.

Reforms encountered little problems in the Commission, but as we will show, the debate in the Council was highly contentious.

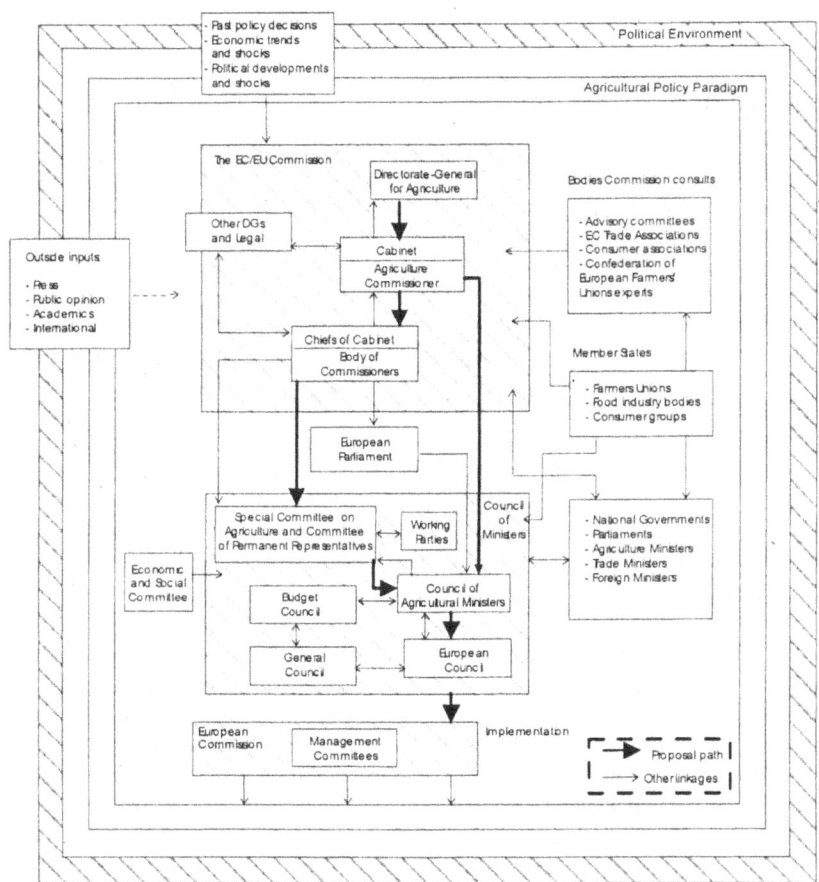

Figure 6.1: Decision-making Process for EC/EU Agricultural Policy Formation at the time of the MacSharry Reform

Immediately after the failure of the Heysel summit, rumors began to circulate that Commissioner Ray MacSharry was about to introduce a new plan to reform the CAP.[87] Even to the extent that people took these rumors seriously, doubt existed about how conscientiously the Agriculture Commissioner would pursue CAP reform. Even if he were to take a vigorous stand, could he possibly get a reform proposal through the Agriculture Council?

---

[87] For a report of these rumors, see *Agra Europe*, December 14, 1990: P/2.

Perhaps there would have been less surprise if the inner workings of the Directorate-General for Agriculture (DGVI) had been more transparent and if the Uruguay Round negotiations had not been such an overwhelming event in the months leading up to the Heysel stadium conference. MacSharry had begun to work on a CAP reform proposal shortly after he became Agriculture Commissioner in January 1989. He conducted weekly meetings with members of his cabinet and with senior members of the DGVI staff, including Director General Guy Legras, to consider the problems of the CAP, and what could be done to alleviate them (interview).[88] The group was particularly concerned about budget pressures and the building of EC agricultural stocks.[89] The starting question for the discussion was whether the existing price support mechanism could be maintained. It was concluded that prices would have to be cut, and a planning group was established to develop a new reform proposal seven or eight months prior to the Heysel conference. The members of the planning group were not directly involved in the Uruguay Round negotiations. Thus the CAP reform planning process proceeded on a separate track from the Uruguay Round process, though MacSharry and Legras maintained a close personal involvement in both processes (interview).

A DGVI Paper Catalyzes the CAP Reform Debate

The DGVI paper was dated December 6 1990, the day the Heysel Stadium Conference ended in failure. It was leaked to *Agra Europe*, which published the details in its January 18, 1991 issue (*Agra Europe*, January 18,1991: P/1 and E/1). The paper recommended significant price cuts for which farmers would receive direct payments based on the area farmed and average regional yields. These compensatory payments would be modulated, so as to favor small farmers. For cereals, the suggested price cut amounted to 35 per cent, compensated in full for the first 30 hectares, with compensation reduced by 25 per cent on the next 50 hectares and by 35 per cent on additional land. For dairy, the paper recommended an intervention price cut of 10 percent. It also recommended a cut in quotas of 4.5 percent on average, with no quota cut for farms producing less than 200,000 kg annually, and a 10 per cent cut for farms producing more than 200,000 kg a year. For beef, DGVI recommended an intervention price cut of 15 per cent, with an increased premium for male animals. The paper also included recommendations for accompanying agri-environment and early retirement measures.

---

[88] MacSharry's team consisted of MacSharry, his Deputy *Chef de Cabinet*, Paddy Hennessy, Commission President Delors' personal agricultural expert, Jacques Demarty and Guy Legras, the Director-General for Agriculture. The size of the group was apparently kept small in order to avoid leaks.

[89] MacSharry was reportedly shocked by a Commission study that showed that approximately 50 percent of the CAP was spent inefficiently, and that 80 percent of support went to the largest 20 percent of farmers. This apparently helped convince MacSharry that the distribution of agricultural support required reform.

Initial Reactions in the Commission and Council to the MacSharry Proposals

The DGVI proposal was presented for discussion in the Commission (*Agra Europe* January 25, 1991: P/1). The document contained the basic principles for reform, but with all the figures on price cuts and quota reductions carefully removed. MacSharry warned the Commission that the stabilizers introduced in 1988 had only had a "marginal effect" in reducing the levels of support expenditure and in improving the competitiveness of EC agriculture (*Agra Europe*, January 18, 1991: P/1). He listed as priorities: the reduction of existing production quotas; price cuts, with compensatory payments targeted at smaller farmers; and extensification aid to protect the rural environment. The Commissioner said that it was nonsense trying to help small farmers through price supports since only 6 percent of the cereal producers were responsible for two-thirds of the output, and since 10 percent of beef producers produced more than half of the beef output (*Agra Europe*, January 18, 1991: P/1). It was reported that MacSharry had a solid base of support from Commissioners Bangemann, Andriessen, Brittan, Christopherson and Millan (*Agra Europe*, January 18, 1991: P/1). However, powerful opposition was indicated from a group led by Commission President Delors, which advocated CAP "modification" rather than reform.

The Commission paper was further distilled to 13 pages for submission to the Agriculture Council. MacSharry told the Council that the CAP faced an impending financing crisis, with spending for 1991 coming dangerously close to the "agricultural guideline" of 32 billion ECU (*Agra Europe*, January 25, 1991: P/1). He added that unless corrective action was taken, the "guideline" could be exceeded in 1991, which would be very difficult to defend. He said that both price cuts and quota reductions were "unavoidable"; and, that measures to cut expenditures should be aimed at the top 10 percent of the farmers responsible for the bulk of production, who would be asked to fend more for themselves. Asking large farmers to take the brunt of the sacrifice was not discriminating against the productive sector, but rather reorienting support to share the burden more fairly (*Agra Europe*, January 25, 1991: P/1). The Commissioner said that reforms must have the triple objective of controlling expenditure, increasing the competitiveness of EC agriculture and maintaining the rural population. "I believe that we must try to keep the maximum number of farmers on the land," said MacSharry. "There is no other way to preserve the natural environment, traditional landscape and a model of agriculture based on the family farm. The policy must now recognize that the farmer fulfils a double function of producing food and of protecting the environment and the countryside" (*Agra Europe*, January 25, 1991: P/1-P/2).

The EC farm ministers gave MacSharry's yet unfinished reform plans a very cool reception. The strongest opposition came from the UK, Netherlands and Denmark, claiming that placing the burden of reform on larger farmers would discriminate against their producers (*Agra Europe*, January 25, 1991: E/1). The size of the envisaged price cuts was so great that Council President Rene Steichen (the Luxembourg farm minister) lamented, "nobody is terribly thrilled by these proposals" (*Agra Europe*, January 25, 1991: E/1).

The February 1991 Commission "Reflections" Paper

On February 1, the Commission released its "Reflections" paper, designed as a framework within which to focus the reform debate in the Commission and Council. This paper maintained the basic principles for reform set forth in the DGVI paper, but did not make specific recommendations for price and quota cuts or for compensatory payments to farmers. The "Reflections" document defended the concept of modulated support, with larger farmers asked to pay a bigger share of the burden, noting that support through public funds should aim at correcting inequalities by supporting those who derive fewer advantages from the market (*Agra Europe*, February 14, 1991: E/3). However, it was vague about the criteria, mentioning only that modulation should be based on such factors as size, income, regional situation and other relevant factors (*Agra Europe*, February 15, 1991: E/2). The paper emphasized the importance of an active rural development policy to keep farmers on the land in the context of price cuts and quota reductions. It went so far as to say that rural development should include support for other forms of economic activity in addition to farming which help to maintain rural populations and strengthen the economy of rural areas (*Agra Europe*, January 14, 1991: E/1). However, the "Reflections" paper made it clear that the MacSharry reform package would not include an examination of the adequacy of structural fund intervention to promote rural development, as that would be part of the overall review of structural policy scheduled later in 1991.

The Agricultural Council gave only limited attention to the "Reflections" paper in the spring of 1991, as the farm ministers were pre-occupied with the annual price fixing debate, but it soon became clear that the chances for reform had not been improved by the watering down of the DGVI proposals. Ominously, the German government declared its opposition to the reform package, primarily because of the proposed price cuts. German farm minister Ignaz Kiechle indicated that he had serious problems with the MacSharry plan (see *Agra Europe*, February 8, 1991: P/4). Kiechle complained that he was being asked to support a plan with little real substance. He did not like the use of the word "competitive". With whom should EC members be competitive - with each other, or with third countries? It did not seem reasonable to him to expect EC agriculture to compete with the and Australia - countries with enormous areas devoted to large-scale food production. Kiechle seriously objected to the assumption that small farms were good and large farms bad. Germany liked some elements of the proposal such as the encouragement of set-aside, extensification and the view of farmers as protectors of the rural environment. But, what was MacSharry trying to achieve? If he was trying to raise farm incomes, who was going to pay for it? He was not mollified that the "Reflections" paper was more vague than the December DGVI paper - in fact, this made him more suspicious. The French agriculture minister also objected to the MacSharry reforms, but for different reasons: he was strongly opposed to the proposed set-asides (Webber (1997), p.37).

The Commission Publishes Detailed Reform Proposals in July 1991

The release of detailed Commission proposals was delayed both by the price debate and by reported pressure from the French government. The French did not think that the EC should propose "unilateral" concessions in the form of a CAP reform paper in advance of the GATT Uruguay Round agreement (*Agra Europe*, June 14, 1991: P/1). Commission President Delors also counseled delay, as he wanted the June Luxembourg summit to focus on political and monetary union, not reform of the CAP (*Agra Europe*, June 21, 1991: E/1) The MacSharry proposals were finally published on July 1, 1991 as Commission document COM (91) 285/3. The reforms proposed were significantly weaker than those suggested in the unpublished December 1990 DGVI paper. The price cut for cereals had been reduced to 30 percent, with compensatory payments paid in full to all farmers. There was no modulation based on farm size (*Agra Europe*, July 5, 1991: P/4). Dairy quotas were to be cut by four percent across the board, though member states were given the option of redistributing one percent of the quota cut to extensive dairy holdings in mountain and less favored areas. The beef intervention price cut was still 15 percent, though premia for individual animals had been increased. Accompanying agri-environmental, early retirement and afforestation measures were retained.

All EC farm ministers raised fierce objections to the July 1 CAP reform proposals when they met later in the month (*Agra Europe*, July 19, 1991: E/1). However, the Agriculture Council did not reject outright the reform package. The Council President, Dutch farm minister Piet Bukman summed up the general mood, "all delegations agree that if there is no fundamental reform we will have an unbearable situation" (*Agra Europe*, July 19, 1991: E/1).

Every agricultural minister expressed opposition to some or all of MacSharry's proposals, but no consensus developed about a better way to reform the CAP. So, the Council reluctantly took the proposals as a basis for discussion. French minister Louis Mermaz questioned the need for such a drastic cereal price cut and called for the continuation of the concept of Community preference, giving domestic supplies adequate protection on the European market (*Agra Europe*, July 19, 1991: E1-E/2). German Agricultural Minister Ignaz Kiechle questioned whether reducing prices would actually result in reduced production. He also wondered if such substantial cuts were wise before the conclusion of the GATT talks. The British minister, John Gummer, complained that the proposed reforms would penalize the excellence and success of the large, specialist farm to prop up part-time inefficient farms. The Spanish Minister, Pedro Solbes Mira, was generally positive in his response, but made the surprising suggestion that the proposals should cover all products, not just those produced predominantly in Northern areas. The Irish Farm Minister, Michael O'Kennedy called for a more gradual, step-by-step approach. A number of ministers, including those from France, the UK and Denmark wondered whether the Commission estimates of the cost of reform were too low.

Commissioner MacSharry was not discouraged by the reactions to his reform package. He noted that the ministers had been more negative to his price package proposals earlier in the year, but the price package had been approved by an 11-1 majority (*Agra Europe*, June 19, 1991: E/2). He thought his reforms covered the "middle ground" of opinion in the Council; therefore, he was optimistic that the negotiations would yield an agreement. To encourage the Council, he warned that the next year's price package would be very restrictive if no agreement was reached by December.

Approval of the MacSharry Reforms

Debate over the MacSharry reforms went on in the Agricultural Council over the autumn and winter of 1991 and into the spring of 1992 as the ministers haggled over the details. Interestingly, the December 1991 Draft Final Act for the Uruguay Round, tabled by GATT Director-General Arthur Dunkel, appeared to be consistent with MacSharry's proposals, making it likely that a GATT international agricultural trade agreement could be reached if the MacSharry reforms were approved. The Commission tabled several compromise papers in early 1992, in collaboration with the Portuguese Agriculture Council President, Arlindo Cunha, but still a final agreement eluded the Council. Finally, Commissioner MacSharry met with each agriculture minister individually, requesting a list of four or five items most important to the minister. In return for inclusion of these items in the final proposal, he was rewarded with the assurance that each minister would support the Commissioner in achieving reform (interview). The strategy of individual discussions helped to prevent demands from escalating. Arlido Cunha also did a tour of the capitals with his advisors to find out the "bottom line" for each country. The Commission prepared a paper in April 1992, which included something for each minister. The centerpiece of the agreement was a cut in EC cereals prices by 29 percent, with a fully compensated compulsory set-aside of 15 percent. Small farmers with acreages were excused from the set-aside requirement. Germany received an additional side-payment of higher male beef and suckler cow premiums. The Agriculture Council agreed not to cut milk quotas in an unsuccessful effort to gain the support of Italy for the reform package, although in the end, the Italians were unable to block agreement (Coleman and Tangermann (1997), p.21). After an intense five-day Council meeting in May 1992, during which the ministers were largely confined to the meeting facilities, the package was approved.

The CAP reform package was a masterly compromise forged by the Commission with cooperation from the Council Presidency. The main aim of the Commission was to secure the cut in cereal prices that would help to restore competitiveness of EU agriculture and allow participation in trade talks. The Portuguese government had made reform a priority for its six-month presidency. Entrenched national interests had apparently been overshadowed by the need for a resolution. The EU system had proved resilient and responsive to internal and external pressure.

6.2 Analysis of the Reforms

The reforms in the CAP were a reflection of a number of factors, both economic and political. The framework developed in earlier chapters can give some help in sorting out the influence of these factors. The starting point for reform clearly was the CAP as it existed at the end of 1990. But the economic and political environment conditioned the form and extent of the changes and influenced the pace of change.

Failed Past Policy as an Impetus for Reform

The CAP in 1990 was still operating as a policy based on supporting commodity prices well above world market levels, with a system of variable levies to discourage imports unless the world price rose above threshold price levels. The Community supported commodities to maintain prices at or above intervention price levels set by policy. This high price support policy had encouraged domestic production far above EC needs in the 1980s, producing surpluses that could only be disposed on the international market with ever increasing export subsidies. With costs rising constantly, this policy was very expensive, straining the EC budget.

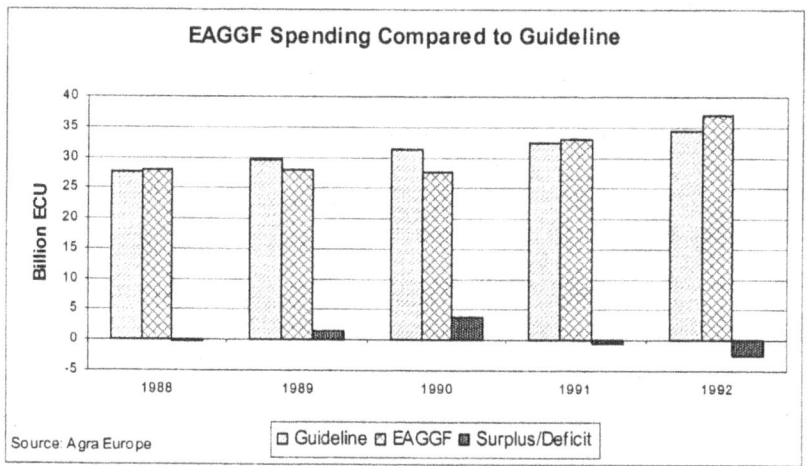

Source: *Agra Europe*, February 8, 1991: P/3
Figure 6.2: EAGGF Spending Compared to Guideline

A first effort to contain the growth of expenditures was made in 1984, when the Community approved a system of dairy quotas. These limited production and cost, but discouraged innovation and left EC dairy products uncompetitive on international markets (see Moyer and Josling (1990), Chapter 4, and Petit *et al.* 1987). Though dairy support expenses had been brought under control, the costs of cereal supports grew rapidly, catalyzing the 1988 agreement to impose budget stabilizers, which set maximum guaranteed quantities for production, and imposed penalties for exceeding these limits. At the same time that stabilizers were imposed, a guideline was established limiting the growth of CAP spending to 74 percent of the rate of growth of the EC GNP. The stabilizers, however, were not very successful in limiting production or in controlling agriculture spending. Moreover, they were very unpopular with farmers.

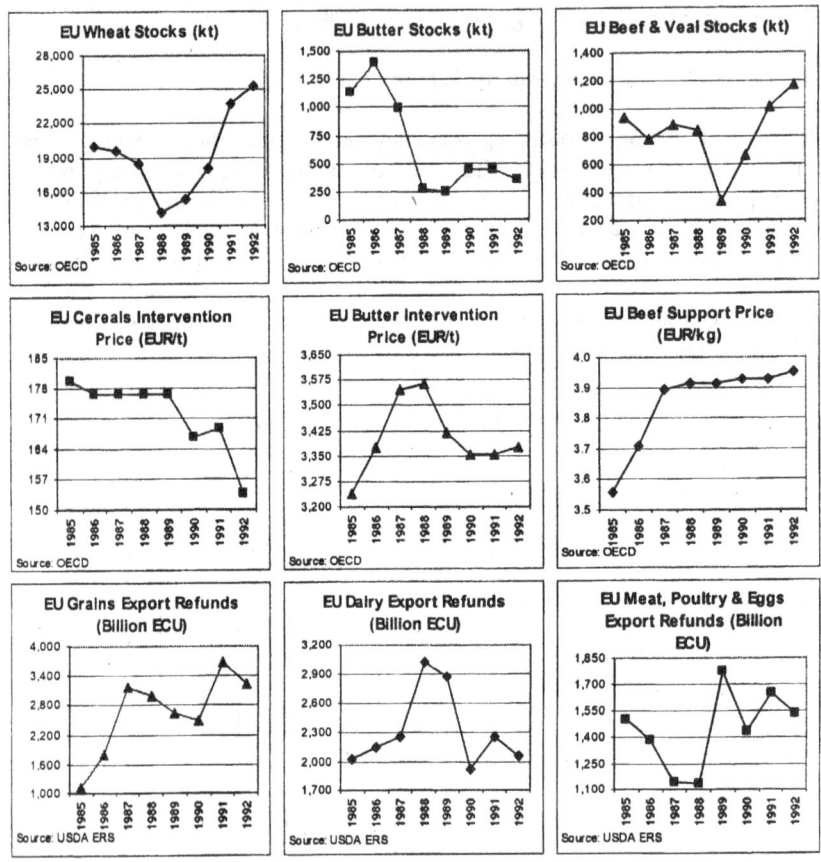

Figure 6.3: EU Cereal, Dairy and Beef Stocks, Intervention Prices and Export Subsidies

Ominous Economic Trends Reinforce the Need for Reform

The rising cost exacerbated the need for fundamental reform of the CAP. As Figure 6.2 shows, CAP expenses were expected to breach the budget guideline in 1991 and to exceed the guideline in 1992.

At the same time, stocks were mounting and export subsidies were increasing, as shown in Figure 6.3. Support prices for cereals and dairy products were reduced over this period but even this did not stop export subsidy costs from rising to threaten the budget compromise.

Farm incomes were not the cause of the crisis. Total agricultural income in the EC had risen steadily, with the aid of CAP price supports, until 1990 (Figure 6.4). This trend was evident in each of the major agricultural producing member states, with only the UK showing a decrease in farm income.

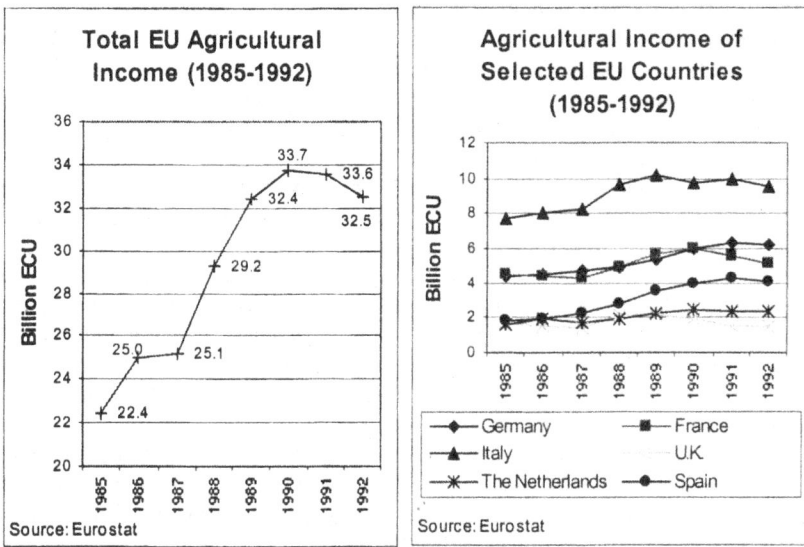

Figure 6.4: EU Agricultural Income (1985-1992)

A large proportion of the EC agriculture budget was not going directly to farmers, but rather for storage and export subsidies. The 1988 budget stabilizers had not been successful in slowing the growth of agricultural productivity or in stopping the growth of CAP spending. A financial crisis loomed in the future. *Agra Europe* reported on January 4, 1991 that the EC then had an exportable surplus of cereals in the range of 35 to 40 million tonnes. Assuming normal weather this surplus could be expected to increase in the next two or three years, nearly doubling the cost of export subsidies from the 1988/89 level to 4 billion ECU. For dairy, declining consumption during the previous two years - both domestically and internationally - had illustrated that, despite six years of quotas, the EC was still producing too much milk in relation to demand (*Agra Europe*, January 4, 1991: P/1). With the Community producing some 13 million tonnes of milk above the level which the domestic market could absorb, current butter and milk powder stocks, respectively at levels of 260,000 tonnes and 335,000 tonnes, would grow rapidly (*Agra Europe*, January 4, 1991: P/1 and January

25, 1991: P/1). Beef policy reform was also needed with record stockpiles of 700,000 tonnes of that commodity hanging over the market.

The Uruguay Round and the Collapse of Communism Generate Other Pressures

The Uruguay Round trade negotiations provided a very strong impetus for the MacSharry reforms. The EC had found itself isolated in the negotiations, under considerable pressure from the US and Cairns Group to reduce import barriers, domestic price supports and export subsidies. It was clear after the failure of the December 1990 Heysel Conference that there would not be a successful outcome to the Uruguay Round without an agreement on agriculture. A Uruguay Round agricultural trade agreement would in turn require significant changes in the CAP.

The collapse of the communist regimes also had important implications for the CAP. The end of communism in Central and Eastern Europe, a region of considerable agricultural potential, raised the possibility that the EC would face increasingly tough new agricultural competitors. Moreover, including the vast agricultural areas of former East Germany into the CAP would considerably increase the budgetary cost. Reunification made Germany by far the largest nation in the EC. Leaders in France and other European countries worried about the possibility that Germany might in the future pursue a more independent policy, particularly in its dealings with the former communist states. This helped galvanize the movement toward building political and monetary union in Europe, culminating in the Maastricht agreement of November 1991. Making a monetary union work would require increased expenditures in the less developed regions of Europe, much of which would go for purposes other than agriculture. With the EC expenditure increases limited to 1.24 percent of GNP, there were pressures to reduce the proportion of the EC budget allocated for the CAP. But the budget constraint, while important for placing reform on the political agenda, disappeared in the consideration of the MacSharry reforms, where policy changes were instituted that increased the cost of the CAP.

The MacSharry reforms were developed in an atmosphere of crisis. Commissioner MacSharry and DGVI staff feared that the CAP would collapse unless it underwent radical change. There was also the prospect of the complete collapse of the Uruguay Round and a subsequent agricultural trade war with the US. Business and financial interests with a stake in the successful completion of the Uruguay Round lobbied EC governments to make the concessions necessary to conclude successfully the agricultural trade negotiations. However, reform of the CAP and the successful completion of the Uruguay Round were not the only concerns of EC decision makers, who were deeply engrossed in creating a deeper and stronger union.

The Multi-Functional Agriculture Paradigm Takes Hold

By 1992, it had become crystal clear that major changes in the CAP were necessary to meet domestic and international needs. But what was needed was the development of a new set of arguments to justify farm policy and garner support for reform. EU

Agriculture Commissioner Ray MacSharry had been developing just such a new approach, which, in effect, marked the first major departure in the EU from the Dependent Agriculture paradigm. Agriculture had to be rescued from continuous budget crisis, or else the sector would be always at the mercy of finance ministers and de-regulators. De-coupling proved to be the solution for the EU, as it had been for the US five years earlier. Moving support prices toward world market levels reduces the obligation to intervene in markets and accumulate surpluses. Budgets can be used for transitional income support and new investment will presumably be based on the lower, more sustainable price levels. Eventually agriculture would become a competitive sector.

The MacSharry reforms provide evidence of the changing approach to agricultural policy in Europe. But the notion of agriculture as a competitive sector did not take hold in Europe to the same extent as in the US. Instead, a new paradigm began to emerge. The theme of agriculture as an environmental steward as well as a provider of raw materials was in fact articulated by the Commission at the same time as it made the case for a move to world market prices. The "Reflections" document that argued the need for reform made the situation clear.

> Sufficient numbers of farmers must be kept on the land. There is no other way to preserve the natural environment, traditional landscapes and a model of agriculture based on the family farm as favoured by society generally. This requires an active rural development policy....
> The farmer fulfils, or at least could and should fulfill, two functions viz firstly that of producing and secondly on protecting the environment in the context of rural development...
> The activity of producing has traditionally been focused on the production of food.
> ... Concern for the environment means that we should support the farmer also as an environmental manager through the use of less-intensive techniques and the implementation of environment-friendly measures (COM (91) 100 Final).

Viewing the farmer not only as a producer but also as a protector of the environment is the hallmark of the new Multi-Functional Agriculture paradigm that was developing in Europe. This paradigm in effect was the reconciliation of the pressures for a competitive agriculture with the political need not to abandon support for rural incomes. If agriculture was to be recompensed for the provision of public goods in rural areas, it might not be necessary to base policy solely on the need to compete with the US in a global food market.

6.3 Assessment of the Reforms

The MacSharry reform debate presents a number of interesting questions for the outside observer that the analytical framework helps us to address. One set of questions deals with the December 1990 DGVI paper. Why was DGVI CAP reform planning started in the spring of 1990 at a time when the agricultural policy community was intensely focused on the Uruguay Round negotiations? Why was the DGVI paper dated the same day that the GATT ministerial at Heysel Stadium was abandoned? Why was the paper leaked, but not officially released? Another set of intriguing questions relates to the content of the MacSharry reform proposals. Why did the proposals move to make the CAP more market oriented, yet have a strong element of supply control? Why did the original recommendations of the DGVI paper contain detailed proposals for price and quota cuts outside the range of political acceptability in the Agriculture Council? Why did the Commission then retreat to a mere statement of principles in its "Reflections" paper? How can we account for the proposed redistribution of support in favor of smaller farmers? Why the strong emphasis on rural development and agri-environmental measures, but no attempt to change the overall structural policies of the EU? A final set of questions deals with MacSharry's bargaining success. How was he able to get a reform package through the Agriculture Council that originally had been opposed by nearly all the farm ministers? Why, when control of CAP expenditures was an original impetus for reform, did the Agriculture Council approve a package that significantly increased the cost of the CAP?

Commission Planning for Reform

Why was the DGVI planning process started in the spring of 1990, and why was the DGVI paper dated the same day as the collapse of the Heysel Stadium conference? The rational actor model is helpful in explaining the impetus for the reform. CAP spending growth was out of control, creating a crisis for the Community. This crisis, obvious by the spring of 1990, had to be addressed if the process of creating a deeper and stronger union was not to be stopped in its tracks. A successful Uruguay Round might mandate CAP reform, but if the negotiations failed, the EC needed to take up CAP reform on its own. These explanations seem consistent with neo-functionalism and the rational actor in that a supra-national institution, the Commission, pursued Community objectives.

Looking at the situation through the lenses of the organizational process model also provides insights into why MacSharry and DGVI took the initiative. The key agricultural policy-makers in the Commission saw the CAP threatened with collapse. Maintaining the CAP, the basis of their power, was a vital interest for them. By moving quickly, they could control the agenda for change, safeguarding the CAP and preserving insofar as possible the DGVI institutional goal of providing maximum benefits to farmers. A situation of crisis creates the maximum incentive for an organization to overcome its normal inertia, inspiring organizational creativity.

The fact the CAP reform internal paper is dated the same day the GATT ministerial was abandoned is itself merely coincidental. It would have taken the DGVI CAP reform planning group some time to complete its analysis, and the proposal was prepared by people not directly involved in the Uruguay Round negotiations. But in a broader sense the coincidence of the dates is significant. The interplay between the linked CAP and GATT bargaining games provides a plausible explanation for the fact that the events were linked. Undoubtedly the proposal had been ready earlier than

December 6, but MacSharry and Legras had every incentive to ensure that this paper was not finalized until after the Heysel conference. If the conference had succeeded, there would still have been a chance to make modifications so that the domestic reforms were consistent with the GATT agreement. If the conference had failed, the domestic reform process could go ahead. The DGVI paper could clearly not have been released before the end of the Heysel conference. Confirmation that the EC was planning far-reaching reform of the CAP would have led other nations to perceive an increased EC win-set in the GATT game, thus weakening the EC bargaining position. Yet, for very different reasons the reform paper could not be dated after the Heysel conference. It would then have appeared to the Agriculture Council as a response to GATT pressures, which would have weakened the chances of getting the reform package approved.

This suggests that MacSharry had a carefully calculated strategy, a view proposed by Tangermann and shared by some of the people interviewed (Tangermann (1996), p.22). According to Tangermann, MacSharry knew that a Uruguay Round agreement could not be ratified by the Agricultural Council at Heysel because greater changes in the CAP were implied than the Council was willing to offer. In game theoretic terms, the EC win-set in the GATT negotiations was too small to overlap the win-sets of the US and the Cairns group (see Coleman and Tangermann, 1997). MacSharry knew that he had to reform the CAP first in order to achieve a successful URA, thus increasing the size of the EC win-set. MacSharry perhaps calculated that the best way to get CAP reform was to come close to reaching a GATT agreement at Heysel, then break off the talks. This would show the Heads of EC governments that a GATT agreement was possible, and lead them to apply pressure on their agricultural ministers to make the necessary changes in the CAP. Having a DGVI CAP reform paper ready for discussion immediately after Heysel is quite consistent with this scenario. Interviews with former senior EU officials confirm this scenario, but add that MacSharry was taking a risk with the Agricultural Council. While acknowledging that MacSharry was a strategic thinker, they do not think he had anything to gain with the Agriculture Council by bringing the agricultural negotiations in the Uruguay Round to the brink, then let them collapse. They believe MacSharry weakened his position with the Council by making positive initiatives at Heysel, when the Council did not want agriculture included in the GATT.

Why was the DGVI document leaked? There are at least two government politics explanations. One of these suggests that MacSharry himself was responsible for the leak. He may have wanted to shock the Council into a serious reform debate by presenting proposals for radical change, which could be weakened as necessary in the subsequent Council deliberations. MacSharry may have felt that he would end up with more reform by starting with a maximal set of recommendations. By leaking the DGVI document rather than formally releasing it, MacSharry would have gained an advantage in that he did not have to accept responsibility for the recommendations. Thus, he could avoid becoming a personal target for attack by the opponents of reform, and at the same time preserve maximum flexibility. Another explanation is that someone opposed to CAP reform leaked the document to embarrass MacSharry. But, if this was the case, why wasn't the document leaked before the conclusion of the Heysel summit, when it would have been far more embarrassing?

The MacSharry Proposals Explained

Why did DGVI planners opt for a market-oriented approach in their recommendations, yet include an element of supply control? The choice of a market-oriented approach can be explained as a rational actor decision. As Coleman and Tangermann describe the situation, the Commission had two goals which the reform proposal had to satisfy: 1) to find a solution to the endemic problems of the CAP; and 2) to provide a way out of the stalemate in the Uruguay Round (see Coleman and Tangermann (1997), pp.17-18). An "autarchic" solution institutionally would have been the easiest path. In controlling supplies through set-asides for cereals and oilseeds, the Community could have significantly reduced export subsidies. But, this solution created problems in the GATT. The price support system necessary to keep prices high would never have survived a deal on domestic support with the US and Cairns Group. Also, an international agreement to lower tariffs would have made it impossible to maintain high prices to protect farmers' incomes.

A "liberal" solution of letting markets determine prices would certainly have been consistent with GATT obligations, but this solution had little political support, because it would have forced many farmers out of business. As Coleman and Tangermann note, the Commission's proposal creatively furthered EC interests in promoting in trade negotiations and in protecting farm income (1997, pp.17-18). Price reductions would promote a GATT agreement and compensatory payments not linked to production would minimize the impact on the countryside. Modulated payments could probably achieve acceptance in the GATT.

The perspectives of organizational process and multi-level governance provide other insights. Looking at the situation through the lenses of the organizational process model, a strict system of supply controls would be complex and difficult for DGVI to administer. A more market-oriented CAP would present less difficult problems. The mix of market-orientation and supply control probably reflects the Commission's recognition of the importance of intergovernmental politics. To get CAP reforms through the Agriculture Council, the support of both France and Germany would be required. France, with a strong lobby of large efficient cereal growers and with an historic "mission" to export, could accept price cuts, but would oppose supply controls. Germany could accept supply controls, but would oppose uncompensated price cuts. A pure market-oriented policy would have been unacceptable to either Germany or France. Most of the farms in what had been West Germany were small and inefficient and many would have had difficulty surviving in an open market environment. The farms in what had been East Germany were large, but still very inefficient. They too would have had trouble competing. In France, while the large cereal growers could compete internationally, there were many small farmers who could not compete. A partially market-oriented policy, with compensated price cuts and limited supply controls, might meet both French and German concerns.

Why did the DGVI paper contain such detailed recommendations for price and quota cuts outside the range of political acceptability in the Agriculture Council? The rational actor analyst would surmise that the DGVI planning group was given a broad mandate to analyze the factors behind the crisis in the CAP and to recommend the best solutions, which could then be modified by MacSharry and Legras to make them more acceptable to the Agriculture Council. In support of this interpretation, the DGVI recommendations seem well-designed to meet the problem of overproduction. The recommendations for compensatory payments implied an increase in the CAP budget at a time of perceived budget crisis. The autumn Agriculture Council debate over MacSharry's Uruguay Round recommendation for a 30 percent reduction in support had shown that the price for approval was compensation to farmers for their losses. This suggests that the planning group took into account political considerations, and that it calculated an increase in the CAP budget would be easier to achieve than forcing uncompensated price cuts through the Council.

Why did the DGVI proposal emphasize redistribution of support in favor of smaller farmers, when this would probably produce a firestorm in the Agriculture Council? The Commission as a rational actor could see modulation in compensatory payments would cost less than full compensation for all farmers. Modulation had an advantage for reducing production in that it limited payments to the largest farmers responsible for the bulk of the surplus. Focusing on the government politics of the Commission produces a different explanation. Commissioner MacSharry thought it was inappropriate that 20 percent of the EC farmers received 80 percent of the benefits.[90] As a bargaining move, he might get the Council to approve a redistribution of benefits, by arguing that small farmers would be forced out of business by the necessary market-oriented reforms. Only by modulating benefits could the EC both undertake reform and achieve the goal of keeping the maximum numbers of farmers on the land. The interplay between the Uruguay Round GATT game and the CAP game suggests another explanation. While price and quota cuts were consistent with the EC meeting the requirements of an international agricultural trade agreement, compensatory payments probably would not meet the green box criteria of acceptability. However, modulated payments would be easier to sell than unmodulated ones.

Why did the reform package include accompanying rural development, agri-environment, early retirement and afforestation measures, and why did MacSharry not attempt to modify the EC structural policies? We gain some insights into the answers to these questions by looking at the Commission as a rational actor. Since the major thrust of the proposed reforms was to make the CAP more market-oriented, measures would be needed to improve the efficiency of the farming sector. An early retirement option would facilitate the structural transformation by providing an opportunity for many marginal producers to leave. The afforestation program, by removing marginal land from production, also would promote efficiency. It is more difficult to argue that

---

[90] The statement that 20 percent of the farmers receive 80 percent of the benefits was used frequently by the Commission, but never substantiated.

the agri-environment schemes would improve farm efficiency, but it could improve sustainability. Government politics suggests a more persuasive explanation. In selling his vision of agricultural reform, which implied increased CAP expenditures, MacSharry had to appeal to prime ministers, finance ministers, and the general public. With the Multi-Functional Agriculture Paradigm taking hold, a good way to do this was to emphasize that the proposed reforms enhanced the role of the farmer as the protector of the countryside. The inclusion of rural development and agri-environmental schemes made this argument more plausible. Also, these schemes would probably be GATT acceptable.

The explanation for the non-inclusion of EC structural policies in the reform package probably lies partly in the bureaucratic politics of the Commission and partly in the intergovernmental politics of the Agriculture Council. Including structural policy, not scheduled for review at that time, would have meant extensive bargaining with Directorates General of the Commission responsible for regional and social policy as well as with the Agriculture Council. This would have appreciably increased the bargaining costs of gaining Commission approval. At the Council level, any attempt to change structural policies would have weakened the chances for support of the reform package from the Mediterranean country governments, which would have seen a threat to their structural funds.

Why did the Commission retreat from the details of the DGVI paper to a mere statement of principles in its "Reflections" paper. This can be explained as a bargaining requisite of the two-level CAP bargaining game. It was pretty clear from the initial hostile reactions of the Agriculture Council that the DGVI recommendations had little chance of approval. Thus, the Commission win-set was too small; it did not overlap the win-sets of the member governments. By retreating to a statement of principles, MacSharry was increasing the Commission's win-set by providing the flexibility to adjust proposal details to satisfy the demands of individual governments. A pullback on support modulation also can be seen as an effort to allow the Commission win-set to overlap with the win-sets of member states. Modulation incurred the opposition of UK, the Netherlands and Denmark, the nations otherwise most supportive of market-oriented reform. France and Germany also had reservations. Network analysis provides another perspective. The detailed DGVI proposals implied major changes to the CAP, undoubtedly threatening from the perspective of national farm organizations. By retreating from details, the Commission may have hoped to reduce the intensity of opposition from farm groups, making the task easier of selling MacSharry reforms to the Agriculture Council.

Getting the MacSharry Reforms Through the Agriculture Council

How was MacSharry able to get his reform package through the Agriculture Council, which had opposed the original proposals with near unanimity? We gain insights by examining several dimensions of government politics. An institutionalist perspective is helpful in explaining how the EC decision-making structure influenced the process. Only the Commission can formulate proposals to the Council. The farm ministers knew the CAP had to be reformed, but had only MacSharry's proposal to consider. MacSharry had the bargaining advantage of controlling the agenda. This advantage was limited by the Agriculture Council norm of seeking consensus before acting on important questions. MacSharry was constrained to produce a proposal that would achieve acceptance through consensus. The Council President's support for MacSharry was important in producing consensus in the critical final stages of bargaining. The Portuguese agriculture minister, Arlindo Cunha, used very effectively the prerogatives of the Presidency to take the initiative in informal conversations, and in a tour of national capitals to see what was acceptable to the various member states and then develop compromise proposals (see Moyer and Josling (1990), Chap 2, on the powers of the Council Presidency). He helped bridge the gap between MacSharry and the member states by suggesting a compromise price cut of 27 percent instead of MacSharry's proposed 35 percent (Colman and Tangermann (1997), p.21). This facilitated the final compromise price cut of 29 percent.

Commissioner MacSharry deserves credit as an effective bargainer. He was careful not to be too strongly committed to the details of the DGVI paper, which gave him room for maneuver. He used this flexibility skillfully in manipulating the reform provisions so that each farm minister could claim some measure of victory in the final outcome. He showed toughness in moving the process along, when, for example he threatened reduced price supports in his next price package if no reform agreement was reached. MacSharry's bargaining leeway may have been increased in the early stages of the reform process, when France and Germany disagreed in their reactions to the Commission paper (Webber (1997), pp.37-38).

The prospects for MacSharry's proposals improved when Chancellor Kohl and President Mitterrand reached an "informal understanding" in early 1991 to put the Uruguay Round "on hold" and first reform the CAP (Webber (1997), p.38; Webber (1999), p.53). According to Webber, they agreed that in line with the Commission's (and also the French) approach, Germany would not veto a cereal price cut, and that, in turn, France would not ultimately block a new GATT agreement, or would at least display "good will" in the Uruguay Round negotiations (Webber (1997), p.38; Webber (1999), p.53). Agreement between Germany and France almost always achieves acceptance among other EU nations. These nations combined have the economic power resources to bring most other EU members along. But relative power is not the only explanation. Germany and France have rather different interests in agriculture and trade issues, and as Weber suggests, their agreement often represents the "median" position of the member states as a whole (Webber (1997), p.64). The importance of the French-German "informal understanding" shows the importance of intergovernmentalism, although the interplay between this agreement and MacSharry's proposals would support a multi-level governance explanation.

Synergistic linkage with the GATT game also contributed to the Agriculture Council's acceptance of the MacSharry reforms in the CAP game (see Coleman and Tangermann, 1997). The EC Commission regarded successful completion of the Uruguay Round as important for promoting the economic health of Europe. In Germany, the stakes were even higher. Sentiment was strong in most important sectors of the German economy, except for agriculture, for a new international trade agreement. Though opinion was more divided in France, strong elements of the business sector wanted a positive outcome to the Round. It was clear to all that successful completion of the trade negotiations required reform of the CAP. Reform had had to occur soon as a time deadline was approaching, with the November 1992, US Presidential election, and the expiration of US Fast Track negotiating authority.

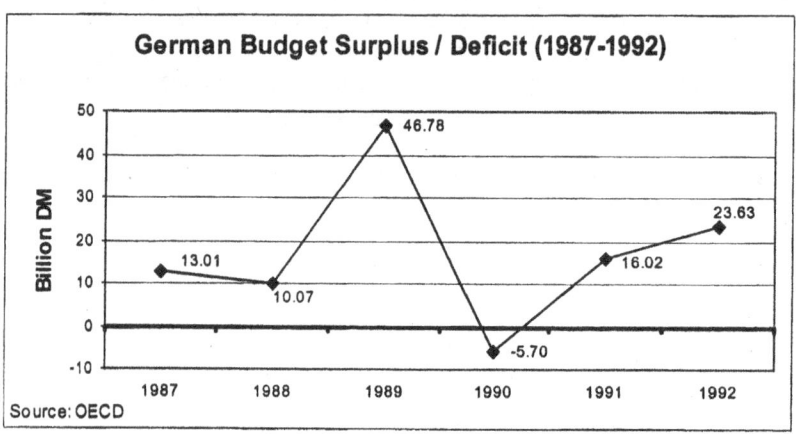

Figure 6.5: German Budget Surplus / Deficit (1987-1992)

Thus the Uruguay Round placed enormous pressure on the Commission, France and Germany to expedite reform of the CAP. The international pressure reinforced the domestic CAP game budget pressure to control the growth of spending for agriculture. The German government was particularly sensitive to the spending problem, because, as the principal net contributor to the EC budget, Germany would have to bear the lion's share of increased expenditures for agriculture. The timing was particularly bad. With a large and uncharacteristic domestic budget deficit in 1990 caused by the necessity of huge expenditures to integrate former East Germany into the Republic, the German government could not contemplate increasing its contribution to the EC (Figure 6.5). The combined need to save the Uruguay Round and control the EC budget created an impetus for Chancellor Kohl and the German cabinet to subordinate agriculture to broader national interests, and hence push Agriculture Minister Kiechle to accept the MacSharry proposals (see Patterson (1997), pp.156-161).

Agricultural interests in France were overruled for different reasons. The "no reform and no discussion of reform" position of the FNSEA and the French agriculture ministry left the response to MacSharry up to the Finance Ministry, the Foreign Ministry, and the Prime Minister's office (the three agencies of the Interministerial committee) (Coleman, Atkinson and Montpetit (1997), p.476). These agencies took a broader view of French interests than did the agricultural community. They were more concerned about the agricultural spending problem, and they wanted the Uruguay Round to succeed. The French government was able to gain the support of the French cereal growers, who had increased their strength sufficiently to be able to take positions independent of the FNSEA. They could accept price cuts and do quite well in both European and world markets (Coleman, Atkinson and Montpetit (1997), p.477).[91]

Finally, why did the Commission, EC heads of government and finance ministers allow the agricultural ministers to approve a final reform package that considerably increased the cost of the CAP, when part of the initial impetus for reform was the out-of-control growth of agricultural spending? Looking at the government politics of this multi-level governance situation, one can see that building a winning coalition in the Agriculture Council required the Commission to make a series of modifications to its original budget-prudent ideas, each of which added to the costs of the reform. One can get an idea of the Commission's original aims from the December 1990 DGVI internal document leaked to the press (see Coleman and Tangermann (1997), p.18). The proposed modulation of compensatory payments and the proposed uncompensated set-asides, both designed to favor the smaller farmer, would have kept budget costs of reform manageable.[92] But, the costs of reform escalated significantly as modulation for price cuts was weakened then eliminated to gain the support of the United Kingdom, the Netherlands and Denmark, and as MacSharry's proposal was modified to pay compensation for land set aside.

But why did the projected cost increase not catalyze a strong negative response from Prime Ministers and Finance Ministers? In part, this might have been because the long-term costs of the reform plan were uncertain. MacSharry was proposing a very different way of supporting farm income. There was no evidence from the past to validate cost projections. For example it was difficult to refute the Commission's July 1991 arguments, that while the proposal would increase CAP spending by 2.24 billion ECU, the reform would eventually result in lower costs over time as the surpluses of grain, dairy products and meat declined.[93] It was also hard to assess the accuracy of such predictions as one that appeared in *Agra Europe* on July 19, 1991, "the guarantee budget for the CAP in 1997 would increase to 37.3 billion ECU. This is well up on the 1991 level of 32.5 billion ECU but well down on the estimated cost of 42.7 billion ECU expected in 1997 if there are no reforms" (p.E/1, quoted by Patterson (1997), p.155). The problem of assessing costs was complicated by the fact that the MacSharry proposals went through a series of iterations. It would not have been easy for busy Prime Ministers and Finance Ministers to keep up with changing cost estimates.

---

[91] Roeder-Rynning argues that the imposition of EC agriculture spending guidelines in 1988, by limiting the ability of the Agriculture Council to grant across-the-board price increases, weakened the ability of the FNSEA to speak for all farmers, encouraging dissident groups such as the cereal producers to pursue their own agendas.

[92] Full compensation would go to farms under 30ha, 75 percent to those between 31 and 80 ha, and 65 percent to those over 80 ha. Farms under 30 ha would not have been required to set-aside land; those between 31 and 80 ha would have been required to set aside 25 percent; and those larger than 80 ha would have been required to set aside 35 percent (Coleman and Tangermann (1997), p.18).

[93] See Patterson (1997), p.155. Also, *Agra Europe*, 5 July 1991: P/4 and 19 July 1991: P/2.

The synergistic linkage between the GATT game and the CAP game also helps to explain why the budget cost of the MacSharry reforms did not undermine approval. All of the members of the EU wanted a Uruguay Round Agreement, and it was clear that this required CAP reform. Thus, the need for a successful completion of the GATT talks increased national win-sets in the CAP reform game. There was only the MacSharry reform proposal on the table. Developing a different proposal would have been impossible before the expiration of US Fast Track authority in 1993. The choice was either to approve the MacSharry proposal or allow the Uruguay Round to fail. National governments still had two options: 1) to get tough with the Agriculture Ministers and insist that they approve a less expensive reform package; 2) accept the package as approved by the Agriculture Council, and ignore or rationalize away the cost issue. The first option was a political non-starter in that it would have incurred the wrath of the European farm lobbies. It would not have worked, given the continuing importance of consensus in the Agriculture Council, unless every member government had been willing to exert such pressure, which was out of the realm of possibility. The second option had more appeal. A more expensive CAP would be an acceptable price to pay for a GATT agreement, particularly since the cost increase might be contained in the medium to long run. Also, the domestic political fall-out from increased CAP spending appeared minuscule compared to a full-fledged confrontation with the farm lobby.

6.4 Conclusion

The MacSharry reforms established a new path for the Common Agricultural Policy in that they shifted the primary instrument for supporting farmer income from price supports to compensatory payments. This change had been brought about both by the perceived unsustainability of an unreformed CAP, the resultant undermining of the Dependent Agriculture Paradigm and by the realization that a successful Uruguay Round could not be completed without CAP reform. The timing of the reform was galvanized by the need to complete the Uruguay Round before the 1992 US Presidential election and expiration shortly thereafter of US Fast Track negotiating authority, and by a developing EC budget crisis. The enhanced status of rural development and agri-environmental measures evidence the developing strength of the Multi-functional Agriculture paradigm. Commissioner Ray MacSharry recognized the inevitability of change and took the initiative to have DGVI develop proposals which would both maintain the CAP and allow for successful completion of the GATT negotiations. Thus, DGVI and the farm policy community were able to maintain control of EC agricultural policy and to limit the damage of reform to farm interests. The price of an agreement, given the practice of seeking unanimity in the Agriculture Council, was to increase the budget cost of the CAP at a time of impending budget crisis. But, the need to complete the Uruguay Round provided an impetus for the EC to sacrifice budget limits for CAP reform. Expanding the budget was not much of a burden for the many EC members who were net recipients, but was very difficult for

Germany, the largest net contributor. But, Germany's stake in the Uruguay Round was so large that it was willing to pay the price.

With approval of the MacSharry reforms, the EC win-set in the Uruguay Round negotiations significantly increased. It now became possible to contemplate concessions on domestic price supports, import barriers and export subsidies that would allow a successful outcome to the negotiations. In the next chapter we will see how the negotiations were brought to conclusion.

Chapter 7

Reform Revived: The Dunkel Draft, the Blair House Accord and the WTO Agreement on Agriculture

7.1 Introduction

The collapse of the Heysel meeting marked a low point in the Uruguay Round negotiations and stimulated renewed efforts by the protagonists to reach some measure of agreement and hence rescue the talks from failure. The months after the failed Ministerial were absorbed with these intense diplomatic efforts. Few new ideas were introduced, and the negotiations became more political and less technocratic. Agreement on the structure of an agricultural package did not occur until February 1991, when the EU indicated that it could live with the outlines of the US (and Cairns Group) position on the scope of an eventual package.[94] This opened the way for diplomacy and compromise rather than posturing. The efforts were essentially devoted first to securing a bilateral deal between the US and the EU and then developing the details of an agreement that would apply to all the participating countries. Finally the agricultural package had to be put back into the overall Uruguay Round Agreement. This could only happen after the EU had secured substantial modifications in its own internal agricultural policy so as to be able to live with the changes implied by a GATT agreement. How this EU policy change led to the completion of the Uruguay Round is an important aspect of the story of farm policy reform in the 1990s, and is the subject of this chapter.

7.2 MacSharry Reform Unlocks the Door

The connection between the CAP reform proposals made by Commissioner MacSharry and the isolation of the EU at Heysel is an example of the complex linkage between domestic and trade policies in agriculture. The same day that the Ministerial was breaking up, a document began circulating in another part of Brussels with some ideas that would in effect rescue the GATT negotiations. The first discussion document on

---

[94] The European Community became the European Union with the coming into force of the Maastricht Treaty in November 1993. This chapter and subsequent ones will therefore use the term EU rather than EC.

what became the MacSharry reform of the CAP outlined a scheme for moving away from almost total reliance on price supports, operated largely at the border, toward a system of lower prices supplemented by direct payments. The significance for the GATT talks was obvious to even the most casual observer. By essentially choosing a US-style policy for the major arable crops - lower market prices supplemented with payments from the treasury - the EU could lower external protection, reduce export subsidies and claim to have moved toward "decoupled" domestic support. On the other hand, the domestic reform document was not produced primarily as a trade policy proposal. The linkage between domestic reform and trade policy changes operates at several different levels. To understand these levels it is useful to look at the process, which brought about the conclusion of the Uruguay Round negotiations.

The Heysel meeting had collapsed essentially because the EU could not accept the proposal for specific constraints on export subsidies. The circulation of the first draft of a reform package that would allow the EU to reduce export subsidies, by dropping support prices and paying compensation payments (see Chapter 6), was an indication that there was light at the end of the tunnel. In February 1991, at a meeting in Geneva, the Commission finally allowed discussion of export subsidies to proceed where previously such a topic had been blocked by pressure from the French government. Meanwhile, Arthur Dunkel, the Director General of the GATT, engaged in yet more "shuttle diplomacy" to evaluate the position of the parties, as he had done two years earlier after the Montreal meeting had also ended in failure. Much of the year was taken up by translating the negotiating ideas into treaty text. The details of a potential agricultural settlement were initially incorporated into the "Draft Final Act" of December 1991, submitted by Arthur Dunkel on his own initiative, and usually called the Dunkel Draft. The Dunkel Draft kept the tripartite structure of "market access", "export competition", and "domestic support" which had been incorporated in the De Zeeuw draft of June 1990 (as discussed in Chapter 4) and introduced a timetable for liberalization of support and protection. The Dunkel Draft was not, however, immediately acceptable to the EU, whose agricultural ministers still considered it too much an attack on the CAP.

The way to an agreement was finally stimulated by the rather speedy progress of the MacSharry reform package. The EU Commission saw this reform package as allowing them to react to the intensifying pressure to accept the Dunkel Draft as a basis for negotiations and at the same time to be modernizing the CAP and putting a check on the upward drift of budget cost. Technical discussions started up again in Geneva, and the details were discussed of what the Dunkel proposals would mean to each of the major parties. Meetings took place among various combinations of countries, including US-EC bilaterals, meetings that included Japan, Australia and Canada (the "quint"), and a "group of eight" in which some other Cairns Group countries, including Argentina, were represented. The major political breakthrough came when the EU Council of (Agricultural) Ministers passed the MacSharry reforms in June 1992 (see Chapter 6). This finally allowed EU negotiators to engage in serious talks with the US and other countries.

7.3 Bilateralism in Action: The Blair House Accord

The Blair House discussion on agriculture was the culmination of a set of negotiations that had started in early 1992. Technical discussions between the US and the EC had been held under the umbrella of the New Transatlantic Agenda, agreed between the Bush administration and the EC. This attempt to improve the climate of transatlantic economic (and political) relations in the aftermath of the Cold War had relatively few successes to its credit. Helping along the agricultural talks was one of these successes. The Bush administration was keen to get agreement on the Round in an election year, and in any case his Fast Track authority from Congress was about to expire. In addition, the EU was concerned that a Clinton victory could add new uncertainty to negotiating with the US. Negotiations came to a head in late October in Chicago, when the US and the EU negotiators met in a hotel to settle their differences. They were still talking when election day arrived in the US, and the Agriculture Secretary, Edward Madigan, had to leave to vote. During this hiatus, Ray MacSharry, the Agricultural Commissioner, received a phone call from Jacques Delors, the President of the European Commission, to indicate that he should remain firm on export subsidies. Although widely interpreted as intervention on behalf of the French government, which would have been somewhat improper in view of his position as a European official, it is just as likely that Delors was concerned about the difficulties in getting an agreement through the Agricultural Council. In any event, MacSharry returned to Brussels and wrote a letter of resignation to Delors, asking to be relieved of the agricultural negotiating portfolio (though not the role of Agricultural Commissioner). Delors initially asked Andriessen to take back that portfolio, but was not prepared to give him adequate support. MacSharry finally resumed his position and returned to Washington for a last attempt at an agreement that was almost within reach in Chicago.

To add an incentive to settle the agricultural component of the Uruguay Round, an old trade dispute from the earlier years of the GATT had once more become a transatlantic irritant. The dispute was over the EU's oilseeds policy, which the US claimed was contrary to GATT articles and also "nullified and impaired" the benefits that the US had expected to enjoy as a result of binding oilseed tariffs in the Dillon Round (1960-62). The fact that the EU had bound its tariffs on oilseeds meant that it could not introduce a "typical" CAP market regime for those commodities, with variable levies protecting a target domestic price level. Instead the EU chose to pay direct payments to oilseed crushers to encourage them to use domestic oilseeds. A GATT panel found that this violated Article III, the national treatment provision, and that the rights of the US had indeed been impaired. The oilseed dispute had taken on a symbolic importance even beyond its considerable commercial impact. It was regarded in the US as a test case for whether the multilateral process could actually constrain a popular domestic program. The EU had used the opportunity to experiment with a new type of policy instrument, direct payments to farmers, to get around the problem that processor payments constituted discrimination against imported oilseeds. But when the panel was recalled to rule on the new policy, they decided that impairment still existed. As a consequence, the US announced at the end of the abortive Chicago talks that it

Reform Revived: The Dunkel Draft, the Blair House Accord and the WTO 121

would impose sanctions (on $300 million of trade) on imported French and Italian wine, to come into effect at the end of 1992. The obvious solution was to fold the resolution of the oilseed dispute into the conclusion of the agricultural discussions in the Uruguay Round.[95]

The extra incentive given by the threat of sanctions was enough to make negotiators come back for a final session in Washington in November 1992. The venue was Blair House, a building across from the White House used for visiting dignitaries. The participants were Ray MacSharry and Frans Andriessen on the EC side of the table, accompanied by advisors including Mary Minch; and Edward Madigan and Carla Hills, on the US side, advised by Joe O'Meara and Julius Katz. Negotiations were intense, but the compatibility of the personalities of the principals overcame the policy differences.[96] Agreement was reached on November 20, 1992, on a package that was to later form the basis for the Uruguay Round Agreement on Agriculture.

Three elements appear to have combined to make the Blair House negotiations a success. First, the ground had been well prepared. Detailed discussions at the technical and professional level left the politicians well informed about the impact of various outcomes. Second, MacSharry had been successful in retaining support from domestic interests even while he was looking for ways to reach agreement. He had emerged from the Heysel meeting as someone fully determined to defend the integrity of the CAP against the attacks from the US and the Cairns Group. Meanwhile he had pulled off a remarkable "internal" reform of the CAP in May 1992 that incidentally gave him flexibility in the trade negotiations. It was therefore easier for him to build on the two achievements by coming to terms with the US to resolve the oilseed and the UR issues.

This deal finally allowed the EU to accept the disciplines on export subsidies, though the cut-back was to be less than proposed in the Dunkel Draft, and gave assurance that the MacSharry compensations, along with the US deficiency payments, were protected from challenge in the "blue box" and would not have to be cut back. In addition it weakened the discipline of the AMS constraint by aggregation over all commodities, and introduced a "peace clause" sheltering the fundamentals of the CAP from further challenge if the policy did not deviate too much from the present situation.

In an interesting juxtaposition between the dispute settlement process and the trade negotiation machinery, a compromise settling the long-running oilseed subsidies conflict was rolled into the package and agreed. In the end the domestic program yielded to the force of the GATT rules and the imperative for reaching an agreement. But for this to happen it had to be part of a package, to allow the domestic interests to be reconciled.

---

[95] Besides the fact that the two issues were politically linked, settlement of the oilseed conflict would imply that the grain policy reforms instituted by MacSharry were also GATT-compatible.

[96] It may not be completely irrelevant that four of the negotiators were either Irish or claimed some Irish roots.

7.4 The Accord Revisited: Blair House II

The final stage of the negotiations involved translating the Blair House bilateral deal into a multilateral agreement that would satisfy all parties to the negotiations, and at the same time be an acceptable part of a broader package of trade reforms involving other sectors. In the event, the Accord itself also had to be refined by the last minute negotiations (known as Blair House II) in December 1993.

The actors had changed by the second act of the play. At the end of 1992 the term of the "activist" Commission led by Jacques Delors expired. The new Commissioner for Agriculture was Rene Steichen, from Luxembourg. The 1992 election in the US had ushered in the first Clinton Administration, and Carla Hills was replaced by Mickey Kantor as US Trade Representative. The new President was granted an extension of Fast Track authority by Congress for a period of two years, so that he could among other things wrap up the Round.

Talks between the EU and the US on the outstanding issues continued through most of 1993. Negotiations focused on the French objection to the treatment of export subsidies in the original Blair House deal. The US was determined not to open up the Blair House Accord for renegotiation: the EU was equally determined that some reinterpretation be agreed to make the compact domestically acceptable. Finally, in late 1993 a compromise was reached which delayed the cuts in export subsidies for a period so as to allow the EU to remove the overhang of stocks without a collapse in prices. This allowed the Uruguay Round to be brought to a close, and the Agreement on Agriculture went into effect in 1995.

7.5 Explaining Negotiating Success

While the earlier phase of the Uruguay Round had been marked by failures to reach agreement at Montreal and Heysel, as we have discussed in Chapter 4, the later phase resulted in successful conclusion of the Blair House I and Blair House II agreements. We now turn to a discussion of what made success possible.

The Road to an Agreement at Blair House

For Blair House I it will be necessary to explain the content of the agreement and why it took nearly two years after the Heysel failure to produce success. We will argue that for the incompatible US and EC winsets highlighted at Heysel to converge sufficiently to allow agreement (level 1in the three level GATT game), the bargaining outcomes for the US and EU (level 2) and in EC member governments (level 3), also would have to change. This would involve high bargaining costs. The failure at Heysel was itself one factor helping to catalyze the necessary changes. Heysel had made it clear that the Uruguay Round could not be successfully concluded without an agricultural trade agreement. The importance of a successful Uruguay Round for stimulating the EU and US economies at a time of economic stagnation (an economic trend) was sufficiently great that agricultural trade policy got the attention of top-level officials who normally do not involve themselves heavily in agricultural policy. Business lobbies with a stake in a successful trade agreement also brought their weight to bear more than usual, but they were countered by farm lobbies who feared that a GATT accord would endanger the benefits they received from domestic agricultural policy.

The larger winset of the US (which implied less agonizing changes) and the relative simplicity of the US policy process, made the adjustment far easier in the US than in the EU. The EU adjustment was eased by the adoption of the MacSharry reforms in the CAP game, which increased the EC's winset in the GATT game (Coleman and Tangermann, 1997). However, a successful agricultural trade agreement had to wait until the CAP reform debate was resolved. Elections in the US and France affected the timing of the Blair House agreements as did the referenda on the Maastricht agreement in Denmark and France. Finally we will argue that both Blair House agreements were facilitated by skillful negotiators committed to using all the leeway they had to achieve a successful agricultural trade agreement. This leeway was enhanced by intergovernmental politics where the governments of Germany and France disagreed on acceptable sacrifices for an agricultural trade agreement. For Blair House I, there was the additional benefit of having an engaged GATT Director-General to mediate US-EC differences.

The GATT agricultural trade negotiations resume The GATT agricultural trade negotiations resumed in February 1991, two months after the Heysel failure, with the positive US reaction to the initial announcement of the proposed MacSharry reforms of the CAP, and the European Commission's willingness to negotiate separate commitments for domestic supports, import barriers and export subsidies. The Commission was able to add again the separate consideration of export subsidies, previously stricken in the November 1990 Council mandate, because of the change in the bargaining arena and an interesting interplay between the Commission, the General Affairs Council and the Agriculture Council. The Commissioner for External Relations, Frans Andriessen aimed at a rapid resumption of the negotiations, and declared that the General Affairs Council had granted the Commission the authority to negotiate (Vahl (1997), p.157).[97] According to Andriessen, the Concessions made at Heysel were still valid. This position was contested by France and Ireland, endorsed by the Luxembourg Presidency. The Agriculture Council insisted that the EC stick to the November 1990 mandate (Vahl (1997), p.158). However, at the February meeting of the General Affairs Council, the majority appeared to back Andriessen.[98] In a declaration, the Council reiterated the need to resume the GATT negotiations on a

---

[97] Andriessen apparently was hoping a synergy between the GATT and CAP negotiations similar to that predicted by Putnam. He wanted to negotiate an international deal to facilitate domestic reform. This reflected a different philosophy from MacSharry, who felt than domestic reform should go first (interview).

[98] The United Kingdom, the Netherlands, Denmark, and to some extent Germany and Spain wanted a more flexible negotiating position (Vahl (1997), p.157).

rapid, balanced agreement, and called on the Commission to act accordingly (Vahl (1997), pp.157-158). Even though the French government had been informed of the Commission plans, it made no effort to block this move. One participant in the process thought that the prospect of the compensatory payments proposed by the MacSharry reforms of the CAP made it easier for the French government to accept discussion of export subsidy limits (interview). At another level, a French effort at this stage to prevent discussion of export subsidies would have opened a breach with the German government which wanted prompt action to conclude the Uruguay Round.

Different attitudes in France and Germany There were profound differences in the attitudes and politics of civil society in France and Germany toward trade liberalization and the importance of the protection of agriculture (see Webber (1997), p.35). In Germany, the German Farmers Union *Deutscher Bauernverband* (DBV), was the only relevant organized interest that opposed trade liberalization. Organized business interests were very active to ensure that conflicts over agricultural trade did not lead to the collapse of the Uruguay Round. All political parties, from the moderate right to the Greens on the left were in basic support of trade liberalization. At the government level, the German agriculture ministry tended to align itself with the farm lobby, while other ministries, particularly the economics ministry, which had responsibility for foreign trade, favored making major concessions in agriculture if necessary to achieve a GATT agreement. Chancellor Kohl thought a successful conclusion to the GATT Round was critical for the German economy, but he hesitated in making agriculture concessions because of his desire to maintain the German-French alliance and because of the importance of the farm vote to the CDU/CSU coalition.

The situation in France was very different. The political Right and Left were divided over the Uruguay Round between strong opponents to liberalization and moderate supporters (see Webber (1997), p.35). The principal peak organization of business CNPF (*Confederation Nationale du Patronat Francais)*, the French National Employers Confederation, was split between liberal and protectionist member associations. Trade unions were also divided. Farmers associations were united in their opposition to agricultural trade liberalization. Public opinion was hostile toward trade liberalization, particularly agricultural trade liberalization, placing pressure on the government to stand firm, even if this meant collapse of the Uruguay Round. The French government was adamant in wanting to preserve the CAP and to avoid making any commitments that would interfere with France's ability to export agricultural products.

With different agricultural interests and a different domestic political climate, it was not easy to hold the French-German alliance together on the Uruguay Round. Chancellor Kohl and President Mitterrand met in February 1991, in the presence of their agricultural advisors, to discuss how to deal with CAP reform and with the GATT (Webber (1997), p.38). They are reported to have reached an "informal understanding" on both procedure and policy content (Webber (1997), p.38). On procedure, they apparently agreed to put the Uruguay Round "on hold" and to first reform the CAP. On content, they are thought to have agreed that the German government should accept a cereal price cut in the CAP and that in return, France would not block a Uruguay Round agreement (Webber (1997), p.38). Other informal discussions were taking place. Shortly after the Uruguay Round negotiations resumed, the US and EC negotiators, who established a good working relationship, began holding secret meetings to try to bridge their differences (interviews). These were held more or less monthly, discussing all the topics in dispute. Each side would throw out ideas of the order - if I were to do so and so, how would you react? Sometimes the group was expanded to include the Japanese and Australian negotiators so that the negotiations would not be perceived as exclusively bi-lateral. The frequency of these meetings increased at critical points in the negotiations. These meetings were enormously helpful in preparing for the Blair House I agreement. Had they been publicized, the freedom of the negotiators to explore various options could have been seriously constrained by political pressures generated by European and American farm lobbies.

Renewal of Fast Track Authority gives a boost to negotiations The Uruguay Round received a boost during the spring of 1991 when the US Congress granted President Bush's request for a two-year extension of Fast Track negotiating authority. Even though the CAP reform debate was the primary focus for the remainder of the year, steady progress was made in the agricultural trade negotiations. In the early June annual ministerial session of the OECD, Commissioner Andriessen argued that the time for compromise had come (Vahl (1997), p.158). The communique issued at the end of this conference mentioned the end of 1991 as the date for concluding the Uruguay Round negotiations. This date was confirmed by the EC's Ministers for Foreign Trade and the European Council (Vahl (1997), p.138). The GATT Director-General, Arthur Dunkel developed a more detailed work program called "Options in the Agricultural Negotiations" (Vahl (1997), p.138). This was accepted without reservation by Andriessen, but MacSharry had reservations, merely describing the document as a useful reference for the future (Vahl (1997), p.138). What seemed evident at this stage was that Andriessen, backed by the trade ministers was pushing very hard for a GATT agreement, while MacSharry, backed by the Agriculture Council, was holding back pending the results of the CAP reform debate.

The Commission certainly saw the links between the CAP reform debate and the Uruguay Round, even though this was formally denied. Both Andriessen and MacSharry knew that the trade negotiations would benefit from the proposed CAP reforms. MacSharry was very insistent on including future EC compensatory payments in the Uruguay Round Green Box of permitted measures (Vahl (1997), p.58). Though Andriessen and MacSharry took somewhat different positions, as they represented different interests, they both gained a certain amount of leeway because of the divisions among and within the EC member countries.

The Dunkel Draft Final Agreement The agricultural trade negotiating process was prodded by GATT Director-General Dunkel at the end of September, when he announced that the final negotiations had commenced. He informed the negotiating parties that he was going to prepare a document providing a status report on all dossiers as of mid-November (Paeman and Bensch (1995), p.199). This speeded up the informal negotiations between the US and EC and got top level attention on both sides. At an EU-US summit on November 9, 1991, President Bush made a significant move toward the EC position by lowering US demands for cuts to 35 percent for export subsidies and 30 percent for other areas, to be implemented in five or six years.[99] By December, it was reported that the EU was prepared to raise its offer to cut domestic subsidies to match the 30 percent proposed by the US, though using different base years (consistent with what seemed a likely outcome of the CAP reform debate) (*Financial Times*, Dec. 23, 1991). President Bush had more bargaining flexibility than the EC Commission. With Fast Track authority, he could change the US negotiating stance without consulting congress. The EC Commission had to clear major changes with the divided Council of Ministers. The US and EC negotiators reportedly also came close to resolving the export subsidy dispute to the point where the US was asking for a mixture of quantitative and budgetary cuts which would allow the EC to export 11 million tons of wheat annually, while the EC seemed willing to make cuts allowing export of 13-15 million tons (*Financial Times*, Dec. 12, 1991).

The December Dunkel "Draft Final Act," (DFA) to which we have previously referred, reflected the results of the GATT Director-General's consultations with a cross section of the GATT membership. It covered all areas of the negotiations. For agriculture, it called for reductions over six years of 20 percent in internal support, 36 percent in external protection (with tariffication and a 15 percent minimum decrease) and a decrease in export subsidies of 35 percent in budget spending and 24 percent in volume of subsidized exports (see Paeman and Bensch (1995), pp.244-245). Reactions among GATT members were varied. The US position was that the DFA contained the basic elements needed to complete the Uruguay Round (see Paeman and Bensch (1995), pp.201-201). Japan, Switzerland and the Nordic countries considered that the DFA required revision. But, Cairns Group members Australia, Argentina and Brazil warned their negotiating partners not to call into question a text that they felt to be the embodiment of a very precarious balance. In Geneva, the spokesman for the developing countries held that though the text did not take sufficiently into account the concerns of the developing countries that it represented an important step forward in the negotiations.

Reactions to the DFA in the EC were themselves quite varied. French Prime Minister Edith Cresson denounced the draft as an American Diktat, some 50 hours before the paper was actually finalized (Paeman and Bensch (1995), p.202). Ireland also rejected the document. Agriculture Commissioner MacSharry reportedly called certain elements in the agricultural text unacceptable, notably no mention of rebalancing, or of direct aid to income as a Green Box measure (Vahl (1997), p.164). However, most EC members were willing to accept the DFA as a basis for

---

[99] Present at the meeting were US President Bush, Commission President Delors and Dutch Prime Minister Ruud Lubbers, on behalf of the Council Presidency.

negotiations, but criticized the agricultural section in particular (Vahl (1997), p.165). The position of the European Council taken at its Dec. 21 meeting was that agriculture chapter of the DFA called into question the very fundamentals of the CAP and needed modification (Paeman and Bensch (1995), p.202).

The DFA served as a focus for the agricultural trade negotiations as they continued into the spring of 1992, as there was no viable alternative. With the end of the CAP reform process in sight, there was guarded optimism that an agreement could be quickly reached. During a joint meeting of the EC Trade and Agriculture Ministers on January 11-12, 1992, Agriculture Commissioner MacSharry commented that he saw no reason why the deadline for the completion of the Uruguay Round by Easter could not be met (*Agra Europe*, Jan. 17, 1992: P/1). To move the process forward, President Bush in March put new agricultural proposals to Commission President Jacque Delors, which were reported to involve a more flexible treatment of income support (Vahl (1997), p.188). German Chancellor Kohl in return submitted a proposal, which also had the support of French President Mitterrand, asking the US to freeze the export of cereal substitutes to the EC in return for limits of subsidized EC exports (Vahl, 1997, p.188). No breakthrough was reached, but the outlook appeared promising. Yet, the French government watched the negotiations with growing apprehension, fearing that the Commission would "sacrifice" subsidized exports to save its income support scheme (Vahl (1997), p.186).

Referendum delays negotiating endgame With the completion of CAP reform in May, there were hopes that the agricultural trade negotiations could be soon concluded. However, this expectation proved overly optimistic. Massive demonstrations by French farmers protesting the MacSharry reforms increased French cautiousness about a GATT deal. When the Danish electorate rejected the Maastricht Agreement in a June, French President Mitterrand decided to put the Maastricht Agreement to a September referendum in France. The vote was expected to be close, so the French government wanted to put the GATT negotiations "on hold" until after the referendum. It was generally felt desirable not to give anti-Europeans more arguments with which to oppose progress toward further integration. And no internationally acceptable agreement of agriculture would ever find favor with the French farm lobby (Paeman and Bensch (1995), p.212).

At the G-7 meeting in July British Prime Minister John Major arranged private meetings between President Bush and European leaders, and tried to initiate the outline of a compromise (Vahl (1997), p.189). However, no agreement was reached with each side waiting for the other to make the first move. Bush and Mitterrand were both wary of open discussion in the G-7 as both faced major elections soon afterward. For Mitterrand, it was the September 20 Maastricht referendum and for Bush, the November Presidential election.

Following France's narrow approval of the Maastricht referendum things began to move quickly. On September 25, Commission President Jacques Delors received an urgent letter from President Bush calling for the resumption of talks (Paeman and Bensch (1995), p.213). Coming as it did in the midst of a Presidential campaign gave an indication of the high priority which Bush gave to a successful Uruguay Round. The plea for urgency resonated in Europe because of the imminent expiration of US Fast track authority, the increasing likelihood that Bush would lose the Presidential election and the uncertainty about Bill Clinton's stance on trade issues (interview). By now there was near consensus among EU governments, except for France, of the need to bring the GATT talks to a quick conclusion. The European Council, meeting on October 17, requested that the Commission work to bring the negotiations to conclusion before the end of the year within the framework of its mandate (Vahl (1997), p.192). France, apprehensive that too much would be given away took the position that the Commission should not go beyond what the EC Agricultural Ministers had explicitly sanctioned (Vahl (1997), p.192). British Prime Minister John Major reacted by stressing the Commission's authority to negotiate (Vahl (1997), p.192). Agriculture Commissioner Ray MacSharry indicated that the EC was ready to compromise, provided that its key demands were met (Vahl (1997), p.191).

US and EU trade negotiators met several times in October, and, though progress was made, agreement was still elusive. John Major, representing the Commission Presidency, then requested the November meeting in Chicago between MacSharry and Madigan to force a political breakthrough. MacSharry's brief resignation as chief agricultural trade negotiator after the failure of the meeting actually strengthened his position. In the ensuing intra-Commission conflict over the issue MacSharry emerged as victor, his authority vis-à-vis Delors strengthened, and with greater latitude to negotiate a deal with the Americans (Webber (1997), p.41). France was unable to obtain a qualified majority in the Council (of foreign and trade ministers) in favor of its demand for counter-retaliation against the threatened US trade sanctions. The *Financial Times* reported, "France had pulled out every stop to get Germany to back delay on the GATT, arguing that the government would fall and rioting would ensue if the agricultural subsidy cuts in the Uruguay Round were agreed (November 12, 1992). However, on this occasion, the German government aligned itself with Britain, Denmark, Holland, Luxembourg and Italy in insisting on a conciliatory approach toward the US (Webber (1997), p.41).

When US and EU negotiators met again at Blair House, the expectations were high in both Europe and America that an agreement could be reached. Yet, the bargaining was difficult. There were splits between and within both delegations. The account of Julius Katz, the Deputy US Trade representative is insightful.

> The Blair House meeting was wild, tension ridden and funny at times... [the meeting] ran over the course of twenty-four hours, with proposals and counter-proposals. Late in the afternoon, the stalemate seemed unresolvable. Part of the problem was that splits had developed within the delegations. MacSharry and Hills were more willing than were Andriessen and Madigan. The latter was concerned that the American farm groups would oppose the deal. After a series of conversations between individuals and groups, using every room on the first floor of Blair House, an understanding emerged which everyone could support, except Madigan. This led to delaying the decision overnight. Hills, Madigan and Katz met with Baker, Scowcroft and Eagleburger. It was agreed to put the decision to

President Bush early the next morning. Overnight Katz contacted various farm groups and reached one of Dean Kleckner's people who telephoned him in Australia and got his endorsement. The next morning Katz spoke to the head of the Soybean association (ASA) who said he was disappointed ("a bitter pill"), but acknowledged that we had done the best we could and said that ASA would not oppose the agreement.[100]

The politics in the US turned out to be so complex that President Bush had to make the final decision.

The Blair House Agreement still bore a resemblance to the Dunkel DFA in that the proposed reductions in internal support and external barriers were unchanged, with reductions over six years respectively of 20 percent and 36 percent. The export subsidy reductions remained at 36 percent in budget spending, but were reduced from 24 to 21 percent in volume. A new "blue box" was created shielding EC compensatory payments and US deficiency payments from domestic support reductions. The Peace Clause sheltering the fundamentals of the CAP from further GATT challenge was given a duration of six years. To settle the oilseeds issue, the EC made a commitment to reduce the base area sown to oilseeds in the 1989-91 period by 15 percent in 1993 and at least 10 percent in succeeding years.

Blair House stirs opposition in France The politics of EU acceptance of the Blair House agreement turned out to be much more complicated than US acceptance. MacSharry and Andriessen had made concessions at Blair House for which they did not have prior approval from the Council. However, they felt that they needed to take the lead and that they could sell Blair House to the Council, thus creating the synergistic effect predicted by Putnam, where an international agreement (level 1) would allow otherwise unachievable results in the Council (level 2) (see Webber (1997), p.42). The Commission accepted Blair House arguing that it was compatible with the MacSharry CAP reforms, but there was trouble in the Council of Ministers. Most EC member states were willing to go ahead with implementation of Blair House, some with reservations, but the news of the deal was greeted with outrage in France, where farming groups accused the Commission of selling out the interests of European agriculture under US pressure. The French government threatened that it would block the deal when it came up for approval, invoking the Luxembourg Compromise if necessary, and asked that the GATT agricultural trade talks be frozen until agreement had been reached in all other sectors.[101]

---

[100] Correspondence with the authors December 18, 1997. The individuals identified by Katz held the following positions: Carla Hills – US Trade Representative; Lawrence Eagleburger – US Deputy Secretary of State; James Baker – US Secretary of State; Brent Scowcroft – US Presidential National Security Advisor; Dean Kleckner, President of the American Farm Bureau.

[101] Though the Luxembourg Compromise, agreed by the Council in January 1966, when France returned to participation after a six months absence, has no legal status, there is still a possibility that the majority of the Council of Ministers would support the right of any member to block

The Commission, to forestall the veto threat, declared that the Blair House agreement would only be submitted to the Council as part of a final Uruguay Round agreement. Then, further aggravating the French, the Commission went ahead and submitted trade lists to the GATT in Geneva, allowing the EC to participate in the final dash to complete the Uruguay Round before the end of the Bush administration. The French government made an intense effort to mobilize support for its position among other EC members. It received sympathy from the governments of Ireland, Italy, Spain, Portugal, Greece and Belgium, worried that the Blair House agreement would conflict with CAP reform. However, none of these governments was willing to endanger the completion of the GATT talks. France made a particular effort to persuade its ally Germany. On December 7, a Franco-German summit was held in Bonn, but the two parties could not reach full agreement on Blair House. The German position was to implement the deal in the framework of CAP reform whereas the French government maintained that the deal was not compatible with CAP reform (Vahl (1997), p.197).

The Commission went ahead with its participation in the Geneva GATT talks, assuming that the Blair House agreement would stand, and the French government, while strenuously objecting, was unwilling to bring the situation to the point of crisis. President Mitterrand found himself between a rock and a hard place. On the one hand he faced a parliamentary election in March of 1993 and the socialists were highly unpopular. With 20 percent of the French electorate deriving income from agriculture, directly or indirectly, the risk of the socialists losing the election was greatly increased if Mitterrand did not block Blair House (Vahl (1997), p.217). On the other hand, an attempt to invoke the Luxembourg compromise would create a crisis in the EC, endangering the Maastricht agreement and dashing the hopes for deepening European integration.

There was too much to accomplish to complete the Uruguay Round before the Bush administration left office, at which point the negotiations were temporarily in limbo until the Clinton administration could decide how to proceed. It would take some time for the new US Trade representative, Mickey Kantor and new Secretary of Agriculture, Mike Espy to get fully up to speed on GATT issues and to establish rapport with their new EC counterparts, Sir Leon Brittan and Rene Steichen. The Commission was also reluctant to press the GATT talks until after the French election.

Blair House II – Accommodating the French

Both sides in the French political campaign thought the Blair House accords ought to be re-negotiated on the grounds that it gave too much away to the US Jacques Chirac, the conservative coalition leader, even went so far as tell an election rally that France should resort to an "empty chair" policy in the EC to block a GATT agreement which went against its agricultural interests (*Agra Europe*, March 12,1993: P/1). The pre-election atmosphere was so bad in France that the European Commission postponed

---

Council action if 'vital' national interests are involved. This was demonstrated most recently when Greece blocked the agriculture price package.

submitting the oilseed part of the Blair House Agreement (not part of the GATT) to a vote in the Council of Ministers out of fear that the French government would use the Luxembourg compromise to block approval.

Interestingly, throughout this period, the European Commission vigorously defended the Blair House agreement. This was true, even for Guy Legras, the Commission's Director General for Agriculture, who was French. He insisted that the EC's prospective GATT Commitments could be accommodated within already approved CAP reform. He was especially dismissive of French suspicions about the Commission's calculations on CAP/GATT compatibility, accusing Paris of creating a "nightmare scenario" (*Agra Europe*, March 12, 1993: E/3).

The general atmosphere for the Uruguay Round improved in April after the conservative coalition won a landslide victory in the French parliamentary elections. France's new Prime Minister, the moderate Gaullist, Eduard Balladur, signaled a move away from extreme election campaign positions on both the oilseeds issue and the GATT negotiations. Sources close to Balladur said that the government was not willing to risk a crisis in the EC or in the GATT talks and that he wanted "trade peace" with Washington. "We don't want to bring the roof down," said an aide to Balladur. "We are looking for solutions without provoking a crisis" (*Agra Europe*, April 8, 1993: P/1). There was speculation in Brussels that Balladur could accept the Blair House agreement, avoiding responsibility by blaming his predecessor (Paeman and Bensch (1995), p.238).

However, this speculation ignored political realities in France. During the election campaign many of the leading names of the new majority had vociferously denounced both the Blair House agreement and the government that had been powerless to prevent it. Now that the conservatives were in power it was very difficult to reverse course (Webber (1997), p.44). Besides, the new government counted farmers as a core electoral clientele.

The Balladur government decided to pursue a "double track" policy on the Blair House accord (see Webber (1997), p.44). On the one hand, to show good will, and because it was a "good deal" for the EU, France would accept the oilseeds component of the agreement (Webber (1997), p.44). On the other, France would continue to insist on the renegotiation of the GATT component of the Blair House agreement, declaring that the overall accord was "unacceptable in its present form," with the need for rebalancing with respect to cereal substitutes and an upward adjustment in export subsidy limits.

Supporters of the GATT breathed a sign of relief when the new French Agriculture Minister, Jean Puech, announced at the end of April that France would accept the oilseeds agreement in return for an improvement in set-aside compensation (*Agra Europe*, April 30, 1993: E/3). Even though this demand added to an already strained EC agriculture budget, it was approved by the other agriculture ministers in May as part of the annual price package (*Agra Europe*, May 28, 1993: E/1). Approval of the oilseeds deal was critical for the GATT, because rejection would guarantee US retaliatory sanctions that would scuttle the Uruguay Round talks.

Pursuing the other leg of its strategy, France demanded a meeting of a "Jumbo" council of EU foreign ministers, trade ministers and agricultural ministers to discuss re-opening negotiations on Blair House. This request was reluctantly granted by the Commission and by other governments. The key to French success at this meeting would be to elicit support from the German government. This would not be an easy task, as the Kohl government did not want to do anything that might delay or endanger an overall GATT agreement. The internal balance in the Kohl government had shifted in the pro-GATT direction with the January, 1993 resignation of hard-line agriculture minister Ignaz Kiechle and his replacement by Jochen Borchert, who was less hostile to Blair House.

At first, the German government appeared deaf to Balladur's pleas for support. To make his case personally, Balladur traveled to Bonn in August to try to turn Kohl around and enlist his support to oblige the Commission to try to re-negotiate the Blair House agreement with the US (Webber (1997), p.44). He apparently made two arguments that strengthened the elements in the German government supporting the French position (see Webber (1997), pp.44-46). One of these arguments was that unless Blair House was re-opened, he would either have to "veto" the agreement, or his government would fall. Either way the Uruguay Round would have collapsed: an outcome precipitating a crisis in the EC as well as in trans-Atlantic relations. The other argument which had an impact on the Germans was that the Blair House export subsidy limits might lead to increased French cereal exports to Germany, thus harming German farmers. Following the summit, the German position, expressed in meetings at the ministerial level between the two governments, apparently shifted to getting France to moderate its demands, emphasizing how important it was that the GATT talks be concluded successfully (Webber (1997), p.47).[102]

The Jumbo Council meeting on September 20, billed as an EC showdown on the agricultural dossier of the Uruguay Round, displayed elements of a major drama. French farmers conducted massive demonstrations as a lead-in to the meeting to make sure that the ministers understood their displeasure (see *Financial Times*, Sept. 20, 1993). The meeting developed quickly into a confrontation between External Affairs Commissioner Brittan and French Foreign Minister Alain Juppe (see Webber (1997), p.48). Brittan refused to try to renegotiate the Blair House agreement, although he referred to the possibility of trying to clarify issues. Juppe took a tough stance, insisting on re-opening negotiations. Emotions ran high. At one point, Juppe was reported to have described Brittan as a "petty official who had overstepped his brief"

---

[102] Not only was the French government subject to German pressures to moderate its positions, but it also received strong messages from French business interests that a GATT failure would adversely affect their interests. By this time, the stakes of a multilateral trade deal were so high in France that the making of policy on agriculture in the GATT had been taken away from the Ministry of Agriculture, which worked closely with farm organizations, and placed in the hands of the Interministerial consisting of offices of the President, Prime Minister and the ministries of foreign affairs, finance, industry and agriculture. Thus, the voice of the farm lobby in the agricultural policy process was greatly weakened and the voice of industry strengthened (see Epstein, 1997).

(*Agra Europe*, Sept. 24, 1992: E/1). At another point, UK Foreign Secretary Douglas Hurd implied that his government would boycott EC Councils if the Community's agricultural problems blocked a GATT deal. The French position was backed more or less by the Southern member states and Ireland, but opposed by the UK, Holland and Luxembourg (Webber (1997), p.49). The German Foreign Minister, Klaus Kinkel clearly took Brittan's side at the outset, saying that Germany opposed re-negotiation but was ready to support consultations designed to 'clarify' the accord (Webber (1997), p.49).

The balance in the Council began to shift when Juppe moderated his demand for re-negotiation, saying that the actual conduct of talks with the US and their outcome was more important than how the talks were labeled (Webber (1997), p.49). At this point, the German delegation shifted its position in support of the French. Then, efforts turned to coming up with a compromise position that would win the approval of the other EC members that had sided with Brittan. The compromise that emerged was that "amplifications and clarifications" would be sought on a number of areas of concern to France and the other delegations. These areas included the Peace Clause, cereal substitutes, aggregation of products and disposal of stocks (*Agra Europe*, Sept. 24, 1993: E/1). Brittan emerged with bargaining leeway because most of the EC members wanted the GATT talks to succeed.

Sir Leon Brittan then commenced what became an extended series of meetings with his counterpart, US Trade Representative Mickey Kantor. The US, then in the midst of the Congressional debate to approve the North American Free Trade Agreement, at first refused to re-open the Blair House agreements. However, after NAFTA had been ratified on November 17, the US agreed to discuss EC concerns. Finally, on December 5, Kantor and Brittan announced that they had reached an agreement modifying the Blair House accords, which they hoped would open the way to the successful completion of the Uruguay Round (*Financial Times*, Dec. 6, 1993, p.3). This agreement included US concessions that went a good way toward meeting French demands. More specifically, the two parties agreed first to exempt Europe's existing 25 million tonnes cereals stockpile from the Blair House accord. Second, they agreed to switch the base year from which subsidized exports must be reined in from the 1986-89 average to 1992. Since subsidized EU cereal exports rose from 17 million tonnes during the initial base period to over 20 million tonnes in 1992, the switch greatly reduced the impact of the Blair House accord, and over the six year life of the agreement would Europe (principally France) to export an additional 8m tonnes of cereals.[103] Third, they agreed to extend from six to nine years the "peace clause." The price paid by the EU for these US concessions included market access for US pork, grains, dairy products and "specialty crops" - which include nuts, vegetables, processed turkey and almonds. Since these concessions were not expected to yield significant new export opportunities for the US, the EC gave ground by trimming tariffs on a number of manufactured goods. The outcome was a win-win situation.

---

[103] The agreement also allowed the US more subsidized exports than would have been possible under the Blair House Agreement - to the chagrin of the Cairns Group.

Both sides could proclaim victory. France accepted the agreement after receiving some reassurances that additional measures would be taken if the agricultural deal turned out to be incompatible with CAP reform. Thus the way was cleared for the successful completion of the Uruguay Round.

7.6 The URAA and Domestic Policy Reform

The Uruguay Round Agreement on Agriculture (URAA) established a set of completely new and more operational rules for agriculture. In particular, it resulted in a legally effective binding of tariff rates for agricultural goods and imposed constraints on the most trade-distorting types of agricultural policies used throughout the world. This fact in itself is a major change in the way in which agriculture is treated in the GATT. In the past, governments had considerable scope to design and pursue their agricultural policies as they saw fit for domestic interests and to treat agriculture as a special case under trade rules. As a result, the GATT did not effectively constrain most of the government actions in agriculture that impacted trade. After the Uruguay Round, governments had to observe binding commitments they had accepted under international law. These bindings covered nearly all border measures, both on the import and on the export side, and they also applied to the total of trade-distorting domestic support, to the extent that this support has a noticeable effect on international trade. The implications for domestic policy are discussed below. But it is hard to overestimate the significance of this fundamental change in the scope of the trade rules. An important sector in world trade, which had escaped most GATT disciplines since the inception of the General Agreement, was now for the first time effectively brought under control.

The relationship between the Agreement on Agriculture and domestic policy is best understood by considering the three major areas on which negotiations focused - import access, export competition, and domestic support. In each of these three areas, two approaches were applied: the definition of new rules and the reduction in levels of support and protection. The reduction schedules contained the specific "concessions" on market access and commitments on export and domestic subsidies. Each substantive area included a set of safeguards, guarantees and accommodations that were necessary to get agreement. In addition, a Peace Clause, was negotiated which gave countries certain assurances against challenges under GATT rules. The provisions of the agreement apply less stringently to developing countries under the principle of "Special and Differential Treatment." A separate Agreement on Sanitary and Phytosanitary Measures (known as the SPS Agreement) was also concluded, with somewhat more indirect impact on domestic policy.[104]

---

[104] See Josling, Tangermann and Warley (1996) for a full account of the Agreement: the text is to be found in WTO (1996). Commentary on the implementation of the Agreement is to be found in IATRC (1997).

7.7 Market Access

Perhaps the most far-reaching element in the Agreement was the change in the rules regarding market access. With a few temporary derogations, all participating countries agreed to convert all existing non-tariff barriers (along with unbound tariffs) into bound duties and not to introduce new non-tariff measures. The new bound tariffs, as well as tariffs bound earlier, were to be reduced by 36 percent over the six-year implementation period (1995 to 2000), on a simple (unweighted) average basis, with a minimum rate of reduction of 15 percent for each tariff line. The agreement to convert all non-tariff import barriers to bound tariffs took agricultural trade a big step toward the treatment of manufactures within the GATT. It also represented a major constraint on the operation of domestic policy instruments.[105]

Domestic policies and trade policies act in tandem to support domestic markets and increase farm receipts. Border measures are needed to prevent imports from undercutting national markets. Domestic measures traditionally have focused on the marketing of the domestic crop or livestock product, either fixing a price at which public or private agents buy from farmers or controlling supplies on to the market to raise the price. But fixing a domestic price is of little use if consumers can merely buy from abroad. Border controls are therefore needed as a backup to the domestic price policy. Controlling quantities similarly is ineffective in raising price if imports can come in to substitute for domestic production. Once again the control at the border is an important part of the policy. Free trade would obviously limit the use of domestic price policies and render domestic quantity controls ineffectual. A fixed tariff has a less dramatic impact but moves in the same direction. It limits the effectiveness of both price-fixing policies and quantity-control instruments. The introduction of fixed tariffs in the URAA effectively puts a limit on domestic price policies and a strong constraint on the usefulness of quantity control policies. The full impact of these constraints will not be felt until the level of tariffs is reduced to a much lower level, in subsequent rounds of WTO negotiations. But the fact that the rule has been established has changed permanently the context in which domestic agricultural policy is formulated. The linkage between market access and domestic policy has other aspects. To secure minimum trade gains when tariffs were bound at prohibitively high levels, and to counter the ability of state trading import agencies to restrict trade, the agreement provided in cases of tariffication for "minimum access opportunities", generally a share of the domestic market rising from 3 percent to 5 percent of consumption. The introduction of so-called Tariff Rate Quotas (TRQs) was intended to provide for this access, as well as to ensure continued access for pre-existing quotas where exporters enjoyed preferential market access in the past. Although importation of these minimum quantities was not guaranteed, to ensure an incentive to fill these quotas, "low or minimal duties" were to be charged on these imports. The impact on domestic policy

---

[105] For a discussion of the merits of tariffication for the trade system see IATRC (1989).

varies by commodity. But in those cases where domestic quotas exists, such as with milk and sugar in the EU, dairy products in Canada and sugar in the US, the operation of the TRQs has been important in the development of the domestic market. The system of non-reciprocal commodity preferences given to selected developing countries by both the EU and the US are themselves operated through the TRQ system: increasingly it is being realized that the URAA has important impacts on the way in which such programs are administered.

7.8 Export Competition

The ability of countries to define and control export subsidies in agriculture was one of the main issues under discussion in the negotiation. It was among the most contentious items of disagreement between the US and the EU in the negotiations. The Agreement for the first time imposed a ban on new export subsidies, though existing subsidies were allowed to continue subject to agreed reductions. The Schedules establish the level of such subsidies deemed to exist in the base period. Based on these past levels of export subsidization, countries have accepted legally binding commitments regarding maximum export subsidization in the future. Hence, for the first time there can no longer be any doubts as to what (maximum) level of export subsidies a country can grant in agricultural trade. Under the Agreement, countries accepted commitments leading to a reduction in expenditure on export subsidies of 36 percent as well as a reduction in the quantity of subsidized exports by 21 percent during the six-year implementation period. To provide some flexibility, countries have been able to shift their export subsidy commitments between individual years of the implementation period. Export credit schemes were not included in the commitments, and countries have not yet been able to agree on their limitation.

The link between export subsidies and domestic market support is almost as fundamental as that between market access and domestic price and quantity controls. In the absence of the ability to dispose of surpluses, domestic markets are in danger of collapse from occasional or regular oversupply. Competitive exporters, whose domestic market price is at the level of the world market price do not need such aids. But whenever prices are set at a higher level it is as important to have an outlet for surpluses as it is to stop the inroad of competitive imports. Thus restraining the ability of countries to set prices for export items at too high a level represents a fundamental change in the nature of domestic farm policy. Once again the impact of this constraint will become clearer as the level of export subsidies allowed is reduced in further negotiations.

7.9 Domestic Support

The most innovative feature of the Agreement was the negotiation of a set of rules for and commitments for domestic support policies, though in practice the near-term influence of this innovation is likely to be modest. Given the nature of the link between domestic agricultural policies and international trade, the fact that GATT commitments now impose quantitative constraints on certain types of domestic support is itself significant. The impact has already had an effect on the development of domestic policies in both the EU and the US and is likely to continue to do so in the future. The domestic support commitments could with little exaggeration be called the first multilateral agricultural policy.

The nature of the constraint on domestic support warrants some explanation. The variable constrained under the "domestic support" commitments includes both expenditure on domestic subsidies and the value of administered market price maintenance, measured against fixed external reference prices of the base period. This domestic support is measured by the Aggregate Measurement of Support (AMS), which can be aggregated over both policy instruments and commodities. The Agreement specified the method of calculation of the AMS, required countries to enter their base period (1986-88) AMS in their Schedules, and sets the rate of reduction of 20 percent over the six-year implementation period, resulting in annual AMS commitments specified in the country Schedules.

However, rather than binding all policies, measures "with no, or at most minimal, trade distortion effects or effects on production" were exempted from reduction commitments under the AMS approach (and indeed not included in the AMS calculation). This "green box" was defined in both general form and in terms of a list of eligible policies which included measures such as advisory services, domestic food aid, decoupled income support, income insurance and safety-net programs, set-aside payments (if land is retired for a minimum of three years), regional and environmental aids and those that encourage early-retirement. In addition to the green box policies, a *de minimis* provision exempted support below five percent of the value of production of any given commodity. "Green-box" policies are not actionable for purposes of GATT challenges (see the discussion of the Peace Clause, below). Policies that are not accepted as "green" automatically become subject to reduction commitments (i.e., are included in an "amber" box) as a part of the AMS.

As a result of the Blair House Accord between the United States and the EU, another exemption was agreed. It was decided that neither the US deficiency payments (as authorized under the 1990 Farm Bill) nor the compensation payments under the MacSharry reforms of the Common Agricultural Policy of the EU need to be included in the AMS calculation. In this way, both the US and the EU escaped the reduction commitment on major aspects of their domestic policy. The wording chosen for this exclusion (called the "blue box") exempted "direct payments under production-limiting programs" provided that they are made on the basis of fixed area and yield (or number of head for livestock) or on a maximum of 85 percent of base level of production. Another important consequence of the Blair House Accord was the decision to make domestic support commitments not product-specific but sector-wide, thus allowing some heavily subsidized sectors to avoid the disciplines of the AMS constraint.

The significance for domestic farm policy of the amber, blue and green boxes is obviously more direct than the significance of the market access and export competition aspects of the URAA. A framework now exists for the direct challenge of domestic policies of other countries if they give support in a particular way (deemed to be trade distorting) above a particular level. The fact that challenges have not been made is itself evidence of the extent to which domestic policies have generally been restrained to comply with the URAA. It is not so much that the URAA dictated changes that were reluctantly adopted by domestic legislatures. It was more that domestic policy changes were endorsed by the WTO and given a legitimacy that makes it difficult for countries to return to the types of policies that were the major cause of trade problems in the 1980s. International acceptance of green (and blue) box policies has made reform both easier and less controversial. The fact that the "new" policies have also found domestic acceptance has undoubtedly helped to avoid clashes between domestic and international agendas.

Though the significance is relatively direct, the actual impact of the domestic support commitments (at least for the US and the EU but also for most of the OECD countries) has been relatively little. The process of domestic policy reform has in effect rendered the already relatively small AMS reductions minimally binding. Few countries have made full use of their amber box allowance. But ironically this can be interpreted as an indication that a shift to green box policies has taken place enough to make the amber box less restrictive than it would otherwise have been.

7.10 The "Peace Clause"

As an incentive for countries to accept the new disciplines and commitments on domestic support and export subsidies, it was agreed that policies that conform to the new rules are sheltered from international challenge under the GATT. The Due Restraint provisions, known as the Peace Clause, valid during the implementation period, state that "green box" policies (in accordance with Annex 2 of the Agreement) are non-actionable for purposes of countervailing duties and other GATT challenges; domestic support that conforms with commitments, including "blue box" payments under production-limiting programs (i.e. US deficiency payments and EU compensation payments) is subject to the imposition of countervailing duties only if they can be shown to have caused injury, and is exempt from other WTO challenges as long as support does not exceed the level operative in 1992; and export subsidies within the constraints of the Agreement are exempt from most WTO challenge and subject to countervailing duties only if they cause injury.[106]

---

[106] The injury provision already exists in the GATT rules on countervailing duties and is not a new feature of the Uruguay Round. The other GATT challenges include "nullification and impairment" of a country's GATT obligations and "serious prejudice" to another country's interests, usually in third markets.

The Peace Clause is a particularly interesting part of the URAA. In effect it provides shelter from challenge for most if not all of the domestic farm policies of the WTO members so long as they are within the constraints of the blue and green boxes, as well as giving less generous protection to allowable export subsidies. Without such a provision it is doubtful whether the EU could have agreed to the constraints on the CAP indicated by the URAA. The prospect of having first to tailor the CAP instruments to the new rules and then to have them be subject to countervailing duties and WTO challenges would seem like double jeopardy. The price for allowing the new rules was to be relieved from additional hazards of legal redress.

7.11 Experience with the Implementation of the Agreement

So far the Uruguay Round Agreement on Agriculture seems to have been implemented with reasonable diligence by both the EU and the US, as well as by other countries, as they assimilated its provisions into legislation and practice. Over all the main thrusts of the Agreement, the move to tariffs as the only import barrier, the binding of existing export subsidies, and the categorization of domestic support measures by their trade-restrictiveness have proceeded smoothly. The revisions to the agreement that are currently being discussed are more in the nature of completing and tidying up rather than correcting significant mistakes. It is useful to consider how the URAA impacted on US and EU policy before discussing the implications for the policy process.

7.12 Effect of the URAA on Domestic Policy in the United States

The United States has been able to implement the provisions of the Uruguay Round Agreement on Agriculture with relatively little change in domestic policies. In this regard the experience of the US has been different from that of the EU, where the impacts were more immediate.[107] Indeed it was useful to secure the domestic political support for the outcome of the Round that the US appeared to have gained access to other markets for agricultural products while not relinquishing the responsibility for policy making to international negotiations. Nevertheless the Agreement has had some impact on policy developments and has at the least encouraged changes that have been implemented for largely domestic reasons. And these domestic policy changes in turn have had the effect of increasing the significance of international trade negotiations on domestic policy.

The market access provisions in the Uruguay Round Agreement on Agriculture did not lead to a dramatic opening up of the US market for agricultural goods. For many products trade barriers were low before the Round, while for the few "sensitive" items such as dairy products and sugar liberalization was modest. Conversion of non-

---

[107] More detail of the implementation of the Agreement in the US is given in the chapter by Sumner in IATRC (1997).

tariff barriers to tariffs took place in several sectors, notably in beef, where "voluntary export restraints" (to avoid the imposition of quantitative restrictions) had been used to bolster the domestic market over parts of the cattle cycle, and in dairy, where non-tariff import barriers had been widely used to control milk product markets. In these cases TRQs were established to maintain access (beef) and provide for minimum access (dairy) along the lines of the Agreement. Above-quota tariffs remain high for the sensitive goods. Although tariff levels for all agricultural goods were cut on average by 36 percent over the period up to 2000, the US took advantage of the minimum allowable cut of 15 percent for dairy and sugar products. This leaves action on these commodities a natural focus for the next round of negotiations.

Implementation of the Agreement had one impact that was significant in terms of domestic policy. Section 22 of the Agricultural Adjustment Act, which gave the President the mandate to use quantitative controls whenever imports threatened domestic support programs, was removed. This in turn removed the need for the waiver from GATT rules that had been in effect since 1956. The importance of this is symbolic: it indicates that even the US has agreed to allow the operation of international trade under agreed rules to impinge upon domestic programs. But it also has a real impact, in that the ability to use quantitative restrictions on domestic production to raise domestic prices is now significantly curtailed.

Export subsidy programs in the US were also subject to the cuts agreed in the Round. However the rise in world prices in the two years after the Agreement came into effect, in 1995 and 1996, meant that export subsidies for cereals naturally declined. But the enthusiasm for using export subsidies in any case declined, and Congressional appropriation for subsidies has actually decreased substantially in recent years. The Export Enhancement Program (EEP) is unlikely to be used to its fully authorized level in the near future. This is a major change from the attitude that export subsidies are necessary aspects of commercial policy to be used to maintain market shares and prevent the EU and other exporters from undercutting US sales abroad.

As was expected, the Uruguay Round Agreement has had little impact on US domestic support programs such as the deficiency payments scheme for cereals. That was ensured by the Blair House deal which allowed both the US and the EU to shelter their direct payments in the "blue box" reserved for payments linked to supply control programs. Even without this it is unlikely that the level of payments would have violated the AMS limits that had as a base a period of higher subsidies. Moreover, even the very indirect restraints of the "blue box" were made redundant for the US by the substantial changes in domestic policy embodied in the FAIR Act of 1996.

7.13 Implementation in the European Union

The EU had to reform its Common Agricultural Policy (CAP) in 1992 in order to be able to agree to the Uruguay Round outcome. Unlike in the US, where the Uruguay Round had relatively little impact on the operation of domestic policy, the EU has had to make still more changes since that time in order to implement the terms of the

Agreement. Nevertheless the policy changes were kept to a minimum by various devices that have preserved much of the instrumentalities of the CAP. The cereals market, for example, is still protected by a variant of the variable levy, as a result of the bilateral deal at Blair House (later multilateralised) that the duty paid price of imports should not exceed 155 percent of the intervention price (the prevailing threshold price).[108] Similarly with the import duties for fruits and vegetables, the use of tariffs conditional upon the relationship of import prices to predetermined "entry" prices acts much as the previous policy of supplementary duties triggered by reference prices.[109]

Not only have the mechanisms determining market access changed little, the ease of access into the EU has improved only marginally. TRQs exist in a number of products, but for the most part these reflect "current access" (i.e. the bilateral agreements that the EU has had with a number of overseas countries). In those cases where new "minimum access" quotas have been opened up, they have often gone to countries with which the EU has trade agreements. The above-quota tariffs are often prohibitive, as were the threshold prices that they replaced, and true market access awaits the next round of trade negotiations. In some cases market access actually declined as a result of tariffication.[110]

On the export side the picture has been very different. It was always known that the constraints on export subsidies negotiated in the Round were likely to be the most binding on the EU: that is why the agreement on such constraints was so difficult to achieve. This has proved to be the case. For a number of products, wheat, sugar, beef and cheese in particular, the export subsidy constraints have already dictated domestic policy decisions. However, in the case of wheat, the high world prices "rescued" the policy from the constraints of the WTO schedule in 1995 and 1996, as the need for export subsidies temporarily waned. The ability of the EU to "bank" some of the export subsidy allowance enabled it to avoid some of the adjustment that otherwise would have been necessary. And in the case of cheese, the export restriction has to some extent been circumvented by the production of processed cheese in bond through the use of already "exported" butter and skimmed milk combined with imported cheese.[111]

The CAP reform of 1992 was clearly a major domestic farm policy change. It allowed the Uruguay Round to be completed. It would therefore be unrealistic to expect that the URAA would produce a further change in domestic policy as a part of

---

[108] There was a long dispute, now settled, between the US and Canada and the EU on the issue of whether the maximum duty-paid price should apply to each transaction (as the Agreement appeared to say) or to all transactions at a particular time. Clearly there would have been major implications for the incentive to ship different qualities of grain.

[109] If the import price is less than 92 percent of the "entry" price then a high (often prohibitive) tariff applies. (See the chapter by Tangermann in IATRC (1997).

[110] This was particularly the case where levies were previously tied to domestic cereal prices, as with pigmeat. CAP reform had already reduced import levies on pigmeat, but they went back up again when based on the tariff equivalent in the WTO base period. See IATRC (1997).

[111] See IATRC (1997).

the implementation of the agreement. Indeed the deal secured at Blair House to place the MacSharry compensation payments in the "blue box", implying that they did not count toward the level of support that needed to be reduced (and are sheltered by the Peace Clause from most WTO challenges unless they are increased), ensured that the EU stayed well within the AMS constraint. The pressure for domestic policy change has not so far been enough to move the main mechanisms of the CAP away from the 1992 reform mechanisms. The issue for the next round will be whether the EU can change its method of allocating the compensation payments so as not to need the blue box at all.

7.14   Explanations for the Success of the Round

The Uruguay Round clearly achieved much, even if it did not live up to everyone's expectations. But what were the ingredients of a successful trade round? Why was agreement possible in 1993 when it was not possible at the end of 1990? The answer seems to lie not in skillful negotiations or in the desire to put trade relations above domestic political concerns. The URAA was possible because it provided a useful counterpart to the paradigm changes that were taking places in domestic policy. It encouraged such changes and locked them in. The new trade rules were consistent with the model of agricultural policy that was taking over domestic political discussion in the United States. In other words the Competitive Agriculture paradigm implied a view of a stable and open world market (a "level playing field") that was relatively unhampered by high tariffs, export subsidies, and trade distorting domestic support. For some countries, such as those in the Cairns Group, the new paradigm formed a prominent part of the rhetoric of their negotiating stance. The US, with its strong export interest, had broadly gone along with the trade implications of the new paradigm though at the same time sheltering import competing sectors such as dairy and sugar from the implications of a more competitive world market. In others, including the EU, the Competitive Agriculture paradigm was being absorbed only slowly and with considerable domestic resistance. Eventually the Multifunctionality paradigm emerged as a way of reconciling these international pressures with the perceived political necessity of maintaining income support for European agriculture. But at the time of the Marrakesh Agreement one would have had to conclude that EU farming was headed towards an era of intense competition on world markets.

The Uruguay Round, in addition to reinforcing the paradigm shifts in domestic farm policy, helped to internationalize policy making in the agricultural area. Developed country governments spent almost ten years, from the setting up of the GATT Agriculture Committee and the OECD Trade Mandate to the final agreement in Marrakesh, discussing and debating their farm policies and their trade impacts. Although there were intense disagreements over this period, it nevertheless represented a major departure from the period of non-transparent domestic policies and closed decision processes. A realist view of this process would presumably focus on the fact that concessions came reluctantly and with great pressure. Governments did not give up any sovereignty over agricultural policy, though they agreed to a set of rules that would constrain their action in return for the constraints on that of others.

But this explanation may short-change the role of institutions in the process. It is relevant, for instance, to ask what role did the GATT, as an institution, play in brokering a deal? The Secretariat itself constituted a small group of lawyers and economists whose main function was to service the delegates, keep straight the paperwork and organize meetings. Little actual policy advocacy took place during the Round, though considerable expertise existed if needed by delegates. However, the activities of the Secretariat clearly became more important as the negotiations developed. Some control over the agenda was maintained particularly as national politicians rotated into and out of trade positions. The Director General intervened personally in the negotiations on two crucial occasions.[112] But in addition to the activities of the Secretariat, the body of ambassadors in Geneva who did much of the negotiating, acted as a permanent "institution" with collective memory, standard operating procedures and even common objectives that may not always have reflected those of their political bosses in the capitals.

---

[112] The role of Arthur Dunkel was particularly critical, both in terms of his efforts to keep the negotiation process going and his active interest in the substance. Peter Sutherland added political weight, after his appointment, that facilitated the final agreement.

Chapter 8

The FAIR Act of 1996 - Decoupling Payments from Production

8.1 The Development of the FAIR ACT

With the Uruguay Round complete and the World Trade Organization underway, agricultural policy reform efforts shifted back to the domestic arena. New domestic action came first in the US, where new legislation was needed with the expiration in 1995 of the 1990 farm bill. Since US agricultural policy, with the changes instituted in the 1990, seemed well within the parameters set by the Uruguay Round Agricultural Agreement, there really were no strong international pressures for further reform. However, as we shall see, the changing US domestic situation catalyzed significant new reform.

The Republican Party won a stunning victory in the 1994 congressional election, winning control of both Houses of Congress. This was the first time that the GOP had controlled the House of Representatives for 40 years. The new majority, with 76 freshman legislators, was committed to the House Republican "Contract with America" campaign agenda. This agenda stressed fiscal discipline, lower taxes and the devolution of government from the federal level back to the states. All Federal entitlement programs including agriculture would be under scrutiny (see Schertz and Doering (1999), p.8). This chapter describes the development of the 1996 Farm Bill, known as the Federal Agriculture Improvement Reform (FAIR) Act, and the impact that it had on farm policy reform.

The FAIR Act introduced fundamental changes in US farm policy, in the direction of further de-coupling income support from production. Target prices, deficiency payments, and the Acreage Reduction Program (ARP) were eliminated. Farmers who had participated in government support programs in any one of the last five years were given the freedom to grow whatever they wanted, except fruits and vegetables, on land previously part of their commodity program base acreage. Instead of deficiency payments, producers would receive guaranteed, fixed declining government payments under seven year production flexibility contracts (PFCs) for 1996-2002. Payments would be based on 85 percent of their base acreage and program yield regardless of market conditions. Participating farmers had to adhere to environmental protection requirements for erodible land and wetlands.

The FAIR Act of 1996 - Decoupling Payments from Production

The Clinton Administration Develops its Recommendations

The process of developing the Clinton administration farm bill recommendations in 1995 was very similar to the process employed by the Bush administration in 1990. Issues were discussed in USDA soon after the completion of the Uruguay Round, in January 1994. Secretary Mike Espy began the formal planning process with a meeting in September 1994. Task forces were assigned to examine specific issue areas and they reported to a central planning committee. There was much greater involvement of agencies outside USDA in the planning process than in 1990. The White House took a much greater interest than in previous farm bills, insisting on greater market orientation. The Office of Management and Budget played a significant role. The Environmental Protection Agency (EPA) participated on issues related to conservation and the environment, as did the Department of the Interior and the Council on Environmental Quality. The Council of Economic Advisors and the Department of State participated on trade issues. The Department of the Treasury participated on some issues. The planning process was also influenced by a series of farm bill forums held around the country. The task forces met during the fall of 1994, producing a large number of papers. The central planning group met weekly from January of 1995 preparing the administration recommendations. The new Secretary of Agriculture, Dan Glickman, joined the discussions after he was confirmed in March 1995.[113]

While the USDA planning process was in its final stages, in February 1995, the President submitted a five-year budget to Congress supportive of agricultural spending.[114] This proposed budget continued to fund deficiency payments, which the Office of Management and Budget (OMB) projected to decline as prices rose due to strong market demand. Funding was also provided for the CRP, which Congress was expected to re-authorize. The budget imposed fiscal discipline by requiring a $1.5 billion reduction in commodity policy outlays in the years 1998-2000, but did not specify how this saving would be achieved.

In May 1995, the administration sent its recommendations to Congress as a set of guidelines.[115] These called for maintaining the traditional program structure of target prices and loan rates, modified to increase flexibility, allowing farmers to plant their base acreages in any program crops without losing program benefits. The guidelines recommended that the percentage of non-payment acres should be increased from the 15 percent specified in the 1990 Farm Bill to achieve a portion of the necessary reductions in outlays recommended in the President's FY 1996 budget. They also recommended extension of the Conservation Reserve and Wetlands Reserve programs. Overall, the guidelines did not depart greatly from the *status quo* of the 1990 farm bill, though they foresaw a gradual transition to a more market-oriented farm sector.

---

[113] Secretary of Agriculture Mike Espy resigned in December 1994.

[114] For detailed discussions of the development of the farm bill see Orden, Paarlberg and Roe, (1999), CQ Almanac (1995 & 1996), and Schertz and Doering (1999).

[115] The "Blue Book," 1995 Farm Bill: Guidance of the Administration, USDA, May 1995.

Gradual change was seen as beneficial to the economic stability of farmers and ranchers.

Formulation of the Farm Bill in Congress

The passage of the FAIR Act through the US Congress is one of the more unusual and surprising developments in farm policy in recent years. Though the outlook at first was for a *status quo* farm bill, a path-breaking new decoupling initiative by House Agriculture Committee Chairman Pat Roberts (R-KS) called "Freedom to Farm" built up a groundswell of support and became the centerpiece of the FAIR Act.

First Initiatives in the Senate

The new Republican chairman of the Senate Agriculture committee, Richard Lugar of Indiana, had a much more aggressive agenda for agricultural policy reform than the administration. After the 1994 election, Lugar indicated that he wanted to make a thorough reevaluation of the objectives of farm programs and of the policies designed to achieve these objectives. In December, he circulated a list of 53 critical questions that he intended to address in Senate hearings, soliciting ideas from a very broad audience of 1000, including farmers, academics and agri-business executives. He received significant feedback, but no consensus appeared in the views expressed. Most of the 135 responses suggested limited adjustments to one or another existing program. However, a small number called for major changes.[116]

In February and March 1995, well before he received the administration's recommendations, Senator Lugar held public hearings on the new farm bill. He employed a different process than the one employed in 1990, when each day's hearing was devoted to a particular set of issues, beginning with a USDA witness, followed by testimony from various interested groups. Lugar wanted to provoke a broader debate in 1995, so he didn't begin with USDA, but instead invited a broad diversity of witnesses to express their views to the committee. General dissatisfaction with existing farm programs stood out in the hearings. Farmers wanted more flexibility in planting and they disliked required unpaid ARP set-asides, although they supported voluntary CRP paid set-asides on fragile land (interview).[117] Another theme was the benefit to the US of expanded agricultural production. Testimony indicated an increased international demand for food in the future. If the US did not respond to this demand, it would be

---

[116] Among the suggestions for radical change were two arguing that commodity programs should be revised dramatically. Other suggestions were lowering target prices, linking benefits to the income of recipients rather than to production, fewer constraints on the use of farmland, and expansion of the Conservation Reserve Program (CRP) (Schertz and Doering (1999), p.20).

[117] A poll administered by Harold Guither of the University of Illinois in 1994 indicated that farmers across the country were almost evenly divided on which course to take, with 41 percent saying they were prepared to phase out current programs, 37 percent favoring the present system and another 11 percent wanting some other solution (*St. Louis Post Dispatch*, March 23, 1994).

filled by other nations. Since the US could respond more efficiently than other nations, it made sense for the US to increase its capacity.[118] Lugar, a free-market conservative, made an initial reform proposal to save $15 billion from anticipated expenditures over five years by eliminating the EEP and by lowering target prices by three percent a year. However, this proposal did not attract much support from either Republican or Democrat members of the Senate Agriculture Committee, who were not inclined to make major changes in farm policy. The Committee hesitated to draft farm legislation, awaiting approval of a congressional budget resolution.

A Slower Response in the House Agriculture Committee

The House Agriculture Committee was slow to get organized, so unaccustomed were the Republicans to majority party status. It took time to select a new staff and to redefine the committee's jurisdiction with the new House leadership. The atmosphere was extremely partisan, reflecting the bitter 1994 electoral campaign. Republicans knew they could expect little help from committee Democrats in developing a new farm bill.

The committee chairmanship was assumed by Pat Roberts, a congressman from the Kansas wheat belt who previously had been one of the staunchest defenders of the *status-quo* in farm policy. Roberts defended existing programs in the early stages of the 1995 Farm Bill debate, but he knew irresistible pressures for change would come from the budget-conscious House Republican leadership.[119] For Roberts, it was a question of damage control - how to limit the harm to agriculture. He had three principle objectives: to ensure that farm commodity programs were not singled out for disproportionate budget cuts; to ensure that any farm spending cuts went toward deficit reduction; and, to seek relief for farmers from what he called the tidal wave of environmental mandates (Orden, Paarlberg and Roe (1999), p.129).

Roberts presented these objectives as part of a new "policy ledger" for agriculture after consulting with the majority in his committee and the House Republican leadership (Orden, Paarlberg and Roe (1999), p.129). On the negative side, he foresaw less federal support for farmers, and possibly, elimination of domestic supply restrictions affecting sugar and peanuts. On the positive side, farmers would receive lower taxes and interest rates from a package of debt reductions, including tax relief and higher health-care reductions. Farm policy would become less burdensome by increasing planting flexibility on base acreage and by eliminating the requirement for unpaid ARP set-asides. Roberts anticipated the renewal of the CRP program, which

---

[118] This theme had previously been given a significant boost with the preparation and astute promotion of a study prepared by Abel, Daft and Early, a Washington DC area consulting firm (May 1994). This study sponsored by the National Grain and Feed Association through its foundation had the support of 185 companies, most of whose profits were geared substantially to volume of commodities handled or processed (Schertz and Doering (1999), p.4).

[119] According to one of the people interviewed, Roberts was told that he was not going to be allowed to be a defender of the old order.

would have a positive effect on commodity prices and provide some assured income for farmers.

Roberts convinced the House leadership that holding its majority after the 1996 elections might depend on taking a supportive approach to agriculture in the new farm bill. His case was strengthened by his assertion that 33 of the 76 freshman Republican members of the House (including 24 who had defeated Democrat incumbents) came from districts with strong agricultural constituencies (Orden, Paarlberg and Roe (1999), p.130). He won an early victory to retain food stamps as a federal entitlement, in spite of the House Republican commitment to turn welfare programs over to states in the form of block grants. This helped ensure continued support for farm programs from urban legislators.

As a first step to developing new farm legislation, Roberts held about 20 regional hearings around the country.[120] In an unusual move for the House, these hearings were held by the full Agriculture committee, rather than by the subcommittees. In the hearings, farmers expressed general dissatisfaction with current commodity programs. They did not like the restrictions on their ability to plant implied by base acreages; they did not like required uncompensated annual acreage reductions (ARPs); and, they had become convinced that deficiency payments did not provide a very good safety net. However, they did like the Conservation Reserve Program.

Getting a Congressional Budget Resolution

In a departure from previous farm bills, the Republican majority revised procedures subordinating the agriculture committees to the budget process. First, congress would approve a budget resolution, with an amount allocated for farm spending. Then the agriculture committees would be asked to develop farm legislation as part of a budget reconciliation bill, keeping spending within the pre-established limits of the budget resolution. This departed significantly from the process in 1990, when legislators only knew the binding budget constraint when the farm bill got to the House-Senate Conference. The Senate and House Budget Committees approved their versions of the fiscal 1996 budget resolution during the week of May 8, 1995 (1995 CQ Almanac, p.350). The House Budget Committee approved a plan to cut farm programs by $9 billion over five years, with additional cuts to come in 2001 and 2002. This figure had been cut from an initial recommendation of $16 billion through the efforts of Representative Roberts and his supporters. Roberts also obtained a non-binding amendment that linked together the two sides of his policy ledger (Orden, Paarlberg and Roe (1999), p.182). This amendment opened the agricultural budget to re-examination if other Republican promises were not delivered. The Senate Budget Committee approved a non-binding "sense of the Senate" resolution that farm subsidies should be cut no more than $5.6 billion over five years, with other

---

[120] This was a different strategy from the Senate Agriculture Committee, which held its hearings in Washington.

agricultural cuts to come out of nutrition programs. These cuts were far less than the $15 billion proposed by Senator Lugar.

As a final budget resolution developed, the Republican leadership, determined to balance the budget, shifted its emphasis to seven-year estimates. On June 29, Congress agreed on a budget resolution aimed at balancing the budget over seven years. The Agriculture Committees were instructed to find $13.4 billion in farm program cuts as their contribution to the budget reconciliation package that would be assembled later in the year (1995 CQ Almanac, p.350).

The "Freedom to Farm" Initiative

Congressman Roberts and the Agriculture Committee majority staff had many discussions about how to ensure maximum benefits for farmers in the prevailing atmosphere of fiscal stringency. They were looking for ways to achieve budget cuts, yet reduce ARPs and increase planting flexibility for farmers. In one of these discussions, direct payments to farmers not tied to the production were suggested (interview). This would allow ARP land to be brought back into production without budgetary cost.[121] Direct payments had worked for the CRP, why wouldn't they work for land actually farmed? This thinking was reinforced in staff discussions with the grain industry, which gave its support.[122] Armed with knowledge that farmers and agri-business were ready for a change in policy, the staff prepared the "Freedom to Farm" memorandum.

The "Freedom to Farm" memorandum was circulated to members of the House Agriculture Committee in early June, 1995, as an unsigned three page outline of a reform proposal (see Orden, Paarlberg and Roe (1999), p.132; also Schertz and Doering (1999), p.34).[123] This proposal outline was designed to ensure that farmers received the $43 billion level of spending projected by the CBO budget baseline of February 1995, less the cuts mandated in the congressional budget resolution.[124] It presented a straight-forward alternative to existing programs for feedgrains, wheat, cotton and rice. Farmers would receive a guaranteed annual income, with payments determined by past program participation. These guaranteed payments would be made regardless of the level of market prices and would not be linked to production. In exchange for the payments, farmers would be required to maintain previously developed conservation plans. With payments decoupled from prices and production, there would be no need for base acreages and ARP unpaid set-asides. Payments would decline over a seven-year "transition" period until 2002.

---

[121] Under the existing system a budget cost would be assessed for bringing ARP land back into production to cover loans and deficiency payments for the crops produced as a result.

[122] The support of the grain industry for fixed direct payments could not be publicized. To let farmers know that the grain industry favored an idea would have guaranteed a negative reaction, given the distrust of farmers for agri-business.

[123] The text of the anonymous "Freedom to Farm" memo can be found in Schertz and Doering (1999), p.155.

[124] The budget baseline represented projected farm spending under the 1990 farm bill.

"Freedom to Farm" had considerable intrinsic appeal, and hence attracted a great deal of attention. For farmers, this proposal offered guaranteed income, providing a better safety net than deficiency payments in cases of natural disaster, such as the 1988 drought and the 1993 Midwest floods. In disaster situation, prices would rise and deficiency payments would fall, but producers most affected with small crops could not reap the benefits of high prices. Broadening the appeal to farmers, commodity prices were rising in 1996, so producers would receive more in the short run from production flexibility contracts than they would from deficiency payments calculated at the target price levels of the 1990 farm bill. Under "Freedom to Farm", the chances appeared better that farmers could receive the full funding provided by the February, 1995, CBO budget guideline, than under the continuation of existing programs. Farmers would also benefit from reduced paperwork required to receive deficiency payments.

"Freedom to Farm" was attractive to policy-makers in that it capped the entitlements to farmers, remedying a problem with previous farm bills, which had gone over budget when deficiency payments were higher than anticipated. "Freedom to Farm" also looked promising in that it continued the trend to greater market orientation, and would promote US farm exports. The proposal thus was consistent with agricultural trade liberalization. Decoupling payments from production would allow to US to go beyond the requirements of the Uruguay Round Agreement on Agriculture in reducing domestic support and export subsidies. This would put the US in a good position to demand the end of the "Blue Box" and export subsidies in the 1999 trade round (see Chapter 10).

"Freedom to Farm" had a special appeal to Congressman Roberts, although he was cautious in embracing the concept.[125] Some of his constituents were in the painful position of having to return deficiency payment cash advances for wheat as a result of rising commodity prices (Orden, Paarlberg and Roe (1990), p.134). Kansas farmers hardly could afford to return deficiency payments. Having spent the money, they were unable to take advantage of rising prices because of weather damage to their crops. Farmers receiving de-coupled payments would not have to face the prospect of returning them.

The House Agriculture Committee Considers "Freedom to Farm"

The "Freedom to Farm" initiative had gathered sufficient support for Roberts to introduce it as a formal bill in late July. By this stage, more detail had been added to the Memo's outline. Payments offered over a seven-year "transition" period would decline from $7.6 billion in 1996 to $5.2 billion in 2001. The bill provided for the reauthorization of the Export Enhancement program, and the retention of non-recourse Commodity Credit Corporation loans. However, loan rates would be set at 70 percent of the "Olympic" five-year rolling average, instead of the 85 percent provided in the

---

[125] Roberts was very mindful of the contentiousness of the Boschwitz-Boren proposal for decoupling in the 1985 Farm Bill debate.

1990 farm bill. In introducing the legislation Roberts announced that he would spend the summer recess advocating his proposal and gauging the reaction of farmers, then hold a formal markup session when Congress reconvened in September (Orden, Paarlberg and Roe (1999), p.135).

When Congress returned in September, in a departure from the usual process, the "Freedom to Farm" proposal went to the full House Agriculture committee, which had the task of developing farm legislation for inclusion in the budget reconciliation act, without prior consideration by any sub-committee. Roberts gave the sub-committees a chance to discuss how to implement the cuts mandated by the congressional budget resolution, but they declined to participate in this painful process.

By the time the House Agriculture Committee began its hearings in September, "Freedom to Farm" had generated both strong support and strong opposition. The proposal won praise from regional and national newspapers. It also earned the enthusiastic support of the Coalition for a Competitive Food and Agricultural System, a coalition of 125 agri-business companies and trade associations with an interest in agriculture. It received the endorsement of the Kansas Farm Bureau, but other farm organizations remained non-committal (Orden, Paarlberg and Roe (1999), p.138). Neither the American Farm Bureau nor any of the national commodity associations endorsed the proposal. Strong opposition came from cotton and rice producers and processors, who were concerned that the full planting flexibility allowed by "Freedom to Farm" would damage their industries.[126]

The proponents of the *status quo* mobilized around an alternative farm bill proposed on September 15 by Bill Emerson (R-MO) and Larry Combest (R-Tex.), which retained existing support mechanisms for deficiency payment crops, including slight program modifications acceptable to sugar and peanut producers. This bill also extended the regional milk-marketing orders that set formula-driven regional price differentials (Orden, Paarlberg and Roe (1999), p.139). The bulk of $13.4 billion budget saving assigned by the congressional budget resolution would be achieved by raising non-payment acres to 30 percent. Other cost reductions would be induced by changes in voluntary set-aside programs, the peanut program, dairy supports, EEP, the CRP and federal crop insurance.

Roberts worried about the strength of the *status quo* forces, whose position was fortified by the administration recommendations and the Cochran bill in the Senate, which like the Emerson-Combest bill, preserved existing commodity support programs. To strengthen his position for changing the *status quo*, Roberts invoked the support of the new House Republican leadership. He argued that the leadership was unwilling to re-authorize farm programs without significant reforms - particularly a cap on future payments and some deregulation of production (Orden, Paarlberg and Roe (1999), p.139). To make the threat credible, he circulated a letter signed by Speaker Newt Gingrich, Majority Leader Dick Armey (R-TX), and Majority Whip Tom DeLay (R-TX), which indicated possible intervention to impose changes to agricultural policy through the leadership's control of the budget process unless the agriculture committee

---

[126] It was feared that cotton and rice acreage would be increased, resulting in lower prices.

reported sweeping reform (Orden, Paarlberg and Roe (1999), p.139). This authority was based on a rarely-used provision of the Congressional Budget Act of 1974 allowing amendments to budget legislation from the House floor whenever an authorizing committee failed to offer a bill achieving the savings specified in a budget resolution (Orden, Paarlberg and Roe (1999), p.139).

As the House Agriculture committee began its deliberations, Roberts introduced a new version of his Freedom to Farm Act, divided into four subtitles (Orden Paarlberg and Roe (1999), pp.192-93). The first sub-title suspended the permanent 1949 law until 2002, and authorized de-coupled payments for feedgrains, wheat cotton and rice. The total allocated for payments had been reduced somewhat to $38.4 billion for seven fiscal years (declining from $6 billion in 1996 to $4.4 billion in 2002. The second subtitle deregulated the dairy industry. Marketing orders and the dairy price support program were ended. Decoupled ("freedom to milk") contractual payments would be paid to dairy farmers on the basis of their historic production levels. A recourse loan program was established, with loan rates at 90 percent of market prices. The third sub-title extended the sugar and peanut programs through 2002 in an effort to win support for "Freedom to Farm" from these constituencies to counterbalance the opposition from the cotton and rice industries. The fourth subtitle re-authorized the CRP at the existing level of 36.4 million acres, but with annual rental rates at 75 percent of previous values. EEP expenditure authority was reduced below Uruguay Round limits for the years 1996-2000, but restored to maximum levels for 2001-2002.

With both Roberts and Emerson-Combest bills on the floor for debate, the House Agriculture committee faced a clear choice between maintaining deficiency payments or shifting to de-coupled income support. But, the fate of the two bills may have depended on Roberts' generous provisions for sugar and inclusion by Emerson of dairy provisions opposed in the Midwest (Orden, Paarlberg and Roe (1999), p.141). When Emerson-Combest came up for a vote, 18 Democrats, led by cotton farmers Cal Dooley of California and Charles Stenholm of Texas rallied in support. However, the proposal failed, 23-26, with both Democrats and Republicans divided. Emerson and Combest were able to win support from only three other Republicans in addition to 18 Democrats. However, Democrats from the upper Midwest opposed the measure, in part because of the dairy proposals.

After the Emerson-Combest proposal was defeated, the committee turned to the Roberts bill. The committee was under tremendous pressure from the House Republican leadership to pass "Freedom to Farm", but cotton lobbyists argued strongly in opposition. When the vote was taken, the Roberts bill failed by a vote of 22-27, with all 22 Democrats voting in opposition. Joining the Democrats were five Republicans, including Emerson and Combest. Before a hushed committee room, Roberts recessed the session, caucused privately with Republicans and then came back to announce that the committee had failed to reach a consensus. For Roberts, a potential Senate candidate, the vote was a major public setback. Yet, he refused to make more concessions to win votes, and predicted that his bill would be the vehicle in the House for budget reconciliation.

Development of a Traditional Farm Bill in the Senate

The Senate proceeded in a different direction than the House in developing farm legislation. After the passage of the congressional budget resolution, Senator Lugar retreated from his advocacy of drastic spending cuts and began to hint that the Senate would pass a farm bill not much different than the 1990 legislation (Orden, Paarlberg and Roe (1999), p.136). While Lugar was deciding what to do, Senator Thad Cochran (R-MS) and 14 co-sponsors from the Senate Agriculture Committee introduced the Agricultural Competitiveness Act, a traditional farm bill. Under this bill, uncapped deficiency payments tied to base acreages were retained for wheat, feed grains, cotton and rice, while support prices for sugar and peanuts were kept at 1995 levels. Budget savings would be achieved by increasing non-payment acres for deficiency payment products, and by imposing modest reforms for sugar and peanuts.

Senate Democrats, led by Senator Tom Daschle (SD), presented their own proposal, which established a two-tier payments mechanism for wheat and feedgrains, with the quantity of output eligible for deficiency payments limited so that support was targeted to mid-sized farms. This proposal raised loan rates to 95 percent of the Olympic moving average of past market prices. Planting flexibility was increased by combining separate commodity base acreages into a single farm program base. Expenditures for farm programs were capped at $7 billion per year and the Secretary of Agriculture was given broad authority to use ARP supply controls and other interventionist measures if expenditures were projected to exceed authorized levels.

Senator Lugar worked to build bi-partisan consensus. This was a necessity in the Senate, where 60 votes are needed to cut-off a filibuster. The Senate Agriculture Committee worked through the August recess trying to reach common ground on meeting the requirements of the budget resolution. When Lugar was informed of "Freedom to Farm," he encouraged Pat Roberts to proceed in the House, although he could not push the proposal in the Senate because of opposition from Senators from cotton and rice producing states, particularly Senator Cochran (interview).

As the budget reconciliation deadline approached in late September, with consensus still beyond reach, Lugar announced that he would insist on four farm policy reforms. These included minimal budget savings of $13.4 billion; elimination of the authority for ARPs; increased planting flexibility; and support reductions for sugar and peanuts commensurate with support reductions in other commodities (Orden, Paarlberg and Roe (1999), p.142). In an effort to bridge regional differences, he offered "Freedom to Farm" payments for feedgrains and wheat, with traditional deficiency payments for cotton and rice. Lugar was willing to compromise to reach consensus.

After ten days of difficult negotiations the Senate Agriculture Committee approved the budget reconciliation proposal (see Orden, Paarlberg and Roe (1999), p.143). Deficiency payments and crop-specific bases were to be retained for all crops, with nonpayment acres increased to 30 percent. Authority for unpaid annual ARP set-asides was to be eliminated, with a cap set on maximum per unit deficiency payments to offset the projected cost of ending ARP programs. Wheat and feedgrain producers would have received increased planting flexibility, while restrictive base acreage planting requirements were to be maintained for cotton and rice. Loan rates were retained at 85 percent of the Olympic moving average of past prices, with marketing loans retained for cotton and rice. Only slight reductions in support would have been imposed for sugar and peanuts. Milk marketing orders were to be retained along with regional price differentials, while CRP expenditures were to be capped.

The Budget Reconciliation

Lugar's bill passed the Senate with only minor amendment, but still there was no agricultural budget reconciliation bill approved by the House. Following the stalemate in the House Agriculture Committee, Roberts negotiated for a week to resolve the differences among Republicans, and when these negotiations failed, he fulfilled the threat made in the letter from the leadership circulated earlier to the committee.[127] He announced that the committee would abrogate its budget responsibility and hand over decisions to the leadership of the House. A period of complex negotiations followed, where Gingrich and his lieutenants tried to figure out how they could insert "Freedom to Farm" into the budget reconciliation bill without losing the Republican votes necessary to pass the measure. The GOP leadership felt the need for quick action, as the budget negotiations were behind schedule, and they feared loss of the policy initiative. Finally an agreement was reached when they assured legislators opposed to "Freedom to Farm," representing cotton, sugar and rice constituencies, that their concerns would be addressed in the Conference.

After days of intense infighting over dairy, sugar, peanuts and conservation, the Conferees reached agreement on the agricultural provisions of the budget reconciliation bill. Roberts' "Freedom to Farm" won approval, with contract payments set for $5.5 billion in 1996, $5.8 billion in 1997, then declining to $4.0 billion by 2002. Producers of feedgrains, wheat, cotton and rice were given planting flexibility, extended to allow production of fruits and vegetables on 15 percent of base acreage. This bill would have eliminated authority for ARP set-asides and repealed the Agricultural Act of 1949 as permanent legislation. Rising farm prices strengthened Roberts' bargaining hand. He argued successfully that "Freedom to Farm" would ensure more benefits for farmers than deficiency payments by better capturing the budget baseline (Orden, Paarlberg and Roe (1999), p.148). With prices rising, deficiency payments would decline, but "Freedom to Farm" payments would be guaranteed.

Other agricultural provisions in the conference budget reconciliation bill included setting loan rates at 85 percent of the five-year Olympic moving average of past

---

[127] In the letter signed by Congressmen Richard R. Armey, (R-Tex.), Newt Gingrich (R-GA) and Tom DeLay (R-Tex), the leadership expressed hope that the Agriculture Committee would approve "Freedom to Farm," a measure "consistent with the goals of the new Republican Congress." The letter stated that the leadership would consider two alternatives, "If the committee fails to report such reforms...." The first would be to bring "a farm bill to the floor... under an open rule." The second would be to "replace the committee's legislation with true reforms before reconciliation is considered on the floor" (Schertz and Doering (1999), p.67).

market prices and the continuation of marketing loans, with loan rates capped at 1995 levels. These provisions were concessions to cotton and rice interests. The conferees continued the peanut and sugar programs, lowering peanut price supports somewhat, and requiring sugar processors to repay government loans when imports dropped to less than 1.5 million tons per year. Dairy was so contentious that no agreement could be reached, so the final reconciliation bill contained no dairy provisions. In a printed statement, Senator Lugar noted, "We are producing for a worldwide market that has a strong demand for what we do. We are changing the premise of farming from the 1930s, when we were afraid of oversupply and felt the need to control supply" (1995 CQ Almanac, pp.3-55).

A Presidential Veto

Both Houses of Congress passed the Budget Reconciliation Conference report by partisan majorities, but President Clinton vetoed the legislation on December 7, 1995. A budget crisis ensued when the President would not concede to the budget demands of the Republican congress, leading to two partial government shutdowns as 1995 came to a close.

During this period, new budget estimates from the Congressional Budget office narrowed the gap between the administration and Republican estimates of the budget deficit. These estimates also projected Commodity Credit Corporation commodity and export expenditures decreasing over the next seven years from $56.6 billion to $48.8 billion (Orden, Paarlberg and Roe (1999), p.151). These estimates were largely based on higher market price expectations and lower deficiency payments. The new estimates reduced the projected budget savings of "Freedom to Farm," from $13.4 billion to $4.5 billion, but Roberts was able to get credit from the Republican leadership for the "savings" caused by increased prices.

The reduced estimates of government farm budget savings paradoxically put the Democrats in something of a bind. They still criticized "Freedom to Farm" for cutting farm spending too much. But these arguments began to ring hollow as it became increasingly apparent that "Freedom to Farm" would provide more support to farmers than deficiency payments, at least in the short run. Having made the case that Roberts' plan was too stingy, they could not easily shift to the argument that "Freedom to Farm" would provide windfall profits.

Efforts to Resurrect Farm Legislation

As 1996 began, the pressures to pass a farm bill mounted rapidly. Provisions of the 1990 Farm Bill were beginning to expire, and farmers needed to know under what rules they were operating when making their planting decisions for 1996. Legislation had to be passed before the beginning of the winter wheat harvest in April, otherwise the harvest would be conducted under the permanent 1949 farm law, which would triple loan rates and create havoc in commodity markets. There was talk of extending the 1990 Farm Bill for another year, but this was strongly opposed by Congressman Roberts. Such an extension would probably delay a new farm bill until after the 1996

Presidential election, when a new 1996 budget baseline would be used. This would be less favorable to farmers in that farm spending was decreasing because of rising commodity prices (Schertz & Doering (1999), p.90).

Congressman Roberts introduced in January the agricultural provisions from the failed budget reconciliation as the free-standing Agricultural Market Transition Act. By this time rising commodity prices had taken much of the wind out of the opposition. "Freedom to Farm" now had the endorsement of the American Farm Bureau, while the cotton and rice interests were shifting toward support. This bill added a dairy title that would end price-support programs for butter and nonfat dry milk, and the Department of Agriculture would have to consolidate the nation's system of milk marketing orders within two years.[128] In other provisions, the bill would have repealed much of the 1949 permanent farm law, and have extended the peanut and sugar price-support programs for seven years, with some changes in allotments and loan rates. Successful amendments were added to extend the Food for Peace Program (PL-480) and to give farmers greater leeway in taking their lands out of the Conservation Reserve Program. The House Agriculture Committee approved this bill on January 30. Overall, the bill was projected to cost $44 billion, close to the projected expense of the expired programs, though the House Republican leadership seemed less concerned with budget savings than before the failed budget reconciliation.

The Senate operated under greater pressures for quick action than the House. Both Senator Lugar and Majority leader Bob Dole were running for President and wanted a farm bill approved before the February Iowa caucuses. The debate over farm policy had all along been less partisan than in the House. A compromise was almost worked out between Senators Lugar and Democrats from the corn belt and Great Plains, which would have accepted a plan by Senator Daschle (D-S.D.) to provide a non-refundable advance payment to farmers each year equal to 40 percent of a payment based on historical subsidies. The other 60 percent would be linked to market prices and county yields. However, Republicans forced their leader to back off and the tentative agreement collapsed.[129]

Senator Leahy (D-Vt), the former chairman, then jumped into the breach and worked out an agreement with Lugar that the Republicans accepted. The Lugar-Leahy compromise retained "Freedom to Farm" declining fixed payments and eliminated ARP programs. In other provisions, it gave farmers increased planting flexibility, retained marketing loans, capped commodity loan rates, capped export subsidies, and

---

[128] A regional series of price supports that tended to favor Northeastern and Southeastern producers over those in the upper Midwest.

[129] Schertz and Doering (1999) provide several possible reasons for the collapse. There may have been a collective judgment on the part of the Republicans that Senator Daschle's demands for not filibustering were too high and that they would prefer to hang tough with "Freedom to Farm." With continued strong commodity prices, they may have thought constituent pressures supporting "Freedom to Farm: might nudge a sufficient number of Democrats to vote for Roberts' plan. There was also the possibility that the Republicans became aware that Senator Leahy (R-Vt.) would be willing to make a better deal accepting "Freedom to Farm" (p.96) (see also, Hosansky (1996)).

re-authorized, with some modifications, the sugar and peanut price-support programs for seven years. This bill did not propose major changes in dairy price supports. It did not include the provision for a commission to make recommendations about future government involvement in agriculture. The Senate bill had a much broader scope than the House bill. As a price for supporting "Freedom to Farm," Leahy insisted on re-authorizing nutrition, trade, credit and other programs, which would have brought the total authorization to $50 billion. Senator Lugar brought the bill directly to the floor of the Senate without formal approval by the Senate Agriculture Committee, where it passed easily by a vote of 74-26.

The Lugar-Leahy compromise created potential problems with the House Republican leadership, both with regard to the increased proposed expenditures and the welfare and conservation provisions. Reauthorization of food-stamps in the farm bill was a blow to Republican plans for welfare reform. The conservation provisions seemed in conflict with the Republican commitment to fewer mandates and less government intervention. Roberts had hoped to avoid these problems by focusing narrowly on de-coupled payments and commodity policy, while holding other aspects of farm policy for a later separate farm bill. He also wanted to lock in payments to farmers before confronting environmental and nutrition issues (Schertz and Doering (1999), p.111). But, the Senate bill forced him to abandon this strategy.

Roberts brought the Agricultural Market Transition Act to the floor of the House after the February 1996 recess, under a rule that allowed just 16 amendments rather than the 75 requested. The central elements of "Freedom to Farm," were easily accepted, including declining fixed payments, the end of deficiency payments and the end of ARP programs. Amendments to end the peanut and sugar programs were rejected, respectively by the close votes of 209-212 and 208-217. For dairy, marketing orders were retained, although the number of marketing regions was reduced. The narrow commodity focus of the Agriculture Committee was broadened to include re-authorization of the CRP for seven years and creation of a new Environmental Quality Incentive program. Provisions were adopted to re-authorize trade programs, and to fund restoration of the Everglades.

The FAIR Act

By the time the House passed its farm legislation, most of the uncertainty about future farm policy had dissipated. Widespread support now existed for shifting commodity programs into de-coupled declining contract payments now labeled as production flexibility contracts (PFCs). With the pressing need for a new farm bill, even the Democratic administration showed a willingness to acquiesce when Secretary of Agriculture Dan Glickman indicated that the President would not veto the farm bill because of de-coupling alone. Glickman, however, did have concerns about the safety net, and about conservation, nutrition and rural development programs. The GOP leadership, in need of a legislative victory with elections approaching, had no alternative except to compromise. In the Conference, Roberts had to abandon his plans for a second farm bill and add conservation and nutrition titles that ran counter to House Republican proposals for deregulation and budget restraint. Agreement was reached to re-authorize the CRP at 1995 levels, with an early out for some acreage. The legislation re-authorized the food stamp program for two years, while the welfare reform debate proceeded. Other nutrition programs were extended for seven years. The price supports for butter, powder and cheese were phased out over four years and the 33 milk marketing orders were consolidated to 10-14. Several of the Senate's conservation measures were adopted, including a $50 million wildlife habitat program. The approved farm bill gave the Secretary of Agriculture greater flexibility in assessing penalties under the "Swampbuster" program and authorized $300 million for the Fund for Rural development, over three years. Roberts was forced to concede on retaining the permanent 1949 farm law, but he got his provision to establish a Commission to recommend future farm policy.

The Federal Agriculture Improvement and Reform (FAIR) Act, as approved by the Conference, was scored by the Congressional Budget Office as saving $2 billion from the December 1996 baseline and was hailed by the GOP leadership as imposing budget discipline. It passed by overwhelming majorities of 318-89 in the House and 74-26 in the Senate. President Clinton signed the FAIR Act on April 4 in a low-key ceremony.

8.2 Analysis

The "Freedom to Farm" reforms introduced in the FAIR Act instituted a major shift in farm subsidies away from the quantity of commodities produced toward direct income support. This was a situation where an innovative idea resonated with the economic and political environments. The analytical framework developed in Chapter 2 is helpful in explaining how and why "Freedom to Farm" became a central part of the FAIR Act.

The Legacy of the 1990 Farm Bill

The 1990 Farm Bill established the concept of "triple-base", giving farmers authority to plant any crop they wanted on 15 percent of their base acreage, in return for forgoing government deficiency payments. The remainder of their land could be planted in program crops eligible for deficiency payments or set-aside under ARP programs. This policy, as we have noted in Chapter 5, had been implemented to lower the costs of deficiency payments at a time of large government deficits, and to give farmers greater production flexibility, so that they could better respond to market demands. "Triple-base" had been somewhat successful in accomplishing these objectives, but the 1990 Farm Bill went way over budget, largely because of high disaster payments, peaking after the major Midwest farm belt floods in 1993. Though farmers liked the flexibility of triple-base, they were unhappy about the increasing percentage of their land not eligible for government payments. This unhappiness focused on the ARP program. Farmers felt that if the government wanted a market oriented farm policy they should be able to plant all of their land. They were joined by input producers, elevator operators and traders, whose businesses would benefit from increased planted acreage.

Another salient aspect of the 1990 Farm Bill was the emphasis on the environment. Elements included the continuation of the Conservation Reserve Program (CRP), the establishment of a wetlands reserve program, the continuation of swamp-buster provisions keeping wetlands out of agricultural production, and other environmental provisions which producers had to meet to qualify for government payments. These provisions were certainly popular with the environmental lobby, though farmers resented government environmental regulations impinging on their freedom. Farmers liked the CRP because it provided a guaranteed income. However, agribusiness had reservations to the extent that the CRP kept good farmland out of production. As noted previously, the success of the CRP, with contract payments to farmers for taking land out of production, helped in selling the idea of production flexibility contract payments under "Freedom to Farm."

Budget and Trade Deficits Cast a Shadow

Perhaps the most important economic trend at the time of the 1995-6 Farm Bill debate was the chronic federal budget deficit, which was still running at about $200 billion in 1995 (Figure 8.1).

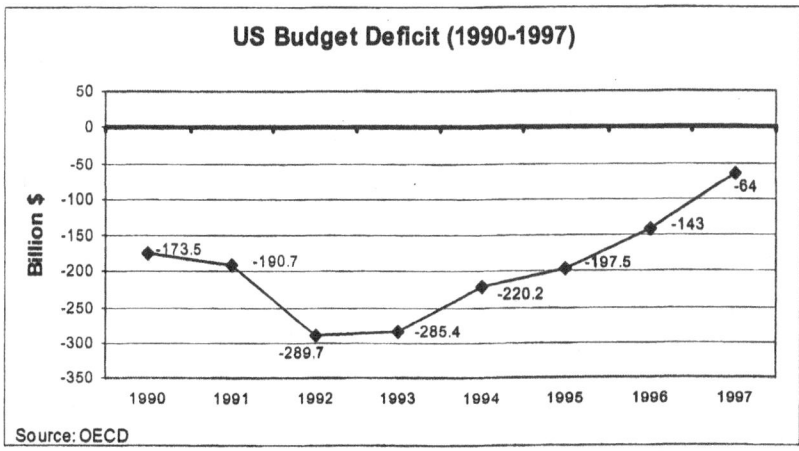

Figure 8.1: US Budget Deficit (1990-1997)

Debt reduction was a high priority in Washington, particularly in the newly elected Republican congress. It was a lower priority in the Clinton administration, which did not feel it had received credit in the 1994 congressional election for its earlier efforts to bring the budget into balance.

The balance of trade was also in chronic deficit, although the positive agricultural balance was one of the bright spots in an otherwise not so rosy picture. Agricultural exports were rising rapidly, largely because of the economic boom in Asia (see Figure 8.2).

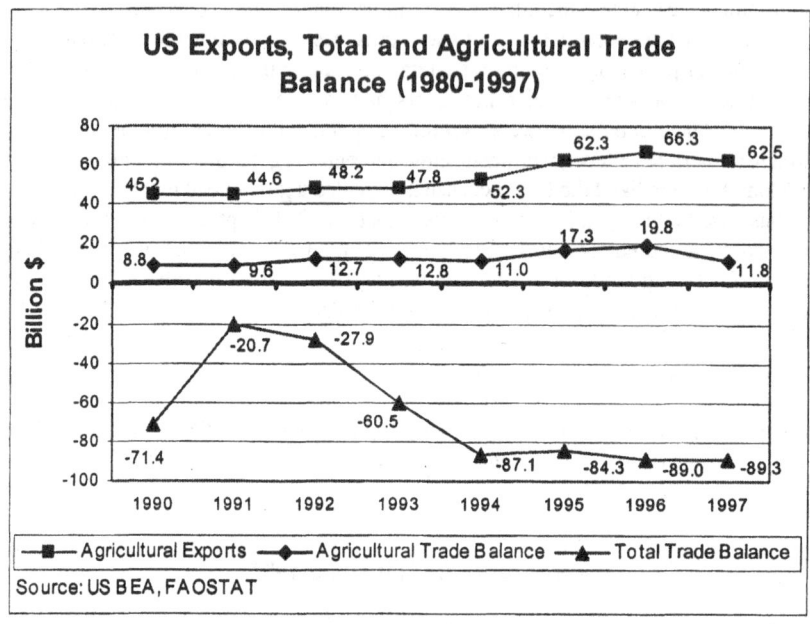

Figure 8.2: US Agricultural Exports, Total Trade Balance and Agricultural Trade Balance (1990-1997)

Commodity prices were also rising because of the increased export demand, and reduced supply, caused in part by the widespread 1993 flood damage in the Midwest corn belt (an economic shock).[130] They peaked in 1995 but stayed high during the period of discussion of the Farm Bill (Figure 8.3).

Perhaps the most important political development was Republican control of both houses of Congress, gained in the 1994 election. The GOP victory was particularly significant in the House, where the Republicans had been in the minority for 40 years. The House Republicans had run using as a manifesto their "Contract with America," which called for smaller government, less government federal government regulation, reduction of federal entitlements, tax cuts and return of power to the states. The election campaign created a highly partisan atmosphere in Congress, particularly in the House.

---

[130] The flood damage also contributed to the 1990 Farm Bill cost overruns, by increasing payments for disaster assistance.

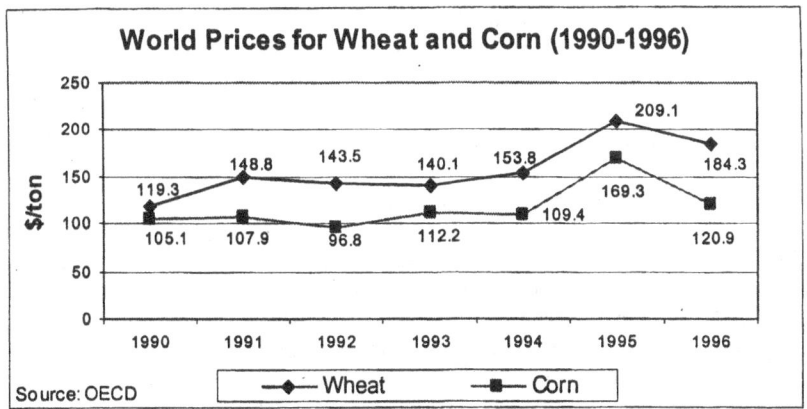

Figure 8.3: World Prices for Wheat and Corn (1990-1996)

The Importance of GOP Control of Congress and the Uruguay Round Agricultural Agreement

The successful completion of the Uruguay Round Agreement on Agriculture (URAA) in January 1994 was another important political development. This agreement did not however provide immediate constraints for US agricultural policy, in that US deficiency payments were "blue box" payments. Also, the 1990 US Farm Bill and increasing commodity prices allowed the US to meet the Uruguay Round limits on domestic and export subsidies and on import barriers. The URAA improved the outlook for increased US agricultural exports, with the prospect of more open international markets.

An Opportune Moment for Change

The political environment in 1995 was unusually conducive to significant change in US agricultural policy. Something had to be done about the budget deficit and now Congress had a strong Republican majority committed to cutting government spending, with federal entitlements as a target. The environment for reform was particularly strong in the House, with 76 new Republican congressmen committed to the "Contract with America", and with new leadership and staffs never previously in power, and hence with no personal commitment to existing policy.

The political environment was open to change in agricultural policy, but it did not dictate what kind of change. However, consensus developed on certain parameters. Spending on farm programs had to be cut and future cost overruns had to be controlled. Farmers should be given more flexibility and ARP programs should be curtailed. Both of these objectives were consistent with increasing the market orientation of farm policy, while increased flexibility could allow expenditure cuts.

The elimination of ARPs was problematic in that the cost of the agricultural budget would be increased.[131] Any significant policy change would have to overcome the cumbersome congressional policy process, structurally biased toward maintaining the *status quo* (see Moyer and Josling, 1990). It would also need to overcome a wide variety of well-placed commodity groups, with a strong interest in existing policy.

The Competitive Agriculture Paradigm Triumphant

The Competitive Agriculture paradigm was stronger in 1995 in the US agricultural policy community than it had ever been before. Consensus existed by this time that the future prosperity of US agriculture depended on international markets. Given increased agricultural productivity, the federal government simply could not afford the cost of supporting an agriculture protected from international competition. Exports must continue to increase and that could not succeed in the long run without trade liberalization and the reduction of domestic trade-distorting subsidies. The successful completion of the Uruguay Round Agreement on Agriculture strengthened this paradigm. It became easier to argue for domestic legislation consistent with the liberalization of international trade than to argue for a policy that distorted markets or interfered with US international competitiveness.

The Changing Influence of Lobbies

The outside political inputs were pretty much the same as they had been for the 1985 and 1990 farm bills, with one important exception. As before, a wide variety of commodity groups and general farm organizations attempted to influence the policy process. The commodity groups, including the corn growers, wheat growers and cotton growers came into the debate as strong supporters of existing commodity programs and deficiency payments, in which they had a vested interest. But, as we will discuss later in this chapter, "Freedom to Farm" had an appeal, which weakened their support for existing programs. Also, as we noted in Chapter 2, the influence of the commodity groups was waning as a result of the congressional reforms of the 1970s. The Farm Bureau, supportive of the Uruguay Round agreement and willing to move toward greater market orientation, eventually became a supporter of "Freedom to Farm." A wide variety of environmental and conservation groups attempted to have their views integrated into the forthcoming legislation. These groups had been influential in the 1985 and 1990 farm bills in establishing the CRP program and in inserting swampbuster and other environmental provisions. However, the Republican victory in the 1994 congressional elections presented a less receptive environment, with the priority for less government regulation. The environmentalists exercised little influence in the House Agriculture committee, but had strong support on the House floor. In addition,

---

[131] Crops grown on ARP land brought back in production would be eligible for loans and deficiency payments.

The FAIR Act of 1996 - Decoupling Payments from Production

they had a very strong advocate in the Senate Agriculture committee in Senator Leahy (D-VT).

The principle difference from previous farm bill debates in the outside political inputs was the activity of the Coalition for a Competitive Food and Agricultural System, a group of 125 diverse agri-business companies and trade associations that managed to become a player in the farm policy network (Appendix). These companies had never coalesced together to make a collective farm bill effort, though individual agri-business companies lobbied Congress and the administration. But, in the summer of 1994, a group of representatives from agri-business and trade associations agreed to organize to promote a more market and export oriented farm policy. The Coalition, whose membership accepted the Competitive Agriculture paradigm, maintained that supply control policies are counter-productive, that annual acreage reduction programs should be eliminated, and that the Conservation Reserve Program should be reformed to focus on land truly environmentally sensitive (see Coalition Update March 17, 1995). This group accepted the need for an income safety net, but believed that any safety net program should be price and production neutral. It also believed that loan rates should be set at levels not to compromise US competitiveness in global markets.

The coalition made effective use of the previously mentioned Abel, Daft and Early study (1994) in promoting its position. This study argued that although world markets for agricultural commodities were growing rapidly, the US could not get the share of the increase offered by American agricultural productivity because of land set-asides. While the US was taking good farmland out of production to keep prices up, other countries were expanding their production to meet the increased world demand. Thus, supply control programs were having a negative impact on jobs, income and the overall economy.

In its arguments, the Coalition emphasized that agriculture "doesn't begin and end on the farm" (Rauch (1995), p.215). It noted that while the agriculture sector comprises up 16 percent of the economy, only about an eighth of that amount is made up by farm revenue, with the rest generated by agri-business. Thus, farm bills should not focus exclusively on aiding farmers, but should consider as well other agriculture interests.

The Coalition became an early supporter of "Freedom to Farm." It undertook a major two-pronged effort: to educate the agricultural community at the grass roots and to engage in direct lobbying of legislators. The coalition prepared position papers on a wide variety of subjects, which were widely disseminated, and it gave many press briefings. Members spoke at a wide variety of farming conferences, met with farm organizations and the editorial boards of newspapers and made the coalition's positions clear to every congressional office on Capitol Hill.

Continuity in the Policy Process

The structure of the decision-making process had not changed significantly from the 1990 Farm Bill debate. The same bureaucratic interests in USDA, including the Agricultural Stabilization and Conservation Service and the Foreign Agricultural Service, participated in the formulations of both farm bills, although the political appointees changed with the new administration in 1993. The process of developing the administration recommendations in 1995 was comparable to the 1990 Farm Bill process, except for greater involvement by other Executive agencies and the White House.

The House and Senate Agriculture Committees were the central actors in preparing both 1990 and 1995 farm bills, although control of the committees had changed hands from the Democrat to Republican Parties. As we have mentioned, one major change in the congressional procedure was establishing strict budget limits early in the legislative session, with the farm bill included in the budget reconciliation. This forced both Senate and House Agriculture committee to confront major cuts in the agriculture budget earlier in the process than for the 1990 farm, thus creating an environment conducive to the development of the "Freedom to Farm" proposal. Another change was the writing of farm legislation in the full House Agriculture Committee rather than in sub-committees. This weakened considerably the influence of the commodity groups, though it remains to be seen how permanent is this change.

8.3 Assessment

There are many intriguing questions about the FAIR Act, particularly about how "Freedom to Farm" became part of this legislation, which our analytical framework helps us to address. One set of questions deals with the posture of the Clinton administration. Why did the administration recommend only incremental changes to the 1990 farm bill? Why were the recommendations even more general than those of the Bush administration for the 1990 farm bill? Why did the administration wait until May of 1995 to submit its recommendation? Why did the administration not take a more active role attempting to shape the legislation during the congressional debate? Why did President Clinton sign the FAIR Act containing "Freedom to Farm" when he had vetoed the budget reconciliation containing similar provisions? A second set of questions deals with the congressional process. Why did Senator Lugar begin the committee process by calling for major cuts in target prices? Why was the "Freedom to Farm" initiative launched in the House rather than in the Senate? Was "Freedom to Farm" really a new idea, or an elaboration of an existing idea? Why did "Freedom to Farm" pick up such momentum during the summer and fall of 1995? How was Pat Roberts able to get "Freedom to Farm" attached to the budget reconciliation, after rejection by the House Agriculture Committee? Why in the FAIR Act were sugar, dairy and peanut programs left very much intact? Other questions for analysis have to do with the influence of the Uruguay Round on the FAIR Act and with the importance of individual congressional leaders.

The Clinton Administration and the 1996 Farm Bill

Why did the Clinton administration, in its "Blue book," advocate only incremental change to agricultural policy in a time of budget crisis. The incrementalism is partially explained by organizational process and partly explained by government politics. The administration, believing that it had not received much credit in the 1994 congressional elections for its budget cutting efforts, signaled that it was not going to take the initiative for major new budget cuts. It was prepared to let the new GOP leadership take the political heat for further budget cuts. In the absence of a strong mandate to cut spending, there was little incentive to introduce drastic agricultural policy changes. Absent pressure to change, bureaucratic processes usually come up with recommendations which continue the current policy, making adjustments at the margin, as this minimizes bargaining costs.

The recommended adjustment to the 1990 Farm Bill to increase planting flexibility and market orientation was certainly influenced by the desire to control the growth of agricultural spending. It was also influenced by the increasing trend in farm exports and the administration view that the climate was ripe for further export increases in the future. This view was fueled by economic growth in Asia and the successful conclusion of the Uruguay Round. The administration viewed agricultural policy through the lenses of the Competitive Agriculture paradigm, but felt constrained to adjust policy gradually.

Why were the administration recommendations for the 1996 Farm Bill even more general than the 1990 recommendations? We gain insights by looking through the lenses of the government politics model. Neither the Bush nor Clinton administrations wanted to recommend a detailed farm bill which could become a political target in a Congress controlled by the other party, as had happened with President Reagan's farm bill proposals in 1981 and 1985. The Clinton administration had further reason to stand back in 1995, given the increased partisanship in the House, with its majority committed to the "Contract with America."

Why were the administration's recommendations submitted only in May 1995, when the farm bill debate was well-underway in Congress, rather than in February, at the beginning of the legislative session, as Secretary Yeutter had done in 1990? The lateness of the Clinton administration proposals is partly explained by the transition in leadership at the Department of Agriculture. Following the forced resignation of Secretary Mike Espy in late 1994, the finalizing of recommendations had to await the confirmation of his successor, Dan Glickman, which did not take place until March 1995. Also, the greater involvement of the White House and other executive agencies may have slowed down the planning process.

Why did the administration, having submitted its recommendations, not attempt in an active way to influence the development of the farm bill? Schertz and Doering note that the President's behavior on farm legislation paralleled his relaxed approach on the budget reconciliation, successfully keeping Congress at bay (1999, p.122). But, in contrast to the budget reconciliation bill, there was an imperative to enact a farm bill to avoid reverting to permanent farm legislation with its high price supports. The administration may have taken a passive role assuming that the House and Senate Agriculture Committees would ignore its recommendations as had happened in the past for both Democratic and Republican Presidents. Perhaps, the President decided to sit on the sidelines and let the Republicans take the responsibility for the farm program that developed. This may have been a rational political strategy in that he was not going to get any credit for the legislation that emerged. If "Freedom to Farm" failed, the Republicans would have to take the blame. But, this overlooks the power of the President to stop legislation that he does not like. Perhaps the President would not have been able to write his own provisions into the farm bill, but he probably could have stopped "Freedom to Farm" in the Senate where Democratic support was essential.[132] Schertz and Doering ask why the President never appeared to give any one-person authority to act quickly in negotiating with the hill (1999, p.122). This may have reflected differences (government politics) within the administration. The effect was to undercut Secretary Glickman, when Senate Agriculture Committee Democrats communicated directly with the White House.

Why did the President, after vetoing the budget reconciliation, then send a message through Secretary Glickman, that he would not veto a new farm bill exclusively on the basis of "Freedom to Farm" provisions? One sees a variety of the elements of *government politics* here. Reactions to "Freedom to Farm," within USDA were not monolithic. The bureaucracy, particularly ASCS (which was threatened), was strongly opposed. However, the Chief Economist was generally favorably inclined towards the approach. Other senior USDA officials had mixed feelings. They appreciated the market orientation, and favored limiting the ARP program, believing that these aspects were consistent with increasing US exports to meet the global demand for food, but they were concerned about the impact of "Freedom to Farm" on farming communities. Secretary Glickman was apprehensive about lump-sum payments and the consequences of a catastrophic fall in prices. He was also apprehensive that Producer Flexibility Contract payments would compete for finance with the Fund for Rural America (interview). However, his view moderated over time. Certainly, there was no incentive to sign the budget reconciliation, which had many other measures objectionable to the administration. However, as the new farm bill developed in early 1996, with environmental and other measures pleasing to the administration, the preponderant view was not to veto. Reinforcing this predilection was the pressing need to finalize new farm legislation before the winter wheat harvest began.

Explaining Farm Bill Development in Congress

Why did Senate Agriculture Committee Chairman Richard Lugar come forth with his initial proposal to cut agricultural spending even more drastically than the Senate Budget committee by reducing target prices, anathema to much of the agriculture committee. At first blush, this would appear not to be a politically astute proposal, although it could be seen as a rational option for promoting the market and export orientation of US agricultural policy. Another view is that Lugar floated an extreme proposal to jump-start the debate for reform, without expecting his proposal to succeed. This view is supported by the fact that Lugar backed down from his proposal

---

[132] President Clinton did almost stop "Freedom to Farm" when he vetoed the budget reconciliation bill, but his action was probably primarily because of other provisions in the bill.

rather quickly; he was open to other ideas, and worked to build consensus within his committee. He perhaps helped create the momentum for reform later picked up by Congressman Roberts.

Did "Freedom to Farm" really represent a new idea for agricultural policy? We would argue that "Freedom to Farm" was not a completely new idea, but developed existing ideas further. Decoupling payments from production had been discussed in the 1985 Farm Bill debate in the context of the Boschwitz-Boren proposal, but had been rejected as too radical a change of policy in a time of farm crisis. The 1995 legislation took a step toward de-coupling with its "50-92" (later "0-85") provision (see Chapter 5). The CRP program, established at the same time, provided contract payments for taking land out of production. Positive feedback from these experiments in de-coupling influenced the thinking of the House Agriculture Committee staff members who developed "Freedom to Farm."

Why did "Freedom to Farm" have its origins in the House Agriculture Committee, rather than in the Senate, and why was it endorsed so enthusiastically by Congressman Roberts, who previously had been one of the strongest defenders of the status-quo? There are institutional (organizational process) and political (government politics) reasons why the environment in the House Agriculture Committee was more hospitable than in the Senate Agriculture Committee to a de-coupling proposal such as "Freedom to Farm." With only one third of the seats open in 1994 (compared to the entire House), there were fewer new members and hence more of a commitment in the Senate to the *status quo*. The newly elected Republicans in the House felt they had a mandate for change under the "Contract with America". There was no such mandate in the Senate. The Republicans in the House had a majority of 27-22 on the House Agriculture Committee, while their majority in the Senate was only 10-8. If the Democrats were united and one Republican Senator defected, the Senate committee would be at loggerheads. The rice and cotton lobbies were strong supporters of existing programs, and undoubtedly would have blocked "Freedom to Farm" through their representatives, notably Senator Cochran. Senator Lugar recognized this when he encouraged Pat Roberts to proceed with "Freedom to Farm" in the House, while Lugar went ahead with a traditional farm bill in the Senate. Even if "Freedom to Farm" could have cleared the Senate Agriculture Committee in the summer of 1995, it would undoubtedly have been stopped on the floor, where it would have taken 60 votes to stop a filibuster.

Congressman Roberts' support for "Freedom to Farm" can best be explained as a rational choice decision. Roberts became an advocate when he was convinced that de-coupled income payments better served the interests of farmers than existing commodity policy, particularly in his Kansas constituency, yet was consistent with the Republican mandate to reduce government regulation. Deficiency payments were notably unpredictable. With prices rising as they were in 1995, there was a very good chance that payments to farmers would decrease. "Freedom to Farm" would better enable farmers to "capture the baseline," of previous government support. Pre-set declining payments, from Roberts' perspective, appeared to provide a better safety net than deficiency payments. Deficiency payments had not provided much assistance to farmers during the drought of 1988 and the floods of 1993, when crops were small and prices were low. Finally, the situation of Kansas farmers in the spring of 1995 must have weighed heavily on his thinking. Prices were rising, which meant that farmers would have to pay back advances on deficiency payments. But that would have created great hardship, since wheat crops had been damaged by a late spring frost and farmers did not have the yields to take advantage of high prices.

One of the more intriguing questions about the "Freedom to Farm" debate is why the proposal picked up so much momentum over the summer of 1995, earning the endorsement of groups previously both friendly and hostile to traditional farm policy. The proposal even gained favorable reviews from both *The Washington Post* and *The New York Times*. The "Freedom to Farm" concept had broad appeal because it could be interpreted in many ways, and appeared supportive of diverse values. This facilitated partisan mutual adjustment, where an option is especially attractive if it can be seen as the means to a variety of ends (Lindblom, 1959). "Freedom to Farm" had an appeal to farmers because it reduced uncertainty about government payments and offered more flexibility in what they could plant. With rising prices, it offered more financial support than deficiency payments. It had an attraction to agri-business in that ARP acreage reduction programs would be ended. "Freedom to Farm" allowed the farm lobby and agri-business to overcome a conflict implicit in the deficiency payments regime over the value of annual set-asides. For the advocates of liberal trade, production flexibility contracts were advantageous in that farm income payments were decoupled from production, thus making US agricultural production more responsive to the demands of the international market. In international trade negotiations, the US could push for the abolition of the "Blue Box." "Freedom to Farm" appealed to the budget guardians in that it would cap farm entitlements and could cut government spending on agriculture. This concept had an attraction to the people opposed to farm subsidies, in that it signaled the end of New Deal farm programs, and might be a transition to the end of farm entitlements. Overall, "Freedom to Farm," was a potent bargaining vehicle for building a farm policy consistent with the Competitive Agriculture paradigm.

How was Congressman Roberts able to steer "Freedom to Farm" through the House in the Budget Reconciliation Act, after not being able to gain the approval of his committee? Government politics provides a persuasive explanation. Roberts generated strong support for "Freedom to Farm," in the new Republican leadership, including Speaker Gingrich (R-GA) and House Majority Leader Armey (R-TX). This support was certainly influenced by the tone of "Freedom to Farm," which signified less government regulation, less interference in the economy and a cap on farm entitlements. The leadership saw the potential for promoting a farm bill with "Freedom to Farm" provisions as a significant legislative accomplishment consistent with the "Contract with America." It helped in gaining Speaker Gingrich's support that the peanut interests in his district would not be disturbed. Dick Armey could see Roberts' plan as the beginning of the end of federal farm subsidy programs.

Roberts was able to maintain leadership support even after the budget reconciliation bill was vetoed, when it became clear that his now free-standing farm legislation would lead to far smaller reductions in government expenditures for agriculture than originally anticipated. The leadership probably stayed in Roberts corner because he had convinced Gingrich and the others that a future Republican majority in the House depended on the newly elected congressmen with agricultural constituencies retaining their seats.[133] But this may only have been part of the story. Budget considerations became less pressing after the failed reconciliation. Deserting Roberts at that stage might have delayed the farm bill, with highly negative political reverberations. If the leadership had backed away from Roberts, it probably would have had to get involved in the intricate details of farm legislation, an overwhelming enterprise at this time of confrontation with the President.

Another factor leading to House approval of "Freedom to Farm" in the budget reconciliation, and also contributing to Senate acceptance, was the muting of commodity group resistance. The commodity groups, with a big stake in deficiency payments, initially were wary of Roberts' proposal, which, by de-coupling payments from production, potentially undercut their political influence. As we have noted, the cotton and rice commodity groups initially strongly opposed "Freedom to Farm." However, as commodity prices rose during the farm bill debate, and as it became clear that farmers would gain more from Production Flexibility Contract (PFC) payments than from deficiency payments using 1990 Farm Bill target prices, the commodity groups had to reassess their positions.[134]

During this reassessment, "Freedom to Farm" built up strong support at the grass-roots level that the Washington-based lobbyists could not ignore. The corngrowers became supporters of "Freedom to Farm" fairly early in the debate, while the wheatgrowers always remained divided. But, it was shift of the cotton and rice lobbies that provided the key to congressional approval. Their opposition had prevented Roberts from achieving a majority in his committee and prevented Lugar from pushing Roberts' proposal in the Senate. There is some evidence that the efforts of the Coalition for a Competitive Food and Marketing System contributed to the change in position of these lobbies.[135] Looking at the situation from the perspective of network analysis, we can see that acceptance of "Freedom to Farm" was aided by the loss of cohesiveness in the farm policy network, that previously has been strongly committed to deficiency payments. Roberts' work became far easier when the commodity groups shifted to or supported or muted their opposition to his proposal, and when the supportive Coalition for a Competitive Food and Agricultural System entered the network.

How do we account for the fact that the FAIR Act combined "Freedom to Farm" with retention of the 1949 permanent farm legislation and with the retention of

---

[133] At one stage Roberts took 55 freshman and sophomore congressmen in to see Gingrich to convince him that their seats were in jeopardy if agricultural spending was cut too drastically.

[134] This is extensively covered in Orden, Paarlberg and Roe, 1999, chapter 4.

[135] John Baize, an oilseeds consultant/lobbyist, with close links to the coalition is reported to have been very helpful in shifting the Cotton Council from opposition to support of "Freedom to Farm," by calling up cotton growers and encouraging them to "do the math." The Broiler Council, a member of the Coalition did considerable legwork in selling "Freedom to Farm" in the South.

commodity loan rates at 85 percent of the five-year Olympic average? Why were sugar and peanut programs continued? And, why was the dairy program partially preserved? Why were the Conservation Reserve Program and various environmental programs reauthorized? Looking through the lenses of the government politics model, one can see that these provisions were necessary for forming a winning coalition, representing partisan mutual adjustment. The 1949 permanent farm law and higher loan rates than Roberts envisioned were added to reassure legislators worried about a radical departure from traditional farm policy. Roberts needed the votes of the peanut, sugar and dairy producers to get his program, even though they were inconsistent with the spirit of "Freedom to Farm." The Conservation Reserve program had very broad support, and like "Freedom to Farm," reduced the uncertainty among farmers about their income.[136] Adding environmental provisions had become essential when Senator Lugar needed an alliance with Senator Leahy to break the threat of a filibuster by Senator Dashchle and other "prairie populists."

The Impact of the Uruguay Round

What impact did the Uruguay Round Agreement on Agriculture (URAA) have on the 1996 farm bill? We would argue that while the FAIR Act was primarily influenced by domestic factors, the URAA did have an influence. This was complex in that there were both liberal and illiberal elements. Orden, Paarlberg and Roe have shown that the 1994 Republican congressional election victory and rising commodity prices were the two factors most responsible for the decoupling of farm payments from production in the FAIR Act (1999). The URAA did not provide meaningful constraints in that the US had already fulfilled its commitments to reduce domestic price supports, import barriers and export subsidies, prior to the 1996 Farm Bill debate. The need to gain congressional votes to pass the Uruguay Round Agreement implementing legislation may in fact have strengthened *status quo* US farm policy. Secretary of Agriculture Mike Espy and Alice Rivlin, the Acting Director of the Office of Management and Budget, sent a letter to the chairmen and ranking minority members of the Agriculture Committees in September 1994 (while the implementation legislation was under debate). This letter contained assurances of support for export subsidy programs, the expansion of the purposes of these programs, and a "full continuation" of the CRP. It also promised maintenance of discretionary spending on USDA agricultural programs, and increases of $600 million in GATT-allowed "greenbox" and other activities to promote exports of US farm products (Schertz and Doering (1999), p.15).

Our interviews indicated that the URAA increased the legitimacy of the Competitive Agriculture Paradigm, which strengthened the advocates of "Freedom to Farm." As one individual influential in the congressional process put it:

---

[136] It would appear that the environmentalists and their allies won over the Coalition for a Competitive Food and Agriculture System who wanted to downsize the CRP program.

The successful completion of the Uruguay Round gave all of us confidence in what we were doing and was a boost to morale. [The] Uruguay [Round] was very important in that it brought agriculture into the world trade regime and promotes agricultural trade. The world will have to increase its agricultural yields three times in the foreseeable future. The US can provide much of what is needed. It won't work to see people starve. Agriculture is an engine of growth. The movement away from supply management in the 1996 Farm Bill reflects the influence of the Uruguay Round (interview).

The URAA promise that exports would thrive in a more open world market did nothing to decrease support for the Export Enhancement Program, which still was seen as a "bargaining chip" to get other nations to lower their import barriers and export subsidies.[137] However, this promise also reinforced those who supported decoupling. In this respect, the URAA may have increased the unity and effectiveness of the Coalition for a Competitive Food and Agricultural System. Conversely, the URAA put the forces for strengthening existing commodity programs on the defensive. It became untenable to argue for a farm policy that advocated increasing import barriers, target prices or loan rates above 1995 levels. This undercut the "prairie populists" who would have liked to see farm policy move in that direction.

The origins of "Freedom to Farm" had more to do with "capturing the baseline" for farmers than in expanding international trade. Still, the consistency of "Freedom to Farm" with the trade liberalizing thrust of the Uruguay Round, strengthened Roberts and his supporters. They could argue persuasively that exports would increase with declining PFC payments and the end of ARP programs.

The Leading Roles of Roberts and Lugar

How important was leadership in the development of the FAIR Act reforms? We would argue that even though the economic and political climates were ripe for reform, a very different farm bill would have emerged had Congressmen Roberts and Senator Lugar not chaired the congressional Agriculture committees. Roberts and Lugar had divergent concerns and styles, but they complemented each other in their efforts to produce a new farm bill. Roberts had been a very strong defender of existing farm programs, but had an even stronger underlying goal to do whatever was necessary to get maximum government benefits to farmers. When it became clear that "Freedom to Farm" would further this goal better than the deficiency payments system, he became an advocate and single-mindedly worked to see decoupling included in the farm bill. Lugar, had been a critic of existing farm subsidies and a strong advocate of a market-oriented farm economy. He had a reform proposal of his own to progressively lower deficiency payments, but when this generated little support in the Senate Agriculture Committee, his style was to seek bi-partisan consensus.

---

[137] For a discussion on "bargaining chips" in agricultural trade negotiations, see Orden, Paarlberg and Roe (1999), pp.97-99.

What Roberts and Lugar had in common is that they were both astute legislators. Lugar played an important role in starting a momentum toward reform by asking very broad questions about farm policy in his questionnaire and by soliciting very diverse points of view in Senate Agriculture Committee Hearings. Roberts picked up the ball with "Freedom to Farm," nearly lost it in the House Agriculture Committee, but had build sufficient support among the House leadership that he was allowed to take the extraordinary step of inserting his proposal into the budget reconciliation bill without approval of his committee. Then, when the budget reconciliation was vetoed, he was able to maintain support of the House leadership even when it became clear that "Freedom to Farm" was going to be more expensive than a continuation of the 1990 farm bill. Lugar, though sympathetic to Roberts' proposal, developed a more comprehensive farm bill in the Senate, which preserved the deficiency payments system. When the climate was opportune in January 1996, he was able to broker a bi-partisan deal with Senator Leahy to include "Freedom to Farm" in the Senate bill in return for including provisions on environmental and nutrition programs that were unpopular with Republicans. Then, when the bill got to Conference, Lugar and Roberts were able to get bi-partisan support for the combined package.[138]

There were many points in the process where "Freedom to Farm" could have disappeared from the agenda had there been different leadership. Larry Combest (R-Tex), the second senior Republican on the House Agriculture Committee was the co-sponsor of a proposal very similar to the 1990 Farm Bill that was very nearly approved by the committee. Had he been chairman, "Freedom to Farm" would never have made it onto the agenda. Thad Cochran (R-Miss.), who would have been chairman of the Senate Agriculture Committee in Lugar's absence, was strongly opposed to "Freedom to Farm," in the early stages of the debate.[139] Though his attitude changed as the cotton and rice lobbies came around, it is not clear that he would have inserted "Freedom to Farm" in the Senate farm bill, in which case it might have been lost in Conference.

8.4 Conclusion

The FAIR Act, by abolishing deficiency payments, base acreages and ARP programs, while creating the new policy instrument of production flexibility contracts, established a new path for US agricultural policy. The shift to a new policy path was catalyzed by the budget crisis, which gave the Republicans a potent issue in the 1994

---

[138] Roberts and Lugar appear very much to fit John Kingdon's characterization of policy entrepreneurs. Policy entrepreneurs take advantage of open policy windows, having their proposals at the ready. They seize the opportunity by hooking their solutions to problems or by seeing that proposals from the policy stream are considered when the political conditions are right (see Kingdon (1993) and (1984)).

[139] Senator Jesse Helms (R-N.C.) was senior to Cochran and could have assumed the chairmanship in Lugar's absence, but he would have had to give up his chairmanship of the Senate Foreign Relations committee.

The FAIR Act of 1996 - Decoupling Payments from Production

congressional campaign. When the Republicans won control of both houses of Congress, the commitment to cut the budget deficit required a serious re-appraisal of existing agriculture policy. The importance of the budget constraint was magnified by the change in congressional rules, which forced legislators to include farm legislation in the budget reconciliation bill. The old deficiency payments regime had become unpopular at a time when the outlook for farming looked rosy because of limits on planting flexibility and required ARP set-asides. The "Freedom to Farm" seed planted as an alternative found especially nourishing growing conditions. Decoupling of payments from production was attractive to the Republican congress as a way of reducing government regulation and of reducing the uncertainty of farm entitlements. "Freedom to Farm" was attractive to agri-business in that it ended ARP programs and increased market-orientation. This reform proposal became appealing to an increasingly broad cross-section of farmers as rising commodity prices (with decreasing deficiency payments) made it clear they would receive more government largesse than under the existing 1990 Farm Bill rules. The chairman of the House Agriculture Committee had a strong incentive to promote "Freedom to Farm" in that its provisions would prevent the farmers in his district from having to return deficiency payments at a time when their crops were poor as a result of a late spring frost. Roberts and Lugar were skillful politicians, well-placed to shepherd de-coupled payments through the congressional process. Their work was facilitated in that the consequences of "Freedom to Farm" were uncertain enough to make targeting difficult for the opposition.[140] "Freedom to Farm" developed such a momentum that it could not be stopped, even when it became clear that there would be no budget savings, the original impetus for reform.

The FAIR Act gave the Competitive Agriculture Paradigm a strong foothold in US farm policy. Supply restraints were out and "transition" payments were in. New standard operating procedures were developed to institutionalize the change. Once in place these procedures were would be difficult to reverse, particularly since the beneficiaries of "transition payments" could be counted upon to lobby intensely to preserve their benefits.

Having decoupled payments from production, all US agriculture needed was policy reform in other countries to usher in an era of global competition in farm products. How would the EU respond in its ensuing reassessment of the CAP as part of the Agenda 2000 debate? It is to this response that we turn in the next chapter.

---

[140] One reason why "Freedom to Farm" was difficult for the opposition to target is that there was very little analysis of its consequences. Most of the studies done at the beginning of the farm bill debate had assumed incremental change from the 1990 farm bill. See Conley (1996) and Schertz and Doering (1999), p.17.

Chapter 9

Agenda 2000 - New Reforms for the CAP

9.1 Development of the Commission Reform Proposals

The European Union instituted its Agenda 2000 reforms of the Common Agricultural Policy at the April 1999 Berlin summit. The planning for Agenda 2000 looked ahead in a rapidly changing world to the future impact on the CAP of changing market conditions, the future entry into the EU of the former communist countries in Central and Eastern Europe, and to the implications of the forthcoming WTO agricultural trade negotiations beginning in 1999. The process also had to take into account demands for increased expenditures for agri-environmental and rural development measures. The Agenda 2000 reforms went through a long and convoluted political process before approval, similar to the previous MacSharry reforms. The final reform package expanded the MacSharry reforms by lowering target prices and providing compensatory payments to farmers. It also created a strengthened Pillar II for the CAP, consisting of rural development and agri-environmental measures. This chapter discusses the development of the Agenda 2000 reforms.

Renewed Demands for Reform

Not long after the signing of the Marrakech agreement and the creation of the World Trade Organization in March 1994, demands for further reform of the CAP began to surface. These demands increased in intensity during 1994 and 1995, even though the early feedback indicated that the MacSharry reforms had been successful. The CAP budget seemed under control, markets were in better balance, consumption had increased, stocks disappeared, and, contrary to expectations, farm income increased. But critics questioned how much these positive trends stemmed from MacSharry, and how much they were due to strengthening world markets. What would happen, they asked, when world prices returned to more normal levels? With continued improvements in productivity, would not stocks begin to develop again, and would the EU still be able to export the surplus, without violating the Uruguay Round limits on export subsidies?

The prospect of entry into the EU of the former Communist countries of Central and Eastern Europe (CEEC) raised other serious questions. Four studies commissioned by Sir Leon Brittan in his capacity as Commissioner for External Trade concluded that the financial costs of integrating these countries into the CAP, without further price cuts, would be unacceptably high.[141] If CAP support prices were not reduced, the wrong production signals would be sent, which would contribute to the EU's chronic surpluses. Moreover, if the CEEC countries had to raise their commodity prices significantly upon joining the CAP, higher domestic food costs would result, increasing the stress on financially strapped consumers.

The pressures for further reform of the CAP were resisted at first by DGVI and by the departing Agriculture Commissioner, Rene Steichen. The new Agriculture Commissioner, Franz Fischler was more ambiguous in testimony before the European Parliament's Agricultural Committee, shortly after he assumed office on January 1, 1995. He indicated that his priorities were completing CAP Reform, implementing the GATT accord, and helping to prepare the ground for the expansion of the EU to include the countries of Central and Eastern Europe (*Agra Europe*, Jan 13, 1995: E/1). The pressures on DGVI increased in May, when Commission President Jacques Santer promised plans by the end of the year for "radical reform" of the CAP to meet the challenge of integrating the CEEC countries (*Agra Europe*, May 19, 1995: P/2).

Commissioner Fischler took the initiative as he reacted to the position of the Foreign Affairs Council calling for the early accession to the EU of Hungary, Poland, the Czech Republic, Slovakia and Slovenia, and as he anticipated action on accession at the Madrid summit in December. In early October he instructed DGVI to produce recommendations by the end of the month on the necessary changes for agriculture. (*Agra Europe*, October 6, 1995: P/1). *Agra Europe* reported that Fischler and his cabinet were keen to ensure that their position on the enlargement issue was clearly articulated and under discussion well in advance of the Madrid meeting (*Agra Europe*, Oct. 6, 1995: P/1).

The Commission "Strategy" Document

The DGVI recommendations became the basis for the Commission "Strategy" document, which while short on detailed prescriptions, reached the firm conclusion that the various pressures building on the EU in the next few years - of which Eastern enlargement was just one - would inexorably require further reforms of the CAP. (*Agra Europe*, Nov. 10, 1995: P/1). Some of the other pressures cited were impending budgetary problems, long-term market imbalance in certain sectors, the challenge of a new WTO Round, and internal environmental considerations. The document considered a range of options from maintaining the status quo to "radical reform," although the Commission's preferred approach was a "progressive and gradual adjustment of the policy to develop the reforms already undertaken in 1992." This resonated with Commissioner Fischler's professed desire for an "evolutionary"

---

[141] These studies were by authored Allan Buckwell, Stefan Tangermann, Secondo Tarditi and Louis P. Mahe. See *Agra Europe*, Jan. 20, 1995: E/1-E/2. They provide evidence of a pro-reform *epistemic community* of "professionals with recognized expertise and competence, and an authoritative claim to policy-relevant knowledge, sharing the same normative and principled beliefs, the same causal beliefs, the same notions of validity, and a common enterprise" (see Webber (1997), p.6; also see Haas (1992), p.3).

approach (*Agra Europe*, Nov. 10, 1995: P/1). The "Strategy" document emphasized the need to diversify rural economies, the shortcomings of the EU's regional funds, and the obligation in the Maastricht Treaty to integrate environmental concerns with other EU policies. (Lowe, Rutherford and Baldock (1997), p.1).[142] The report stressed that further reform of the CAP was not imposed on the EU by the impending CEEC accession, but would be necessary in any case as a result of a variety of external and internal pressures. *Agra Europe* noted that this "de-linkage" was made to soothe the sensitivities of agriculture ministers, who had shown resistance in the Uruguay Round to CAP changes imposed from outside the EU (Nov. 10, 1995: P/1).

The Agriculture Council accepted the basic principles for the development of the CAP contained in the "Strategy" document, but indicated that the process of enlargement should entail long transition periods and that the *acquis communautaire* - including the existing principles of agricultural policy - should be respected (*Agra Europe*, Dec.1, 1995: P/1). The European Council endorsed the conclusions of the "Strategy" document at its Madrid meeting in December, and asked the Commission to develop ideas on integrated rural development further (Lowe, Rutherford and Baldock (1997), p.2).

Reform Concepts in DGVI

DGVI Director-General Guy Legras gave an indication of the timing and content of the new reform proposals in June 1996 (*Agra Europe*, June 21, 1996: P/1). He indicated that the Commission would produce a "Reflections" document within the next twelve months, outlining the main principles of the planned reform. Detailed proposals for reform would subsequently be produced, taking into account the reactions of the Agriculture Council. This two-stage procedure was similar to the procedure successfully employed in formulating the MacSharry reforms. Legras made it very clear that the thinking in DGVI was to continue reform along the lines started by MacSharry, when he remarked - "you might call it [the new reform proposal], MacSharry Mark II" (*Agra Europe*, June 21, 1996: P/1). Legras noted that the centrepiece of the reform would be lower cereal price supports, but that the proposals would also include reductions in dairy and beef sector supports. In both the cereals and dairy regime the objective would be to abolish the differential between EU and world market prices, thus making export subsidies largely superfluous and avoiding the

---

[142] Article 130R of the Treaty on European Union (the "Maastricht" Treaty) states the following aims for Community policy on the environment: (i) preserving, protecting and improving the quality of the environment; (ii) protecting human health; (iii) prudent and rational utilization of natural resources; (iv) promoting measures at the international level to deal with regional or worldwide environmental problems. Community policy should aim at *"a high level of protection taking into account the diversity of situations in the various regions of the Community"; "preventative action should be taken, ... environmental damage should as a priority be rectified at the source, and ... the polluter should pay ... Environmental protection requirements must be integrated into the definition and implementation of other Community policies"* (see Tracy (1997), p.43).

limitations on subsidized exports imposed by the Uruguay Round. These limitations would likely be strengthened in the next round of agricultural trade negotiations scheduled to begin in 1999 (*Agra Europe*, June 21, 1996: P/1). It was not made clear how much farmers would be compensated for these price cuts.

Agra Europe reported that the proposals for reform would give new emphasis to agri-environmental measures (June 21, 1996: P/2). One key element in the Commission's preparatory work was the forthcoming conference on agri-environmental policy to be held in Cork, Ireland, in the autumn. Commissioner Fischler indicated that the conference would discuss CAP reform "accompanying measures," stocking levels for livestock and the concept of "cross-compliance" (where the payment of farm subsidies would be made conditional on achieving environmental objectives). The Commissioner sought to develop these ideas into a more coherent agri-environmental strategy for the EU (*Agra Europe*, June 21, 1996: P/2).

The Cork Conference

The November 8-11 1996 Cork Conference was attended by some 500 delegates from both the EU and CEEC states, representing a broad range of interests. The Conference had three stated objectives: 1) current and future challenges facing the EU's rural areas, and the type of European policies needed to meet them; 2) promotion of a fully fledged, multi-sectoral, integrated rural development policy in all rural areas of the Union; and, 3) steps required to improve the implementation of existing European structural programs, moving toward genuine rural development. The climax of the meeting was the production of a statement in the shape and future development of rural policy - the "Cork Declaration" (see Box 9.1). The declaration put rural development at the top of the EU policy agenda, implying expanded programs.[143] It emphasized the importance of including the entire farmed countryside within the scope of rural development, rather than focusing on specific geographic zones. It called for the integration of existing funds to simplify the plethora of policy mechanisms. It advocated greater subsidiarity, transparency and participation in achieving an integrated rural policy.

Even though the conference demonstrated a strong constituency for rural development, the Cork Declaration received a generally cool reception in the EU policy community. In the Agriculture Council, the German, Dutch and Spanish ministers refused to endorse the statement, claiming negative implications for the CAP if the declaration's recommendations were carried out (*Agra Europe*, Dec. 20, 1996: E/5). In a second blow, the December Dublin summit dropped a statement on the Cork Conference from its official conclusions at the behest of the French and German delegations who said it went too far (*Agra Europe*, Dec. 20, 1996: E/5).

---

[143] For discussion of the Cork Conference and its implications, see Lowe, Rutherford and Baldock (1996).

> **The Cork Declaration**
> - Sustainable rural development must be at the top of the EU agenda. It must be the fundamental principle underpinning rural policy.
> - Policy must be multi-disciplinary in concept and multi-sectoral in application. It must apply to all rural areas, with differentiation in favour of areas of greatest need.
> - Support must focus on providing the framework for self-sustaining private and community based initiatives, without re-nationalizing the CAP.
> - Policies must protect and sustain the quality and diversity of rural landscapes.
> - Policy must be de-centralized and should follow the principle of subsidiarity, with a single programme for each region.
> - The use of local financial resources must be encouraged and where necessary the administrative effectiveness of regional and local government organizations must be enhanced.
> - Monitoring must ensure transparency to ensure good use of public funds.
>
> Source: *Agra Europe*, Nov.15, 1996:E/7

Box 9.1: The Cork Declaration

These negative reactions stemmed partly from the Conference itself and partly from the recommendations. The conference was a highly stage-managed affair, which did not allow much participation by the delegates (Lowe, Rutherford and Baldock (1996), p.3). The timing was bad: EU policy makers were at that stage deeply caught up in the BSE crisis, with little time or inclination to come to grips with a common rural policy for the EU. In what was a political mistake, DGXVI (Directorate General for Regional Policy and Cohesion), and Commissioner Monika Wulf-Mathies, responsible for large elements of current rural development programs, were left off the Conference platform, causing serious tensions within the Commission (Lowe, Rutherford and Baldock (1997), p.4). But, probably most serious, the declaration played to the suspicions of *status quo* agricultural interests, who were afraid that a greater emphasis on rural development would take money away from farmers. This doubtless inspired the negative reactions from Germany, France and some of the Mediterranean countries where the rural vote is important (Lowe, Rutherford and Baldock (1996), p.3).

The Agenda 2000 Proposals

In July 1997, the Commission published, "Agenda 2000: For a Stronger and Wider Europe." This document gave a broad outlook for the development of the EU beyond the turn of the Century, the impact of enlargement to include the Central and Eastern

European Countries (CEECs), the financial framework beyond 2000, and proposals for the further reform of the CAP.[144] Agenda 2000 recommended that negotiations should begin immediately with five of the CEECs (Estonia, the Czech Republic, Hungary, Poland and Slovenia) and with Cyprus. Negotiations for the entry of the other five CEECs (Latvia, Lithuania, Slovakia, Romania and Bulgaria) could begin as soon as these countries met certain economic, and in the case of Slovakia, political conditions.

Table 9.1: Agenda 2000: Agricultural Expenditure Projections, Billion Euro, in Current Prices (assumes two per cent inflation per year)

	1999	2000	2001	2002	2003	2004	2005	2006	Total Ex-pend.	%
EU-15 Reformed CAP	41.7	41.6	43.4	45.4	47.3	47.9	47.9	47.9	363.1	91.9
New rural development accompanying measures	-	1.9	2.0	2.0	2.0	2.0	2.1	2.1	14.1	3.6
New Member States										
CAP market measures	-	0.0	0.0	1.1	1.2	1.2	1.3	1.4	6.2	1.6
Specific rural development accompanying measures	-	0.0	0.0	0.6	1.0	1.5	2.0	2.0	7.6	1.9
Pre-accession aid*	-	0.5	0.5	0.6	0.6	0.6	0.6	0.6	4.0	1.0
Total Agricultural Expenditure	41.7	44.0	45.9	49.7	52.1	53.2	53.9	54.5	395.0	
Guideline	45.0	46.7	48.5	50.6	52.6	54.7	56.9	59.2		
Margin	3.3	2.7	2.6	0.9	0.5	1.5	3.0	4.7		

*Equal to 0.5 billion per year at 1997 prices
Source: Adapted from Commission, Agenda 2000 (July 1997), Vol. I, Table 2, in Tracy (1997), p.15.

A new financial framework would be needed to enable the EU to finance its on-going requirements and to integrate the prospective member countries. In a general

---

[144] For discussion of the July 1997 Agenda 2000 proposals see Tracy (1997), especially chapters 1-3, 8.
[145] The EU changed the name of the ECU to the Euro in 1995. The Euro replaced the ECU on 1 January 1999.

atmosphere of financial austerity, the Commission recommended spending restricted to the previously established ceiling of own resources (1.27 per cent of EU GNP), which was to be reached in 1999. Agriculture would constitute the largest item, but spending increases were limited to 74 per cent of the Union's annual GNP growth. During the period from 2000 to 2006, the agricultural spending guideline was projected to grow from 44.1 billion ECU (45 per cent of the EU budget) to 50 billion ECU (43.7 per cent of the EU budget) (see Tracy, (1997), pp.14-15). Structural operations, the second largest expenditure item, were projected to increase from 35.2 billion ECU (36.1 per cent of the EU budget) in 2000, to 42.8 billion ECU (37.3 per cent of the EU budget) in 2006. Of the 275 billion ECU total for structural operations, 45 billion ECU would be allocated to the new member states.

Table 9.1 lists the agricultural expenditure projections of the July 1997, Agenda 2000 proposal. This list is revealing in terms of the Commission's priorities. Of the total 395 billion ECU projected agricultural expenditures between 1999 and 2006, 363.1 billion ECU would be devoted to the "reformed CAP" (pillar I) in the current 15 EU Member States and 6.2 billion ECU in the prospective member states. The combined total would account for 369.3 billion ECU, or 93.5 percent of agricultural expenditures. New rural development and accompanying measures (Pillar II) would receive 14.1 billion ECU in the EU 15 and 7.6 billion ECU in the prospective new Member States, for a total of 21.7 billion ECU or 5.5 percent of agriculture expenditures. These figures make it clear that the proposed expenditures for rural development would constitute only a small fraction of those reserved for the reformed CAP.

Pillar I - Market support The agriculture section of the Agenda 2000 proposal was based on two pillars. Pillar I encompassed market support, while Pillar II consisted of rural development and environmental measures. Under Pillar I, the intervention price for cereals would be reduced from 119.19 ECU/tonne to 95.35 ECU/tonne (a 20 per cent reduction). At the same time, compensatory payments would increase from 54 ECU/tonne to 66 ECU/tonne (a 22 per cent increase), multiplied by the regional cereals yield. However the mandatory set-aside would be set at zero. For beef, Agenda 2000 proposed a gradual reduction of effective market support from 2780 ECU/tonne to 1950 ECU/tonne (a 30 per cent cut), with an increase in direct payments for suckler cows, bulls and steers. For dairy, an extension of the quota regime until 2006 was proposed, with a gradual decrease in support prices of ten per cent. At the same time, a new yearly payment for dairy cows would be introduced at a level of 145 ECU/cow.

Pillar II - Rural development and agri-environmental measures Pillar II of Agenda 2000 comprised a number of different rural development and agri-environment measures.[146] The Community's Regional Fund, Social Fund, Cohesion Fund and EAGGF Guidance Funds were kept intact. The proposal did not recommend the

---

[146] For a detailed discussion of EU structural, rural development and environmental policies prior to Agenda 2000 and of the impact of Agenda 2000, see Tracy (1997), Chapter 3.

creation of a rural fund, but made much more explicit the importance of rural development, and would have increased the use of the agriculture Guarantee Fund (market support) for this purpose. Rural development measures were envisaged as distinctly farmer-oriented and fit into two general categories: RD1, which included agri-environment, afforestation, early retirement and the less-favored area scheme; and RD2 (modernization and diversification), investment in agricultural holdings, establishment of young farmers, training, investment in processing and marketing facilities, forestry, adaptation and development of rural areas. Wherever possible the principle of "subsidiarity" (making decisions at the appropriate de-centralized level) would be applied. The number of structural objectives was reduced from five to three, with much of the funding shifted to the EAGGF Guarantee Fund (see Tracy (1997), p.46).

Objectives 1 and 2 included specific rural development components.[147] Objective 1, which was unchanged, included the development and structural adjustment of regions lagging behind (defined as areas in which per capita GNP is less than 75 percent of the Community's average for the last three years) was kept intact. The Regional Fund, Social Fund and EAGGF guidance would continue to support integrated programs. However, the guarantee section of EAGGF would have taken over the responsibility for a number of measures currently financed by "Guidance", including assistance to farmers in less-favored areas. The proposed "Objective 2" dealt with economic and social restructuring in other regions suffering from structural problems. These would include areas undergoing economic change in industry and services, crisis-hit areas dependent on the fishing industry, urban areas in difficulty, and declining rural areas. The EAGGF Guarantee Fund would be used with the other funds for programs in rural areas. Programs would favor economic diversification, with increased support for small and medium-sized enterprises and innovation, with greater emphasis on vocational training, local development and protection of the environment (Tracy (1997), p.46).

Rural development measures outside areas covered by objectives 1 and 2 would be applied horizontally and implemented in a decentralized way at the appropriate level, at the initiative of member states. The Commission apparently intended that programs should be applied to broad regions, such as the German Lander or the French regions (Tracy (1997), p.47). Each region would select from a "menu" the measures that best fit its needs. Box 9.2 gives a summary of the proposed rural development measures and their sources of financing.

---

[147] Objective 3 would aim, on a "horizontal" basis for regions not covered by objectives 1 or 2, at *"the development of human resources."* It would give priority to improving access to employment, the development of learning and promotion of local employment opportunities (see Tracy (1997), p.46).

> **Agenda 2000 - Rural Development**
> - **Simplification**: One regulation instead of nine
> - **Subsidiarity**: More flexibility for Member States and Regions
> - **Measures**:
>   RD1: agri-environment, afforestation, early retirement, Less Favored Areas
>   RD2: (modernization and diversification): investment in agricultural holdings, establishment of young farmers, training, investment in processing and marketing facilities, forestry, adaptation and development of rural area
> - **Objective 1 regions**
>   RD1   financed by EAGGF Guarantee
>   RD2   financed by EAGGF Guidance and integrated into structural fund programming
> - **Objective 2 regions**
>   RD1 and RD2 financed by EAGGF Guarantee
>   RD2   under the legal framework of the General Structural Funds Regulation
> - **All other rural areas**
>   RD1 and RD2 financed by EAGGF Guarantee
>   Single programme per Member State (region)
>
> Source: European Commission DGVI

Box 9.2: Agenda 2000: Rural Development

The July, 1997 Agenda 2000 proposal declared a prominent role for agri-environmental instruments and would have "reinforced and extended" relevant measures (Tracy (1997), p.48). It made three suggestions. First, the Commission should develop a proposal on "cross-compliance," enabling Member States to make direct payments conditional on the respect for environmental provisions. Second, account could be taken of the "overlap between less-favored areas and areas of high nature value." This suggests that the current support system, based on livestock numbers or specified crop areas per farm, might gradually be transformed into an instrument "to maintain and promote low input systems." Third, "targeted agri-environmental measures should be re-enforced and encouraged through increased budgetary resources, and where necessary, higher co-financing rates" (Tracy (1997), p.48). This would apply particularly to "services which call for an extra effort by farmers such as organic farming, maintenance of semi-natural habitats, traditional orchards or hedgerows, continuation of alpine cattle keeping, upkeep of wetlands." However, Agenda 2000 provided no specific provision for financing these measures.

9.2 The Agenda 2000 Debate

Reactions in the Agriculture Council

Not surprisingly, the initial reactions of the Council of Ministers to the Agenda 2000 proposals were quite mixed. The farm ministers from the UK, Sweden and Denmark backed the general direction of Commissioner Fischler's proposal, but said the reforms should have gone further. The UK and Sweden indicated disappointment that milk quotas would be retained until 2006, while Sweden also called for compensation payments to be phased out over time (*Agra Europe*, July 25, 1997: E/1). Denmark indicated that the dairy price cut should be larger than the ten per cent proposed by the Commission, that compensation should be much lower and targeted on the dairy sector, and that greater emphasis should be given to the environment, animal welfare and consumers (*Agra Europe*, July 25, 1997: E/1). The Irish farm minister said he supported the broad direction of CAP reform proposed by the Commission, though he had misgiving over the financial effects on farmers, whom he wanted compensated for any price cuts (*Agra Europe*, July 25, 1997: E/1).

The German agriculture minister, Jochen Borchert, led the opposition, saying that he could see "very few positive things" about the proposal (*Agra Europe*, July 25, 1997: E/1). He warned that acceptance of the Commission's plan would mean a 15-20 percent drop in the income of German farmers. He challenged the assumptions that the next WTO Round would lead automatically to price cuts and that enlargement would further increase production surpluses (*Agra Europe*, July 25, 1997: E/2). He also attacked the logic of the proposed dairy reforms, saying that it made no sense maintaining quotas designed to keep prices high until 2006, while at the same time proposing a milk price cut. He received support from the farm ministers of Belgium and Luxembourg, while the Austrian minister questioned the need for price cuts.

France and the Southern members of the EU also expressed reservations about the proposal. The French farm minister, Louis LePensac, told journalists that initial calculation indicated the Commission proposal would have a "negative effect" on the income of French farmers (*Agra Europe*, July 25, 1997: E/2). He wanted a fairer distribution between sectors and between farmers, and announced that the French ministry of agriculture was working on a modulation system. He also criticized the Commission for ceding ground to the EU's WTO partners on agricultural price cuts before the next round of negotiations, an argument later taken up by the German agricultural minister. Ministers from the southern EU member states criticized the proposals for not giving enough attention to Mediterranean products, although Commissioner Fischler had said he hoped to have proposals for tobacco and olive oil ready by the end of the year (*Agra Europe*, July 25, 1997: E/2). The Italian minister criticized the Commission for ignoring the effects of enlargement on Mediterranean products.

The Agriculture Council intensively debated Agenda 2000 in a series of meetings held during the Autumn of 1997. In these discussions it became evident that the road to approval would still be a long uphill struggle, although the majority of Ministers accepted the need for reform and backed the general approach put forward by Commissioner Fischler (*Agra Europe*, Oct. 24, 1997: P/1). There was general agreement that beef support price cuts were inevitable, though there remained disagreement over the size of the cuts and over the extent of compensation.[148] Germany wanted smaller cuts, while the UK and Sweden called for larger ones. Germany, Austria, Spain, Finland insisted on full compensation, while the UK and Sweden said that compensation should be phased out. Greece, Spain, Italy and the Netherlands said that compensation was discriminatory.

For dairy reform, a large number of member states argued that a ten percent cut in milk prices would not be enough to deal with potential problems with the dairy market, and therefore not worth amending the regime (*Agra Europe*, Oct. 24, 1997: E/1). However, the UK, Italy, Sweden and Denmark wanted the quota system abolished. A number of member states, led by the Dutch, insisted that any compensation for a milk price cut should be based on quota allocation, not animal numbers, to avoid the possibility of countries with high milk yields losing out. For cereals, a majority of the agriculture ministers demanded full compensation for the proposed 20 percent price cut, rather than the 50 percent compensation proposed by the Commission (*Agra Europe*, Oct. 24, 1997: E/2). The UK, Sweden and Denmark said that compensation should be phased out. A number of states, led by the French, expressed concern that plans to end a specific payment for oilseeds could drastically reduce production in the EU and cause a surge in cereal output. There was also strong opposition to plans to exclude silage maize from a reformed arable support regime.

The Farm ministers were extremely cautious in forming opinions about the Commission's rural development proposals, perhaps in part because they did not fully recognize the implications (*Agra Europe*, Sept. 19, 1997: P/3). However, certain elements were seriously questioned. The German agriculture minister, backed by the Dutch and Belgian ministers, argued against the Commission's plan to finance rural development projects from the "guarantee" section of the agriculture budget, claiming that rural development would lose out to spending on market supports (*Agra Europe*, Sept. 26, 1997: E/1). A number of ministers were concerned about the abolition of the special Structural Funds category for rural areas (Objective 5b). They feared that this meant that rural areas would be forced to compete for funds with industrial areas under a new objective 2 (*Agra Europe*, Sept. 26, 1997: E/1).

Commissioner Fischler's Response

Commissioner Fischler vigorously defended the Commission's Agenda 2000 proposals in meetings of the Agricultural Council and in various public forums. In a September, 1997, full page article in the German newspaper, *Frankfurter Allgemeine Zeitung*, he argued that "acting as though everything would stay the same as in the past without reform is verging on a lie" (*Agra Europe*, Aug. 29, 1997: P/3). He pointed out that Europe risked losing its status as the "biggest player" on the world market if it failed to

---

[148] See *Agra Europe*, Oct. 24, 1997: P/2 for a summary of national positions.

cut prices. Price cuts would reduce reliance on export refunds increasingly squeezed by the Uruguay Round commitment. He warned that the EU, with a stagnant domestic market, should go down the road of "moderate liberalization" so as not to pass up valuable customers in Asia (*Agra Europe*, Aug. 29, 1997: P/3). He rejected the view that immediate reform of the CAP before the next WTO Round represents "submission" to the US and other trade partners. He noted, "the [proposed] reforms are not premature submissiveness on our part, but making use of the existing regime to be able to sell our products on the world market" (*Agra Europe*, Aug. 29, 1997: P/4). He stated that protection of farm incomes remained the main objective of agricultural policy and predicted that the envisaged reforms would improve the welfare of farmers.

The European Farming Model

From the very origins of the European Community, there had been a strong concern that the survival of the family farm was essential for sustaining rural communities and well-managed landscapes (Potter (1998), p.1). The Commission defined this concern in its 1991 paper on *The Development and Future of the CAP*: "sufficient farmers must be kept on the land. There is no other way to preserve the natural environment, traditional landscapes and a model of agriculture as favoured by society generally" (CEC (1991), p.9). Potter notes that for many in Europe this idea connects with the long-standing debate about the dangerous social consequences of agricultural decline and land abandonment, which in France is known as "desertification" (Potter (1998), p.8). Preserving family farms to protect the landscape provided a publicly defensible set of arguments with which to justify the retention of agricultural support (Potter (1998), p.9).

Hence, it is not surprising that the opponents of agricultural policy reform built on this argument to define a European Model of Farming as a weapon against Agenda 2000. The Committee of Agricultural Organizations in the EU (COPA) came up with a rather detailed formulation:

> In Europe not only does agriculture involve production of healthy, good quality products for use as foodstuff or non-foods, it also plays an essential role in land use and town and country planning and in employment, creating activities in the rural sphere, and preserving natural resources, the environment and the beauty of the landscape. Moreover, through the export of agricultural products and foodstuffs, it contributes not only to the balance of trade in the European Union but also to the balance of foodstuffs at worldwide level via food aid (COPA (1997), p.2).

COPA argued that in order to develop the European Farming Model, all proposals for reform of the CAP needed to fulfil a rather long set of criteria, which included:

- guarantee an increase in farm incomes comparable to those of other socio-professional categories;
- allow European agriculture to continue to fulfill its multi-functional role;

- as a main world producer of healthy and quality agricultural products for use as foodstuffs and for non-food purposes within the European Union as well as for exports, and:
- remain the backbone of rural regions for employment, town and country planning, preserving the landscape, environmental protection and maintaining the social fabric
- promote continued improvements in structures and efficiency in the agricultural sector
- maintain European identity by highlighting the role of agriculture in society and applying it as the basis of the European position in the forthcoming WTO negotiations (COPA, 1997, pp.2-3).

COPA and other groups opposed to CAP reform saw the European Farming Model through the lenses of the Multifunctional Agriculture paradigm. Greater market orientation, as envisaged in Agenda 2000 would endanger the small family farmer, thus risking the destruction of the rural landscape and rural society. Using the forthcoming WTO talks as a justification for commodity price cuts was inappropriate, when the Commission should be holding the line against liberalization in the WTO, as a requisite of preserving European rural life.

Interestingly, the concept of the European model of farming was powerful enough and general enough to be appropriated by the proponents of Agenda 2000 as well as the opponents. Commissioner Fischler employed it frequently. In a September 1997 article in the *Frankfurter Allgemeine Zeitung*, Fischler argued that the revised CAP would establish a level playing field for EU farmers, rewarding them for the intangible services they provide, such as care of the countryside. He noted that overseas competitors are not expected to deliver equivalent services (*Agra Europe*, August 29, 1997: P/4). He stated that the EU would defend its higher environmental and food health standards in the WTO to ensure that EU farmers were not hamstrung in the face of imports from countries with more lax rules.

The Luxembourg Summit

At the end of their Autumn 1997 discussion of the Agenda 2000 proposals, the Agriculture Ministers agreed on a common stance, which was set forth in a position paper approved by the Luxembourg summit in December.[149] This paper provided the impetus for the Commission to develop the proposed Agenda 2000 regulations, released in March, 1998. The position paper gave a broad assent to the general direction of the Agenda 2000 proposals, but did not contain much on their substance (*Agra Europe*, Nov. 21, 1997: EP/1). Reform was seen in the context of preserving the European Model of Farming:

---

[149] The Spanish agriculture minister demurred, arguing that expenditures under the CAP guideline should be confined to the current 15 members of the EU.

Agenda 2000 - New Reforms for the CAP

The Council has therefore set its sights on equipping Europe with a brand of agriculture capable of coping successfully with the challenges of the 21st century... To meet these challenges, it [the Council] is firmly resolved to continue developing the existing model of European agriculture and act to assert its identity both inside and outside the European Union (*Agra Europe*, Nov. 21, 1997: A/1).

The approach involving mainly a combination of reduced price-support measures and compensation through direct aid as well as flanking measures remains generally valid.... The details of reform in the various sectors concerned need to be designed in such a way as to arrive at economically sound, viable solutions which are socially acceptable, make it possible to insure fair incomes, to strike a fair balance between production sectors, producers and regions and to avoid distortion of competition (*Agra Europe*, Nov. 21, 1997: A/1).

Striving for greater competitiveness must however, take second place, and will in due course be reconciled as best it can with the model of European agriculture referred to earlier (*Agra Europe*, Nov. 21, 1997: A/1).

Thus the Agriculture Council and the European Council told Commissioner Fischler and DGVI that it was fine to go ahead and develop draft regulations based on the Agenda 2000 proposals, but to ensure that they were consistent with preserving the European model of farming.

The Fischler Tour of National Capitals

While the Agriculture Council debated Agenda 2000 in the Autumn of 1997, Agriculture Commissioner Fischler embarked on a tour of every EU capital to meet with farmers, representatives of the food processing industry and government officials. His stated mission was to explain what impact the reform proposals would have and how they would be implemented (*Agra Europe*, Sept. 12, 1997: E/2). It was evident that he wanted a reading of the political acceptability of his proposals. In the course of his tour, he proceeded to negotiate various elements of Agenda 2000 with national governments individually in an attempt to make the general proposal more palatable. In this respect, he was following the precedent set by Ray MacSharry in 1992, but at an earlier stage of the process. The tour sounded a cautionary note for Fischler. He found strong sentiments to maintain the *status quo* with only slight modifications to the CAP (*Agra Europe*, Jan. 9, 1998: A/1).

The March 1998 Draft Agenda 2000 Regulations

The Commission's March 1998 draft regulations added detail to the July 1997 proposals, but there were some changes. Direct payment for silage cereals was included to mollify the group of nations led by Germany strongly opposed to its exclusion. Direct payments for beef suckler cows, bulls and steers were increased to make the proposed market price reduction more acceptable. The proposed support price reduction for milk was increased to 15 per cent to accommodate milk processors and the governments that had thought a ten percent price reduction insufficient to be worth the trouble of changing the dairy regime. At the same time milk quotas would have been increased by two per cent, with half of the increase going to mountainous areas and Nordic zones, and with priority for the other half given to young farmers. National envelopes would have been created for both the beef and dairy industries allowing national governments to allocate 30 per cent of beef and dairy support aid schemes as they see fit. This made the proposals more acceptable to Germany, the Netherlands and Italy, which would have lost from the shift to direct payments because of existing limits on herd sizes *(Agra Europe,* Feb. 20, 1998: EP/1). France and Ireland also backed this scheme to allow them to target funds.

The proposed Agenda 2000 regulations added a digressive overall ceiling on aid payments to individual farmers, which would perhaps help to deal with growing public disenchantment with payments for large farmers. Total aid payments between 100,000 and 200,000 ECU would be reduced by 20 percent, with payments over 200,000 ECU reduced by 25 percent. National governments, in addition, could reduce direct aid payments by 20 percent "where appropriate," if the labor force used on their holdings "falls short of limits to be determined." In a move calculated to increase support among environmentalists, a cross-compliance option was added where governments could introduce environmental requirements as a condition for direct payments. Governments would be directed to provide measures to reduce direct payments to farmers who fail to demonstrate their active role in maintaining rural areas by undertaking genuine farming activities. Funds saved from cross-compliance and modulation would remain available to member states as additional support for agri-environmental measures.

The proposed rural development regulation would have established an integrated legal framework for farm and rural development and agri-environmental measures to be co-financed by the "Guarantee" section of the agriculture budget (see Lowe and Ward 1998). The regulation would be applied across the whole of the European Union and funds would be allocated on the basis of multi-annual programs prepared, "at the most appropriate geographical level" within member states. This proposed regulation incorporated several existing CAP measures: structural adjustment of the farming sector (investment in agricultural holdings, establishment of young farmers, training, early retirement); support for farming in less-favored areas; remuneration for agri-environmental activities; support for investments in processing and marketing facilities and forestry measures. It also included one distinctly new set of measures for promoting the "adaptation and development of rural areas" incorporated in Article 31.

Article 31 contained some measures which are strictly farm development - land improvement, re-parcelling; setting up farm relief and farm management services; agricultural water resources management; and restoring agricultural production potential damaged by natural disasters (see Lowe and Ward (1998), pp.23-24). It also included some non-farm rural development measures, including: renovation and development of villages and protection of the natural heritage; development and improvement of the rural infrastructure; and encouragement for tourist and craft activities. There were also a number of other measures where it was unclear whether they would apply exclusively to farm-related developments, or could be applied to non-farm activities. These were marketing of quality products; improvement of living conditions; diversification of activities to provide multiple activities or alternative incomes; preservation of the environment and management of rural areas; and financial engineering.

Reactions to the Proposed Agenda 2000 Regulations

The Commission's proposed regulations got a rough ride at a special meeting of the Agriculture Council called at the end of March, 1998. *Agra Europe* reported that the detailed reforms were even more unacceptable than the outlined policy changes released the previous July (*Agra Europe*, Apr. 3, 1998: EP/1). The Commission's plan, not to compensate fully for cuts in support prices and the planned size of the price cuts, sparked opposition. The proposals to give member states more flexibility in allocating aid payments also were roundly criticized on grounds that they would lead to distortions of competition between producers in different member states. The Commission's plans to award extra milk quota to countries with dairy farmers in mountain areas were also attacked.

The German farm minister Jochem Borchert led the assault on the proposed regulations arguing that the Commission's reforms would lead to higher expenditure, lower incomes for farmers, more red tape and a greater dependence on aid payments (*Agra Europe*, Apr. 3, 1998: EP/1). He was especially critical of the plan to cut milk prices by 15 percent and of the need for a 20 percent cut in cereal prices. Louis Le Pensac, the French farm minister, asked Fischler to rethink his proposal, warning that the higher direct aids could be swept away in the next round of WTO talks (*Agra Europe*, Apr. 3, 1998: EP/3). He also objected to the proposed milk price cut as a start to dismantling the milk quota regime. The Irish farm minister, Joe Walsh, rejected the Commission's proposals outright saying that "major Irish economic interests are at stake," as beef and milk were more important to Ireland than to any other state (*Agra Europe*, Apr. 3, 1998: EP/1).

The only real support for the proposed regulations came from the UK, Sweden and Denmark. Still, it would have been dangerous to infer too much from the Agriculture Council debate, with real negotiations several months away. The EU member countries had every incentive to protect their negotiating positions at this stage to enhance their bargaining advantages. There was also an issue of responsibility. As one official put it in an interview, "Half of the present Ministers of Agriculture will no longer be in office when the final vote is taken. Hence ministers feel that they have nothing to lose by taking an extreme position."

Yet, in spite of the opposition to the proposals, most EU members accepted the thrust of Fischler's policy changes. This suggested that the negotiations, when they really began after the German election in September, 1998, would focus on the size of price cuts, compensation and the political appeal of greater national control over aid payments (*Agra Europe*, Apr. 3, 1998: EP/1).

The Agenda 2000 Endgame

A new factor came into play during the summer of 1998 as the German election campaign heated up. Germany's 20 billion ECU net budget contribution became an election issue when the Social Democratic Party (SPD) put the Kohl government on the defensive by demanding a reduction (see Table 9.2). Any reduction in Germany's budget contribution would have implied new limits on CAP spending, unless other EU governments increased their contributions. The contribution issue carried over to EU budget discussions, where the government of Germany, the largest net-contributor, insisted on a reduction in its contributions. The salience of these demands increased when the Social Democratic (SPD) - Green Party coalition, headed by Gerhard Schroder, came to power after winning the October 1998 German Parliamentary election. Other EU members were not responsive to the German demands. The French government was not willing to increase its budget contribution, and the British government insisted on maintaining its budget rebate.

Attention turned to ways that agricultural spending could be controlled as a way of assuaging German concerns about the EU budget. One suggestion was to cut spending on structural programs, but this was strongly opposed by the Spanish government. Co-financing provided another option, where a portion of CAP costs would be shifted to national treasuries. This might make national agriculture ministries more responsible in resisting increases in agricultural spending, but it might also constitute a first step in the re-nationalization of EU agriculture policy.[150] The German government favored this option, but the French government was unalterably opposed. Degressivity of payments constituted a third alternative, where agricultural support levels would gradually be reduced over time. This alternative garnered support from the British and French governments, but was strongly opposed by the German government.[151] Modulation provided a fourth option, where payment limits would be established for individual farmers; or, payments would be reduced with increasing farm size. This option received strong opposition from both British and German governments.

---

[150] The European Commission issued, in October, 1998, a document on the future of the EU's own resources, in which co-financing was described as one option, and where quantitative implications of co-financing were analyzed.

[151] It has been suggested that the proposal to make payments digressive over time was introduced by France as a tactical move, mainly to counter the German proposal for co-financing. In this it was successful, as in the end neither of the two proposals was accepted. But placing digressivity on the table may have a longer-term effect in decreasing farmer confidence in the reliability of payments.

Table 9.2: EU Budget Payments and Receipts (1996)

EU Budget Payments and Receipts for 1996 (million ECU)			
	Net payments	Receipts	Net position
Germany	20,766.9	9,872.0	-10,894.9
Netherlands	4,435.7	1,988.9	-2,446.8
UK	8,227.1	5,951.1	-2,276.0
Italy	8,935.2	7,532.9	-1,402.4
Belgium	2,743.0	1,996.8	-746.2
Sweden	1,957.4	1,204.9	-752.5
France	12,410.9	11,951.1	-459.8
Austria	1,872.6	1,600.4	-272.2
Luxembourg	163.2	83.9	-79.3
Finland	961.3	988.4	27.1
Denmark	1,359.9	1,553.3	193.4
Ireland	710.2	2,970.5	2,260.3
Portugal	906.1	3,680.4	2,774.3
Greece	1,107.1	5,039.8	3,932.7
Spain	4,538.9	10,511.1	5,972.2

Note: Payments are own resources income, net of UK budget rebate. Receipts are funds paid to Member States to cover operating expenses.
Source: *Agra Europe*, January 2, 1998: A/1

The Agriculture Council rushed to complete the details of the final Agenda 2000 package over the winter of 1998-99 before the Finance Ministers set stringent limits on agricultural spending. There was a general sense that the reform package would survive the forthcoming Berlin summit of March 1999 intact, given the complexity of the agriculture package, and the lack of knowledge of the details outside DGVI and national agriculture ministries.

After a marathon stop-start meeting lasting some two-and-half weeks, the Agriculture Council seemed to have agreed on a deal for reforming the CAP (see *Agra Europe*, March 12, 1999). No formal vote was taken, although the German Presidency declared a qualified majority of member states backing the compromise (*Agra Europe*, March 12, 1999: EP/1). This "agreement" roughly resembled the Commission's Agenda 2000 draft regulations, but included some significant concessions in all policy sectors (see Table 9.3). For cereals, the proposed 20 percent price cut was watered down to take place in two steps instead of one, while a 10 percent set-aside was approved compared to the originally proposed zero percent. For beef, the proposed intervention price cut was decreased from 30 percent to 20 percent, in three stages instead of one. For dairy, the proposed 15 percent price cut was phased in over three years beginning in 2003 instead of occurring in one step after approval of the reform package. This agreement had a potential problem in that costs over the seven year reform period were estimated at 312.5 billion Euro, well over the 307.5 billion Euro agreed by the EU heads of government at the February 26, 1999 informal Petersburg summit (*Agra Europe*, March 12, 1999: EP/3).

Table 9.3: Comparison of MacSharry and Agenda 2000 Reforms

	MacSharry Reforms (1992)	Agenda 2000 Proposal (July 1997)	Agenda 2000 Regulation (March 1998)	Agricultural Council Package (March 11, 1999)	European Council (March 26, 1999)
Cereals	30% price cut with compensation rising to 45 ECU/tonne in 1996 set-aside 15% (0% for small farmers)	20% price cut in one step; compensation 66 ECU/tonne set-aside 0%	20% price cut in one step compensation 66 ECU/tonne set-aside 0%	20% price cut in two steps (2000 and 2001) compensation 66 Euro/ tonne; set-aside 10% until 2001, then 0%	15% price cut in two steps (2000 and 2001); compensation 63 Euro/tonne; set-aside fixed at 10% until 2006
Beef	Intervention price cut 15% animal premiums increased	Intervention price cut 30% animal premiums increased	Intervention price cut 30% animal premiums increased national envelopes	Intervention price cut 20% in three stages from 2000 animal premiums increased national envelopes	Intervention price cut 20% in three stages from 2000 animal premiums increased national envelopes
Dairy	Quotas extended to 2000	Support prices cut 10%; compensation payments increased	Support prices cut 15%; 2% increase in milk quotas continue quotas until 2006; compensation payments increased	Support prices cut 15% phased in over three years beginning in 2003; quotas increased 1.5%, with special increases for Italy, Greece, Spain, Ireland & Northern Ireland; review quota regime in 2003 with aim to allow quota regime to expire in 2006; compensation payments increased	Reform delayed until 2005/06 15% price cut begins then as does the 1.5% quota increase; special quota increases begin in 2000; no commitment to review quota system

The European Council, after 20 hours of difficult and sometimes acrimonious debate among the 15 member countries, finally brought to conclusion the Agenda 2000 negotiations on the budget, the CAP and structural funds. But the Agriculture Council compromise "agreement" on the CAP did not hold up when French President Chirac announced serious opposition (see *Agra Europe*, March 26, 1999 and *Financial Times*, March 27, 1999: various articles). After fierce debate, a further weakened CAP reform package was approved which seemed more aligned with Chirac's ideas. The cereals price cut was reduced from 20 percent to 15 percent, and dairy reform was delayed until 2005-2006, at which time the 15 percent price cut and 1.5 percent quota increase will begin. At the same time, the European Council imposed strict new limits on farm spending. Total agricultural spending (excluding rural development and veterinary measures) will be kept at the 1999 level in real terms, at an average annual expenditure of EUR 40.5 billion plus an annual inflation increase of two percent.

9.3 Analysis of the Agenda 2000 Proposal

Agenda 2000 continued and intensified the MacSharry reforms of the Common Agricultural Policy. The new reforms further de-coupled farm subsidies from production and elevated the status of rural development to become a second pillar of the CAP. This chapter now turns to the task of how and why the EU decided to continue down the MacSharry reform path.

The Solid Path Established by the MacSharry Reforms

The MacSharry reforms had moved the CAP toward greater international market orientation by cutting prices for cereals, oilseeds and protein crops. At the same time, they established the principle of compensatory payments to farmers to offset losses caused by price cuts. The MacSharry reforms contributed to economic trends in a number of ways. The compensatory payments made the growth of CAP spending greater than it otherwise would have been in a period high international prices and booming international markets. But, the price cuts and set-asides helped slow the growth of cereal production, which, in turn, contributed to the decline of intervention stocks (Figure 9.1). Incomes for cereal farmers also rose with farmers receiving unexpectedly high prices for their products in addition to their compensatory payments. The Commission, in June 1996, estimated that arable farmers had been over-compensated by 8.5 billion ECU (*Agra Europe*, June 13, 1997: E/1).

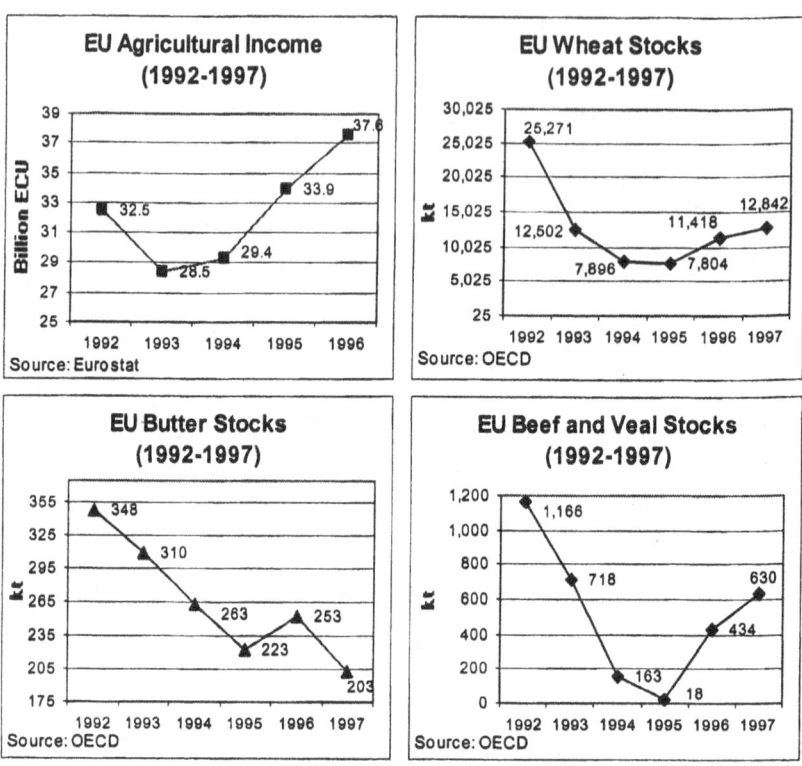

Figure 9.1: EU Agricultural Income Levels and Intervention Stocks (1992-1997)

The MacSharry reforms also influenced the political environment and the policy paradigm for Agenda 2000. European farmers and the European farm lobby, largely hostile to the reforms at their inception, had come to accept them by 1997, partly because EU farm income had risen for three straight years (9.3 percent in 1994, 5.2 percent in 1995 and 5.5 percent in 1996) (*Agra Europe*, March 20, 1998: EP/13). The compensatory payments proved much more popular than anticipated in the farm community, partly because they reduced farmers' uncertainty by providing an assured income over time, and partly because of the windfall profits. At the policy-making level, the MacSharry reforms were viewed as highly successful, providing a model for further reforms, even though spending on farm policies continued to rise (Figure 9.2).

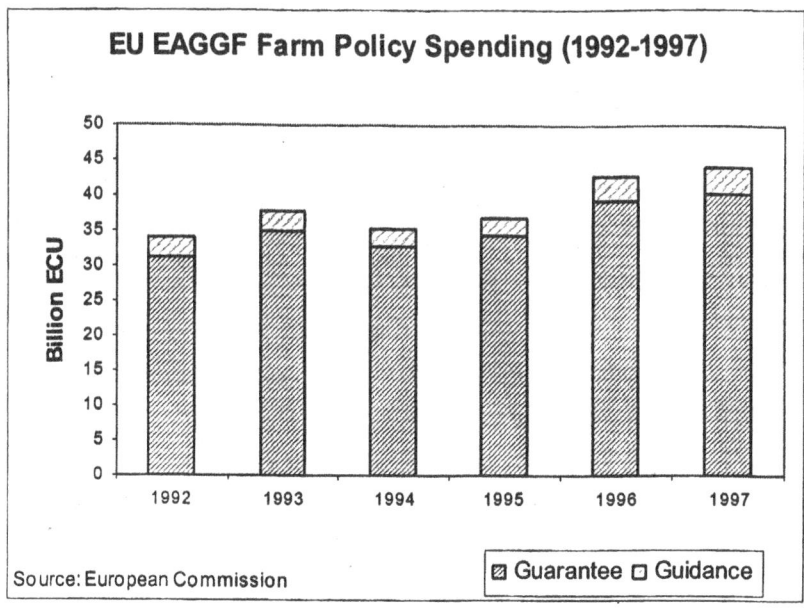

Figure 9.2: EU EAGGF Farm Policy Spending (1992-1997)

The MacSharry reforms contributed to the shift in the EU away from the Dependent Agriculture paradigm by recognizing the importance of bringing EU commodity prices closer to world market levels. This helped establish new values around which to base the Community agricultural policy debate. Even the opponents of reform would henceforth have to deal with world market orientation, centering their arguments around why EU prices should not conform to world prices. The perceived success of the MacSharry reforms strengthened the hands of the proponents of reform. EU acceptance of the Uruguay Round Agreement on Agriculture was not only a previous policy decision influencing the development of Agenda 2000, but also an important political development. Rules were established which set limits on domestic price supports, import barriers and export subsidies, and which committed the EU to the WTO international dispute settlement process for agriculture. Before the expiration of the "Peace Clause" in 2003, only the rules limiting export subsidies would create serious problems for the CAP as reformed by MacSharry. Yet, the Uruguay Round had a significant impact on the development of the Agenda 2000 proposals. It contributed to the shift away from the Dependent Agriculture paradigm in that it brought agriculture into the general GATT/WTO liberal trade regime. It influenced the political environment by bringing GATT/WTO considerations to the forefront in the thinking of policy makers and lobbyists. The new rules had an impact on the way various groups defined their interests, and even had a direct effect on the decision-making process in that only GATT/WTO compatible policy options could be considered. The impetus for further reform was increased by the URAA commitment to begin another round of international trade negotiations in 1999, with goal of increasing liberalization. The fear that the CAP would be attacked piece by piece in the GATT/WTO dispute settlement process when the "peace clause" expired provided a further impetus for reform.

The Constraints from Rising Costs and Subsidies

The escalating cost of EU agricultural policy was one of the most important economic factors setting the CAP reform process in motion previous to Agenda 2000, though as we have seen, the MacSharry reforms ended up costing more than the unreformed policy (see Chapter 6).

Figure 9.3 shows the cost of the CAP increasing under the MacSharry reforms and projected to continue rising until 2006. But, the overall cost of the CAP was less than the budget guideline for agricultural expenditures set in 1988, with the gap projected to grow from 2003 to 2006. Thus, Agenda 2000 was not catalyzed by an actual spending crisis. However, there was a real risk that the spending guideline would be breached by the cost of integrating the CEEC into the CAP or by a downturn in world prices.

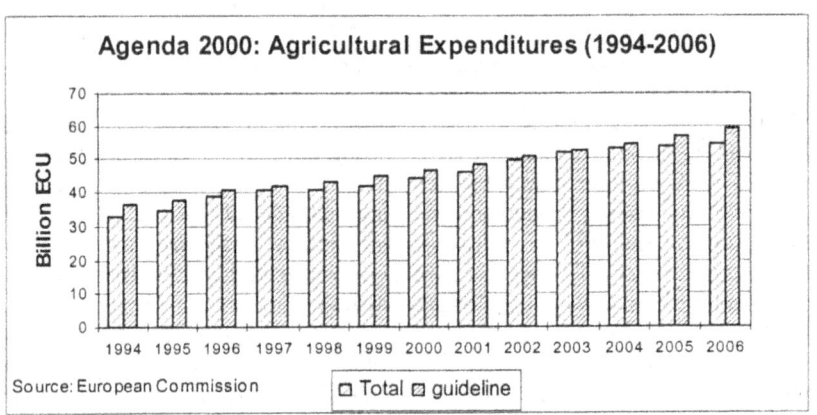

Figure 9.3: Agenda 2000: Projected Agricultural Expenditures (1994-2006)

The potential difficulty in receiving approval from the Council of Ministers for an increase in the agriculture spending guideline is revealed by the distribution of EU budgetary payments and receipts among EU Member States at the time Agenda 2000 was formulated (see Table 9.2). Nine of the current EU members had become net contributors to the EC budget, including the four largest members (Germany, UK, Italy and France) and would resist an increase in their financial obligations. The governments of Germany, in particular, had an incentive to limit EU spending, with a net contribution to the EU budget of 10.9 billion ECU.

Agenda 2000 - New Reforms for the CAP

The developers of Agenda 2000 could not overlook how CAP money was spent. Support for arable crops (cereals, oilseeds and protein crops) consumed 16.4 billion ECU in 1996 or 41.9 per cent of the CAP budget. Commissioner Fischler tried unsuccessfully to get the Council of Agriculture Ministers to cut spending on compensatory payments for arable crops at the same time that Agenda 2000 was formulated, because of perceived over-compensation and the need to cover the enormous costs of dealing with the BSE crisis.

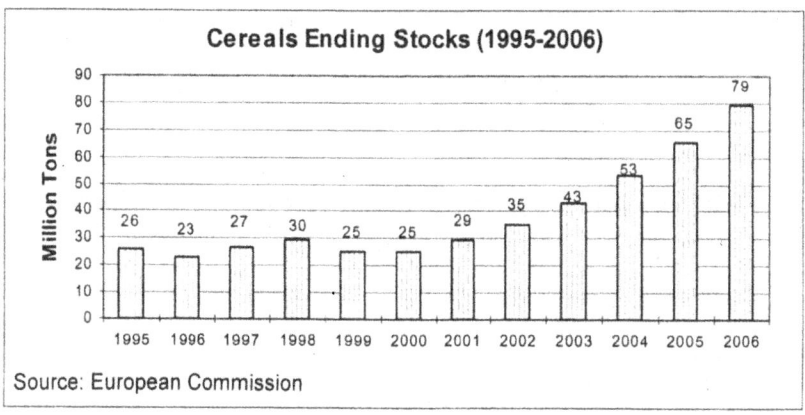

Figure 9.4: Commission Projections of Ending Cereals Stocks (1995-2006)

The potential growth of commodity stocks was another concern. Even though cereal and beef commodity stocks were down in 1996, the Commission projected huge increases after the turn of the century, as shown in Figure 9.4 and Figure 9.5. The Commission predicted that beef and veal stocks would rise to 1.5 million tons by 2006, while cereal stocks would rise to 79.3 million tons. The beef problem stemmed largely from the BSE crisis, which had dramatically lowered domestic EU demand by 15-20 percent (see *Agra Europe*, March 27, 1998: A/1). International demand for EU meats had also declined precipitously, reflecting fear of BSE infected meat. Though domestic consumption was expected to recover somewhat by the end of the century, the EU still faced a gradual decline in domestic consumption of 0.4 percent annually, as people changed their diets to eat less red meat. International demand was projected to increase in the new century, but the Commission expected that this increased demand would be met by exports from the US and Australia. EU exports of beef would be limited by continued fears about BSE as much as by Uruguay Round export constraints.

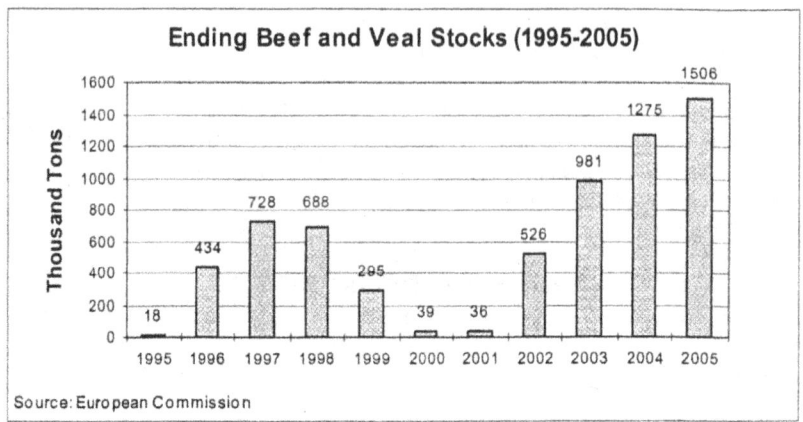

Figure 9.5: Commission Projections of Ending Beef and Veal Stocks (1995-2005)

The projected cereal problem was based on the assumption that productivity and production would continue to increase steadily as a result of improved agricultural technology, even with 17.5 percent of the cereal land set-aside. Domestic consumption would rise at a much slower rate, thus leaving a growing surplus to export. Figure 9.6 shows that after the year 2000, the wheat surplus was projected to be so large that it could not be exported without breaching Uruguay Round export subsidy limits.

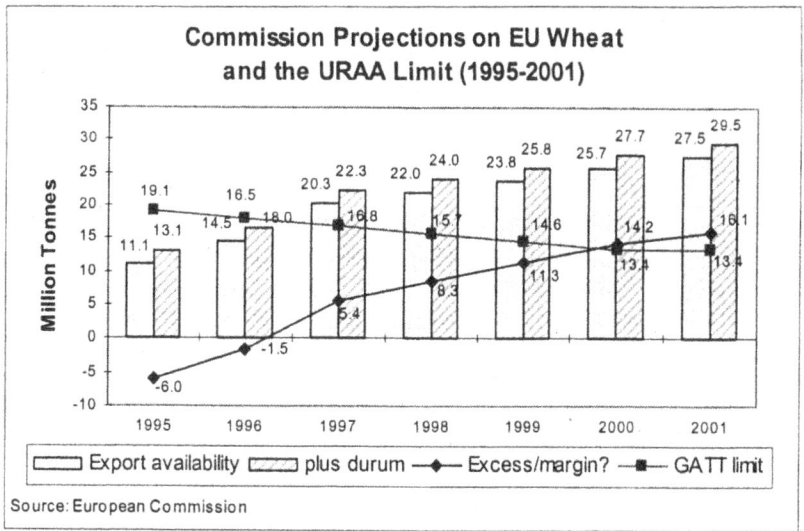

Figure 9.6: Commission Projections on EU Wheat Exports and the URAA Limit

The projected increases in cereal and beef stocks, though not an immediate crisis, presented a strong case for further reform of the CAP. The case was strengthened by projections of large increases in growth in annual demand for agricultural commodities in developing countries. With an unchanged CAP, Uruguay Round export constraints would limit the EU's ability to export its surplus to meet this demand, with the probable result that the EU would lose market share in the developing countries.

Dealing with the Collapse of Communism and the Maastricht Treaty

The Commission planners formulating Agenda 2000 had to consider a number of political developments. The importance of the Uruguay Round Agreement on Agriculture has already been discussed. Another highly significant development was the collapse of the Soviet empire in Central and Eastern Europe, followed by democratization in the various countries freed from Soviet influence. There were strong reasons to integrate these countries into the EU, where membership would promote both stability and democracy. A larger EU would make a stronger presence in the global political arena. Over the long term, the larger internal market would provide important economic advantages. However, the financial costs of bringing the CEEC into the EU would be very high. The demands on the EU regional, social and cohesion funds would be considerable in promoting the structural change necessary for integration. The increased cost of the CAP, both in term of "Guidance" and "Guarantee" funds, would be great. Dirk Ahner, head of the DGVI unit developing Agenda 2000, told the January 1997 Oxford Farming Conference that he estimated the cost to the EU budget would be 12-13 billion ECU, if all 10 associated CEECs joined the current CAP together in 2000 (*Agra Europe*, Jan. 10, 1997: E/1). Compensatory payments would consume about half of the additional spending. Ahner also noted that the EU stock build-up problem would be exacerbated if CEEC output were added to that of the EU 15 without reforming the CAP, even though he considered that the risks of a post-accession production explosion had been exaggerated in some quarters (*Agra Europe*, Jan. 10, 1997: E/1).

The Maastricht Treaty was another political development of some significance. This treaty had initiated the process leading to monetary union in 1999. The monetary union process did not influence the CAP directly, but became the high priority issue for Prime Ministers and Foreign Ministers, diverting attention away from agricultural policy. The Maastricht treaty had importance in another sense: it made protection of the environment an important policy objective in the EU. Article 113R specified that ... *environmental protection requirements must be integrated into the definition and implementation of other Community policies* (Tracy (1997), p.43). This was not in itself an impetus for reform of the CAP, but meant that consideration of the environment had to be taken into account in any further reforms.

Another political development, the 1996 US FAIR Act, attracted the attention of EU planners of Agenda 2000 (see Chapter 8). The FAIR Act, by further de-coupling payments from production, raised the possibility of more aggressive US competition for international export markets - competition which the EU could not meet without either lowering prices or exceeding Uruguay Round export subsidy limits (see Moyer, 1996). It also indicated that the US, with deficiency payments abolished, would make the Uruguay Round "Blue Box" a target in the next WTO agricultural trade negotiations. If the "Blue Box" were abolished, EU compensatory payments would probably be illegal under WTO rules, so the EU planners of Agenda 2000 had an incentive to create a structure for the CAP which could adjust to this possibility.

An Environment Conducive to Further Reform

Much about the political environment and policy paradigm for the Agenda 2000 planning process in the spring of 1997 can be inferred from our discussion of past policies, economic trends/shocks and political developments. The Commission perceived a need to further reform the CAP along the lines begun by the MacSharry reforms, though this need had to compete for attention at top levels with monetary union. The CAP did not face imminent crisis, but convincing evidence existed of the need for change to meet EU WTO obligations, to prepare for the next round of WTO agricultural trade talks, and to allow the integration into the EU of the CEEC. The Commission had accepted the Multi-Functional Agriculture paradigm, and had received support from the European Council with acceptance of the Commission's "Strategy" paper at the December 1995 Madrid summit. There was general consensus that the CAP should better take into account the protection of the environment, though no consensus had emerged about exactly what should be done. The Commission had made a commitment to give more attention to rural development in agricultural policy, but the priority of rural development for the heads of government had been made questionable by the rejection of the Cork Declaration at the December 1996 summit.

The political environment for reform in 1997 was also influenced by a number of deadlines. The EU's structural policies would expire at the turn of the century, mandating a policy reassessment. Dairy quotas also were scheduled to expire in 2000, requiring action on dairy policy. Finally, the WTO agricultural trade negotiations were scheduled to begin by the end of 1999, necessitating the development of an EU negotiating position.

The Decision-making Process, the Actors and Their Interests

The July 1997 Agenda 2000 proposal was a Commission document, so required no opinion in advance from the European Parliament or the approval of the Council of Ministers. However, since any reforms would need approval by the Agriculture Council, the Commission had a strong incentive to listen closely to the views of national governments and the farm lobby. Also, given the probability of strong farm lobby resistance to further reforms of the CAP, the Commission had an incentive to listen to views from outside the farm community to build as strong a constituency as possible for its proposals. Within the Commission, Agriculture Commissioner Fischler and DGVI had the dominant position, since they had the responsibility for developing the proposal. DGXVI (regional policy) also would have to be consulted to the extent that the reform proposals dealt with structural policy.

The future policy objectives for the CAP listed in Agenda 2000 (see Box 9.3) give some sense of the Commission's view of Community interests. It is interesting to note how significantly these objectives differed from the objectives for the Common Agricultural Policy listed in Article 39 of the 1957 Treaty of Rome:

Agricultural Policy Objectives

Treaty of Rome (Art 39)
a. to increase agricultural productivity by promoting technical progress and by ensuring the rational development of agricultural production and the optimum utilization of the factors of production, in particular labor
b. thus to insure a fair standard of living for the agricultural community, in particular by increasing the individual earnings of persons engaged in agriculture
c. to stabilize markets
d. to ensure the availability of supplies
e. to ensure that supplies reach consumers at reasonable prices

Agenda 2000
a. to improve the Union's competitiveness through lower prices
b. to guarantee the safety and quality of food to consumers
c. to ensure stable incomes and a fair standard of living for the agricultural community
d. to make its production methods environmentally friendly and respect animal welfare
e. to seem to create alternative income and employment opportunities for farmers and their families

Box 9.3: Agricultural Policy Objectives

The only original objective referred to was that of ensuring a fair standard of living for farmers. Increasing agricultural productivity, market stabilization, supply availability, and reasonable consumer prices had been "replaced" by food safety and quality, protection of the environment, animal welfare and alternative income opportunities for farmers and their families. This change in priorities is indicative of the EU shift from the Dependent Agriculture paradigm to the Multi-Functional Agriculture paradigm.

DGVI had parochial organizational interests, which it would likely superimpose on EU interests in its decision-making. First, it had in interest in preserving the CAP, as this provides the reason for existence of a Directorate-General for Agriculture, and serves as a basis for its power. Second, DGVI had an interest in keeping the CAP running smoothly, avoiding crisis if possible. Poor functioning of the CAP and the existence of crisis would likely bring prime ministers and finance ministers into the agricultural policy process, diminishing DGVI's influence. Third, DGVI had an interest in protecting agriculture's share of the EU budget.

Agenda 2000 - New Reforms for the CAP

Lobbies and Public Opinion Influencing the Process

Brussels lobbies had generally predictable positions on CAP reform, but were hindered from focusing their efforts until the Agenda 2000 proposal was released, since they could not know in advance exactly what the proposal would contain. The farm lobby, was wary of change, though generally accepting the MacSharry reforms, and (with some reluctance) the Uruguay Round agreement. This lobby was skeptical of agri-environmental measures, fearing that these would impose new burdens on farmers, and was concerned that rural development measures might divert CAP funds away from support of farm products. The British NFU was an exception in that it favored reform of the CAP. The seed, farm chemical and fertilizer producers had an interest in greater market orientation, with reduced set-asides to increase their business, while the food processing industry wanted prices lowered. The consumer lobby favored reform but was not well-organized and did not have much clout.

One group - the environmental lobby - deserves special mention, because for the first time it had become well organized in Brussels, and had earned respect in DGVI among the people formulating Agenda 2000 (interview). This lobby, including representatives from the World Wildlife Fund, Birdlife International, the European Environmental Bureau and the European Forum for Nature Conservation and Pastoralism, exercised influence by providing scientific information, new ideas and policy options, by making skillful use of the media to raise the profile of environmental issues, and by hosting seminars for the Commission. Generally, the environmentalists favored cuts in prices and compensatory payments to farmers, so that more money could be devoted to agri-environmental measures and rural development.[152]

The Commission in a study released in August 1997 gave some indication of the climate of public opinion on further CAP reform (*Agra Europe*, Aug. 8, 1997:E/4). This study found that the 1992 reforms had increased public opposition to the way farmers are supported. It warned that this dissatisfaction outside the farming community would threaten the long-term prospects of compensatory aids. The Commission noted, "The public has difficulty in understanding why aids are given for not cultivating the land without requiring good cultivation practices" (*Agra Europe*, Aug. 8, 1997: E/4). "This raises doubts about how long the direct aids can be justified if producers do not have to provide a specific service to society" (*Agra Europe*, Aug. 8, 1997: E/4). The study suggests that cereal growers will have to farm in a way more acceptable to the general public in the future. If compensation payments are to be continued in the future, they should be linked to protecting the environment and/or maintaining the countryside. The Commission also found that the general European public did not easily accept the biggest landowners receiving the largest amount of aid, which was clearly happening under the MacSharry reforms.

---

[152] There was not much of a rural development lobby except for the environmentalists.

Explaining Member State Reactions

It was not entirely clear in advance of the release of Agenda 2000 how individual Member governments would react. The initial response would probably come from agriculture ministries, whose acquiescence would be important, as the Agricultural Council would need to approve any reforms to the CAP. With the Agricultural Council as the primary forum for debate, the Commission could probably not gain acceptance of any proposal that significantly cut farmer benefits. As with the MacSharry reforms, farmers would have to receive compensation for price cuts. Farm ministries were also wary of new rural development initiatives that might take money away from farmers. The European Council's rejection of the Cork declaration further indicated the need for caution on rural development. EU Member countries had rather divergent views on reform. The UK, Denmark and Sweden wanted to make the CAP more market-oriented. French opinion was divided between the efficient cereal growers of the Paris basin, who could compete internationally, and the more marginal farmers in other regions of the country, who saw greater market liberalization as a threat to their survival. The Mediterranean countries, particularly Spain, were primarily concerned with maintaining the benefits they were receiving from EU structural programs. Germany strongly supported the CAP status quo, with the mindset of the agricultural ministry still firmly locked in the Dependent Agriculture paradigm. The dominant farm interests were still those of the small farmers in what had been West Germany. These interests were threatened by greater openness to global markets. German dairy interests were adamantly opposed to any change in the system of dairy quotas. One could expect the Kohl government to take the side of the farm lobby, at least until the September 1998 election, given the critical importance for the CDU/CSU of the farm vote.[153]

9.4 Assessment

Approval of the Agenda 2000 farm policy reforms evidences the acceptance within the EU farm policy community of the Multi-Functional Agriculture paradigm. We consider in more detail in the next section the impetus for the Agenda 2000 reforms, the Commission "Reflections" paper, the sponsorship of the Cork Conference by the Agriculture Commissioner and DGVI, the content of the Agenda 2000 proposals, the modifications made in the draft regulations, and the weakening of reform by the European Council.

---

[153] This situation changed significantly after the German election, when Schroder became Chancellor and Funke became agriculture minister.

Agenda 2000 - New Reforms for the CAP

The Commission "Strategy" Paper

What catalyzed the development of the Agenda 2000 proposals? The impetus for the November 1995 "Strategy" Paper outlining reforms of the CAP beyond MacSharry can best be explained by looking at the situation through the lenses of the organizational process and government politics models. DGVI was quite happy with the MacSharry reforms, and the statements of Commissioner Fischler and Director-General Legras repeatedly stated that they saw no reason to go further. But, when the Commission decided that change was necessary, DGVI responded with alacrity in developing the "Strategy" Paper. DGVI had an interest in responding to the Commission initiative to maintain control over what changes would occur. DGVI had bargaining advantages in the Commission reform debate in that it could set the agenda and outline the direction for change.

How can one explain the content of the Commission's "strategy" paper? Consonant with the rational actor, DGVI analyzed the problems the CAP would face in the future, and developed options, ranging from maintaining the status quo to "radical reform." The recommendation to make a "progressive and gradual adjustment ... to develop the reforms undertaken in 1992," could reflect the desire of an organization (DGVI) to maintain its standard operating procedures, making the minimum adjustments necessary to deal with a policy problem. This recommendation could also reflect a DGVI view that an incremental approach would be easiest to sell to the Agriculture Council, since it minimized bargaining costs, providing the possibility of reaching agreement on specific measures without having to reach agreement on policy goals.

The Cork Conference

Why did DGVI and Commissioner Fischler take the initiative in planning the Cork Conference? From the standpoint of the rational actor, one can see Fischler and DGVI looking analytically at the internal impact of a more market-oriented CAP, and concluding that devoting more resources to rural development would cushion the shock and help farmers make the adjustment. Looking at the situation from the perspective of Organizational Process, one could see DGVI, worried about the political vulnerability of compensatory payments, viewing rural development as a more acceptable means of channeling support to farmers. This would protect the share of the EU budget devoted to agricultural spending and the influence of the Directorate-General for Agriculture.

The government politics model offers several insights. The first centers on the bureaucratic politics of the Commission. Previously, the responsibility for structural programs in rural areas had been divided between DGVI and DGXVI (regional development). By launching a successful initiative, DGVI would strengthen its hand, perhaps gaining full control over structural spending in rural areas. Another political dimension focuses on the two-level CAP reform game between the Commission and the governments of member countries, which would be played out in the Council of

Agricultural Ministers. Rural development is a concept with considerable public appeal (it is extremely difficult for anyone to come out and say that he or she is opposed to rural development). If rural development could be integrated into a CAP reform proposal, the proposal might stand a better chance of gaining the support of otherwise skeptical Member governments, particularly Germany and France, which had strong societal commitments to maintaining the integrity of rural areas. A rural development initiative would also be helpful in linking the CAP strategy in the EU with the 1999 WTO agricultural trade talks. With the passage of the 1996 US FAIR Act, the "Blue Box" seemed a certain target for challenge in the WTO talks. In this context, rural development funding would be much easier to defend as "Green Box" measures than compensatory payments. A rural development initiative would allow the EU an alternative means of supporting farmers should compensatory payments be declared WTO illegal, and hence would allow the EU to avoid international political isolation by having to defend the "Blue Box."

The Cork Conference can be seen as part of the Commissioner Fischler's strategy to build a base of support for the DGVI rural development ideas, building a momentum difficult for heads of government to resist at the subsequent Dublin summit. A summit endorsement of these ideas would strengthen the Commission's hand with the Agriculture Council for making rural development a major component of its forthcoming Agenda 2000 proposal. Unfortunately, the timing of the Cork Conference was bad as it came at the height of the BSE crisis, which had become the pre-eminent policy issue. The Commission's planning for the Conference was flawed in that it presented its own point of view to the community of rural development experts, who had expected the Conference to be an open forum for deliberation. It is not clear whether the summit would have endorsed the Cork declaration, had it not been for the BSE crisis and the dissatisfaction of some of the participants with the organization of the Cork Conference, but these factors militated against endorsement. The failure of the summit to endorse the Cork Declaration created a strong political incentive for Commissioner Fischler and DGVI to pull back from their rural development initiative and to weaken its emphasis in Agenda 2000.

Agenda 2000 Proposals

How can we understand the proposed reforms of Agenda 2000? One can largely explain the content of the Commission's July 1997 Agenda 2000 proposals as the product of a calculating rational actor thinking of the long-term interests of the EU, where these interests were partially defined by economic trends and political developments. One can also see parochial interests of DGVI in play as predicted by the organizational process model. The options considered by the central actor were constrained by the two level CAP bargaining game going on among EU institutions and Member governments. They were also constrained in anticipation of a new WTO game linked to the CAP game. The Agenda 2000 proposals differ only incrementally from the MacSharry reforms, an outcome consistent with bargaining and Lindblom's partisan mutual adjustment.

Consistent with the rational actor model, the Commission planning process, which produced Agenda 2000, was highly centralized in a small DGVI planning group. This group analyzed market trends, the Uruguay Round Agreement on Agriculture, the US FAIR Act, and the expansion of the EU to include the CEEC, as they would have an impact on the CAP in the future. The planners speculated about issues likely to be raised in the next WTO talks and asked how well prepared the EU would be to deal with these issues. They considered the EU's rural development and agri-environmental interests. Also, consonant with the rational actor, DGVI commissioned an independent study by experts, led by Professor Allan Buckwell, which provided both ideas and an analytical frame of reference to aid the DGVI planning group in its analysis.[154] The DGVI planning group interacted closely with the Buckwell group at meetings before Agenda 2000 was prepared.

However, many aspects of the Agenda 2000 proposals are hard to explain as decisions of a rational actor. Why, for instance, was the recommended change only incremental - MacSharry Mark II? Why were dairy quotas continued and the recommended price cuts for milk insufficient to allow the EU to compete internationally without export subsidies? Why was 90 percent of the proposed agricultural budget devoted to market support and compensatory payments, transferring an enormous amount of money from taxpayers to a mere 7 million farmers - a very small percentage of the population? Why were compensatory payments not made transitional, as their continuation would increase the cost of the CAP budget and create problems for the integration of the CEEC into the EU? How could it be argued that the EU was preparing for the next WTO agricultural trade negotiations, when it expanded compensatory payments, which clearly did not meet "Green Box" criteria? Why were agri-environmental and rural development schemes given prominence in the objectives for Agenda 2000, but with little funding allocated for their implementation? Why was rural development assistance centered almost exclusively on farmers - a minority and declining part of the rural population?

Organizational process analysis is helpful in answering these questions. DGVI, the organization that prepared Agenda 2000, has a primary purpose to promote the welfare of farmers, its main constituency. Supporting farm income is a deeply ingrained value resistant to change. Thus, it is not surprising that such a large percentage of Agenda 2000 is devoted to market support and compensatory payments. It is also not surprising that farmers were the primary focus of rural development. The recognition of the importance of agri-environmental measures and rural development, with funding coming from the "guarantee" section of the CAP budget, may well be a sign of how DGVI saw its interests evolving in the future. As mentioned in the analysis of the Cork Conference, funding for agri-environmental and rural development is likely to be more defensible in the future than compensatory payments. DGVI may well have seen it prudent to have agri-environmental and rural development initiatives

---

[154] There was another study conducted by the section of DGVI responsible for rural development. These studies provide further evidence of a pro-CAP reform *epistemic community* in the EU.

in place, which could be expanded in the future to justify maintenance of DGVI's share of the EU budget. Organizational process may account for part of the incrementalism of Agenda 2000. The general perception in the Commission was that the MacSharry reforms had been successful in achieving their objectives and had been accepted by farmers. If more reform was necessary, why not use MacSharry as a template? There would be less uncertainty about the outcome than with a new approach to reform.

The government politics model and network analysis are also helpful in filling out the explanation for the incrementalism of Agenda 2000. The expected resistance to change from the farm constituencies and the Agriculture Council constrained the Commission to reject radical change in the "strategy" paper and propose instead a "progressive and gradual adjustment" in reforming the CAP. Incremental change would reduce pain and uncertainty, thus greatly reducing the opposition in the farm policy network. The acceptance of the "strategy" paper by the European Council set the parameters for the subsequent proposals. Departing from this structure would have been difficult to justify and would have vastly increased the bargaining costs of gaining approval for Agenda 2000 in the Agriculture Council.

The complexity of the rural development section of Agenda 2000, with funding coming from regional, social, agricultural "guidance" and agricultural "guarantee" funds, rather than a single rural fund, as Commissioner Fischler had desired, can be explained by the bureaucratic politics of the Commission. Control over the EU structural funds was divided between DGVI and DGXVI. Each of these agencies successfully fought to maintain control of its share of the budgetary pie.

Government Politics in the form of two-level CAP game politics between EU institutions and Member governments provides insights into why Agenda 2000 was such a large and complex package. The Commission thought it would be easier to get a big package through the Council of Ministers than a small one, in that a big package could contain items benefiting all Member states (interview). Two-level CAP game politics contributes to our understanding about why Agenda 2000 expands compensatory payments to farmers, with no hint that these payments would diminish in the future. Both of these examples show how interested the Commission was in enhancing the win-sets of the Member State agricultural ministers to facilitate approval of the new reforms in the Agriculture Council.

Two-level game analysis also provides an explanation for the Commission's emphasis on enhancing the "multi-functionality" of farms and preserving traditional farm life as part of the national heritage. The Commission wanted to reassure interests in France and Germany who saw a greater market orientation as a threat to rural life.[155] The Commission's timidity in changing the milk quota system and in lowering milk price supports appears as an effort to appeal to the politically important German dairy farmers, who had a vested interest in maintaining the CAP *status quo*. Bringing the proposal within the win-sets of both France and Germany was absolutely essential,

---

[155] See articles by Gisela Hendricks and Helene Delorme in Kjeldahl and Tracy, 1994.

because Agenda 2000 could not survive the Agriculture Council debate without the support of the French-German alliance.[156]

The explicit reference to preparing for the 1999 WTO agricultural trade negotiations provides evidence of how the Commission thought the Agenda 2000 game would be linked to the forthcoming WTO game. Approval of Agenda 2000 would allow the Commission credibly to tell other WTO members that the EU had gone as far as it could go with agricultural reform. This could be seen as an attempt to explicitly define a narrow EU win-set, which would strengthen the EU hand for preserving the "Blue Box," while having liberalized domestic price supports and reduced the need for export subsidies.

Agenda 2000 Draft Regulations

How can we explain the modifications made in the March, 1998 draft regulations to the July 1997 Agenda 2000 proposals? The government politics model provides insights. In the two-level CAP bargaining game, the new provisions adding direct payments for sileage cereal, and for increasing payments for beef suckler cows, bulls and steers, can be understood as part of a Commission effort to fine-tune its proposals. This would bring them within the win-sets of Member governments that had expressed concern about the original provisions. The increased dairy price cut, along with milk quota increase and national envelopes for beef and dairy industries also seemed designed to mollify the opposition of member governments. The digressive overall ceiling on aid payments to individual farmers appears as an attempt to bolster public support for the CAP. The addition of cross-compliance can be understood as an attempt to court the increasingly important environmental lobby.

The rural development provisions can be understood partly as an effort to increase support for Agenda 2000 in the EU, and partly as a way of creating a contingency for modifying the CAP in response to future WTO challenges. Even though the proposed funding for rural development was very small compared to the funding for market support, a way would be created for re-channeling market support funding in a changing political climate. The growing strength of the environmental lobby and the growing interest of environmentalists in agricultural issues were harbingers of such change. The forthcoming WTO talks could conceivably provide a real impetus. If the EU should fail to preserve the "Blue Box," to shelter its compensatory payments from GATT challenge, there would be every incentive to shift funding to the activities specified in the rural development regulations, which would be much easier to defend as "Green Box" payments.

---

[156] See Webber (1998) on the importance of the French-German alliance for CAP decisions in the early years of the EC and in the 1990s.

Final Weakening of the Agenda 2000 CAP Reform Package

Two questions seem important for explaining the attenuation of the Agenda 2000 agricultural reform package. First, why did the Agriculture Council water-down the Commission recommendations in its "final compromise," after long dialogue with the Commission and receiving a variety of concessions? Second, why did the European Council weaken the Agriculture Council "final agreement"? The intergovernmentalism variant of the government politics model is helpful in finding the answers. The actions by the Agriculture Council would seem to represent the usual last-minute concessions to farm interests in an attempt to build consensus among the agriculture ministers for a final agreement. Institutionally, this was almost inevitable, given the EU decision-making process which allows Agriculture Ministers to decide agricultural policy, and which has a well-established norm of seeking unanimity prior to Agriculture Council action on major issues.

The weakening of the Agriculture Council "final agreement" is more interesting, since it was unexpected. Historically, the heads of government had been far tougher on agriculture than the farm ministers. The explanation starts with the intransigence of French President Chirac. This, in itself was not surprising, given Chirac's long-standing strong ties to the French farm community (he had once been agriculture minister), and his dependence of the support of agricultural interests in his cohabitation with a Socialist controlled government and parliament. The French President's position was aided by the overspending of the agreed budgetary limits implied by the Agriculture Council agreement by 6.9 billion Euro.[157] With none of the EU governments willing to increase its contribution, the question became one of how to reduce the growth of CAP spending. Chirac's proposal to reduce the cereal price cuts and to delay the dairy reforms would accomplish this, and was further helped by the fact that one or more EU Member countries were blocking all the alternatives, including co-financing, degressivity and modulation. Thus, concern with the future costs of the CAP, previously an impetus for planning reform, paradoxically, now became an obstacle to change.

At first, Chirac stood alone, but he was adamant, and the other heads of government caved in for a variety of reasons. The political environment favored Chirac. The entire Commission had resigned the previous week under pressure from the European Parliament, and NATO had just begun bombing Serbia because of Serbia's behavior in Kosovo. It was thus absolutely essential that the European Council act decisively. German Chancellor Gerhard Schroder was in no position to fight Chirac, given the recent disarray of his government, with the resignation of Finance Minister Oscar Lafontaine, and the embarrassment that would have ensued if the European Council had failed to reach an agreement during the German Presidency. The British might have been expected to fight for CAP reform under normal circumstances, but Prime Minister Tony Blair was fighting to preserve the UK budget

---

[157] The EU changed the name of the ECU to the Euro in 1995. The Euro replaced the ECU on 1 January 1999.

rebate. He wanted to increase the structural funds allotted to the depressed areas of Cornwall, South Yorkshire, West Wales and the valleys, highlands and Islands of Scotland and Northern Ireland. Spain went along with the deal when Germany agreed that there should be no cut in cohesion funds that Spain received. Special regional aid packages insured the support of Portugal and Belgium, while Italy had already been bought off with a special milk quota increase.

9.5 Conclusion

Agenda 2000 did not establish a new reform path for the CAP, but rather continued down the path established by the MacSharry reforms. This was not surprising given that policies establishing a new path tend to generate positive feedback. There was no sense of imminent crisis to provide the impetus for radical change. Farm income had increased, commodity stocks were down and farmers liked their compensatory payments. The Commission knew that further changes in the CAP would be required to limit rising costs, while maintaining international market share without exceeding URAA export subsidy limits. Pursuing the MacSharry path was attractive in that the bargaining costs of incremental change appeared manageable, implementation was feasible and the consequences were predictable.

With the domestic policy changes of the FAIR Act and Agenda 2000, the focus of reform shifted again to the international arena and the new round of WTO agricultural trade negotiations beginning in 1999. How would these negotiations proceed? In what way would they be influenced by the FAIR Act and Agenda 2000 reforms. The next chapter deals with these questions.

Chapter 10

The 2000 Agricultural Negotiations

10.1 Introduction

A new round of agricultural negotiations was launched on March 24, 2000 in Geneva. The WTO Agriculture Committee, meeting in "special session", decided on a timetable for the first phase of the talks. On May 9, 2000, Jorge Voto-Bernales was appointed as Chairman of the Agriculture Committee for the initial stage of the WTO agricultural negotiations. The WTO Director-General, Mike Moore, remarked on the "constructive and businesslike" manner in which delegates had conducted the first meeting, and said that the "goodwill" shown at the meeting was a good omen for the talks. Starting the talks, of course, is easier than bringing them to a successful conclusion, but after the chaos in Seattle any good news was welcomed in trade circles. The first phase of the talks concluded with a "stocktaking" of the proposals for the negotiations, in June 2001, and moved onto the "second phase" of the talks, elaborating on the "modalities that could be used to achieve the objectives. The talks were given a boost by the successful outcome of the Doha WTO Ministerial in November 2001. An ambitious timetable was established for the remainder of the negotiations, that included agreeing on the modalities by March 2003 and presenting draft schedules incorporating the obligations implied by such modalities by the time of the next Ministerial, scheduled for later in 2003.

The breakdown of the Seattle Ministerial in December 1999 had posed an interesting dilemma for the scheduled agricultural talks. The postponement of the start of a new round of trade negotiations would not in itself have delayed the start of the agricultural round: the Uruguay Round Agreement on Agriculture (URAA) mandated further negotiations by the end of 1999.[158] But the lack of agreement on a more general round left the built-in agenda to languish without political impetus. The time between Seattle and the Doha Ministerial was taken up with the task of mending fences, including rebuilding confidence in the WTO system. It was not a propitious time to be conducting the agricultural negotiations in the absence of a political stimulus. The success of Doha energized the negotiations and finally offered the possibility of real progress in the agricultural talks.

---

[158] World Trade Organisation (WTO) members agreed, "that negotiations for continuing the process [of substantial progressive reductions in support and protection] will be initiated one year before the end of the implementation period [2000]" (Article 20, URAA). Agriculture is thus an integral part of the "Built-in Agenda" which was agreed in the Uruguay Round.

In spite of the hesitant start, WTO members were rather well prepared for the current round of agricultural talks. The ground had been thoroughly tilled and the seeds scattered. Countries began to formulate their overall approach to the round, and to define their expectations for agriculture, well before the Seattle meeting. Many tabled papers in the WTO General Council in the weeks before the Ministerial outlining their positions. In addition, over seventy papers had been prepared in the context of the "Analysis and Information Exchange" process authorized at the Singapore WTO Ministerial and conducted informally by the Committee on Agriculture.[159] Countries were ready to start the agricultural talks if they had got the appropriate signal from Seattle. This does not mean that the talks would have been easy even with an enthusiastic launch of a major round. The prospect of stalemate or of minimal progress on agriculture was always on the cards. But in the aftermath of Seattle it was doubtful whether any significant progress could have beeen achieved in agriculture in the absence of a more general set of trade talks.[160]

Agriculture did not cause the collapse of the Seattle Ministerial. Indeed, had other factors not intervened the agricultural talks might have been launched with some momentum. The EU, for instance, was on the brink of agreeing to wording in the agricultural paragraphs of the declaration that would have excluded the phrase "multifunctionality" from the draft, and would have stated that the objective of the negotiations was to move "in the direction" of removing export subsidies.[161] But the EU made it clear after the breakdown of the talks that these concessions would have to be negotiated afresh if the rest of the package was not agreed.

This current round of agricultural talks is different in many respects from the Uruguay Round or its predecessors. In some ways the task of the negotiators is more clear-cut, in large part because of the transparency introduced by the Uruguay Round Agreement on Agriculture (URAA). Tariff levels are easier to negotiate than non-tariff barriers, and the defined commitments on export subsidies and domestic support can be subject to further cuts without revisiting the definitions. But clear-cut tasks can also focus opposition. There are several countries that would prefer not to pursue the path toward a more open trade system for agriculture, or at least not be pushed in that direction by international pressure. Moreover, as always, negotiations will take place in the context of contemporary events. These events could overshadow and even derail the talks. The agenda already has been influenced by a number of issues that were not on the table during the Uruguay Round. There is no reason to believe that the agenda will stop shifting just because formal talks are underway.

---

[159] Most of these useful documents are publicly available at the WTO website (www.wto.org).

[160] The US was suspicious that the EU was pushing a broad agenda to avoid the spotlight falling on agriculture. The EU, on the other hand, undoubtedly could have moved more easily on agriculture if other sectors had been included. The impact of single sector negotiations not embedded in a round therefore is to put the focus squarely on agriculture but also to make it more difficult to get a "good" outcome.

[161] Japanese negotiators were reportedly unhappy with what they saw as a capitulation by the EU, leaving themselves and Korea to carry the argument for modest progress in agriculture.

This chapter looks at these talks in the context of the continuing process of farm policy reform. Will the new talks "complete" the process of reform of agricultural trade rules started in the Uruguay Round? Will they lead to significant further liberalization of agricultural markets? Can they act as a catalyst for further domestic reform? Or will they in effect put a brake on such reform, as countries try not to "give away" bargaining chips that could be useful in the endgame for a new agreement in the WTO? Will domestic policy reform give negotiators the flexibility to respond creatively to the challenges of trade reform? Or will the process of domestic reform itself slow to the extent that the WTO talks are bought to a halt? To answer these questions it is necessary to discusses both the substantive issues in the continuation of trade policy reform and their links with domestic policy change.

As always, there are a number of other factors which will condition the pace of the talks, including the ability of the European Commission to secure for itself a constructive mandate for negotiation over the objections of some of the member states; the present lack of "fast track" trade negotiating authority in the US; the recent accession of China to the WTO; and the determination of developing countries to be full partners in the WTO. One should also not forget the impact of the state of commodity markets, which can have a marked effect on the progress of agricultural talks as it impinges on the perceptions and policies of individual countries. Each of these could have a significant bearing on the agricultural talks. But the key determinants are still the prospects for continued reform of farm policy reform in the OECD countries and the extent to which the reform processes in the US and the EU converge or diverge.

10.2 Building on the Uruguay Round Agricultural Agreement

The next round will take as given a decade of serious domestic farm policy reform in most of the industrial countries in the direction of less trade-distorting policies. In this regard it can push ahead with further necessary changes in the trade rules. The overall objective of the current round of agricultural talks is clearly to continue the progress made at the Uruguay Round. This implies negotiations on improved market access, further constraints on export subsidies and, if exporters get their way, some tightening of the rules for domestic support.[162] This can be thought of as the "core" agenda (Josling, 2000) around which a number of other issues have emerged as a result of the experience with the Uruguay Round Agreement, such as the administration of TRQs and the issues of state trading and of export restrictions. But several other items are clamoring for a place on the agenda. These include the sensitive questions of health and food safety, along with a number of environmental issues relating to agriculture and biotechnology. Also important to agriculture will be a resolution of the broader issues of regional trade agreements and preferential trade arrangements.

---

[162] For a fuller discussion of the agenda for the talks see Tangermann and Josling (2000).

Those countries interested in the continued reform of the trade rules, led by the Cairns Group but supported by the US, emphasize the "core" issues such as the liberalization of market access, the reduction or elimination of export subsidies and the containment of domestic support that is given in a way that distorts trade. The general presumption is that the Uruguay Round set the rules but did not go far toward reducing protection. The main task of the next round for these countries is therefore to make a significant step toward the opening up of agricultural markets. However, for those concerned with environmental and food safety issues, these core issues are of less interest. Instead, a rather different set of agenda items is important to the EU, Japan and some developing countries. These issues are closely related to agricultural trade though technically outside the Agreement on Agriculture. These issues include the trade conflicts over Sanitary and Phytosanitary (SPS) measures and the potential conflict over genetically modified foods (GM foods), as well as questions of intellectual property rights. For developing countries there are other issues as important as those in the core, including the question as to whether to press for continued "special and differential treatment" in agricultural rules. For those countries more concerned with food security, issues such as the need to control the use of export restrictions in times of shortage and the ability of countries to take action against imports that threaten to disrupt markets are important, as are the future of trade preferences.

Market Access

The market access negotiations will be at the heart of the next agricultural round.[163] Exporting countries will not consider the talks to be a success unless a substantial step is taken to reduce the high levels of agricultural tariffs.[164] With varying degrees of enthusiasm, countries have endorsed the objective of improving market access. The US has called for an "ambitious" target for expansion of market access: the EU admits that its export interests would be served by an opening of markets but cautions that the process will take time.[165] For the Cairns Group, the negotiations "must result in deep cuts to all tariffs, tariff peaks and tariff escalation".[166] Of the major players Japan is naturally the most reticent, contributing the observation that current tariff levels "reflect particular domestic situations" and that these circumstances should be given due consideration in the negotiations.[167] NGOs are generally less enamored with

---

[163] The issues and options for market access are discussed in detail in Meilke, *et al.* (2001).

[164] A recent study puts the average agricultural tariff at 62 percent (Gibson, *et al.*, 2001).

[165] The EU paper contains the intriguing statement that it should "pursue an active market access policy with a view to eliminating barriers to entry in certain third country markets." Both the US and the EU positions are discussed in more detail below.

[166] See the Cairns Group "Vision" statement transmitted to the WTO as WT/L/263, and the subsequent communiqué from the Buenos Aires meeting of the Cairns Group, WT/L/312. The Cairns Group members are Argentina, Australia, Brazil, Canada, Chile, Colombia, Fiji, Indonesia, New Zealand, Paraguay, Philippines, South Africa, Thailand, and Uruguay.

[167] For details of the Japanese position, see WTO documents WT/GC/W/220 and

market access negotiations, associating such liberalization with globalization and the pressure from multinational firms for ever wider markets over which to spread fixed costs. To many of these pressure groups, market access is a part of the problem rather than the solution. Developing countries tend to stress the importance of expanding market access in the products of export interest to themselves.

Market access improvements reduce the scope for domestic policy. Not only does the height of the tariff determine the protection given to the domestic product but it acts as a constraint for domestic marketing parastatals. Tariff levels for competing goods can have a major market impact, as well as the economic incentives to fill TRQs. But in addition, the techniques of negotiating tariff reductions can have significantly different impacts on domestic policy.[168] Across-the-board tariff cuts seem to be equitable but leave current imbalances in protection in place. Formula reductions cut tariff peaks but are often resisted by those sectors that would have to face the largest tariff cuts. Some countries favor a focus on individual sectors (zero-for-zero arrangements) that allow one to move to tariff (and export subsidy) free trade. This however risks setting up anomalies among competing products. Countries that are reluctant to liberalize often favor the use of "request and offer" negotiating techniques, to enable the process to respond to pressures from individual sectors.

The other aspect of tariff policy that is of importance to domestic policy-makers is the form of the tariff. The URAA mandated a tariff-only regime, but allowed some countries to concoct complex tariffs that involve reference prices and compound rates.[169] Moreover, the Blair House agreement between the US and the EU obliged the EU to impose a maximum duty-paid price for cereals that acts very much like the variable levies which were outlawed in the agreement. Many countries also would like to insist on the use of *ad valorem* tariffs rather than specific duties, which have a somewhat more protective impact when prices are low.

Market access can also be improved by expanding the guaranteed market access (TRQs) that forms a part of the provisions of the Agreement on Agriculture. Some position papers (though not that of the US) mention the importance of expanding TRQs in the next round. The Cairns Group paper says that "trade volumes under tariff rate quotas must be increased substantially". Other countries suggest further improvements in the TRQ system, in addition to the administration of the quotas. As a number of countries recognize in their position papers, the issue of developing a more uniform system for the administration of the TRQs is one of the most urgent tasks for the new agricultural round. TRQs for agricultural imports have created a new wave of governmental interference with trade through licensing procedures and provided a playground for rent-seeking traders - who will in turn have an incentive to lobby for the continuation of the high above-quota tariffs. The question is how to prevent the

---

G/AG/NG/W/91.

[168] For a discussion of tariff reduction options see Josling and Rae (1999).

[169] The EU tariff schedule for fruits and vegetables includes tariffs conditional on whether the offer price is below or above a reference price (IATRC, 1997).

TRQs from interfering any more than necessary with the competitive development of trade.

Export Competition

If the high level of protection sets agriculture apart, the widespread use of export subsidies is perhaps the most disruptive element in the operation of world markets.[170] The practice of subsidizing exports of agricultural products has been constrained by the Uruguay Round, but most of the subsidies are allowed to continue in a reduced form. The main user of export subsidies is the EU: some 90 percent of current expenditure on export subsidies is in the EU (ERS, 2001). But, as the EU points out, other exporters employ export credits and use single-desk sellers, both of which can under certain circumstances give their exporting firms an edge. In this round of negotiations, it will be more difficult than ever to persuade countries who export agricultural goods with little or no subsidy to allow countries such as the EU and the US to continue their market-distorting practices. Developing countries also are generally in favor of the elimination of export subsidies. Only the EU will have great difficulty in agreeing to the dismantlement of export subsidies, though it has already come under considerable pressure to do so.

Elimination of export subsidies would be a major achievement for the agricultural talks. But the pre-requisites for dispensing with export subsidies are a renewed confidence in world markets, with firmer and more stable price levels for the major products, and reduced dependence on intervention buying in domestic policies. The former condition itself depends on the success of the Agreement in increasing trade and reducing protection: removing export subsidies may be the only way to create the conditions under which they are not needed. As for domestic programs, it is possible that practice and sentiment in the EU may have moved further away from the use of market support policies to other instruments by the end of the negotiations (see Chapter 12). If these conditions were met then the current set of negotiations could set a target to phase out export subsidies over a particular transition period.

In the Uruguay Round, export credits were declared to be a form of export subsidy, but it did not prove possible to agree on constraints. The OECD countries have negotiated a code for non-agricultural export credits that puts limits on credit terms and the length of credit extension, but it has not yet been possible to include agriculture in this agreement. This leaves this topic as one to be dealt with in the WTO talks, though some countries have indicated that they do not wish to "pay twice" for getting rid of such policies. It should be possible to agree on the allowable terms for such credit, and hence be able to calculate the magnitude of the subsidy that is involved if softer credit terms are offered. The best way to deal with the subsidy equivalent of such concessionary credit is to charge it against the export subsidy constraints in the schedules.

---

[170] The options for negotiating improved export competition are evaluated in Young, *et al.*, (2001).

The quantification of export subsidies and their reduction has left more visible the distinction between those countries where exports are privately sold from those where a parastatal controls such exports. There is widespread concern in those countries where trade is by private firms that the state trading enterprises can obtain cheap credit from their governments, offer better terms to buyers, and generally compete unfairly with the private trade. To the extent that these practices could be labeled as export subsidies, the issue is one of monitoring and transparency. But some commonly used devices such as price pooling (giving the producer an average price over several destinations or time periods) are also seen as giving the producer an unfair advantage. It might therefore be a matter for negotiation as to whether any constraints need be placed upon STEs with regard to their producer pricing policies.

Different marketing practices among exporters are inevitable, and not in themselves undesirable. But international guidance is needed as to which practices of parastatal export agencies are consistent with agreed conditions of competition and which distort that competition. Now that the more clear-cut kinds of export subsidy have been identified and included in the country schedules of allowable subsidies, the main task of the negotiations will be to clarify the definition as regards the actions of state trading exporters.[171] This would ensure that such actions as dual pricing and price pooling, if deemed to be hidden subsidies, could be counted against the schedule for that country.

In the next Round, several importers are likely to seek to constrain the ability of exporters to restrict supplies. After all restraints on exports are no less inconsistent with an open trade system than restraints on imports. Export taxes should be included under the same qualifications as quantitative restrictions. The argument has already surfaced in connection with the Food Security Declaration appended to the Uruguay Round Agreement (the Ministerial Decision on Measures Concerning the Possible Negative Effects of the Reform Program on Least-Developed and Net Food-Importing Developing Countries). It seems inconsistent to leave in place the possibility of export taxes and quantitative restrictions that have an immediate and harmful impact on developing country food importers.

Domestic Support

It is one of the ironies of the Uruguay Round that, although the biggest conceptual breakthrough was the acceptance by countries that domestic policies were a legitimate concern of trade talks, the actual disciplines imposed on those policies through the reduction of the Aggregate Measure of Support (AMS) were rather weak.[172] The key question for the next Round is therefore whether to strengthen or abandon the attempt

---

[171] In this regard the outcome of the dispute over Canadian dairy exports is useful. The panel report has indicated that the use of special export grades of milk that can be sold at a lower price to processors for export of dairy products constitutes a form of export subsidy under the URAA.

[172] For further details on the domestic support issues in the current talks see Kennedy, *et al.*, (2001).

to constrain domestic policies. Obviously, the answer will have a major impact on the constraints imposed by the trade rules on the process of domestic policy reform.

As mentioned in Chapter 7, the fact that the AMS constraints have not been binding for either the US or the EU does not mean that the domestic support rules have been ineffective. The process of re-instrumentation of domestic support programs, away from those that most impede trade, began as a part of the reforms discussed in earlier chapters. The institution of the "green box" has in itself been useful in two different dimensions: as a guide to what policies are deemed acceptable in terms of trade distortion, and as an indication of the type of policies that can offer a more targeted approach to income problems in the farm sector. The attraction to countries of adopting "green box" policies is both to guard against challenge from trading partners and to avoid being counted toward the AMS. Thus the AMS constraint is of value even if not particularly onerous. The domestic appeal of such "decoupled" policies is that they allow the government to get out of the business of buying, storing and selling farm products for which no commercial market exists. Writing a check to farmers to "compensate" for lower prices is a lot easier than trying to unload surplus products on world markets, in particular when those markets are already oversupplied. And the space in the green box for environmental payments allows governments to pursue other rural objectives than commodity price support with minimal risk of challenge under the WTO.

The green box presently contains a number of policy instruments that, while probably less trade distorting than price or income supports still encourage an expansion of output. Sometimes they are related to such otherwise reasonable programs such as crop insurance, but incidentally increase the incentive to produce by reducing risk. Other programs may be indirectly linked with production even though the main reason for payment is not output. This might be true of certain environmental payments, which could lead to an increase in output. But exporters fear that to re-open the definition of the green box might, however, allow countries to argue that it be expanded to include food security policies and non-decoupled support schemes designed to keep farming in certain areas.

Nor are all countries happy to let governments pay "decoupled" payments and other green box subsidies without constraint. The Cairns Group points out that the "overall levels of support for agriculture remain far in excess of subsidies available to other industries." But their target is primarily the trade-distorting (amber box) policies. Canada, however, indicates that it will seek "an overall limit on the amount of domestic support of all types" (green, blue and amber).

The "blue box" containing the US and EU direct payments which were granted exemption from challenges under the Blair House Agreement was a creature of its time, necessary to get agreement to go ahead with the broader Uruguay Round package. It is, however, still a somewhat awkward bilateral deal not appreciated in other parts of the world. Such an anomaly could possibly be removed in the next round. The policies of the US and the EU themselves are changing for internal reasons. The US FAIR Act goes further than ever before to make the payments to farmers decoupled from output and therefore compatible with the green-box. The EU has considered a similar move as a part of the continued reform started in 1992, as a way of making the CAP consistent with enlargement, but for now the idea has been shelved.[173] The task for the current talks will be made much easier if the EU modifies the direct payments for cereals and oilseeds such that they meet the conditions laid down in the green box. The "blue-box" could then be emptied and locked. But the EU has announced that one of its objectives is to defend the blue box (in essence the compensation payments under the MacSharry and Agenda 2000 reforms) so as to avoid challenge to these policies and their scheduled reduction.

Multifunctionality and the Agricultural Talks

This issue of the size of the green box appears to be where much of the early negotiation rhetoric has been targeted. The argument is usually shrouded in terms of the "multifunctionality" of agriculture.[174] The concept of multifunctionality is not in itself particularly novel, as agriculture has always played a complex role in rural societies, and rural areas have a vital place in national social and political life. But the EU has latched onto the concept as a way of both providing cover in the WTO for policies which it would like to maintain and also providing a rationale for paying farmers in ways that are not tied to commodity output. Exporters are trying to neutralize any impact that the idea might have by pointing out that multifunctionality is not restricted to Europe, though the EU Commission tends to link it to a model of European farming, by implication different from the system of farming in competitor countries.

The basic question remains "what does multifunctionality mean for domestic and trade policy reform?" On the one hand it could merely be a recognition of the fact that a variety of programs will be maintained in most societies which target specific aspects of rural life. For the trade system to be seen to rule out such programs would seem to be as risky, as it would seem to be going against concerns of rural development, environmental protection and animal welfare. This is entirely consistent with the Competitive Agriculture paradigm, which certainly allows for the correction of market failures of a social and environmental kind. On the other hand, if trade-restricting policies were to become the accepted instrument for maintaining multifunctionality then that could signal a regression to the time of expensive commodity market distortions. In effect the multifunctional paradigm would be set against the competitive market paradigm and the trade talks would be the location for the conflict. The EU, however, has never taken the view that trade policies are the only way to preserve

---

[173] The Agenda 2000 reform of the CAP, agreed in 1999, did not change the conditions for the direct payments to cereal farmers. Use of the land in program crops is still required. If new members are admitted under these conditions it is difficult to see how the EU could avoid paying the direct payments to their farmers. This would constitute a large part of the budget cost of extending the CAP to new members.

[174] The term "multifunctionality" does not appear in the Doha text. The UR Agreement on Agriculture, in mandating further reform, specifies that account should be taken of "non-trade concerns." Multifunctionality is assumed by its advocates to being one of these concerns.

multifunctionality. The green box was intended precisely to deal with such rural concerns. An alternative outcome of the talks would be to confirm the criteria for the green box and encourage multifunctional policies to conform rather than opening the green box up to be a repository for an assortment of production related payments.

One change in the constraints on domestic support that would have a significant impact on domestic policy is to make the AMS specific to individual commodities. This was the original intention in the Uruguay Round: it was at the Blair House negotiations between the US and the EU that the notion of aggregating the AMS over all commodities was introduced - essentially to weaken its impact. The AMS could thus be made more binding at a stroke by defining commodity specific amounts of "coupled" price support expenditure that could then be reduced over time.

10.3   The US and the 2000 Round

The US has been an active participant in the current round of talks on agriculture, but it is not clear whether the US will be in a position to take the lead along the path toward further reform. Clearly the outcome of the debate over fast-track negotiating authority will influence the answer to this question. Without fast-track negotiating authority, and with a Congress wary about further attempts to liberalize trade, it is not easy to see a leadership role in the talks. But even with fast track certain hard decisions have to be made. The US will need to offer to others some incentives to allow them to strike a deal on agriculture. In particular, the US is going to have to grant better access in its own markets for some of the commodities which have so far not been opened up to imports. These include sugar, dairy products, peanuts and citrus fruits. Domestic farm interests are going to extract a high price for any significant opening of the market.

In addition, the US is going to have to convince its trading partners that the series of "emergency" payments that a growing budget surplus allowed Congress to grant to farmers is not the end of its traditional commitment to more open markets. Already the US has encountered skepicism from its trading partners, as they perceive an unwillingness to translate the spirit of the trade negotiating position into domestic farm policy. It is not that the WTO constraints are being breached: so far there has been ample room in the amber box for the emergency payments. But the inconsistency of the US arguing for support reductions at a time when support levels are steeply rising in the US, even if still within WTO constraints, has markedly weakened the ability of the US to lead the debate in Geneva. And the issue of whether such emergency payments, at a time when domestic process are weak, are truly in the green box will be a key point of contention in the talks. At the least, the US has given up much of the "high ground" by the large subsidies granted out of the growing budget surplus.

Open markets also imply transparent health regulations, allowing such imports as poultry and fresh fruits and vegetables onto the domestic market subject to meeting the same conditions as imposed on domestic supplies. Regional suppliers, in particular, have begun to press the US to relax some of its technical regulatory barriers. One would expect this pressure to accentuate as a part of the process of opening up US markets to NAFTA partners. Indeed, the putative date for an agreement on free trade in the Western Hemisphere (the FTAA) is only a few years away. But whether the political will is present to support a liberalization of US markets, whether on a regional or global basis, is not certain.

The US views on market access are in any case still somewhat ambiguous. The US has supported the notion of "zero-for-zero" agreements that would accelerate trade liberalization for particular commodity groups (such as oilseeds). This would tend to go against the notion of reducing protection across the board, a technique for reducing tariffs that would force down the high protection for dairy, sugar and peanuts. But the US agrees with the Cairns Group on the need to improve the administration of TRQs and to expand them to increase market access, as well as on the need to make sure that STE importers do not restrict imports and that the safeguard system is not abused. The US has called for the abolition of export subsidies but is more cautious on the curbing of export credits, which form a part of foreign aid policy as well being a convenient way of stimulating exports. The US agrees with both the EU and the Cairns Group that export monopolies should be restrained, though Canada will resist any move in this direction.[175]

On the issue of domestic subsidies the US has indicated that it would like to modify the rules so that all potentially trade-distorting subsidies are restrained. The US proposal calls for the division of subsidies into those that are allowable and those that need to be constrained. One might have thought that this was a way of targeting EU subsidies, as the FAIR Act should have removed the major US crop payments into the green box. But recent event in the US have exploited the ambiguities in the AMS measure, as mentioned above, as farmers were given an additional $6 billion in 1998 at a time of low prices, followed by similar payments in 1999 and in 2000.[176]

10.4   The EU and the 2000 Round

The European Union approaches the new Round of agricultural trade negotiations in somewhat of a quandary. On the one hand the lesson taken by many in Europe from the experience of the Uruguay Round was that the EU had exhausted all its energies defending the CAP from attack that it had no time to develop a positive strategy to pursue changes that it would like to have seen either in trade rules or in the policies of others. The notion that it had already "reformed" the CAP, with dairy quotas in 1984 and a budget ceiling in 1988, was not convincing to its partners. Even after the

---

[175] See the position papers tabled before the negotiating group: G/AG/NG/W/15, G/AG/NG/W/11, and G/AG/NG/W/92.

[176] It should be pointed out that other countries are also in the process of compensating farmers for income losses. However so far this has not taken the form of higher prices, and thus could come under the heading of direct income payments. Such largesse may well, however, encourage farmers to stay in production.

introduction of the MacSharry reforms in 1992 it was clear that the EU still required high border protection to preserve its domestic policy. On the other hand, to have gone into the current talks in a position of strength would have required further reforms in advance of the talks. This was in effect scuppered by the French government when the Agenda 2000 program was watered down at the Berlin summit (see Chapter 9). As a result the EU will need to shift further as the final package becomes clear.[177]

On market access, the EU is reluctant to engage in any sweeping cuts in tariffs. Though an exporter, it still feels under pressure from competing imports of temperate zone goods. As a result it would like to see Asian markets expand, but cannot move too far from its traditional protection of the domestic market. A modest across-the-board reduction in tariffs is likely to be the preferred outcome. But the EU will be vulnerable on the issues of the widespread use of specific tariffs, the use of reference prices for fruits and vegetables and the high degree of excess protection for cereals as afforded by the bound tariff relative to the "maximum duty-paid import price" for cereals that was agreed in the Uruguay Round. The position of the EU on state trading is clear: as the EU has sided with the US to put additional disciplines on such agencies.

On export subsidies the EU position is that they are essential to the clearing of markets at least for the next few years. Whether they could be persuaded to end them in principle is not clear. The Commission would rather not have to use them as instruments of policy, but it would be unacceptable to lose market share too rapidly in the cereals and dairy markets as a result of not being able to lower offer prices.

One of the most contentious issues is likely to be the "size" and "composition" of the green box. For the EU the green box represents a possible way out of the dilemma of how one satisfies political imperatives for the maintenance of farm incomes and at the same time lives within the constraint of the WTO. Payments, perhaps from national sources, aimed at recompensing farmers for the "multifunctionality" of European agriculture are a political necessity. Whether the concept of the green box needs to be amended to include such payments is not clear. And the Commission runs the significant danger of raising the expectations of European farmers that the multifunctionality card can be played to gain more protection at the border – an idea that would certainly deadlock the talks. On the blue box, the EU has defended it in the early stages but can change their own compensation policies without too much inconvenience (and to domestic advantage) to make them compatible with the green box, as did the US in the FAIR Act.

---

[177] The EU position is laid out in documents G/AG/NG/W/17, G/AG/NG/W/34 and G/AG/NG/W/90.

10.5 Timing of the Negotiations

The timeline for the agricultural talks is constrained in part by the process of the negotiations themselves. So far, in the first phase of the negotiations, there have been about 180 papers presented to the Special Sessions of the Agriculture Committee of the WTO. Of these, some 47 are Proposals and the rest are comments. The negotiators undertook a "stocktaking" of these proposals at the meeting in March 2001, thus ending the first phase of the negotiations. The second phase of the negotiations was agreed based on the proposals and any further elaboration that countries might provide. Three Special Sessions of the Committee on Agriculture were held in September and December 2001 and March 2002 along with three "informal" sessions in May and July 2001 and in February 2002. There was a review of progress in March 2002, at which countries reaffirmed their commitment to the Doha timetable. However it was apparent that there was little time before the Fifth Ministerial Conference, to be held in Mexico in the summer or fall of 2003, to agree on the modalities.

Foremost among the factors that could govern the pace of the trade talks is the fate of the Peace Clause. The Agreement on Agriculture specified that the Peace Clause extend for nine years, and hence is due to expire at the end of 2003. Obviously there will be discussion about extending this period of "due restraint". But any country that has to ask for this extension will need to expend negotiating capital to do so. Thus if the EU were to argue for an extension it will have to convince its negotiating partners that such a concession is worthwhile. On the other hand the importance of the Peace Clause should not be overstated. Its main effect is to protect domestic subsidies in the blue and green box from challenge under the Subsidies Agreement. That agreement does indeed seem to restrict sector-specific subsidies fairly rigorously, but the Subsidies Committee would be unlikely to take on the task of refereeing agricultural subsidy conflicts. And it could take years for a raft of challenges to the agricultural policies of the major countries to find its way through the Dispute Settlement Process. Moreover, a high profile case that went against a key agricultural subsidy in either the EU or the US could further weaken the domestic political support for the WTO.

Two caveats should be entered at this stage. First, the number of countries involved in the negotiations is itself a problem. In the past the tendency has been for a small number of countries to meet outside the formal negotiating sessions and discuss compromises. But the number of members that have taken an active interest in the WTO negotiations on agriculture suggests that it will be difficult to exclude countries from the hard bargaining. Secondly, the negotiations will be watched closely by outside (non-governmental) groups, representing producer and consumer interests as well as environmental and human rights groups, who will insist on greater transparency in the name of democracy. The very openness of the process may however slow down the task of reaching an agreement. Though the agricultural agenda was not a main point of contention for most of those in the streets in Seattle, the public scrutiny of proposed deals on agriculture could still become a factor.

The main factor that will govern the pace of the agricultural talks, however, is the progress in the new Round. The agricultural timetable will then inevitably be governed by that of the overall Round. This could slow down the progress toward an agreement but at the same time raise the political stakes. A larger package could be on the table but might have to wait until some of the other difficult negotiating areas caught up with agriculture.

Elements outside the WTO orbit can have a decisive impact on the pace of the negotiations. Three such exogenous factors are worthy of some discussion. One is the pace of domestic farm policy reform, discussed in Chapter 12, below. The US Congress is currently reconciling two versions of a Farm Bill that will be needed sometime within the next year (the FAIR Act govern programs until 2003). At present a continuation of the main instruments introduced in 1996 seems likely, augmented with additional counter-cyclical measures that could present a challenge to the WTO. The EU Commission is to present its "mid-term" review of the CAP in June 2002, and report to the European Council its opinion as to whether further reform is needed in preparation for enlargement to include the countries of Central and Eastern Europe. There is little doubt that significant reform suggestions will emerge. So the articulation of the twin processes of domestic and trade policy reform will be difficult but also crucial. The fact that the trade talks will be proceeding at the same time as domestic policy discussions gives the opportunity for positive synergy if handled correctly. It could of course also confuse and slow down each process.[178] Complicating both domestic policy reform and trade policy reform is the complexity of domestic bargaining processes, with groups that benefit from current policy well-positioned to obstruct change, or to direct it in support of their own parochial interests. As we have seen in our discussions of the Uruguay Round and US and EC/EU domestic reform, these factors make liberalizing change difficult under the best of circumstances.

A second exogenous factor is the timing of elections in major countries. The next year promises to be an active one for political contests. France is entering a major electoral cycle, with votes for the President and both houses of the legislature in the next calendar year. It is unlikely that major controversial decisions such as CAP reform or the end of another WTO round can take place in the lead-up to the polls. On the other hand, a new French government could have more flexibility than the present one to make some difficult decisions. Germany also faces parliamentary elections that will not only determine the political makeup of the Bundestag but also affect the freedom of the Chancellor to carry out trade and agricultural policy reforms.[179] And the US mid-term elections will also constrain the ability of the Executive branch to complete trade deals. This suggests that negotiators will seek a "window" for an agricultural agreement free of imminent elections. If the electoral calendar is any

---

[178] Paarlberg has pointed to this possible negative interaction in the case of the Uruguay Round, but others (Colman and Tangermann, Swinbank and Tanner) have taken the opposite view.

[179] Four smaller countries, Denmark, Ireland, the Netherlands and Sweden also have elections scheduled for the year 2002.

indication, the most propitious time for an agricultural agreement would be in the year 2003, presumably late in the year at the scheduled Ministerial meeting.

A third factor governing the WTO timetable is the progress in regional trade talks. Some skilful coordination is going to be required to ensure that the regional and the multilateral processes do not conflict. The Quebec City Summit of the Americas set a deadline of January 2005 for the completion of negotiations for a Free Trade Area of the Americas. It would obviously make sense for the WTO talks to be over before this time. In the agricultural area, improvement in access into the US agricultural markets by Latin American countries will be one of the most insistent and controversial demands. The US is more likely to be able to yield to some of these demands in the context of a broader trade round, though duty free access for Brazilian poultry, citrus and sugar into the US market may have to be put on a slow track.[180]

On the other side of the Atlantic, EU enlargement for the first wave of six applicants could also be signed, sealed and delivered by 2005. Once again care will be needed to avoid conflicting timetables. The agricultural chapter of the current negotiations could be ready to sign by the end of 2002 (again constrained by the electoral cycle of the EU members). This would be an easier deal to construct if the outcome of the agricultural talks in the WTO round were already known. As this is unlikely to be the case, potential members face the possibility of signing up to alignment with a CAP whose level of protection and possibly even allowable policy instruments are themselves about to change. On the other hand it is also unlikely that enlargement will actually be completed in advance of a conclusion to the agricultural talks. In practice the talks will have to be coordinated in such a way that the new members in effect negotiate on agriculture during 2002 in both Geneva and Brussels.

It is unusually hazardous to speculate about the outcome of the current agricultural talks, but the necessary conditions for success seem to be (a) continuation of the "spirit of Doha," including the engagement of developing countries in the negotiating process and the cooperation between the US and the EU trade negotiators; (b) the support from the politicians and the business community in US and the EU for the agricultural component of the round; (c) the continued pressure from the Cairns Group of smaller agricultural exporters and their ability to gain allies in the developing world; and (d) the return of some form of stability in world agricultural markets so as to be able to focus on longer term issues.

The "spirit of Doha" enabled the WTO to begin an ambitious new program of trade talks. There is no certainty that this spirit will continue for the length of time needed to complete the Agenda. The WTO now has more countries willing to participate actively in the institution and more tasks on its plate. But if it suffers a loss of domestic political support and credibility then its ability to deliver will be

---

[180] Similarly, the completion of a WTO agreement on agriculture could be the opportunity to break the logjam in the talks between the EU and MERCOSUR, which centers around access for Latin American agricultural products. In this regard, a full Round will probably have to tackle the question as to whether agricultural goods can be excluded from a free trade area set up under Article XXIV.

compromised.[181] Or, to put it another way, if the trade negotiating authority of the major actors is too circumscribed by illiberal restraints then no amount of negotiating skill will be enough to reach an acceptable outcome. Thus the US and the EU still have a crucial role to play even if they can no longer determine the agenda. Transatlantic coordination is probable more important now than when the trade talks were a "bilateral" conversation with other countries waiting to approve the outcome.

Support of the private sector is also crucial, both directly as an input into the negotiations and indirectly through pressure on legislators and politicians. The food industry has a major role in explaining the significance of open markets to a well-functioning global food system and rebutting the notion that only large corporations or rich countries gain from freer trade. In this respect some self-discipline may be needed to avoid the appearance of using trade talks to secure commercial advantage or restricting competition. Support of trade liberalization by farm interests is also crucial. Traditionally this has been forthcoming in the exporting countries but in short supply in the importing regions. But efficient suppliers gain ultimately from trade liberalization even in importing countries, though they may lose in the short-term some of the benefits from protection. If the protective walls are already crumbling it may be better to advocate a policy of replacing them with programs that encourage productivity increases.

The Cairns Group played an important role in the Uruguay Round in making sure that the issues of agricultural trade were not swept under the rug. They clearly see their role in the current round as keeping the feet of the EU and the US negotiators to the fire. In the longer run, their objective is to remove the "exceptions" for agriculture so that "normal" WTO rules, on subsidies and market access, apply. However laudable, the best may become the enemy of the good. The immediate goal of getting agreement on the ending of export subsidies is probably feasible and would have almost universal support among developing countries. To push too hard on the rules for domestic support, by denying the legitimacy of widely-held rural policy objectives on the grounds that they may also reflect a protectionist agenda, may be counter-productive. And to be too concerned over the use of food safety standards to protect domestic producers may risk antagonizing the bulk of the population who would reject any weakening of standards in the name of trade liberalization.[182]

---

[181] The parallel with the widening and deepening of the EU is striking. Both face the issue of reforming the decision-making structures as membership is widened, and both have to be concerned with the issues of democratic accountability and legitimacy as they deepen the degree of integration. Hence the importance of the Convention on the Future of Europe as a way of building legitimacy for EU enlargement and the significance of the apparent erosion of support within the US and other countries for further trade liberalization.

[182] Such coalitions between groups with disparate interests are sometimes referred to as "Baptist-bootlegger" coalitions, after the coincidence of interests at the time of Prohibition in the US between those that wanted to ban alcohol for moral reasons and those that profited from the ban. In the current circumstance, the bootleggers may benefit from environmental subsidies or strict health standards but the Baptists have command of the high-ground of public opinion.

Where governments have less control is over the situation on world markets for agricultural goods. The history of trade negotiations is littered with examples of world price developments de-railing the talks at crucial stages. One could argue that low prices push exporting countries into such negotiations, as they correspond to periods of high support costs. But importers may not be able to respond until the prices on the world market rise and the cost of liberalization is reduced. However, it is probably the existence of instability that is more damaging to the case for open markets. Such instability comes less from the spill-over effect of domestic price policy that before, but is still a function of weather and disease problems. How to reduce the impact of those factors without re-introducing market intervention programs is a challenge, though not explicitly for the WTO. But more generally the instability is a result of economic fluctuations and financial perturbations. So the future of the WTO agricultural talks may rest on whether the global economy recovers steadily from the current slump over the next few years and avoids the disruptions that have plagued several Asian and Latin American countries in recent years.

Chapter 11

Reform Compared: Similarities and Differences between the US and EU

11.1 Introduction

The premise of this book has been that fundamental shifts have occurred in the farm policies of both the US and the EU in the period since 1985. However, the changes have reflected different agricultural conditions and different political structures and constraints. This chapter attempts a comparison of the politics and processes of reform of farm policies to identify any similarities that can help to understand the nature of reform and any differences that can highlight the importance of the political and economic context in assessing such reform.

11.2 US and EU Policy Changes Compared

Agricultural policies in the US and EU have faced similar challenges since the 1970s from chronic farm surpluses. These surpluses have been generated by advances in technology leading to steadily increasing yields, exacerbated by government subsidies based on production. Inelastic demand for farm products in both Europe and America has meant that the surpluses cannot be disposed on domestic markets without collapsing prices. The impetus instead has been to seek international markets where demand is more elastic. Overproduction has led to increasing costs for farm policy, in support of a sector of the economy declining both in numbers and as a percentage of GDP, placing hard-to-justify burdens on US and EU budgets.

US and EU agricultural policy-makers have moved in parallel directions in their efforts to deal with surpluses. They have made policy more market and export oriented, with payments increasingly de-coupled from production. Yet, high levels of support have been maintained for farmers in both Europe and America, with the burden of support shifting over time from consumers to taxpayers. Both the US and EU insured farm income at the beginning of this period through a system of domestic price supports kept in place by import controls and intervention buying. The US took a significant first step toward reform in the 1973 farm bill, which, to reduce domestic surpluses and increase exports, eliminated the old price support system for wheat, corn, cotton and rice, bringing domestic prices down to world price levels. Farmers were compensated for lost income with government deficiency payment checks based on the difference between a legislatively set target price and the market price. In return for receiving deficiency payments farmers were required to set aside a portion of their land in uncompensated annual set-asides (ARP) to help maintain market prices. A safety net in the form of a floor price was provided by non-recourse loans; where farmers could gain loan forgiveness in return for forfeiting their crops to the government if the market price dropped below the loan rate.

Reform in the EU came later, at first, took a different direction, then moved to create its own system of deficiency payments. In 1984, the EU, facing rapidly increasing dairy costs and surpluses, responded not by reducing price supports, but rather by imposing supply controls in the form of dairy quotas. In 1988, with rising cereal policy costs and surpluses, the EU was still not able to cut price supports, but it did make a first step toward de-coupling payments from production by establishing maximum guaranteed quantities for cereals and oilseeds, with financial penalties for exceeding these limits. Then, in 1992, with the CAP facing the internal danger of collapse and external pressures for change, the MacSharry reforms lowered support prices for cereals, oilseeds and beef, though not to world market levels. Farmers were given compensatory payments for the income loss caused by the price cuts. These compensatory payments were partially de-coupled from production in that they were based on past regional yields. At the same time, European farmers were required annually to idle a portion of their land. Finally, in 1999, in the Agenda 2000 reforms, the EU further lowered price supports for cereals, oilseeds and beef, at the same time increasing compensatory payments.

Meanwhile, the US began de-coupling of payments from production in the 1985 Farm Bill by freezing the base acreages and yields for which farmers could receive deficiency payments. At the same time congress lowered loan rates (and the floor price) to make US farm products more attractive on the international market. The government went one step further in the 1990 Farm Bill, creating "triple-base," which, to cut farm support costs, excluded 15 percent of base acreages from deficiency payments, allowing farmers to plant whatever they wanted on that land except for fruits an vegetables. Then, in the 1996 FAIR Act, passed by the newly elected Republican congress committed to reducing the role of government, the US went even further than the EU in de-coupling by eliminating deficiency payments, acreage bases and ARP set-asides. Farmers were compensated by fixed "declining" acreage payments based on past crop yields, and given the freedom to plant whatever they wanted on their land (or not to plant at all).

In addition to the trend toward de-coupling, agricultural policy in both the EU and US has given increased emphasis to the environment, and more recently to rural development. This emphasis was first apparent in the 1985 Farm Bill that created the Conservation Reserve Program (CRP) along with sod-buster and swamp-buster measures. These programs have been continued in subsequent US farm legislation. The 1996 FAIR Act also created a new Fund for Rural America, with $300 million authorized to augment existing resources for agricultural research and rural development. In the EU, agri-environmental policy and rural development have been important emphases in both the MacSharry and Agenda 2000 reforms, although funding has been less than 10 percent of that authorized for market support and compensatory payments.

The extent of market-oriented agricultural policy reform in both the US and EU has varied greatly between different commodity sectors. The policy changes have tended to be more significant in commodity sectors with the potential for increased exports (cereals for the EU and cereals, feedgrains, cotton and rice for the US). In some import sensitive sectors, little reform has occurred. Both the US and EU rely heavily on domestic price supports and import barriers to support income for farmers producing sugar and dairy products. The US peanut policy also has not been reformed, relying on import barriers and production quotas.

11.3 The MacSharry and FAIR Act Reforms Compared

To illustrate more sharply the similarities and differences between the principal agricultural policy reforms in the EU and US during the 1990s it is instructive to compare the MacSharry CAP reform with the US FAIR Act. Both reform packages established new paths. Both were developed at a time of policy crisis, although the type of crisis was somewhat different. Both were an attempt to respond to crisis by putting agricultural policy on a more stable footing. In the case of the EU, MacSharry was concerned with a possible collapse of the CAP for budgetary reasons as well as with the standoff in the Uruguay Round: for the US the crisis was the need to reign in the federal budget deficit. Establishing control over farm spending was a key issue helping to catalyze both reforms, but ironically both increased farm spending as a result of the side-payments that had to be made to build winning coalitions. Policy change in both cases required "cash out" compensation to farmers.[183] In both cases, political leaders accepted the possibility of cost increases in order to move down a different policy path. The reform on offer seemed sufficiently important in terms of the long run acceptability of the policy to make the extra cost worthwhile.

In both cases, the impetus for reform came largely from the outside the agricultural sector, though the detail of the reforms were worked out inside the agricultural policy community. These reforms were managed by strong, astute politicians (Ray MacSharry and Pat Roberts), making the most of their respective political and economic environments. In the US, Roberts operated under constraints imposed by the new GOP-controlled Congress and made skillful use of the rising commodity prices to secure a deal that farm groups could support. In the EC, the need to complete the Uruguay Round fitted in well with increasing stocks and export subsidy payments to enable MacSharry to push through a dramatic reform when others before had failed. There is the probability of different policy outcomes had different farm leaders been in place. It is not clear that a weaker Commissioner could have

---

[183] Orden, Paarlberg and Roe (1999) have argued that farm policy is so deeply entrenched that usually the only way it can be significantly reformed is through cashing it out through compensation to farmers, rather than the alternatives of cut-outs, squeeze outs and buyouts.

pushed reforms similar to MacSharry's through a fractious EU Agriculture Council. In the US, a 1996 US Farm Bill with an adjusted deficiency payments system had already passed the Senate, and would probably have been approved by the House except for Roberts' opposition.

11.4 The US and EU Policy Processes Compared

US and EU processes for making agricultural policy are pluralistic, convoluted and compartmentalized. There is no single central policy authority in either region. Power is divided between the Commission and Agriculture Council in the EU, best explained by the Multi-level Governance model. The European Parliament has traditionally exercised less influence over farm policy, but this is beginning to change.[184] Power is shared between the Executive and Congress in the US, with congressional power centered in the House and Senate Agriculture committees. The Agriculture subcommittees of House and Senate Appropriations committees have enormous influence in annual appropriations, but are less influential in formulating longer authorization legislation contained in farm bills, usually formulated every five or six years. Policy is made in both the US and EU by institutions and individuals with close links to farming. The main agencies responsible for making policy recommendations, USDA and the EU Directorate General for Agriculture, are also charged with the administration of farm policy. Members of the House and Senate Agriculture committees almost always have strong farm constituencies. The EU Agriculture Council is made up solely of Member state farm ministers. Farm groups, with open access, have considerable input into the policy process. Outsiders participate much less regularly and generally exercise less influence, partially because they have less access, and partially because they have less at stake in the policy, hence less incentive to master the complex details of agricultural policy.

Agricultural policy decision-making in both the US and EU is best explained by Government Politics and Partisan Mutual Adjustment models, although the Organizational Process and rational actor models provide helpful insights. The bargaining in the US takes place primarily within and between the Senate and House Agriculture committees, and between the congressional agriculture committees and USDA. The bargaining in the EU takes place at two levels: within and between the Commission and Agricultural Councils at the EU level; and within and between agricultural ministries and other ministries at the national level.

---

[184] The European Parliament (EP) has historically had only a limited role in influencing EU farm legislation, as most of the CAP has been regarded as mandatory spending under Article 43 of the Treaty of Rome. For measures covered under Article 43, the parliament can give an opinion, but the Agriculture Council is under no obligation to accept it. The EP can delay action by refusing to give an opinion. With the expansion of the powers of the EP in the Maastricht and Amsterdam Treaties, and the increasing range of issues that come within the scope of farm policy, this situation is changing.

The US Secretary of Agriculture and the EU Agriculture Commissioner have somewhat comparable functions in the policy process. The Secretary and the Commissioner try to set the agenda for legislative debate by submitting planning documents listing issues, goals and recommendations. Policy recommendations usually reflect the "partisan mutual adjustment" between various elements within the farm policy bureaucracy. The EU Agriculture Council tends to take the planning documents more seriously, primarily because the Agricultural Council can only consider proposals originating in the Commission. In the US, any member of congress can submit legislative proposals. The Agriculture Commissioner, knowing that the Agricultural Council will have to react to his proposals, usually tries to consult with Member State governments. The US Secretary of Agriculture has little incentive to consult with Congress, facing the probability that the Agriculture committees will write their own farm bills.

The primary legislative actors are the US House and Senate Agriculture Committees and the EU Council of Agriculture Ministers. The House and Senate Agriculture Committees and the EU Agriculture Council have somewhat analogous roles. The close links between these institutions and the farming community ensures that legislative recommendations will be heavily weighted toward supporting farm interests. In the US the compromises tend to be between commodity interests, whereas in the EU much of the bargaining is between Member States. Decisions are made by simple majority in the Agriculture Committees and by qualified majority in the Agriculture Council, although the Council has a long tradition of seeking consensus in formulating legislation. The need to make deals implies that many side payments will have to be made, resulting in escalating costs as the legislation develops. The EU Agriculture Council president and the US congressional committee chairmen play somewhat similar roles in setting the agendas, controlling meetings and brokering consensus, although the Council president serves only for a six month term, while congressional committee chairmen serve at least for two years, often far longer.

Decisions reached by the EU Agriculture Council and the House and Senate Agriculture Committees can be overridden, but this rarely happens. The farm bills for 1981, 1985, 1990 and 1996, as formulated by the Conference of House and Senate Agriculture Committees, pretty much survived intact on the floors of both Houses. In the EU, the 1984 dairy reforms and the 1992 MacSharry reforms were agreed in the Agriculture Council and survived scrutiny by the European Council, though the 1988 budget stabilizers agreement required intervention by the Heads of Government and the Agenda 2000 package was weakened by the Berlin Summit.[185] Legislation emerging from the US congressional agriculture committees and from the EU Agriculture Council cannot easily be altered because it already represents a balanced compromise between a diversity of interests. Building a consensus for change involves heavy bargaining costs. Moreover, farm legislation involves a myriad of complex

---

[185] The Heads of Government (and Head of State, in the case of France) meet twice a year as the European Council, or Summit. They do not have the ability to pass legislation, but reach agreements that can then be passed back to the Council of Ministers for action.

details, which few outside the agricultural policy community have the incentive to master. This helps to preserve the autonomy of the agricultural policy decision bodies.

This is not to say that the House and Senate Agriculture Committees and the EU Agriculture Council can be oblivious to the concerns of non-farm politicians. Where an issue appears of concern to important actors outside the agricultural policy community, agricultural policy-makers have every reason to take such concern seriously, while responding in a way that ensures that the outcome is most favorable to farm interests. Food Stamp and nutrition programs have become part of US farm bills in part to attract the support from Members of Congress representing urban constituencies, while environment and conservation provisions ensure the support from legislators concerned about environmental issues. In the EU, concern outside the agricultural policy community with farm program spending was an important impetus for both the 1984 dairy reforms and the 1988 budget stabilizers.[186] The strong pressures from interests outside the agricultural policy community to see the Uruguay Round succeed certainly aided Commissioner MacSharry in pushing his reform package through the Agriculture Council. Agenda 2000 reflects the rising influence of environmental groups.

The EU Agriculture Commissioner and the US Secretary of Agriculture play very different roles in the legislative process. With any amendments to Commission proposals needing his support, the Agriculture Commissioner attends Agriculture Council meetings and is in a position to bargain directly with national farm ministers at every stage of the legislative process. The US Secretary of Agriculture, with no power to control the legislative agenda, rarely attends Agriculture Committee sessions, although USDA staff monitor hearings and give advice to Committee members. The Secretary of Agriculture does however gain some bargaining influence near the end of the committee process: if the proposed legislation is too far removed from administrative priorities, he (or she) can threaten a Presidential veto.

Comparable groups have access to the policy process in the US and EU. Farm lobbies probably have the easiest access, though these lobbies are organized rather differently in the US than in Europe. In the US, the dominant farm organizations are commodity-based groups, such as the National Corn Growers Association and the American Soybean Association, although general farm organizations such as the American Farm Bureau Federation (AFB) and the National Farmers Union (NFU) also exercise influence. In the EU, the dominant lobbies are national farmers' organizations, which coordinate activities through the Committee of Agricultural Organizations of the EU (COPA). Commodity groups are not prominent, although organizations such as the Cerealiers de France are now emerging onto the policy scene.

Other groups also have a stake in the outcome of farm policy debates. Agribusiness has good access to policy-making bodies in both US and EU, but firms have tended to operate individually rather the join together for collective lobbying. This situation changed somewhat in the US at the time of the 1996 Farm Bill, with the creation of the Coalition for Competitive Agriculture, which lobbied in support of

---

[186] See Moyer and Josling (1990), chapter 4.

"Freedom to Farm." Consumer groups have had some access to policy makers, both in the US and the EU, but up until the present have not had nearly as much influence as farm lobbies. Farm lobbies have a more apparent stake in farm policy than consumers and are more united in their positions. This may, however, be changing in the EU, with public concern about genetically modified foods, Mad Cow disease, and the outbreak of Foot and Mouth in several countries. In the US the consumer interests have also begun to shape farm policy, with their emphasis on food safety. Environmental lobbies have exercised increasing influence in both Europe and America in recent years. This influence was apparent in the US as early as the 1985 Farm Bill, and in Europe in the 1992 MacSharry reforms. The need to justify continuing de-coupled payments to a skeptical public, where these payments appear as farm welfare, presents an opportunity for environmentalists to insist on a linkage between these payments and action to protect the environment. The increasing emphasis on *Multifunctionality* in the EU appears to legitimate such activity.[187]

Rules, procedures and deadlines are important in both the US and EU policy processes. The EU Agriculture Council has always been constrained by EU rules that do not allow the Union to run a budget deficit. Budget discipline has been weaker in the US: in the debate on the 1990 Farm Bill, the House and Senate Agriculture Committees did not know how much they could spend on farm policy until the bill got to Conference. This did however change with the new budget procedures enacted prior to the 1996 Farm Bill debate, where legislators were told how much they could spend before considering new legislation. In fact, these new procedures were instrumental in the development of "Freedom to Farm."[188] The US trend from budget surplus to deficit may restrain future US farm spending, while the budget ceiling established in the March 1999 Berlin summit has tightened the spending constraint in the EU.

For agricultural trade policy, Fast Track procedures have given US negotiators considerable leeway in advancing proposals, since bargaining moves did not require clearance with congress. The absence of such procedures in the EU, with new initiatives requiring approval by the Article 113 (now Article 133) committee, and often by the Agriculture and General Affairs Councils, has limited the leeway of EU trade negotiators.

US trade negotiators lost much of their negotiating credibility after the completion of the Uruguay Round, when Congress refused to renew Fast Track Authority. While the House approved, by one vote, new Trade Promotion Authority (as a successor to Fast Track) late in 2001, the Senate has not yet acted on their own fast track bill.

The ability to deviate from standard procedures can sometimes be important in promoting reform proposals. "Freedom to Farm" would have been dead, after rejection by the House Agriculture Committee, if the House leadership had not allowed Pat Roberts to insert this proposal into the budget reconciliation bill. Sometimes the legislative calendar has to be accelerated for farm reform legislation. The 1992 US

---

[187] The impact of these changes in the future is discussed in the next chapter.
[188] See chapter 8 and Orden, Paarlberg and Roe (1999), pp.186-187.

presidential election and the expiration shortly thereafter of Fast Track negotiating authority provided a crucial deadline for the completion of the Uruguay Round negotiations. The need to reach an agricultural trade agreement with the US before this deadline provided an impetus for the EU Agriculture Council to reach agreement on the MacSharry reforms during the spring of 1992. The expiration of the provisions of the 1990 Farm bill at the end of 1995, and the need to have new provisions in place before the 1996 planting season, provided an effective deadline for concluding the FAIR Act debate. With the legislation developed so close to this deadline, major changes on the floor of Congress or a Presidential veto were not easy to contemplate.

Elections seem to have had a very different impact on agricultural policy reform in the US than in the EU. In the US, the effect has tended to be positive, while the effect has tended to be negative in the EU. With the approach of the 1992 Presidential election, President Bush used his leverage to expedite a Uruguay Round agreement. The Republican victory in the 1994 congressional elections proved catalytic for the development of the FAIR Act. In the EU, the 1990 German parliamentary election worked to delay the development on an EC agricultural trade proposal for the Heysel Stadium conference, contributing to the Conference's failure. The April 1993 French parliamentary election stiffened the French government's resistance to the Blair House I agreement and French demands leading to Blair House II. The October 1988 German election seems to have delayed final agreement on Agenda 2000 until the March 1999 Berlin summit. Perhaps the difference is that the electorate in the US has seen liberal reform more positively than the electorate in the EU.

11.5 Comparison of the Impact of Trade Negotiations on EU and US Domestic Policy Reform

There was an expectation in the Reagan Administration in the US, and perhaps also in some parts of the EU Commission, that the Uruguay Round agricultural trade negotiations might produce an agreement mandating domestic reform not possible to achieve at home. The belief was based on the idea that international negotiations would be conducted by trade policy officials more favorable to trade liberalization than farm policy officials with close links to farm lobbies. If a liberal trade agreement could be reached, it was thought that the outcome of this GATT negotiation would be reflected in changes in domestic US agricultural policy and in the CAP. Pressure would be generated to make domestic policy consistent with the international agreement, reflecting the two-level game synergy predicted by Putnam (Putnam, 1988). However, it became clear early in the Round that this expectation was little more than wishful thinking. Officials from USDA and the EU Directorate-General for Agriculture dominated the international agricultural trade negotiations, and no "end-run" on farm policy was possible. In part this was because these agencies alone had the expertise to understand the myriad complexities of agricultural policy, and in part because EU and US farm lobbies were strong enough to ensure full agricultural policy representation in the talks. The trade negotiations, rather than leading domestic agricultural policy reform, often lagged behind. This was well illustrated by the failure of the December 1990 Heysel Ministerial Conference. Agriculture trade negotiations nearly collapsed because EU negotiators had insufficient leeway from the Agriculture Council to accept lowering of domestic price supports, import barriers and export subsidies sufficient to allow agreement with the Cairns Group and the United States.

Yet, the Heysel failure illustrates how international pressures can be effective. By threatening the collapse of the entire Uruguay Round, the stalemate created pressures inside the EU to reform the CAP in such a way that a Uruguay Round agreement could be reached. The MacSharry Reforms, which emerged from the EU policy process at this stage then allowed the Blair House Accord between the EU and US to be reached in December 1992. The Blair House agreement as modified by the Blair House II negotiations a year later became the basis for the Uruguay Round Agreement on Agriculture. The domestic policy process retained its autonomy but had to act within a set of international constraints that in the end forced action.

The Uruguay Round Agreement on Agriculture had even more clear-cut impact on the Agenda 2000 reforms. It provided an impetus and rationale for further price cuts as export subsidies were getting perilously close to the URAA limits. It also reinforced the argument for further decoupling of support from agricultural production and ruled out consideration of any policy options that would have increased import barriers or domestic price supports. The problem was that with another set of agricultural talks due to start, it was not clear whether reforms undertaken for domestic reasons would get full "credit" at the international bargaining table.

The Uruguay Round Agreement on Agriculture also had a complex effect on the 1996 US Farm Bill debate, injecting both liberal and illiberal elements into the discussion. The URAA did not provide significant constraints on domestic programs, import barriers or export subsidies, as the US was well within its commitments in these areas as a result of firmer world prices and policy changes since the base period for reductions. The promises made to Members of Congress in return for their support of the Uruguay Round implementing legislation may have strengthened even more the *status quo* in US farm policy. But the URAA did have an effect on the terms of the debate. It increased the legitimacy of the Competitive Agriculture paradigm, strengthening the hand of groups who wanted to de-couple payments from production under "Freedom to Farm," and placing the defenders of existing commodity programs on the defensive. The prospect that exports would thrive in a more open world market, however, did little to decrease support for the Export Enhancement Program, which was seen as a "bargaining chip" to promote further international trade liberalization. The URAA will set parameters for both the 2002 US farm bill debate and the 2003 CAP policy review. Both the US and EU will be constrained not to adopt domestic measures inconsistent with their Uruguay Round commitments. They will have every incentive to shift their support for farmers more into "green box" payments.

11.6 Lessons for the Causes and Consequences of Reform

This analysis emphasized similarities in the factors that triggered agricultural policy reform in the US and EU in the 1990s. First, as was evident in the reforms of the 1980s, it takes a crisis to produce significant change. Agriculture policy is deeply entrenched and reflects considerable built-in bureaucratic inertia. It thus takes a major jolt to bring about more than incremental change. In the EU, there was a farm program crisis prior to the 1984 dairy reforms, the 1988 budget stabilizers and the 1992 MacSharry reforms. There was no sense of immediate crisis catalyzing the Agenda 2000 debate, but Agenda 2000 did not represent a new policy departure, but rather an intensification of the MacSharry reforms.[189] However, the Commission view was that without action in the present a crisis would develop in the future. The anticipatory action of Agenda 2000 may also reflect lessons learned from the previous reform efforts. By taking the initiative early, the Agriculture Commissioner and Directorate-General for Agriculture could prepare their proposals more thoroughly. In the US, there was no sense of crisis at the time of the 1981 or 1990 Farm Bill debates, and the policy outcome was incremental change. By contrast, the 1985 and 1996 Farm Bill debates occurred in the context of crisis, and the changes were more significant.

In our earlier book we noted the link between budget pressures and reform (Moyer and Josling, 1990). A tight budget situation tends to create a zero-sum game between various policy sectors competing for available resources. A projected increase in agricultural spending means less funding will be available for something else. If agriculture spending threatens to exceed its allocated share of the budget, outside actors are likely to be drawn into the agricultural policy process, thus stimulating change. Out-of-control farm spending was certainly a major factor in the EU 1984 EU dairy and 1988 budget stabilizer reforms. It was also a factor in the freezing of base acres and yields in the 1985 US Farm Bill and the creation of "triple-base" in the 1990 Farm Bill. A major goal of these reforms was to contain the growth of farm spending. The link between budgets and farm policy reform since 1990 has been somewhat different. A projected crisis in farm spending was certainly important in stimulating the Commission to prepare the MacSharry reform proposals. However, the spending crisis did not materialize and the reforms in the event cost more than the previous policy. The US budget crisis was also a major factor galvanizing reform in the 1996 US Farm Bill debate. But both the FAIR Act reforms and the MacSharry reforms, cost the government more that the existing policy. The Agenda 2000 reforms were not galvanized by a budget crisis, although the planners were concerned that agricultural spending would breach the spending guideline in the years ahead. Interestingly, the prospect that the Agenda 2000 reforms would increase the cost of the CAP provided

---

[189] It was argued by one reviewer of this manuscript that Agenda 2000 produced significant change in the "philosophy" behind agriculture policy, establishing the Competitive Agriculture Paradigm for the major crop sector of the EU in essentially doing away with the need to subsidize cereal exports. That this could be achieved in the absence of crisis reflected the leadership of Commissioner Fischler who believed in reform in its own right.

French President Chirac with a rationale for weakening the reforms. In a context where no member country government was prepared to contemplate increasing its budgetary contribution, the French managed to argue that the EU could not afford a deeper reform at this time.

It would thus appear that neither US nor EU policy-makers are willing or able to impose reforms that inflict pain on farmers except when such reform can be defended as essential for resolving a budget crisis. This is evidence of the continuing strength of the farm lobby and of support for farmers among the general public.

Why did EU and US policy-makers approve the expenditure increasing MacSharry and FAIR Act reforms, undertaken in the context of budget crisis? In the case of the MacSharry reforms, the originally proposed modulation of compensatory payments and proposed uncompensated set-asides would have kept costs manageable, but the requirement of building a winning coalition in the Agriculture Council forced costs upward as modulation was eliminated and compensation was added for set-asides. EU prime ministers and finance ministers accepted the increase because they needed CAP reform to ensure the successful completion of the Uruguay Round, and there were no other feasible reform options on the table. The approval was made easier because future cost estimates for the MacSharry reforms were uncertain, with at least the possibility that costs would decline over time as surpluses of grain, dairy products and meat declined.

Analogous factors were at work in the case of the FAIR Act reforms. "Freedom to Farm" as originally proposed would have resulted in savings from February 1995 projections of what the extension of the 1990 Farm Bill would have cost. However, costs increased considerably as side payments were made to ensure the support of important farm constituencies. At the same time rising prices decreased the projected costs of an extension of the existing legislation (the 1990 Farm Bill). The Republican congressional leadership accepted FAIR because it needed a farm bill, with the 1996 planting season approaching, and there was no feasible alternative. The GOP leadership also needed to have an important legislative accomplishment in an election year. The budget pressures were actually relieved when President Clinton vetoed the budget reconciliation bill and "Freedom to Farm" was integrated into free-standing farm legislation. As with the MacSharry reforms, the cost factor could also be discounted because of uncertainty. Besides, the FAIR act offered the prospect of capping farm spending. Policy-makers could allow increases in farm program costs in the absence of a public outcry about farm spending either in the EU or US This may be attributed partly to the strong continuing public support for farmers, but also to the fact that the public was not following either reform debate closely. Among those who did know what was being debated, there was a general willingness to try something "new" that might help deal with the seemingly endless farm policy problem.

Neither the EU nor the US has been successful in targeting benefits on the basis of farm size. As noted in Chapter 6, the EU tried unsuccessfully to modulate farm payments to the advantage of smaller farms in the MacSharry reforms. Various proposals to limit farm programs and to target farm payments are also regularly considered in US farm bills. Targeting proposals have universally failed, and while payment limits have been established, they have been weak and easy to circumvent. Two factors would appear to be at work here. First, as one would expect from the public choice literature, large farmers, who have the most at stake in continuing to receive farm benefits, tend to be heavily engaged in debates over farm legislation and tend to dominate farm lobbies. Second, the need for a high degree of consensus in both the EU Agriculture Council and the US House and Senate Agriculture Committees makes it very difficult to proceed without the support of large farmers. Middle-sized and small farmers recognize that they are receiving less than larger farmers, but if the farm community is divided and farm legislation fails, they get nothing at all.

11.7 Evidence of Paradigm Shifts in US and EU Policy Changes

Earlier chapters have pointed to the shift in paradigms underlying farm policy on both sides of the Atlantic. This presents another dimension within which to compare the policy changes. The policy shifts represented by the MacSharry and FAIR Act reforms were accompanied by paradigm shifts, which both facilitated the reforms and were legitimized by the reforms. It was clear well before these reforms that the old Dependent Agriculture paradigm was not working. Basing farm payments on production resulted in chronic surpluses that were expensive to store and dispose. Surplus disposal using export subsidies distorted international markets, creating international trade conflict. Attempts to deal with the surplus problem through supply controls were not very efficient and were unpopular with farmers. Even if a nation succeeded in maintaining high domestic prices to support farm income through supply controls, competitiveness was lost on international markets. Only a new approach which de-coupled payments from production would reduce the incentive to produce surpluses, allowing price signals from international and national markets to determine domestic production. The old paradigm became untenable well before either the MacSharry reform of the CAP or the US FAIR Act, and while this reality was not sufficient in itself to catalyze a change in policy direction, it contributed to a policy environment conducive to policy reform.

It is not surprising that the US and the EU developed different new paradigms. The US agricultural sector, with generally large and efficient farms was generally well structured to compete on international markets, with minimal price supports, import barriers and export subsidies. Hence, the Competitive Agriculture paradigm fit the industry very well. The EU, with a much greater number of small farms, could not fully open its market to competition without either forcing many of the farmers off the land or paying higher compensatory payments than the budget could stand. With a much more densely crowded population and many picturesque old villages, preservation of the countryside assumed a much greater importance in the EU than in the US. The Multi-Functional Agriculture paradigm seemed appropriate for this situation in that it provided a rationale for not completely opening the European market to international competition. It had the added advantage that payment to farmers to protect and enhance the environment could be defended in the WTO as "green box."

The MacSharry and FAIR Act reforms legitimated the new paradigms in the sense that the policy changes were consistent with the new thinking. The new thinking became entrenched as the policy changes became institutionalized in organizational standard operating procedures and as they developed a constituency among the beneficiaries of compensatory payments. As the new paradigms became established, they increasingly provided the reference arguments for evaluation of farm policy.

Paradigm shifts are not easy. One problem is that policies get "locked in" to a political and administrative process that makes change difficult. Often the development of a policy will preclude changes to another "path", at least without considerable political and adjustment cost. This suggests a string "path dependency" in agricultural policies. The agricultural policies of both the US and EU exhibit symptoms of this path dependency. The EU kept its system of price supports in place until the MacSharry reforms of 1992 and the US kept its deficiency payments system until the 1996 FAIR Act. The Agenda 2000 reforms did not depart substantively from the MacSharry reforms, and it looks at the time of this writing in March 2002 that the 2002 US farm bill will continue the de-coupled payments of the FAIR Act.[190] However, the new US farm bill will probably backtrack a bit toward the Dependent Agriculture paradigm by creating new counter-cyclical payments that will kick in when market prices fall below a certain point.[191] The new US legislation will also probably move incrementally toward the Multifunctional Agriculture paradigm by increasing environmental payments.[192] Both the MacSharry reforms and the FAIR Act involved high bargaining costs. It is easier to adjust them than to sink the additional bargaining costs to set policy off in a new direction. The compensatory payments of both reforms have benefited farm interests who now do not want to give them up. USDA and the EU Directorate-General for Agriculture have spent time developing standard operating procedures to implement the reforms. It will be much easier to adjust these procedures than to develop new ones. Sufficient feedback has been received from the MacSharry reform and the FAIR Act to eliminate much of the uncertainty about their consequences. Setting policy off in a new direction would introduce more uncertainty than continuing the present policy. Thus EU and US policy-makers appear to have every incentive to maintain the current direction of policy for the foreseeable future. Whether they will be able to do so is the subject of the next chapter.

---

[190] Both the House and Senate farm bills, passed, respectively, in October 2001, and February 2002, contain provisions to continue fixed payments to farmers, so that it is unlikely that the House-Senate Conference will eliminate them. The Senate bill has a $275,000 limit on the total payments that a farmer may receive from government programs, which is half of the limit in the FAIR Act. This cut was catalyzed by the Washington based Environmental Working Group posting on its web page the payments given to individual farmers over the past five years. However, with the House continuing the existing limit, it is questionable whether the Senate cut will survive the conference.

[191] New counter-cyclical payments are in both House and Senate bills.

[192] Both House and Senate bills increase funding for conservation programs.

Chapter 12

The Future of Agricultural Policy Reform in the EU and the US

12.1 Introduction

The previous chapters have described the process of agricultural policy reform over the decade of the 1990s. Significant changes have occurred in entrenched policies that warrant the label of reform. One important question that one must ask of the recent policy changes in the industrial countries, in particular in the EU and the US, is whether the reforms are "permanent" or just the latest twist in the endless saga of these programs. If a policy change is merely a short term expedient masquerading as reform, the tendency will be to revert to type as soon as conditions allow. Will farm policies in the EU and the US in, say, ten years time look like an evolution of the current reformed policies, or will they resemble the policies of the early and mid 1980s? Should current policies be thought of as the latest variant of the old entitlement approach to farm programs, based on the old paradigm of a Dependent Agriculture? Or are they the manifestation of the Competitive Agriculture paradigm, which takes the government out of supporting commodity prices and making farming decisions, and where necessary "buys out" the political obligation to commodity and farm groups. Or will the Multifunctional Agriculture paradigm come to prevail, with agriculture the guardian of the countryside, rewarded for environmental services as much as the production of raw material for the food industry? Or perhaps there are new paradigms emerging, that focus on the farm sector as an integral part of a global food chain, where national boundaries are an inconvenience and support programs an irrelevance; or that link the choice of food consumed to the environment in a holistic way so that lifestyles and farming practices become intertwined in a "new age" awareness of the cultural significance of food.

Continued reform depends on a combination of political and economic circumstances. These include a receptive climate for reform as well as the absence of any event that would derail the process. Circumstances also require that political systems work reasonably well to reflect changing social views. This chapter examines the conditions under which one might expect US and EU farm policy reform to continue but also sounds a note of caution that the possibility of a return to at least some of the old-style policies cannot be entirely ruled out.

12.2 The Climate for Further Reform of Agricultural Policies

The climate for the reform of farm policies includes both political and economic conditions. Among the political conditions are the strength of the farm lobby, support for farmers among the general public, the support (tacit in most cases) of non-agricultural politicians for programs that grant farmers specific benefits, and the overall willingness of the government to intervene in the market to help particular sectors. The economic conditions include a confidence in the stability of world markets, the financial health of the farm sector, the ability of the government to fund rural programs and the nature of structural developments in the farm and food sector. These dimensions will have an important bearing on the likelihood of further reform in EU and US policies.

The Strength of the Farm Lobby

Though farm populations continue to decline in both EU and the US, the farm lobby remains a formidable force. Farm organizations are well-organized, understand the complexities of agricultural policy and have vast experience working with agricultural policy-makers. Both US and EU agricultural policy processes are structured in such a way to be highly responsive to the farm lobby, with the principal decisions made in the EU Council of Agriculture Ministers and the US congressional agriculture committees, whose members usually have strong agricultural constituencies. There are very strong mutually supportive linkages between the farm lobby, farm policy bureaucrats and farm policy legislators. It has never been easy to challenge the farm lobby in the political arena, because of the strong public support for farmers in both Europe and America, but as we will see below this may be changing, particularly in Europe. Farm votes can be critical in close elections, and may be important for the 2002 elections in France and Germany. In the US, the currently closely divided congress leaves both parties competing for farm votes in the 2002 congressional elections. A major factor in the strength of the farm lobby is its unity. A tight budget situation tends to divide the farm lobby as various elements fight over their share of the available largesse. Loose budget constraints, on the other hand, tend to unify the farm lobby, as the budgetary pie is large enough to accommodate the demands of multiple farm constituencies.

Support for Farm Policies

Perhaps the most striking development in recent months has been the apparent rapid decline in the support for farm policies in the EU. The public perception seems to have changed somewhat dramatically from a general view that the CAP is a necessary, if expensive, policy for support of farming to an association of the CAP with unhealthy and dangerous excesses in intensive agriculture. Of course a change in public perception of this type does not show up immediately in changed policies. And in any case such changes can be reversed by skilful public relations. But in this case there is reason to think that the change is more enduring. The main political parties in Europe seem to be moving behind the idea of radical changes in the CAP so as to respond to public concerns.

The "green" agenda has taken on an increased prominence, with supporters leading the agriculture ministries in Germany, Denmark and Sweden. This agenda emphasizes such things as quality output, food safety, animal welfare and environmentally friendly food production. Supporters would shift government subsidies away from market support to such things as organic farming, enhancement of the environment on farms and rural development. Indeed, the German Agriculture Ministry has been renamed the Ministry for Consumer Protection, Food and Agriculture and the UK Ministry of Food and Farming has been recast as the Department for Environment, Food and Rural Affairs. What is not yet clear is how unified the newly strengthened consumer and "green" lobbies will be, and how insistent on reform of the CAP. Will they be willing to commit the same kinds of resources to change the CAP that the farm lobby will commit to preserve the CAP? The public choice literature would suggest that this is questionable.

Continuation of Economic Reforms

There were several important developments in economic policy that made the context for agricultural trade policy reform very different in the 1990s from that of the early 1980s. The most important of these was the wave of economic reform that swept over almost all countries after the mid-1980s. By 1986 a few countries (such as Chile and New Zealand) had started down the road to more liberal policies, but for most the issues of deregulation, privatization, structural adjustment and macroeconomic reform were still being debated. The Berlin Wall still separated the two parts of Germany, and the Iron Curtain divided Europe. Centrally Planned Economies ran their own type of trade policy based on complete state control. In such circumstances few would have given much hope that the call in the Uruguay Round for more market orientation in agriculture would have received much more than lip-service by most countries of the world.

As we have seen, agricultural policy reform took root in the majority of OECD countries, leading to the conclusion of the Uruguay Round in 1993. Some consolidation has taken place since that time, with the FAIR Act taking a significant step down the reform path and the EU's Agenda 2000 taking a more hesitant move in the same direction. But the issue remains whether the political move toward economic reform has lost momentum. If so, the process of dragging a reluctant agricultural sector toward a deregulated future could itself falter.

Even if the neo-liberal policy shift has run out of steam, the context for the multilateral talks on agricultural trade that began in 2000 is very different. In particular, developing countries now have a very different view of their own role in the global economy. Very few countries have not embarked on a program of reform, either of their own making or at the suggestion of lending and financing agencies. Reform of international trade policies was a key part of the economic reform in all countries. The majority of the former centrally-planned economies have now abandoned the attempt to control trade. No-one queries any more the objective to introduce market disciplines to agriculture. Governments regularly call for the development of competitive agriculture sectors able to sell into world markets or to hold their own against imports from abroad. Government assistance is often still needed for those who cannot achieve the status of international competitiveness, but this assistance is tightly constrained by budget pressures and usually of limited duration. To be sure imports of farm products are still taxed, often quite highly, but the justification often revolves around issues of unfair competition from dumped products and the need for time to adjust rather than the determination to keep out all competitors for the local product. In other words the general assumption adopted by most governments today is that agriculture must live by the same rules as other sectors. If competitive, it will flourish: if not, it must adjust or wither. Under these conditions trade talks can take on a much more constructive tone. Of course there will be continued tension between importers trying to regulate the pace of market opening and exporters trying to push them to go faster. But that is very different from the emotional confrontations in earlier decades between those that considered domestic agriculture beyond the reach of international trade talks and those that wanted to expose such ideas to ridicule.

The multilateral trade system should arguably be in better shape than in the mid 1980s, the last time that a decision was made to start a major round of trade negotiations. Perhaps the most significant aspect of the transformation of the trade system has been its shift from being essentially a "club" for the developed countries, with a fringe of developing countries loosely adhering to the rules and largely disenfranchised from the decision process, to a global set of rules covering most of world trade and with much wider responsibilities and participation. This change from a glorified OECD to a mini-UN has been difficult and contentious. The crunch came in Seattle, when the developing countries made the decision to resist the efforts of the US and the EU to settle the agenda for a new round by the old bilateral processes. The Doha meeting was the first WTO ministerial where the developing countries had a major influence on the outcome, and the resulting trade round has been crowned the "Doha Development Agenda."

The transformation is not yet complete, nor may it be without problems. It is not clear whether the rich countries, particularly Congressional and business opinion in the US, are ready to negotiate and agree to an outcome that effectively redresses the imbalance among countries that was perceived to have emerged from the Uruguay Round. But to look for further concessions from developing countries without major changes in the developed country trade policies is to court deadlock. And the developing countries themselves have not been particularly consistent about how to use their new-found responsibility. Latin America is still generally in the lead in pushing for market opening in the developed countries, while Asia is more concerned with preserving the ability of developing countries to shelter domestic industry. African nations fear marginalization and the further exploitation of domestic resources without any significant outside investment in the more dynamic sectors of the new global economy.

The impact on agriculture is likely to be important. The greatest potential for growth in agricultural exports in the next decade is likely to come from the developing countries. Developing countries all agree among themselves that protectionism in the OECD countries denies them markets for their farm and food products. Developments that are considered in the west as being trade-friendly, such as the decoupling of farm support from commodity prices and the introduction of a science test in health and safety regulations are widely considered by developing countries to be ways of retaining protection. The unwillingness of the developed countries to open up markets in this current round would convince the developing countries that the apparent willingness to share responsibility for the trade system does not extend to making difficult domestic decisions in the area of agriculture.

Global Agricultural Market Developments

The situation in agricultural markets and the context in which agricultural policy will be formed in the future may also be somewhat different from that which accompanied the reforms of the 1980s, though superficial similarities are evident. The current round of trade negotiations is being held in a period of low prices for the major farm products not unlike that which prevailed in 1986, at the start of the Uruguay Round. At that time world markets were in a state of acute disarray as a result of domestic farm policies that were essentially out of control. World prices were at the lowest levels for years and farm program costs were at an all-time high. US agricultural exports had fallen dramatically from their peak in the early 1980s, and the EU was picking up market share with aggressive subsidies. In effect the US and the EU were in a trade war. Even agricultural ministers, often the last to admit the scale of the problem, became convinced that something should be done to improve the workings of the market, if it was not to collapse altogether under the weight of unwanted surpluses. The mood was to "do something" about agricultural trade. The issue even made it to the agenda of the Economic Summit in Tokyo in 1986, when President Reagan lectured his fellow leaders on the disarray in world agricultural markets.

Now, in the midst of the current round, the world market for agricultural commodities continues to be depressed and demand for farm products remains weak. Commodity prices were generally firmer over the 1990s relative to the depressed levels of the mid 1980s. For most of the major commodities there had been adequate market outlets over the decade, much of that due to strong growth in Asia. US exports of farm goods reached record levels in 1996, exceeding even those of the export boom in the early 1980s. In 1995 and 1996 cereal markets reacted to a perceived shortage of stocks and sent prices to their highest levels for five years. But in 1997 the Asian financial crisis sent export demand in the US falling strongly. Prices dipped and farm incomes weakened. US policy-makers responded with emergency relief paid from a now growing budget surplus. The circumstances were in place for a return to the protectionism of the 1980s, with a combination of import restrictions and intervention in domestic markets.

However, the response of governments has been rather different on this occasion. No government in the OECD has resorted to import protection. Export subsidies fell below the allowable levels in the first half of the 1990s as a result of high prices and strong demand, but have not in general been increased in the past three years. Trade disputes between the US and the EU and between the US and Japan continue, but the issues are now to do with health and safety standards rather than market shares. In short, the major governments are resisting the temptation to go back towards a Dependent Agriculture, with high border protection. The Uruguay Round apparently has changed behavior, whether out of conviction or just the higher cost of implementing trade disruptive policies.

This poses a dilemma for agricultural trade reform. Can further steps only be taken if there is a crisis in agricultural markets or another explosion of spending on farm programs? It is possible that the crisis of the mid 1980s may have been needed to stimulate countries to undertake reform. A more benign state of agricultural markets may therefore translate into reduced incentives to continue the reform process. On the other hand, a period of calm in world markets may actually be the best time to push ahead with the reform. If commodity prices recover in the next few years the combination of low prices to attract political attention and higher prices to allay some of the fears of the farm sector may again prove an effective climate for change. If there is the will to continue reform it is likely to be incremental and to continue along the existing path. The experience of the 1980s and 1990s described in this book has shown that it takes a major impetus to implement non-incremental reform and to undertake a new policy path.

Changes in the Composition of World Agricultural Markets

Structural changes in the agricultural and food markets of the world will also have a major impact on the continuation of the process of reform. One of these is the process of intra-industry reorganization that transforms isolated national markets into parts of an integrated global system. This is both driven by firms seeking lower production costs and broader markets over which to spread costs, but is also a consequence of the relaxation of investment and trade regulations. In other words, the food and agricultural sector is not escaping the pressures of globalization that have swept so many parts of the economy.

The most notable indication of this change is that the growth in trade in high value added products is much greater than that in homogeneous bulk products. In 1985 trade in high value added products was barely one half of total agricultural trade. In the year 2000 it was estimated that this share was around three-quarters of agricultural trade. Part of this is due to the effects of rising incomes, as consumers shift away from unprocessed foods. But much of the growth in high value added goods is due to increasing product differentiation as producers and food retailers attempt to convince consumers of the merits of particular geographical locations, recipes and brand names. Goods that were once considered "non-tradable" have found a place in foreign markets for ethnic and exotic foods. Product differentiation, segmentation of the market and quality attribution along with the growth of "non-traditional" trade is the key behind the growth of agricultural exports from many countries in Central and South America as they free up foreign exchange markets and begin enthusiastically to trade. It is also behind much of the rise in US agricultural exports, including to the old, saturated markets of Europe. Europe itself is enjoying a minor export boom in the same types of commodities, breaking out of the trap which for years had made it focus on a few undifferentiated products such as wheat, sugar, skimmed milk powder and butter which could only be sold with heavy subsidies.

This shift in the type of trade raises new issues that need to be resolved. These include the areas of intellectual property rights on seeds and genetic material, geographical origin protection, labeling of organic produce and of goods containing genetically-modified organisms (GMOs), as well as issues of animal and plant health and human safety. The current round of trade negotiations will have to come to grips with these issues. Significant tensions in this area will persist if rules are not clear and widely accepted. Indeed the widespread use of crops that incorporate biotechnology has already collided with the equally widespread fears of consumers, often encouraged by those with other agendas, about their safety. Unless public authorities regain the confidence of the public, trade rules which aim to facilitate trade can themselves lose credibility in the public eye.[193]

In addition to the increase in international trade in processed food products there has been a dramatic rise in the sales of foreign affiliates in the food business. When an international fast food outlet in a foreign country sells a piece of chicken or a hamburger, the transaction is reinforcing the global nature of the food sector. More often than not, the outlet will have purchased some of the ingredients abroad, thus increasing the amount of trade. But capital, technology, managerial know-how and service skills are transmitted to the host country even if all the supplies are purchased locally. Moreover, trade can increase as a result of the changes in taste brought about as a result of the spread of "international" cuisine.[194]

This trade shift toward more processed and differentiated foods also brings different actors into the arena of agricultural trade talks. Agricultural merchants and traders have always played a role, and have generally been in favor of more open markets. Agricultural processors have been much more ambivalent. In exporting countries the processors favor expanded trade, but in importing countries they have often been among the most ardent advocates of domestic self-sufficiency and high capacity. They have tended to take a rather narrow "commodity" view of agriculture and its development. But as these firms themselves become more international, as there product lines expand, and as they have to compete with others that have lower

---

[193] See Josling and Patterson (2001) for a discussion of the regulation of biotechnology in the US and the EU.

[194] It appears that, in the case of food and agricultural products, investment is complementary to rather than a substitute for trade. Though some investment is obviously in place to "jump" a trade barrier, most seems to be part of the search for new markets, taking advantage of economies of scale by spreading managerial and financial assets over a wider market.

raw material costs, they begin to recognize the benefits of allowing the price of raw materials to be determined in the market rather than by politicians. And as trade in consumer-ready foods increases, the desire intensifies to export to markets outside ones own country. This then allows firms to take advantage of economies of scale in processing and manufacturing, further reducing costs.

In the agricultural industry itself, changes are taking place which complement these developments in the food sector. Farms continue to grow larger on average in Japan, the US and Western Europe, as farm amalgamation continues. In the countries of Eastern and Central Europe the state farms are being privatized but are usually kept in parcels of reasonable size. Consolidation in the wholesale trade often encourages farmers to cooperate either with each other or through contractual arrangements with their buyers. As price supports are weakened, the producer has a greater incentive to improve the marketing of the product, through better quality and differentiated characteristics.

Regional Trade Agreements and the Process of Reform

An additional question to ask of the reformed farm policies of the EU and the US is whether they are compatible with the development of regional trade agreements and the process of market integration in the Americas and in Europe. NAFTA made a start in paving the way towards a single agricultural market in North America, and MERCOSUR is pursuing the same path in the South. The 1996 Farm Bill made a significant contribution to this process by reducing the involvement of the government in supporting prices. There is some prospect of an integrated North and South American market in cereals and oilseeds and perhaps red meat in the next few years, as a result of the formation of the Free Trade Area of the Americas (FTAA). Nevertheless there will continue to be frictions over sugar and over fruits and vegetables, as well as over dairy products and poultry, as the competitive Brazilian farm sector competes head on with the US and Canada. In these commodities the 1996 Farm Bill made only a hesitant step towards regional market integration, and it is not clear that the 2002 Farm Bill will go much further in this direction.

In the case of the EU there is little doubt that the MacSharry reform and Agenda 2000 made the economic integration of the European economies, west, central and east, markedly easier. In addition, it offered the possibility of trade agreements with other agricultural exporting areas such as Mexico, South Africa and MERCOSUR. By lowering the price level and compensating with direct payments, it is less likely that the market will have to be kept segmented between east and west. That is not to say that there will not be problems of further integration of agricultural markets. There will always be those in the existing EU that will object to the importation of goods from the new members. After all, French farmers still protest against agricultural imports from Spain, Italy and the United Kingdom on the smallest pretext. But the political imperative to allow the Central European countries access to Western markets will over time allow the economic benefits of specialization and trade within the enlarged EU.

12.3 The Path of US Reform

In the case of the US there is always a lingering doubt about the longevity of the reform engendered by the fact that the underlying legislation, the 1949 Agriculture Act, is still on the books. Failure to enact new legislation in the year 2002 would cause the policy to revert to the permanent legislation. This threat (since the 1949 Act would create an expensive chaos) has been the stimulus for the timely passage of the past many farm bills, but it is not clear how credible it is. It does not appear in late March that this threat will be needed for the 2002 farm legislation. The House passed its version of a new farm bill in October 2001, and the Senate passed its version in February 2002. It seems probable that the differences will be worked out in a House-Senate Conference by mid-2002. The main reason why the failure to repeal the old legislation in 1996 was important was that it missed the opportunity to clear the political decks. The fact that there has to be new legislation is itself an important advantage to those that will argue for the revival of traditional farm programs. The Commission on 21st Century Production Agriculture, set up under the 1996 Farm Bill to consider such issues has generally favored the continuation of the reform process, and it would appear from the Senate and House bills that back-sliding will be limited.

The issue can be put in a more overtly political way. Is it likely that the coalition that has kept farm programs in the US going long after general support in the urban areas had dwindled could reconvene and bring back price supports? The coalition relies on the cohesion of commodity groups despite their widely differing interests, solid support from the (relatively few) Congressmen from overwhelmingly rural constituencies, who generally hold seats on the House and Senate agriculture committees, and the unlikely alliance with those supporting the food stamp program. The coalition is beginning to look shaky. The commodity groups were not united on the occasion of the 1996 Farm Bill. Most of the pressure for the Freedom to Farm Act came from Midwestern cereal and oilseed interests, whereas dairy, sugar, peanuts and other powerful sectors provided lukewarm support or outright opposition. In the end separate deals were cut to placate the sugar and dairy lobbies. They appear more united in the 2002 farm bill debate, wanting quick action, fearing that delay might cause the $73.5 billion in new spending for agricultural programs authorized for the next ten years by the 2002 budget resolution (H Con Res 83) to vanish with the growing budget deficit (CQ Weekly, Dec. 8, 2001, p.2901).

In spite of the decline in the traditional commodity group support for market intervention, significant pressures exist for a return to the programs of the past. Democratic congressmen and those from farm states are still concerned with the ability of the agricultural sector to weather the storm of low world prices. Some would prefer to return to government management of markets; others call for more extensive safety nets and social provisions. The generous funding set aside by the 2002 Budget resolution seems sufficient to sustain farm spending at high levels. Both House and Senate versions of the 2002 farm bill contain provisions to continue the guaranteed payments under Produced Flexibility Contracts and to add counter-cyclical payments to assure farmers of income levels comparable to those with the recent emergency payments. If money is tight, there may be an interesting fight over how much of the available funding to allocate to producer flexibility contracts and how much to allocate to counter-cyclical payments. Even though the budget surplus has been eaten up by the 2001 US recession, tax cuts, and increased government expenditures, the will to impose budgetary discipline declined significantly following the September 11, 2001 terrorist attacks in New York and Washington.

There has been something of a fight between traditional farm interests who now favor both guaranteed and counter-cyclical payments, and environmental and rural development interests, who are dissatisfied with current farm programs, and who seem to accept the Multi-Functional Agriculture paradigm. It would appear that the multi-functional view of agriculture will make some headway in the final 2002 farm legislation, with payments increased for land stewardship. However, efforts to shift funding in a major way away from guaranteed fixed payments have failed up to this point.[195]

There has been another battle in the Senate over the maximum level of subsidies available to individual farmers. The Washington-based Environmental Working Group catalyzed this debate by gaining information on the subsidies paid to individual farmers around the country through the Freedom of Information Act, and then publishing these figures on its web site. The revelation that a relatively small number of farmers were getting enormous subsidies led the Senate by a 66 to 31 vote to limit the maximum amount a farmer can get in federal farm payments to $275,000 (see *The New York Times*, 8 February, 2002). This debate pitted legislators representing cotton and rice interests (with generally large farming operations) against legislators representing cereal and feedgrain interests in the Midwest (with somewhat smaller operations). It is not clear whether this limit will survive the House-Senate Conference, as the House bill contains no new subsidy limit.

Beyond the 2002 farm bill, much will depend on the seriousness of the budget constraint. If money is available to sustain farm spending at the levels of 1998-2000, there will be strong pressures to continue the guaranteed payments under producer flexibility contracts along with counter-cyclical payments and the increased environmental payments likely to be introduced by the 2002 farm bill. If money gets tight, there may be an interesting fight over how much of the available funding to allocate to producer flexibility contracts and how much to allocate to counter-cyclical payments and environmental payments. In this case, the literature on path dependency indicate that it will probably be easier politically to maintain the current course than to revert to the policies of the 1980s, with incremental redistribution over time in favor of spending for land stewardship and rural development. This redistribution may be

---

[195] The House of Representatives in a close vote of 226 to 200, on October 4, 2001, rejected an amendment to redirect $19 billion of the 2002 Budget Resolution $73.1 billion ten-year agricultural spending increase to farmers and communities that reduce pollution from agricultural operations, or set aside more acreage for wetlands, wildlife, hunting and conservation (see *The Washington Post*, 4 October, 2001).

accelerated if US farm spending approaches Uruguay Round limits, or if new limits are agreed in the Doha Round.[196]

12.4   The Path of EU Reform

The changes brought about by the 1992 and 2000 CAP reforms are in general accepted as responsible for an improvement in the market situation in the crops. For this reason, the change is likely to endure. Both internal and external forces will act to keep the policy from backsliding. Internally, the benefits of a lower cereal price are clearly evident to the livestock sector, and the renewed use of domestic grain in animal feed has made market management easier. Externally the WTO Agreement, and the schedules of export subsidies incorporated into the EU's bindings, add up to an effective brake on any significant recidivism. And if the EU is to welcome new members in the next decade, the policy needs to be able to accommodate such changes. The enlargement of the Union will leave little room for the type of policies that the EC6, the EC9 or the EC12 pursued for many years. An EU of up to 27 countries will neither be able to afford the expenditure nor be able to justify the economic costs of such a policy. Of course the CAP could be "rescued" temporarily by the device of a "green wall" around the existing member countries and using border taxes as a way of preserving a higher price level for those countries. But the political implications of this type of solution make it difficult to contemplate. The message would be sent that agriculture is valued highly in the existing members but not in the new members. In other words political reality will require the CAP to change to allow for enlargement, which will in turn lock in the second round of reforms.

When the next stage in CAP reform will come is less easy to predict. The EU Commission was asked, at the 1999 Berlin Summit, to conduct a mid-term review of the success of the Agenda 2000 reform process, which in essence tied the CAP to particular prices, expenditure and instruments until 2006. At present the view is that the Commission will present its review in the second half of 2002, when the French and German elections are safely out of the way. Whether the Commission takes this opportunity to propose major changes or merely mid-course corrections is still unclear. Much will depend on the prospects in 2002 that the EU agriculture budget will exceed the spending ceiling set by the 1999 Berlin summit. If it looks like the CAP budget can be kept within the guidelines, much of the impetus for further reform will be removed. If, on the other hand, breach of the ceiling appears imminent, caused by such factors as low world food prices, decline in the value of the dollar, continued high payments to support the beef market and the need to extend compensatory payments to new members in Central Europe, the pressures for further reform may well be substantial. Another significant factor will be how effective European environmental and consumer

---

[196] The 2002 House bill has a ten-year duration, while the Senate bill sets policy for five years. If the final legislation is for ten years, that will impede efforts to keep farm spending and its allocation on the political agenda.

groups are in mobilizing public dissatisfaction with the CAP into an effective political lobby to shift CAP funding from direct farm income support to support for agri-environment and rural development measures. The outcome of the French and German elections will also be important. Victories by the SPD-Green coalition in the German parliamentary election and by the Socialists in the French presidential and parliamentary elections would bode well for further reform.

12.5   Instruments for the Reformed Policies

If the reforms of the 1990s are to be consolidated, what will be the instruments used in the farm policies of the US and the EU? For the policy reforms to continue there has to be an agreeable set of instruments that address the continued problems of the rural economy. Without such instruments the removal of price supports is essentially dependent upon favorable (i.e. firm) world market price levels. The armory of possible weapons for dealing with rural development, farm income, food safety, environmental protection and social stability is extensive. Unfortunately most of it is untested or tried only on a small scale. In particular, the fate of direct payments, such as those used in the US FAIR Act and the EU's MacSharry payments, is uncertain. Will they become truly portable, attached only to the individual that was first the recipient? That may have some implications for land prices and raise some interesting landlord-tenant problems. Will they become salable? If the payments are portable assets, there is no reason why they should not be sold to others, presumably at a discount reflecting the credibility of the commitment to future payments. If they did become portable and salable, the impact on the rural economy could be significant, as investment shifted from agriculture to other areas. Will they become truly green, being tied to environmental farming practices? This is certainly the way the EU is pointing, but it remains to be seen whether the farm interests will object to the layer of supervision necessary to make significant payments in a fair and effective way. Will farm income stability be dealt with by other instruments? Crop insurance is likely to be one such instrument. But farmers in the US are experimenting with a variety of monetary instruments for offsetting risk, such as the use of options-based contracts. The terms of sale of farm products could over time evolve to include more such contracts. Income insurance and tax equalization schemes can prevent the major swings in income that often beset the farm sector.

12.6   Prospects for Further Reform of Agricultural Trade

There is good reason to believe that the current round of agricultural trade talks could be less contentious and protracted than the last. Although such an optimistic view may depend on the full and timely recovery of the world economy, the signs are in general more favorable than in the years before the Uruguay Round. This improved climate is due largely to the change in the domestic policy environment in the major countries, not least in the EU and US.

It was possible to maintain the traditional farming systems by a combination of basic research into yield-increasing technology, guaranteed markets for undifferentiated raw materials, fixed and profitable margins for processing activities which tended to locate near the production base, and various parastatal marketing agencies in case markets were oversupplied. Trade policy acted as handmaiden to these domestic policies. Tariffs and non-tariff barriers were used by governments as instruments to protect domestic markets from competition from abroad. Globalization brings new challenges and requires new policy approaches. Moreover the old policies often get in the way of those that are needed for the new food system. Nowhere is that more clearly seen than in the trade policies.

The main focus of international trade policy has traditionally been the conditions of access into markets. As globalization has progressed so the scope of trade rules has expanded. The new trade policy environment has a number of different elements. These include the health, safety and environmental rules that ensure quality and acceptability in discriminating markets; codes for the treatment of foreign direct investment; the regulation of conditions of competition; and the codification of the rights granted to the owners of intellectual property.

A global trade system needs global competition laws. This apparently uncontroversial conclusion has had little effect so far on trade policy discussions. Whilst some are calling for full-scale negotiations on international competition policy, others maintain that the most you can do is to make sure that each trading country has its own anti-trust policy in place. But the minimalist approach is unlikely to be satisfactory for very long. The best policy for curbing misuse of market power in any one country is an open trade system. But the very openness of the trade system allows large firms to develop market power in the world market. Global competition policy should be more about market power in world markets than about enforcing competition policy in each national market.

An emerging competition issue is the concentration of market power in the agri-food distribution chain. This has two separate but related aspects. One is the use of market power by public agencies or by parastatals given the ability to act in a restrictive way. This issue of "state trading" is coming to the fore in trade talks. At one extreme it represents a concern among those countries that do not practice state trading that those that do can gain an "unfair" advantage through hidden export subsidies and import barriers. At the other extreme are fundamental systemic issues such the behavior of the state trading entities in China and indeed the extent to which the government still controls, albeit indirectly, all trading decisions in that country. As a major player in agricultural trade markets, the terms under which China is allowed into the World Trade Organization (WTO) will have a significant impact on the rules that can be set for other countries with parastatal agencies active in the market.

The issue of competition also is at the heart of another potential problem facing the agri-food system. Concentration of economic power is not confined to public agencies given monopoly rights in importing or exporting. Private firms can have significant market power to influence prices. Should there be any rules relating to the use of market power in international markets? What are the dangers that the rules are trying to prevent? Is the problem the withholding of supplies to raise the price of commodities? This seems relatively unlikely in the case of basic foods, but could happen with vital supply components. Or is the problem one of dumping and market disruption? The incorporation of anti-dumping rules in a set of more comprehensive competition regulations is the object of many trade economists. Whatever is agreed will have significant implications for global agriculture.

Agricultural trade policy used to be dominated by farm groups and those arguing for more protection. One major shift in the 1980s was the involvement in trade talks of multinational food firms in the negotiations. This trend is likely to continue. First, the processing sector has a strong incentive to look for low-cost supplies. There is therefore the incentive to lobby government for the ability to import those supplies from world markets so as to remain competitive with firms located in countries where prices are lower. In many cases the low cost food suppliers are in the Americas, as are the main competitors in the global market place. Hence one would expect continued pressure from the food industry to allow raw material prices to fall to roughly US levels over a period of years. Given the disinclination of governments to support these prices indefinitely, the inclination of the food industry may well come to dominate in the end.

The tendency for the international food companies to search for low-cost supplies will be reinforced by pressure from those firms that are already operating in several countries. For these firms, including those in the distribution and retailing business, international trade is often intra-firm trade. Any restriction on the movement of food items within the firm will tend to cause problems for the firm, and hence will be resisted.[197] But just as intra-firm movement of goods can be thwarted by government regulations so too can the contractual obligations of firms that have come together in other forms of alliance. One would expect that those firms which have been pioneering supply chains, linking producers in one country to wholesale and retail outlets in another, would also find government restrictions on trade irksome. Thus one might expect these supply chains to add their voice to pressures for trade liberalization.

There is no indication that this process of shifting up the value-added chain is likely to slow down in the near future. The emerging science and practice of biotechnology holds enough tantalizing promise to attract investment even in the face of consumer resistance. There is no indication that the biotechnology revolution has peaked. The key to feeding the world at a reasonable cost is to make full use of the new knowledge and skills in this area. The biotechnology industry is itself undergoing structural change, as large corporations search for the profitable products that will pass the scrutiny of regulators and not be rejected by the public. So far the most important of these products have been cost-reducing, appealing to producers, rather than taste-

---

[197] When European food firms owned production facilities in overseas countries, as a part of the colonial food system, duties and other restrictions were rare. The spread of European food firms into retailing has sometimes been called "Supermercado colonialism".

enhancing. Consumers see little direct benefit for themselves. Hence one can well imagine trade conflicts involving discrimination among suppliers of similar goods depending on the method of production. But biotechnology also makes possible the "design" of foodstuffs with features that could improve their marketability. This development could lead to an increase in trade rather than trade friction, as producers attempt to meet new consumer tastes.

All these changes are in the direction of a more sophisticated agricultural industry aware that the future depends on satisfying a variety of consumer tastes and competing for the consumer dollar with other goods and services. More actors become involved in the political process, and the center of gravity shifts perceptibly away from the primary producer. Policy becomes less "commodity" focused and the emphasis switches to adding value to the raw material and marketing the final product. These changes are crucial to the future of agricultural trade policy reform. In a situation where the "market" is an administered price supported by public purchasing agencies, free trade poses a real threat. In a world where farmers produce for the market, improvement in access to overseas markets compensates in part for more domestic competition. A freer agricultural market no longer means a collapse of prices and mass rural depression. Today it is more likely to spark rural entrepreneurship and healthy market development based on response to the changing food habits of middle-class consumers.

But, measured against all the developments auguring for more open international markets, one needs to consider the potential future impact of the evolving food safety, environment and animal welfare lobbies and the anti-globalization movement. These groups tend to reinforce each other although the food safety, environment, and animal welfare lobbies tend to focus on domestic policy while the anti-globalization movement gives its primary attention to international trade and the WTO. It is at this stage very difficult to predict the future strength of these groups, but we can make some generalizations about the positions they are likely to take.

It appears that none of these groups will be very supportive of a return to the Dependent Agriculture paradigm, with subsidies based on production. The old paradigm promotes intensive production with high use of chemicals and fertilizers. Hence, environmental and consumer critics of farm policy favor policy reforms that reduce price supports and export subsidies, and support measures promoting the multi-functionality of agriculture. But this could mean that they will oppose any further reduction of import barriers, arguing that such barriers are necessary to protect domestic producers from cheap imports produced under conditions not supportive of animal welfare and the environment. This approach could be described as "protected multi-functionality" - reduced price supports, reduced export subsidies, along with expanded rural development and environmental payments, but with retained import barriers.

The anti-globalization lobby's distrust of the WTO is unlikely to impede domestic reform efforts but could present a significant obstacle to liberal reform pursued through international trade negotiations. How serious this barrier will be will depend on the political and economic environment and on how effectively the advocates of trade policy reform can make their case. International trade policy reform will also depend on how much reform is achieved in the domestic arena. If nations are serious about continuing the trend of the past decade, it should be possible to enshrine these commitments in a new WTO trade agreement extending the scope and the reforms started in the Uruguay Round. The 1990s would have proved to be the turning point in the long march toward more liberal agricultural policies.

Bibliography

ABARE (1988). *Agricultural Policies In Japan*. Australian Bureau of Agricultural and Resource Economics, Canberra, Australia.

Abel, Martin, Lynn Daft and Thomas Early (1994). *Large-Scale Land Idling Has Retarded Growth of U.S. Agriculture*. Prepared for National Grain and Feed Foundation.

Adshead, Maura (1996). "Beyond Clientelism: Agricultural Networks in Ireland and the EU," in *West European Politics* vol. 19, no. 3 (July), pp.583-609.

AgraEurope (various issues). Tunbridge Wells, UK: Agra Europe (London) Ltd.

Allison, Graham and Philip Zelikow (1999). *Essence of Decision: Explaining the Cuban Missile Crisis*, 2nd Edition, New York: Longman.

Anon (2001). *Directions for Future Farm Policy*. Commission on 21st Century Production Agriculture, Washington, DC.

Anon (undated). "A New Direction for European Agriculture: The Portuguese contribution to CAP reform" (working document).

Baldock, David and Philip Lowe (1996). "The Development of European Agri-Environment Policy," in M. Whitby, *The European Environment and CAP Reform*, Wallingford, Oxon, UK: CAB International.

Braybrooke, David and Charles E. Lindblom (1963). *A Strategy of Decision: Policy Evaluation as a Social Process*. New York: Free Press of Glencoe.

Buckwell, Allan (1997). "Towards a Common Agricultural and Rural Policy for Europe." *European Economy Reports and Studies*, 5, Office for Official Publications of the European Communities, Luxembourg.

Cloud, David S. (1990). "The Politics of the '90 Farm Bill Revolve Around Budget," *Congressional Quarterly Weekly Report*, May 12, pp. 1468-1470.

Cochrane, Willard W. and C. Ford Runge (1992). *Reforming Farm Policy: Toward a National Agenda*, Ames: Iowa State University Press.

Coleman, William D. and Stefan Tangermann (1997). "Linked Games, International Mediators and Agricultural Trade," paper given at the IATRC Meeting, San Diego, December.

Coleman, William D. and Stefan Tangermann (1997). "Linked Games, Supranational Mediators and Agricultural trade: Analyzing International Influences on Domestic Policy-making" (unpublished manuscript).

Coleman, William D., Grace Skogstad, and Michael Atkinson (1996). "Paradigm Shifts and Policy Networks: Cumulative Change in Agriculture." *Journal of Public Policy*, vol. 16.

Coleman, William D., Michael Atkinson, and Éric Montpetit (1997). "Against Odds: Retrenchment in Agriculture in France and the United States." *World Politics*, vol. 49 (July), pp. 453-481.

Commission of the European Communities (1997) *Agenda 2000. For a Stronger and Wider Union* COM (97) 2000 Final, Office for Official Publications of the European Communities, Luxembourg.

Committee of Agricultural Organisations in the European Union (COPA) (1997). "For a European Model of Agriculture."

Congressional Quarterly (1996). "Highlights of House, Senate Farm Bills." Vol. 54, No.10 (March 9), pp. 653-659.

Congressional Quarterly Almanac (1990, 1995 & 1996).
Conley, Howard H. (1996). "The 1995 Farm Bill: Opportunities and Challenges for Economists." *Journal of Agricultural and Applied Economics*, vol. 28, no.1 (July), pp. 35-44.
COPA-COGECA (1997). "COPA and COGECA's First Reaction to the Commission's Agenda 2000 Proposals for Agriculture."
COPA-COGECA (1998). "COPA and COGECA's Response to the Commission's Agenda 2000 Legislative Proposals for Agriculture."
COPA-COGECA (1998). "The European Model of Agriculture: The Way Ahead."
Daugbjerg, Carsten (1999). "Reforming the CAP: Policy Networks and Broader Institutional Structures," in *Journal of Common Market Studies*, vol. 37, no. 3 (September), pp.407-28.
Delorme, Helene (1994). "French Agricultural Policy Objectives," in Rasmus Kjeldahl and Michael Tracy, ed., *Rationalisation of the Common Agricultural Policy?* Belgium: Agricultural Policy Studies and Copenhagen: Institute of Agricultural Economics.
Department of Agricultural Economics and Food Marketing, University of Newcastle, UK (1998). "Agenda 2000: CAP and Rural Policy Reform: Response and Comments."
Economic Research Service (2001). The Road Ahead: Agricultural Policy Reform in the WTO–Summary Report. Agricultural Economic Report no. 797, U.S. Department of Agriculture, Washington DC, December.
Epstein, Paul (1997). "Beyond Policy Community: French Agriculture and the GATT," *Journal of European Public Policy*, vol. 4, no. 3 (September 1997), pp. 355-372.
Financial Times various issues.
Fraley, Colette (1995). "Glickman Confirmation Hearing Hints Cuts will be Difficult." *Congressional Quarterly*, March 25.
Gardner, Bruce L. (2001). "Benefit-Cost Economics of the FAIR Act," in John A. Schnittker and Neil E. Harl, *Fixing the Farm Bill*, Conference Proceedings, National Press Club, Washington, DC, March 27, pp.31-45.
George, Alexander (1980). *Presidential Decisionmaking in Foreign Policy: The Effective Use of Information and Advice*. Boulder, Colorado: Westview Press.
Gibson, P., J. Wainio, D. Whitley and M. Bohman (2001). *Profiles of Tariffs in Global Agricultural Markets*. AER No. 796. Economic Research Service. U.S. Department of Agriculture. Washington, DC.
Glickman, Dan (2001). "Looking Back to Move Ahead," in John A. Schnittker and Neil E. Harl, *Fixing the Farm Bill*, Conference Proceedings, National Press Club, Washington, DC, March 27, pp. 99-103.
Grant, Wyn (1997). *The Common Agricultural Policy*. New York: St. Martins.
Haas, Peter M. (1992). "Introduction: Epistemic Communities and International Policy Coordination," in *International Organization* vol. 46, no.1 (Winter 1992), pp. 1-35.
Hager, George (1996). "Other GOP Efforts May Fall Along With Budget Talks," *Congressional Quarterly* (February 3), pp. 283-284.
Hagstrom, Jerry (1995). "The Farm Team." *National Journal* vol. 27, no. 26 (July 1), pp. 1705-1709.
Hall, Peter (1993). "Policy Paradigms, Social Learning and the State: The Case of Economic Policymaking in Britain." *Comparative Politics*, vol. 25.
Harl, Neil E. (2001). "Farm Policy Considerations: Introductory Comments, Looking Back to Move Ahead," in John A. Schnittker and Neil E. Harl, *Fixing the Farm Bill*, Conference Proceedings, National Press Club, Washington, DC, March 27, pp. 5-9.
Harl, Neil E. (2001). "The Structural Transformation of the Agricultural Sector," in John A.

Schnittker and Neil E. Harl, *Fixing the Farm Bill*, Conference Proceedings, National Press Club, Washington, DC, March 27, pp.45-57.
Harvey, David R. (1998). "UK Agricultural Development: Policies, Constraints & Issues." Paper prepared for International Symposium of Agricultural Policy in the 21st Century, National Chung Hsing University, Taiwan, ROC, June 11-17.
Hathaway, Dale E. (1987). *Agriculture and the GATT: Rewriting the Rules*, Institute for International Economics, Policy Analyses in International Economics No.20, Washington, DC, September.
Hendricks, Gisela (1994). "German Agricultural Policy Objectives," in Rasmus Kjeldahl and Michael Tracy, ed., *Rationalisation of the Common Agricultural Policy?* Belgium: Agricultural Policy Studies and Copenhagen: Institute of Agricultural Economics.
Hix, Simon (1999). *The Political System of the European Union*. New York: St. Martin's Press.
Hosansky, David (1995a). "Lugar's Farm Plan Poses Test for Fellow Republicans," *Congressional Quarterly*, vol. 53, no. 17(April 29), pp. 1167-1170.
_____ (1995b). "Florida Sugar Growers Edgy as farm Bill Debate Nears," *Congressional Quarterly*, vol. 53 no. 19 (May 13), pp. 1311-1316.
_____ (1995c). "Longstanding Cropland Policy is Fertile Field for Debate," *Congressional Quarterly*, vol. 53, no. 22 (June 3), pp. 1568-1570.
_____ (1995d). "Freshman Republicans Attempt to Fence Off Farm Subsidies," *Congressional Quarterly*, vol. 53, No. 24 (June 17), pp. 1732-1735.
_____ (1995e). "In Farm Bill Debate, GOP Risks Cultivating Enemies," *Congressional Quarterly*, vol. 53, no. 25 (June 24), pp. 1824-1828.
_____ (1996a). "Lawmakers Struggle to Get a Farm Overhaul Bill," *Congressional Quarterly*, vol. 54, no.4 (January 26), pp. 217-218.
_____ (1996b). "House and Senate Assemble Conflicting Farm Bills," *Congressional Quarterly*, vol. 54, no. 5 (February 3), pp. 295-298.
_____ (1996c). "After Intense Maneuvering Senate OKs Farm Proposal," *Congressional Quarterly*, vol. 54, no. 6 (February 10), pp. 355-358.
_____ (1996d). "Opposing Forces Fall in Line to Make or Break the Bill," *Congressional Quarterly*, vol. 54, no. 7 (February 17), pp. 388-390.
_____ (1996e). "House, Senate Move Closer as Bills Go to Conference," *Congressional Quarterly*, vol. 54 no. 9 (March 2), pp. 543-549.
_____ (1996f). "Snare of Competing Interests Entangles Dairy Debate," *Congressional Quarterly*, vol. 54, no.11 (March 16), pp. 691-693.
_____ (1996g). "Farm Policy on the Brink of a New Direction," *Congressional Quarterly*, vol. 54, no. 12 (March 23), pp. 786-788.
_____ (1996h). "House Easily Clears Rewrite of Decades-Old Farm Laws," *Congressional Quarterly*, vol. 54, no.13 (March 30), pp. 874-875.
Hughes, David (ed.) (1994). Breaking with Tradition: Building Partnerships and Alliances in the European Food Industry, Wye College Press, Wye.
Ingersent, K. A. and A.J. Rayner (1999). *Agricultural Policy in Western Europe and the United States*. Cheltenham, UK and Northampton, MA, USA: Edward Elgar.
Ingersent, K. A., A.J. Rayner, and R.C. Hine (1998). *The Reform of the Common Agricultural Policy*. New York: Macmillan Press.
International Agricultural Trade Research Consortium (1989). "Tariffication and Rebalancing." IATRC Commissioned Paper No. 4. St. Paul, MN.
International Agricultural Trade Research Consortium (1997). "Implementation of the Uruguay Round Agreement on Agriculture and Issues for the Next Round of Agricultural Negotiations". IATRC Commissioned Paper No. 12, November.

Jervis, Robert (1976). *Perception and Misperception in International Politics.* Princeton, N.J.: Princeton University Press.

Johnson, D. Gale (1975). *World Agriculture in Disarray.* London: Macmillan.

Josling, Tim (1993). "Agriculture in a World of Trading Blocs." *Australian Journal of Agricultural Economics*, vol. 37. no. 3 (December), pp. 155-79.

Josling, Tim (1998). *Agricultural Trade Policy: Completing the Reform.* Institute for International Economics: Washington, DC.

Josling, Tim (1999). "Globalization of the Agri-Food Industry and its Impact on Agricultural Trade Policy," paper presented to the conference on Agricultural Globalization, Trade and the Environment, University of California at Berkeley, March.

Josling, Tim (1999). "Trends in Agri-markets and Trade Policy," in Meester, Gerritt, Reinout D. Woittiez, and Aart de Zeeuw (eds.) *Plants and Politics*, Wageningen Press, Wageningen.

Josling, Tim (2000). "Competing Paradigms in the OECD and Their Impact on the WTO Agricultural Talks," Paper presented at the Conference Challenging the Agricultural economics Paradigm, held in honor of Luther Tweeten, Sept. 10-11.

Josling, Tim (2001). "The Impact of Food Industry Globalization on Agricultural Trade Policy," in Moss, Charles, Gordon Rausser, Andrew Schmitz, Tim Taylor and David Zilberman (eds.) *Agricultural Globalization, Trade, and the Environment*, Kluwer.

Josling, Tim and Julie Babinard (1999). "The Future of the CAP and Prospects for Change." *European Forum Working Paper,* Institute for International Studies, Stanford University.

Josling, Tim and Lee Ann Patterson (2001). "Regulation of Biotechnology in the US and the EU: Source of Trade Conflict or Opportunity for Cooperation?" Working Paper No. X, European Forum, Institute for International Studies, Stanford University.

Josling, Tim and Allan Rae (1999). "Multilateral Approaches to Market Access Negotiations in Agriculture," paper presented to the World Bank Conference on Agriculture and the WTO, Geneva, 1-2 October.

Josling, Tim, Stefan Tangermann and Thorald K. Warley (1996). *Agriculture in the GATT*, Basingstoke: Macmillan

Kennedy, Lynn, Lars Brink, John Dyck, and Donald MacLaren (2001). *Agriculture in the WTO. Domestic Support: Issues and Options in the Agricultural Negotiations*, IATRC Commissioned Paper #14, Minneapolis, Minnesota, May.

Kingdon, John W. (1984). *Agendas, Alternatives and Public Policies.* Boston: Little Brown.

Kingdon, John W. (1993). "How do Issues Get on Public Policy Agendas?" in *Sociology and the Public Agenda*, Newbury Park, London and New Delhi: Sage, pp. 40-51.

Kjeldahl, Rasmus and Michael Tracy (eds.) (1994). *Rationalisation of the Common Agricultural Policy?* Belgium: Agricultural Policy Studies and Copenhagen: Institute of Agricultural Economics.

Krueger, Anne O. (1992). *The Political Economy of Agricultural Pricing Policy: A Synthesis of the Political Economy in Developing Countries*, A World Bank Comparative Study, The Johns Hopkins University Press, Baltimore.

Levi, Margaret (1997). "A Model, A Method, and a Map: Rational Choice in Comparative and Historical Analysis," in *Comparative Politics: Rationality, Culture and Structure*, Mark I. Lichback and Alan S. Zuckerman (eds.), Cambridge: Cambridge University Press.

Lindblom, Charles E. (1959). "The Science of Muddling Through," *Public Administration Review*, vol. 19, Spring.

Lindblom, Charles E. (1965). *The Intelligence of Democracy.* New York: The Free Press.

Long, Tony (1998). "The Environmental Lobby," in Philip Lowe and Stephen Ward (eds), *British Environmental Policy and Europe: Politics and Policy in Transition.* London and

New York: Routledge.

Lopez, Mauro de Rezende (1997). "Trade Liberalization and Agricultural Reforms in Brazil," Fundacao. G. Vargas, Rio de Janeiro.

Lowe, Philip and Neil Ward, (1998). "A 'Second Pillar' for the CAP? The European Rural Development Regulation and its Implications for the UK." Working Paper 36, Department of Agricultural Economics and Food Marketing, University of Newcastle, UK.

Lowe, Philip, Alastair Rutherford, and David Baldook (1996). "Implications of the Cork Declaration." *ECOS: A Review of Conservation*, vol. 17, no. 3/4.

Madison, Christopher (1990). "Coming a Cropper," *National Journal*, May 5, pp. 1082-1085.

Madison, Christopher (1990). "Raising Hell on Cane," *National Journal*, July 14, pp.1717-1719.

Meester, Gerrit and Frans A. Van Der Zee (1993). "EC Decision-making, Institutions and the Common Agricultural Policy. *European Review of Agricultural Economics*, vol. 20, no.3, pp.131-150.

Meilke, Karl, James Rude, Mary Burfisher, and Maury Bredahl (2001). *Agriculture in the WTO. Market Access: Issues and Options in the Agricultural Negotiations*, IATRC Commissioned Paper #13, Minneapolis, Minnesota, May.

Moravcsik, Andrew (1991). "Negotiating the Single European Act: National Interests and Conventional Statecraft in the European Community," *International Organisation*, vol. 45.

Moyer, Wayne (1993). "The European Community and the GATT Uruguay Round: Preserving the Common Agricultural Policy at All Costs," in Wiliam P. Avery, *World Agriculture and the GATT*. Boulder and London: Lynne Rienner.

Moyer, Wayne (1994). "The Blair House Agreement, Agricultural Trade and the Completion of the Uruguay Round of the GATT," Paper presented at International Studies Association Meetings in Washington, D.C, April 1994.

Moyer, Wayne (1996) "EU and US Agricultural Policies and Their Impact on Bilateral Relations," in Jorg Monar, (ed.), *The New Transatlantic Agenda and the Future of EU-US Relations*. London: Kluwer Law International.

Moyer, Wayne and Tim Josling (1990). *Agricultural Policy Reform: Politics and Process in the EC and USA*. New York and London: Harvester Wheatsheaf, Hemel Hemstead.

Moyer, Wayne and Tim Josling (2001). "Agricultural Policy Reform in the US and EU: The Impact of Shifting Paradigms," Paper presented at European Community Association International Conference, Madison, Wisconsin, May 31-June 2.

Murray, Gail and Natacha Yellachich (1997). "Agenda 2000: WWF Response to the CAP Reform Proposals." (unpublished).

National Journal various issues.

Nelson, Gerald C. (ed.) (2001). *Genetically Modified Organisms in Agriculture: Economics and Politics*, Academic Press, London and San Diego.

North, Douglass C. (1990). *Institutions, Institutional Change and Economic Performance*. Cambridge: Cambridge University Press.

OECD (1994). *Agricultural Policy Reform: New Approaches, The Role of Direct Income Payments*, Organization for Economic Co-operation and Development, Paris.

OECD (1997). *Agricultural Policies in OECD Countries: Measurement of Support and Background Information, 1997*, OECD, Paris.

OECD (1999). *Food Safety and Quality: Trade Considerations*, OECD, Paris.

OECD (1998). *The Future of Food: Long-term Prospects for the Agro-food Sector*, OECD, Paris.

OECD (2001). "Multifuntionality: Towards an Analytical Framework," Paris.
Orden, David (2000). "The Soul of Farm Policy in the 21st Century," Paper presented at the Conference Challenging the Agricultural economics Paradigm, held in honor of Luther Tweeten, Sept. 10-11.
Orden, David (2001). "Policy Options for Import Competing Commodities Consistent with Trade Liberalization," "Looking Back to Move Ahead," in John A. Schnittker and Neil E. Harl, *Fixing the Farm Bill*, Conference Proceedings, National Press Club, Washington, DC, March 27, pp. 83-93.
Orden, David (2001). "Should there be a Federal Farm Income Safety Net?" Paper presented at the 2001 USDA Agricultural Outlook Forum, Arlington, VA, Febrary 22.
Orden, David, Robert Paarlberg, and Terry Roe (1999). *Policy Reform in American Agriculture: Analysis and Prognosis*. Chicago: The University of Chicago Press.
Paarlberg, Robert (2001). "The Political Climate for the Farm Debate: Looking Back to Move Ahead," in John A. Schnittker and Neil E. Harl, *Fixing the Farm Bill*, Conference Proceedings, National Press Club, Washington, DC, March 27, pp. 23-31.
Paeman Hugo, and Alexandra Bensch (1995). *From the GATT to the WTO: The European Community in the Uruguay Round*. Leuven, Belgium: Leuven University Press.
Patterson, Lee Ann (1997). "Agricultural Policy Reform in the European Community: A Three Level Game Analysis," *International Organization*, vol. 51, no. 1 (Winter, 1997).
Petit, Michel, Michele de Benedictis, Denis Britton, Martin de Groot, Wilhelm Henrichsmeyer and Francesco Leshi (1987). *Agricultural Policy Formation in the European Community: The Birth of Milk Quotas and CAP Reform*. Amsterdam: Elsevier.
Pezaros, Pavlos (1999). "The Agenda 2000 CAP Reform Agreement in the Light of Future EU Enlargement," European Institute of Public Administration Working Paper 99/W/02.
Pierson, Paul (2000). "Increasing Returns, Path Dependence, and the Study of Politics," *American Political Science Review*, vol. 94, no.2 (June).
Potter, Clive (1998). *Against the Grain: Agri-Environmental Reform in the United States and the European Union*. Wallingford, OX, UK and New York: CAB International.
Potter, Clive and Matt Lobley (1998). "Landscapes and Livelihoods: Environmental Protection and Agricultural Support in the Wake of Agenda 2000." *Landscape Research*.
Putnam, Robert D. (1998). "Diplomacy and Domestic Politics: the Logic of Two-Level Games." *International Organisation*, vol. 42, no. 3. Summer.
Rauch, Jonathan (1995). "Plowing a New Field," *National Journal*, vol. 27, no. 4 (January 28): 212-216
Ray, Daryll E. (2001). "The Economic Climate for the Farm Bill Debate," in John A. Schnittker and Neil E. Harl, *Fixing the Farm Bill*, Conference Proceedings, National Press Club, Washington, DC, March 27, pp. 9-23.
Richardson, Jeremy (1996). "Policy-making in the EU: Interests, Ideas and Garbage Cans of Primeval Soup," in Jeremy J. Richardson (ed.), *European Union: Power and Policy-making*. London and New York: Routledge.
Ritson, C. and D.R. Harvey (eds.) (1997). *The Common Agricultural Policy*. Wallingford, UK: CAB International.
Robbins, John (2001). *The Food Revolution*, Conari Press, Berkeley, California.
Roberts, Donna, Laurian Unnevehr, Julie Caswell, Ian Sheldon, John Wilson, Tsenehiro Otuski, and David Orden (2001). "Agriculture in the WTO, The Role of Product Attributes in the Agricultural Negotiations," IATRC Commissioned Paper #16, Minneapolis, Minnesota.

Roederer-Rynning, Christilla (2001)."Farm Conflict in France and the Europeanisation of Agricultural Policy," Paper presented at the European Community Studies Association (ECSA) Seventh Biennial International Conference, May 31-June 2, Madison, Wisconsin.

Sandrey, Ron and Russell Reynolds (eds.) (1990). *Farming without Subsidies: New Zealand's Recent Experiences*, MAF, New Zealand.

Schertz, Lyle P. and Otto C. Doering III (1999). *The Making of the 1996 Farm Act.* Ames: Iowa State University Press.

Schnittker, John A. (2001) "Fixing the FAIR Act to Reduce Budget Costs, Looking Back to Move Ahead," in John A. Schnittker and Neil E. Harl, *Fixing the Farm Bill*, Conference Proceedings, National Press Club, Washington, DC, March 27.

Schnittker, John A. and Neil R. Harl (eds.) (2001) *Fixing the Farm Bill:* Conference Proceedings, National Press Club, Washington, DC, March 27.

Schott, Jeffrey J. (1994). *The Uruguay Round: An Assessment*, Institute for International Economics, Washington, November.

Senior Nello, Susan (1984). "An Application of Public Choice Theory to the Question of CAP Reform," *Review of European Economics*, vol.11.

Stenholm, Charles (2001) "Commodity, Environmental and Regulatory Issues in the Farm Bill Debate," in John A. Schnittker and Neil E. Harl, *Fixing the Farm Bill*, Conference Proceedings, National Press Club, Washington, DC, March 27

Swinbank, Alan and Carolyn Tanner (1997). *Farm Policy and Trade Conflict: The Uruguay Round and Common Agricultural Policy Reform.* Ann Arbor: University of Michigan Press.

Tangermann, Stefan (1996). "Implementation of the Uruguay Round Agreement on Agriculture: Issues and Prospects," *Journal of Agricultural Economics*, vol. 47, pp. 315-337.

Tangermann, Stefan (1997). "A Developed Country Perspective of the Agenda for the Next WTO Round of Agricultural Trade Negotiations." Paper presented at a seminar in the Institute of Graduate Studies, Geneva, March 3.

Tangermann, Stefan (1997). "An Ex-post review of the 1992 MacSharry Reform," in K. A. Ingersent, A. J. Rayner and R. C. Hine (eds), *The Reform of the Common Agricultural Policy*. Palgrave, pp. 12-35.

Tangermann, S. (2001). *Agriculture in the WTO: Background to Current Negotiations.* Paper presented at the International Agricultural Trade Research Consortium Annual Meeting, Washington, DC, 18-20 May.

Tangermann, S. and T. Josling (2001). "Issues in the Next Round of WTO Agricultural Negotiations", in J. A. McMahon (ed.), *Trade and Agriculture: Negotiating a New Agreement?* Cameron May Ltd., London.

The Chicago Tribune, Various issues.

The Des Moines Register, Various issues.

The Economist (2001). "From Bad to Worse, Down on the Farm." March 3.

The New York Times, Various issues.

The Saint Louis Post Dispatch, Various issues.

The Wall Street Journal, Various issues.

The Washington Post, Various issues.

Tracy, Michael (1997). *Agricultural Policy in the European Union and Other Market Economies,* second edition. Belgium: Agricultural Policy Studies.

Tweeten, Luther (1999). "Trade, Uncertainty and New Farm Programs," paper presented to the conference on Agricultural Globalization, Trade and the Environment, University of California at Berkeley, March.

Tweeten, Luther and Carl Zulauf (1997). "Public Policy for Agriculture after Commodity Programs," *Review of Agricultural Economics*, vol. 19, no.2, Fall/Winter.
U.S. Department of Agriculture (1995). *The 1995 Farm Bill: Guidance of the Administration.* Washington, DC: USDA.
Vahl, Remco (1997). *Leadership in Disguise: The Role of the European Commission in EC Decision-making on Agriculture in the Uruguay Round.* Aldershot, UK: Ashgate.
Valdés, Alberto (1994). "Agricultural Reforms in Chile and New Zealand: A Review," *Journal of Agricultural Economics*, vol. 45, no. 2, May.
Webber, Douglas (1998). "The Hard Core: The Franco-German Relationship and Agricultural Crisis Politics in the European Union." INSEAD (European Institute of Business Administration.
Webber, Douglas (1999). "Franco-German Bilateralism and Agricultural Politics in the European Union: The Neglected Level," *West European Politics*, vol.22, no. 1 (January): 45-67.
Williamson, John (ed.) (1994). *The Political Economy of Policy Reform*, Institute for International Economics, Washington, DC, January.
Wilson, Donald L. (1990). "How Rich a Harvest for U.S. Farmers?" *National Journal*, June 9, p. 1429.
World Trade Organization (1995). *The Results of the Uruguay Round of Multilateral Trade Negotiations: The Legal Texts,* Geneva: WTO.
World Trade Organization (2000a). *EC Comprehensive Negotiating Proposal*, World Trade Organization, Committee on Agriculture, Special Session, 14 December 2000, G/AG/NG/W/90.
World Trade Organization (2000b). *European Communities Proposal: The Blue Box and Other Support Measures to Agriculture*, World Trade Organization, Committee on Agriculture, Special Session, 28 June 2000, G/AG/NG/W/17.
World Trade Organization (2000c). *Negotiating Proposal by Japan on WTO Agricultural Negotiations*, World Trade Organization, Committee on Agriculture, Special Session, 21 December 2000, G/AG/NG/W/91.
World Trade Organization (2000d). *Note on Domestic Support Reform Negotiations on Agriculture, Submission from the United States*, World Trade Organization, Committee on Agriculture, Special Session, 23 June 2000, G/AG/NG/W/16.
World Trade Organization (2000e). *Proposal for Comprehensive Long-Term Agricultural Trade Reform, Submission from the United States*, World Trade Organization, Committee on Agriculture, Special Session, 23 June 2000, G/AG/NG/W/15.
World Trade Organization (2000f). *WTO Negotiations on Agriculture—Cairns Group Negotiating Proposal: Domestic Support*, World Trade Organization, Committee on Agriculture, Special Session, 22 September 2000, G/AG/NG/W/35.
World Trade Organization (2000g). *WTO Negotiations on Agriculture—Domestic Support: Proposal by Canada*, World Trade Organization, Committee on Agriculture, Special Session, 21 December 2000, G/AG/NG/W/92.
World Trade Organization (2000h). "European Communities Proposal on Export Competition." Committee on Agriculture Special Session. G/AG/NG/W/34. September 18.
World Trade Organization (2000i). "WTO Negotiations on Agriculture: Cairns Group Negotiating Proposal Export Competition." Committee on Agriculture, Special Session, G/AG/NG/W/11, June 16.
World Wildlife Fund (1997). "A New European Community Policy – Sustainable Regional Development."
Yotopoulos, Pan (2001). "Is there a Third Way for Mediterranean Agriculture?" (unpublished).

Young, Linda, Phil Abbott, and Susan Leetmaa (2001). *Agriculture in the WTO. Export Competition: Issues and Options in the Agricultural Negotiations*, IATRC Commissioned Paper #15, Minneapolis, Minnesota, May.

Index

Acreage Reduction Program, 4, 144
acreage reduction programs (ARPs), 80
Agenda 2000, 5, 9, 173-4, 178-80, 182-8, 191-7, 199-211, 220, 223, 230, 233-4, 236-8, 241, 244, 249, 252
Agricultural Market Transition Act, 156-7
amber box, 4, 138, 219
Amsterdam Treaty, 51
Andriessen, Frans, 61, 68, 70-1, 99, 120, 121, 123, 125, 128-9
Argentina, 119, 126, 215
Asia-Pacific Economic Cooperation (APEC), 41
Atlantic Alliance, 73
Australia, 3, 31, 41, 70, 100, 119, 126, 129, 197, 215
Austria, 41, 184

Balanced Budget and Emergency Deficit Control Reaffirmation Act, 86
Balladur, Eduard, 131-2
beef, 5, 39, 41, 46, 56, 98-9, 101-2, 140-1, 176, 180, 184, 187, 189, 191, 197, 199, 209, 252
  lowered support prices, 230
Berlin summit, 5, 174, 191, 223, 235, 236, 252
Blair House, 4, 9, 120, 121-2, 128-33, 137, 140-2, 216, 219, 221, 237
  Blair House Accord, 122, 137
  Blair House I, 4, 121-3, 125, 236
  Blair House II, 4, 122, 128, 236, 237
  timing of Blair House agreements, 123
blue box, 4-5, 7, 121, 129, 137-8, 140, 142, 161, 219, 223
Borchert, Jochen, 132, 183, 189
Brazil, 126, 215
Brussels Conference, 22
budget stabilizers, 12, 14, 103, 105, 233-4, 238
Bush Administration, 61, 79

Bush, George, 61, 63, 68, 79, 85, 90, 120, 125-9, 130, 145, 164-5, 236

Cairns Group, 7, 22, 60-1, 62-4, 70, 72, 106, 110, 118-19, 121, 126, 133, 142, 215-16, 219, 222, 237
Canada, 3, 30-1, 41, 43, 45, 60, 69-70, 119, 136, 141, 215, 219, 222, 249
cereal, *see* grain
Clinton, Bill, 120, 122, 128, 130, 145, 155, 158-159, 164, 165, 166, 239
Closer Economic Relations Agreement, 41
Coalition for a Competitive Food and Agricultural System, 151, 163, 169, 171
Committee of Agricultural Organizations of the EU (COPA), 234
Common Agricultural Policy (CAP), 2-3, 22-3, 29, 30, 35, 41, 53, 54-5, 59, 63, 65- 6, 68, 70, 75, 89, 96-9, 101-16, 118-21, 123-27, 129-31, 134, 137, 139, 140-2, 173-80, 183, 185, 186-8, 190-3, 195-7, 199-211, 220, 222, 225-6, 230, 231-2, 236-40, 243-4, 252-3
  budget, 5
  game, 23
  MacSharry reforms of, 9, 27
  reform of, 22
  stabilizers implemented in, 14
Common Market of the South (MERCOSUR), 41, 226, 249
compensatory payments, 4, 5, 7, 27, 98, 99-101, 110-11, 115-16, 124-5, 129, 174, 180, 193-4, 197, 200, 203, 205-9, 211, 230, 231, 239-41, 252
competitive agriculture paradigm, 33
Conservation Reserve Program (CRP), 80, 83, 85, 95, 145-7, 149, 151-2, 154, 157-9, 162, 167, 170, 230
Cork Declaration, 177, 201, 206
Council of Economic Advisors, 145

Council on Environmental Quality, 145
Cresson, Edith, 126
Czech Republic, 175, 179

dairy, 84, 155
  butter, 105, 141, 156, 158, 248
  milk, 4, 14, 27, 39, 43-4, 102, 105, 136, 140-1, 151-2, 156, 158, 183-4, 187-8, 189, 192, 207-9, 211, 218, 248
    milk powder stocks, 105
  milk quotas, 14, 27, 102, 183, 188, 192
  policy, 4-5, 12, 14, 16-17, 26, 39, 41, 43-6, 56-7, 68, 73, 81-5, 90, 92, 98, 101, 103, 105, 115, 133, 136, 139-40, 142, 151-2, 154-7, 164, 170, 176, 180, 183-4, 188-9, 191-2, 201, 204, 207-10, 218, 221-3, 230, 231, 233-4, 238-9, 249, 250
  products, 4
  quotas, 4, 101, 201
De Zeeuw, 75
De Zeeuw Draft, 69, 75, 119
deficiency payments, 4-5, 14, 17, 26, 38, 84, 93, 95, 121, 129, 137-8, 140, 144-5, 148-50, 152-5, 157-8, 161-2, 167, 168-9, 171-2, 200, 230, 232, 241
Delors, Jacques, 68, 99, 101, 120, 122, 126-8
Denmark, 35, 54, 96, 99, 101, 112, 115, 123, 128, 183-4, 189, 204, 225, 244
Department of State, 50, 145
Department of the Interior, 145
Department of the Treasury, 145
developed countries, 30, 38-40, 43, 46
developing countries, 29, 57, 69, 126, 134, 136, 199, 214-15, 244
Dillon Round, 120
Dole, Bob, 16, 156
domestic price supports, 77, 106, 117, 170, 195, 209, 229, 231, 237
domestic support, 5, 32, 34, 47, 60, 62, 63, 70, 72, 110, 119, 129, 134, 136-40, 142, 150, 213-15, 218-19, 221
Draft Final Act (DFA), 126-7, 129
Dunkel, Arthur, 4, 61, 102, 119, 121, 125, 126, 129

Dunkel Draft, 119

Eastern Europe, 24
Economic and Monetary Union (EMU), 73
Environmental Protection Agency (EPA), 83, 145
Europe, 1, 7- 8, 27, 31, 33-4, 41-2, 46, 70, 73, 97, 107, 113, 115, 128, 133, 175, 178, 185, 187, 220, 222, 229, 234-5, 243-4, 248-9, 252
  Central and Eastern Europe (CEEC), 5, 9, 41, 73, 106, 174-5, 179, 199, 225
European Commission
  Agriculture Council, 16-17, 54-5, 66, 67-9, 71, 74-5, 96-7, 99, 101-2, 108-13, 115-16, 123, 125, 176, 177, 183, 187, 189, 191-2, 201, 205-6, 208-10, 232, 233-7, 239-40
  compensatory payments, 4
  Council of Agriculture Ministers, 18, 26
  Council of Ministers, 21, 23, 50, 54, 65, 74, 96, 126, 129, 131, 183, 196, 201, 208, 233
  Directorate General for Agriculture (DGVI), 18, 21, 26, 51, 53-4, 66, 74-5, 96, 98-100, 101, 107-12, 115, 175-6, 187, 191, 199, 201-8, 232
European Community
  export surplus capacity, 1
European Council, 20, 71, 125, 127-8, 176, 187, 192, 200, 204, 208, 210, 225, 233
European Union
  declining farm population, 2
  expansion, 41
  export subsidies, 5
  integration, 18
Export Enhancement Program (EEP), 4, 81, 83, 140, 171, 237

Farm and Home Administration (FmHA), 84
Farm Bill, 16, 79, 83, 92, 145, 150, 160, 225

Index

1981 Farm Bill, 4, 16, 29, 91, 238
1985 Farm Bill, 4, 12, 16, 29, 60, 77, 80-1, 83, 85-6, 88-90, 92-3, 95, 147, 167, 230, 235, 238
1990 Farm Bill, 4, 5, 9, 77, 78, 80, 81-2, 84-85, 88, 89-95, 137, 144, 145, 149, 150-51, 155, 158-9, 161, 163-5, 169, 172-3, 230, 235, 238-9
1996 Farm Bill, 9, 30, 144, 159, 160, 165, 170-1, 232, 234-5, 237-8, 249-50
2002 Farm Bill, 249
farm lobbies, 3, 13, 26, 53, 66, 74, 116, 123, 125, 234-6, 240
Fast Track, 74, 114, 116, 120, 122, 125-6, 235, 236
Federal Agriculture Improvement and Reform (FAIR) Act, 3, 5, 7-8, 27, 140, 144, 146, 158, 164, 169, 170-3, 200, 206-7, 211, 219, 222-3, 225, 230-1, 236, 238-41, 244, 253
Finland, 41, 184
Fischler, Franz, 175, 177, 183-4, 186, 187, 189, 197, 201, 205-6, 208
fixed bases and yields, 14
Foley, Tom, 16
Foreign Agricultural Service, 50, 69
France, 3, 4, 19, 22, 41, 54, 65, 66, 69, 71, 74-5, 96, 101, 106, 110, 112, 113-14, 123-5, 127-33, 178, 183, 185, 188, 190, 196, 206, 208, 225, 233-4, 243
Freedom to Farm Act, 146, 149, 150-2, 155-6, 158, 162, 164, 166-9, 171-3, 235, 239, 250

General Agreement on Tariffs and Trade (GATT), 2-4, 8, 21-4, 28, 30, 33, 48-51, 53-6, 59, 61-2, 66-70, 72-5, 88, 94-5, 101-2, 108-9, 110-13, 116, 118-35, 137-8, 140, 142, 143, 170, 175, 195, 196, 209, 236, 252
German Farmers Union, 72, 124
Germany, 3, 5, 19, 24, 41, 54, 66, 69, 71, 73-5, 96, 100, 102, 106, 110, 112-14, 117, 123, 124, 128, 130-3, 178, 184, 187, 190, 196, 204, 206, 208, 211, 225, 243, 244

East Germany, 5, 110, 114
Glickman, Dan, 145, 157, 165-6
grain
   cereal, 5, 14, 39, 41, 57, 63-4, 69, 73, 84, 86, 98, 99, 101-2, 105, 110, 113, 115, 125, 127, 131-3, 140, 141, 176, 180, 184, 187, 189, 191-3, 197-9, 203-4, 209-10, 216, 220, 223, 230-1, 246, 249-50, 252
   growers, 203-4
   lowered support prices, 230
   maximum guaranteed quantities for, 230
   producers, 99
   supports, 103
   domestic use in animal feed, 252
   exports, 45
   imports, 46
   industry, 149
   policy, 39
   producers, 95
   stocks, 56
   surpluses, 115, 239
green box, 4, 111, 125-6, 137, 138, 206-7, 209, 219-24, 237, 241

Hellstrom Draft, 64
Hellstrom, Mats, 64
Heysel, 4, 58, 59, 64, 65, 69, 72, 74, 97, 98, 106, 108-10, 118, 119, 121-3, 236, 237
Hills, Carla, 61, 72, 121-2, 128, 129
House Agriculture Committee, 16, 82, 88, 146-7, 149, 151, 154, 156, 164, 167, 172-3, 235
Hungary, 175, 179

import barriers, 7, 56, 61, 70, 72, 77, 88, 106, 117, 123, 135, 140, 161, 170, 171, 195, 231, 237, 240, 254, 256
Intergovernmental Conference (IGC), 73
Italy, 41, 54, 96, 102, 128, 130, 184, 188, 192, 196, 211, 249

Japan, 30, 38, 43-4, 46, 56, 60, 70, 95, 119, 126, 215, 247, 249
   export surplus capacity, 1

Kantor, Mickey, 122, 130, 133